Foundations of Meaningful Educational Assessment

Diann Musial
Northern Illinois University

Gayla Nieminen
Assessment Unlimited

Jay Thomas
Aurora University

Kay Burke
Kay Burke & Associates, LLC

**McGraw-Hill
Higher Education**

Boston   Burr Ridge, IL   Dubuque, IA   New York   San Francisco   St. Louis
Bangkok   Bogotá   Caracas   Kuala Lumpur   Lisbon   London   Madrid   Mexico City
Milan   Montreal   New Delhi   Santiago   Seoul   Singapore   Sydney   Taipei   Toronto

McGraw-Hill
Higher Education

Published by McGraw-Hill, an imprint of The McGraw-Hill Companies, Inc., 1221 Avenue of the Americas, New York, NY 10020. Copyright © 2009. All rights reserved. No part of this publication may be reproduced or distributed in any form or by any means, or stored in a database or retrieval system, without the prior written consent of The McGraw-Hill Companies, Inc., including, but not limited to, in any network or other electronic storage or transmission, or broadcast for distance learning.

This book is printed on acid-free paper.

1 2 3 4 5 6 7 8 9 0 DOC/DOC 0 9 8

ISBN: 978-0-07-340382-3
MHID: 0-07-340382-2

Editor in Chief: *Michael Ryan*
Publisher: *Beth Mejia*
Sponsoring Editor: *David Patterson*
Director of Development: *Dawn Groundwater*
Development Editor: *Anne Reid*
Marketing Manager: *James Headley*
Production Editor: *Alison Meier*
Design Coordinator: *Andrei Pasternak*
Interior Design: *Kay Lieberherr*
Cover Design: *Allister Fein*
Art Editor: *Ayelet Arbel*
Illustrator: *Lotus Art*
Photo Researcher: *Brian J. Pecko*
Production Supervisor: *Tandra Jorgensen*
Composition: *10/12 Palatino by Aptara India*
Printing: *45# New Era Matte, R. R. Donnelley*
Cover: *(top to bottom)* © *BananaStock/PunchStock;* © *BananaStock/PunchStock;* © *Dynamic Graphics/JupiterImages*
Credits: The credits section for this book begins on page 503 and is considered an extension of the copyright page.

Library of Congress Cataloging-in-Publication Data
Foundations of meaningful educational assessment / Diann Musial ... [et al.].
    p. cm.
  Includes bibliographical references and index.
  ISBN-13: 978-0-07-340382-3 (alk. paper)
  ISBN-10: 0-07-340382-2 (alk. paper)
 1. Educational tests and measurements.   I. Musial, Diann.
  LB3051.F68 2009
  371.26—dc22

                                        2007045303

The Internet addresses listed in the text were accurate at the time of publication. The inclusion of a Web site does not indicate an endorsement by the authors or McGraw-Hill, and McGraw-Hill does not guarantee the accuracy of the information presented at these sites.

www.mhhe.com

Contents

Chapter 3

The Social Foundations of Assessment   49

Chapter 5

*Selected-Response
Assessments   107*

Chapter 9

Portfolio Assessment and Rubric Development   237

Chapter 10

Developing Grading Procedures   267

Chapter 12

Using Standardized Achievement Tests as Assessments 331

Chapter 13

Assessment and the Law 359

Chapter 14

Exceptionality and Assessment   397

Chapter 15
Technology and Assessment   425

Preface

Overview

With this text, we offer a readable introduction to assessment and measurement within a classroom context. We have constructed this text to help you understand that assessment is a multidimensional, active process focused on student learning and instructional improvement. We focus on assessment principles and concepts as they apply to teachers and learners within the contemporary classroom. We will help you select, develop, and refine formal and informal assessments that meet the demands of standards-based education and the diverse needs of students.

Among the elements we deem crucial to the text are:

- *A foundations perspective:* How did we get here? Why do we do the things we do in the classroom? With some historical and philosophical context, we have found our teachers are better able to make informed decisions about the place of assessment in their classrooms.

- *A developmental approach:* The text is organized to model your own process as you develop appropriate assessments for your classroom— from planning, through design and execution, to evaluation and reporting.

- *Technology and legal aspects:* Separate chapters are devoted to each of these crucial areas.

- *Self-assessment for reflective practice:* Assessment is not just for students! This final chapter will help you see how you can use assessment to evaluate and improve your practice.

Foundations Perspective

Our textbook provides a foundations perspective for each assessment topic. This approach presents the philosophical, historical, psychological, and sociological underpinnings of assessment to help you better understand and interpret the factors that have shaped classroom assessment. Our experience has been that when our students understand the context of assessment, they are better able to think critically about its place in their classrooms and in their professional practice.

We present this valuable context first by simply describing at the beginning of each chapter the specific foundational perspectives that underlie the topic. We then include some probing questions to help you see the larger issues that can become lost among the many technical details of assessment.

As part of our foundations perspective, we have devoted an entire chapter to the legal issues raised by the assessment process. This chapter is unique to assessment textbooks, and we believe it will deepen your understanding of important complexities that surround assessment.

There are three specific advantages to approaching assessment from a foundations perspective. First, a foundations of education perspective offers a unique philosophical viewpoint that is often missing in discussions of educational assessment. A foundations perspective means that the assumptions, preconceptions, underpinnings, and deep roots of educational assessment are an important part of the discussion. Educational assessment and measurement presuppose an understanding of the nature of knowledge. But before we assess student learning, we as educators do not usually stop to ask: What is knowledge? What does it mean to know something? These are epistemological questions that examine the philosophical foundations of measurement. As educators, we have created ways to assess and measure a number of educational outcomes, but we do not often ask ourselves if we are measuring the truly important outcomes or primarily focusing on the outcomes that we know how to measure. The important outcomes may be difficult to assess. Are we focusing too much on those that can be more easily measured? A foundations perspective requires that we ask ourselves some fundamental questions before plunging into assessment.

The second advantage of a foundations perspective is that it encourages us to examine educational assessment in its historical context. How did the field of assessment evolve? Why is it that we ask certain questions and not others? Why do we prioritize and assess certain skills and content but not others? What historical factors or historical accidents have brought us to our present state?

Finally, a foundations perspective includes a focus on the sociological and psychological environment of classroom work. The theories and models developed by critical thinkers in the social foundations provide insight into the ways that social and cultural norms and institutions affect learners from different backgrounds. These insights will help you develop assessments that are sensitive to the diverse learning needs of students. The psychology of learning and the findings from research in learning theory also have important implications for the effective use of assessment. This perspective is especially critical in making classroom assessment multifaceted, thorough, and grounded in the developmental needs of children.

We use the foundations approach to create a uniquely meaningful context for you as a future teacher. The advantage for you is that you will better understand the many issues that surround your students' lives. You will understand the reasons for assessing one particular learning outcome versus another, as well as the broader implications of assessment. Ultimately, we believe that a foundations approach to assessment will help you select and create more meaningful and appropriate ways of measuring outcomes. It will help you think more deeply and see beyond the immediate results.

Developmental Approach

The developmental approach that we use in this text ensures that ideas and concepts are carefully built throughout the book and that information is presented where it fits naturally into the process of teaching and learning. Early chapters focus on how to determine what you need to know and do within the classroom context and how to plan and develop assessments that relate to instruction.

Following are chapters that show you how to write and select different types of assessments, including selected-response items (true-false, multiple-choice, matching) and student-constructed responses (essays, projects and performances, and so on). We show you how to use observations and interviews to get important information about your students. We also show you a wide variety of ways to capture that information and how to evaluate it using an appropriate rubric.

We explain how to understand the standards movement and its implications for you as a teacher. We discuss exceptionality, grading, and using and interpreting norm-referenced standardized assessments, including statewide assessments. Our chapter on statistical applications presents important and often intimidating concepts in an understandable way using many clarifying examples.

You will find an entire chapter on using technology in classroom assessment, with many valuable ideas. For example, we show you how to create templates for essay tests and research reports that improve and streamline student responses. We demonstrate how to set up e-portfolios for your students and how to use integrated learning systems to support your classroom instruction and assessment.

Our concluding chapter, unique to this textbook, focuses on reflective teacher self-assessment. Here you will learn to use self-reflection to make your classroom instruction more powerful, and you will discover practical ways to help your students become reflective, lifelong learners.

Context and Uses of Assessment

In each chapter, our features "Digging Deeper" and "Resource for Your Assessment Toolkit" support our emphasis on meaningful assessment and practicality. "Digging Deeper" provides important perspectives on contemporary practice and encourages you to reconsider some widely held assumptions about assessment. In Chapter 7, for example, we briefly explore the work of Alfred Binet and Theodore Simon and discuss the influence of their work on modern assessment. Similarly, in Chapter 10 we discuss the surprising relationship between grading and student motivation.

Also in each chapter, "Resource for Your Assessment Toolkit" presents material that will be of immediate practical use to you as a teacher. These resources range from concrete examples of assessment drawn from the classrooms of working teachers to valuable guidelines for thinking about the role of assessment in your classroom. We have taken care to include not only how to develop appropriate assessment but also how to ensure that the assessment matches the unique context of an individual learner within an individual classroom.

Throughout the text we describe how you can help students and parents understand and use assessment results, and we emphasize the ways that you can use assessment feedback to further your own learning. Items to promote further discussion and a short comprehension quiz (with answers at the end of the book) are provided for each chapter, as well as a list of Key Terms and a Summary of the chapter's main topics.

Summary

Foundations of Meaningful Educational Assessment views assessment as the art and science of placing students in a context that brings out their understanding and enables their teacher to record that understanding. The *foundations* perspective acts as a filter through which historical, philosophical, psychological, and social constructs are applied to assessment concepts and practices. Although the foundations perspective examines an array of forces that shape student learning, particular attention is paid to the relationship among assessment, motivation, and learning theory, all of which are cornerstones within psychological foundations. Furthermore, our foundations perspective pays attention to the social context in which students live. We integrate issues of wealth and poverty, bias and prejudice, gender, ethnicity, race, and exceptionalities and try to uncover how these issues influence (both negatively and positively) assessment fairness and equality. This foundations perspective enables future teachers to understand assessment within a larger framework and to make intelligent, ethical decisions.

The *meaningful* focus implies that this text is readable, practical, and applicable to the contemporary classroom and that the topics make sense to teachers, students, and parents alike. The text places assessment issues within the classroom context. As a part of this, we include issues of standards, accountability, and grading.

Finally, assessment is considered multidimensional and includes evaluation, measurement, and developmental issues. We consider assessment and measurement concepts from a variety of perspectives: teachers, students, parents, and others. Learning is the product of complex interactions among student, teacher, family, and society, and student assessment must be sensitive to the variations among learners and their contexts. *Foundations of Meaningful Educational Assessment* encompasses the diverse array of ideas that will lead to the richest and most appropriate use of assessment strategies.

Acknowledgments

We acknowledge our contributors for their expertise in the development of specific chapters:

Annette Johnson (Chapter 10, Developing Grading Procedures)

Jim Lockard, Distinguished Teaching Professor, Northern Illinois University (Chapter 15, Technology and Assessment)

Brenda Lee Love (Chapter 14, Exceptionality and Assessment)

Antoinette S. Mitchell, Vice President, Unit Accreditation, NCATE (Chapter 3, The Social Foundations of Assessment)

Christine Rienstra Kirakofe, Assistant Professor, Northern Illinois University (Chapter 13, Assessment and the Law)

Alice R. Rusevic, Assistant Professor, Aurora University (Chapter 7, Assessment Through Observation and Interview; Chapter 8, Performance-Based Assessment)

Steve Wallace, Assistant Professor, Northern Illinois University (Chapter 11, Statistical Applications to Assessment)

We express deep appreciation to James A. Johnson for his expert guidance in the world of textbook writing and his limitless kindness. We thank Barrie Jean Barrett for her astute suggestions and edits as well as Elizabeth L. Hammerman for her many insights about science instruction and assessment. We acknowledge Annie Reid, our development editor, for her amazing care and precision during the development of the manuscript as well as our senior editor David Patterson whose wise direction and insights have made this work possible. We thank our reviewers for their constructive comments to drafts of the text: Nancy Brown, Oakland University; Marcia Burrell-Ihlow, State University of New York at Oswego; David W. McMullen, Bradley University; Lisa Newland, The University of South Dakota; Louis Roussos, University of Illinois at Urbana-Champaign; Rod Thronson, Carroll College; and Rhea Walker, Winona State University.

In addition, we sincerely thank our families and friends for supporting us throughout the many twists and turns that are part of the creative process. We encourage all of our readers to provide feedback for improving future editions.

Diann Musial
Gayla Nieminen
Jay Thomas
Kay Burke

CHAPTER 1

The Nature of Assessment

Chapter Objectives

After reading and thinking about this chapter, you will be able to:

- **Explain why there are different meanings for assessment.**
- **Describe different metaphors for assessment.**
- **Compare different purposes for assessment.**
- **Describe the characteristics of good assessments, including valid**
- **and reliable evidence gathering and interpretation.**
- **Synthesize and defend definitions and descriptions for assessment.**
- **Understand the ethical issues in assessment and describe methods to assure fairness.**

The concept of *assessment* is packed with all sorts of related ideas. The word itself is often interchanged with other words like *tests, examinations, rubrics, grades, performance reports,* and *evaluations.* Although these terms are related to the concept of assessment, they are by no means the same. It is no wonder that today's learners sometimes agonize over the thought of taking another assessment—for the concept of assessment is often unclear to them. Because assessment has become so intertwined with other concepts, let's reexamine the original meaning of the word and determine which aspects of related terms are appropriate.

One way to uncover the roots of a complex concept like assessment is to consider its language origins. Most English language dictionaries claim that the verb *assess* is derived from the Latin verb *assidere,* which means to "sit beside." What an interesting image this brings to mind! Imagine a learner sitting beside another person who is helping that learner determine what she or he knows or can do. More important, how different is this sitting-beside image from the image of five rows of learners, each hunched over a piece of paper, struggling to choose the correct answers to a list of questions.

In this text, we invite you to participate in a **foundational approach** to assessment. In the foundational approach, assessment concepts are presented from perspectives drawn from philosophy, history, or the social sciences. We believe that these different perspectives will help you be aware of the complexities of assessment, and they will give you a deeper understanding of the issues that arise in assessing learners. These perspectives will help you find your way through the different demands placed on teachers and learners alike.

In this chapter, we begin to employ the disciplines of philosophy and history to clarify underlying concepts of assessment. We introduce metaphors for assessment and show how these metaphors relate to different assessment purposes. We believe that by examining assessment from these basic perspectives you will better understand why assessments look so different and why it is that a person can perform well on one type of assessment and yet struggle with another.

Foundational Questions for Your Consideration

- As a learner, why do you sometimes think an assessment is unfair?
- Do assessments really measure what a learner knows and can do, or do assessments simply measure whether a learner knows what the teacher knows?
- Do you think learners should be allowed to help teachers write assessments? Why or why not?
- Is it a good idea to invite learners to critique an assessment that they have just completed? Why or why not?

Assessment: A Concept at Odds with Itself

Let's begin our study of assessment by considering different metaphors that are linked to the concept. Metaphors provide nuances to definitions, and nuances enrich understanding. You will find that some of the assessment metaphors contrast sharply with others. This happens because assessments are employed for different purposes, and one purpose can conflict with another. By examining the different metaphors and purposes for assessment, you can begin to develop a well-grounded meaning for assessment, which will help you succeed in the world of education and with the many different assessment demands you will face.

Metaphors for Assessment

We have already described one metaphor for assessment, the metaphor of *sitting beside* a learner in an attempt to help the learner understand what he or she knows or is able to do. This image implies that assessment is really a data-gathering activity in which the assessor-teacher interacts with the learner in order to clarify what that learner needs. In other words, the sitting-beside metaphor suggests that simply talking to a learner in an effort to understand the learner's needs or problems is a form of assessment. The setting in this case is relaxed; there is no specific time limit, and the method for collecting information is oral.

Another metaphor for assessment is *judging*. In this metaphor, the assessor is focused on the degree to which a learner has attained some standard, benchmark, or level of achievement. The assessor may require the learner to answer specific questions or perform specific tasks, depending on what that standard or benchmark is. The setting for the assessment also depends on the particular standard or benchmark and may range from simply answering questions on a written test to a demonstration or performance in front of an external audience.

We can also think of assessment as *coaching*. In this metaphor, the assessor is there to help the learner achieve a specific objective. The assessor observes the learner, and if the learner experiences some difficulty, the assessor provides some suggestions concerning how to proceed. Along the way, the assessor gathers information about what the learner knows and can do and also where the learner has difficulty or may need more instruction. The coaching metaphor suggests that assessment occurs as part of the learning process. Just as a coach in sports notices where the players need suggestions and encouragement, so does the classroom teacher assess students as they learn.

All three of these metaphors are legitimate ways of thinking about assessment, and they share a common basis. In each of the metaphors, assessment requires that the learner is placed in a specific setting or context. The context for an assessment has many components that together form an environment intended to enable learners to show what they know or can do. Sometimes the context of an assessment is open-ended, and at other times it is specific and focused.

For example, an open-ended context might ask learners to perform any of a number of possible skills using as much time as they wish, while a more focused assessment might ask learners to perform a specific skill in a specific time and place. The context for an assessment results from a variety of factors—some relating to the setting (time of day, classroom or outdoors, individual or in a group) and others relating to the demands of the assessment (use of notes, timed or untimed, written or oral, open-ended questions or selected response).

Digging Deeper
Democracy and Self-Assessment

John Dewey published *Democracy and Education* in 1916 in an attempt to show how a democratic society was enhanced through an experimentalist approach to education. Dewey believed that both education and democracy are built on the basic principle of the human being in interaction with the environment. According to Dewey, the democratic environment is one that is free of absolutes that block experimental inquiry. He believed schools should establish democratic environments conducive to true experimental inquiry. No subject, custom, or value is so sacrosanct that it should escape critical inquiry. Ideally, the school setting is to be free of coercive and authoritarian practices that might jeopardize freedom of thought and experimentation. In the interaction between the person and the environment, thinking occurs, and, from that, education takes place.

Dewey designed a set of problem-solving steps or reflective experience that approximates a true inquiry. He describes these as follows.

> So much for the general features of a reflective experience. They are (i) perplexity, confusion, doubt, due to the fact that one is implicated in an incomplete situation whose full character is not yet determined; (ii) a conjectural anticipation—a tentative interpretation of the given elements, attributing to them a tendency to effect certain consequences; (iii) a careful survey (examination, inspection, exploration, analysis) of all attainable consideration which will define and clarify the problem in hand; (iv) a consequent elaboration of the tentative hypothesis to make it more precise and more consistent, because squaring with a wider range of facts; (v) taking one stand upon the projected hypothesis as a plan of action which is applied to the existing state of affairs; doing something overtly to bring about the anticipated result and thereby testing the hypothesis. It is the extent and accuracy of steps three and four which mark off a distinctive reflective experience from one on the trial and error plane. They make thinking itself into an experience. (Dewey, 1916, p. 176)

This description of the reflective experience offers a powerful portrait of the type of learning and the type of assessment that should have a prominent place in our schools. As we review the national standards of knowledge, skills, and dispositions that are important to today's learners, keep in mind Dewey's reflective experience and see to what degree the standards are supported by teaching and assessing problem solving according to the five steps outlined above.

The reason you need to consider the cumulative effect of creating a context out of all these pieces is that some contexts will help learners show what they know and can do whereas other contexts will frustrate learners to such a degree that they cannot show what they know and can do. Ultimately, you can think of **assessment** as *the art of placing learners in a context that brings out or clarifies what a learner knows and can do, as well as what a learner may not know or cannot do.*

This underlying view of assessment as the placing of learners in different contexts so that they can easily show you what they know or do not know will be a useful guidepost as you explore the many different purposes and types of assessment tools. If you find yourself puzzled by the terminology and assessment methods, we recommend that you come back to this idea that assessment is the placement of learners in a context that brings out what they know or can do.

Different Purposes for Assessment

One reason that different metaphors are used to understand and describe the concept of assessment is that assessment can occur for different purposes. These different purposes affect the context or the way the assessment will be carried out.

For example, often we assess in order to uncover what a learner knows or is able to do at the end of some period of learning. This type of assessment is called a **summative assessment** because the purpose is to be a summation or summing up of what a learner has achieved. In this type of assessment, learners are often placed in a situation that represents all that they have learned during this period and that requires them to demonstrate the culmination of their learning. For example, they may be required to perform a recital or make a presentation before a group who will ask questions or complete another large, important task that represents what has been learned.

Frequently in the classroom we assess to provide helpful insights to learners so that they can see what they know or do not know or what they can or cannot do. When the purpose of the assessment is to provide helpful feedback so that additional learning can occur, we call this **formative assessment.** Formative assessment also implies that as teachers collect and interpret evidence concerning what a student still needs to know, they adapt their teaching to meet student needs.

At other times, we want to know if a learner simply grasps a specific concept or skill that is part of, or on the way to, a larger meaning or skill set. In this case, a short selected-response quiz or a set of questions all focused on the specific concept or skill is in order.

Or assessments can be used as competitions. For example, we might want to know who is the best speller or the best writer because of a contest or because of a limited number of opportunities. This type of assessment tends to include a variety of different questions so as to challenge the participants with increasingly more difficult problems.

As you can see, it is useful to examine these different purposes of assessment and notice how the different aims affect the way that you set up the environment, create the directions, and select the type of questions you will ask. These different components create a specific type of assessment context. You may discover at least five purposes for assessment.

Assessment as Instruction and Providing Feedback One key purpose for assessment is *to provide feedback to learners*. Some theorists claim that this is the primary purpose for assessment because ultimately assessment should focus on the learners' needs and expectations (Marzano, Pickering, & McTigne, 1993; Stiggins, 2005; Wiggins, 1998). When assessments are used to provide feedback, it is important for the assessor to communicate the assessment results in such a way that the learner can make sense of the information and use it to make decisions about what needs to happen next.

For this reason, a key aspect of assessments that provide feedback is to offer the learner more information than simply the score or the percentage of answers that were correct. Instead, the assessor spends time interpreting the meaning of the score to help learners understand their strengths and limitations as uncovered by this assessment. In general, **feedback** is the underlying purpose that drives classroom assessment. On a regular basis, teachers can assess learners as they dynamically live the life of the classroom. Anecdotal notes, structured observations, tests, quizzes, and short conversations with learners are all typical ways to gather information and provide feedback in the natural context of daily classroom life. In general, these types of assessments are formative.

Assessment as Determining What Learners Need to Learn Next Assessments that are aimed at *finding out what a learner needs to learn next* are formative and tend to be narrowly focused. Often such assessments are used when a discipline lends itself to learning that is sequential. For example, in mathematics a learner needs to understand what a whole number means before that learner can understand how to add whole numbers. For this reason, an assessment that asks questions about whole numbers, followed by questions about whole number addition, followed by questions about whole number subtraction could quickly uncover what a learner knows about whole numbers and what precisely the learner needs to learn next.

Assessment as Diagnosing Learner Difficulties or Misconceptions Sometimes assessments are used *to uncover specific misconceptions that have been identified as typical misunderstandings*. Like FAQs (frequently asked questions), they could be called FMCs for frequently misunderstood concepts, and like FAQs they are specific to a particular learning area. For example, in basic science learners often incorrectly think of surface tension as the force of gravity—a macro force—pulling on liquids. Actually, surface tension is the micro force of molecules attracted to one another. The teacher who is aware of the FMC could assess children by asking them to select the proper meaning of surface tension while providing the force of gravity as a possible answer. This procedure is not intended to trick the learner but rather to allow the teacher to better understand what the learner thinks. Assessing to uncover misconceptions provides a wonderful guide for the teacher to determine how to help the learner relearn or correctly learn a concept. Assessments that focus on uncovering misconceptions are formative.

Assessment as Determining Progress along a Developmental Continuum
Schools are organized by grade levels, and all sorts of expectations for learner achievement have been developed. For example, by first grade, learners are now expected to know the alphabet, to count sequentially to a certain number, and to know how to read a selected cluster of words (as in the Dolch Basic Word Lists). Some assessments are created *to find out how much a learner knows when compared to other learners across the nation at the same grade level.* This type of assessment is *normed*, which means that learners' answers are compared to the answers of other learners of the same age taking the same test. This type of assessment does not provide specific information about what a learner knows or does not know. Rather, it provides a snapshot of where a learner is in comparison to other learners. These types of assessment are summative rather than formative.

Assessment as Program Evaluation or Accountability Another purpose for assessment is *to focus on improving the teaching program* rather than on uncovering the needs of the individual learner. Many school districts are required to use state-developed tests as assessments of the district's learning program. Often, the test scores are analyzed by grade level and by school, and the scores are posted in local newspapers. When assessments focus on accountability to parents and the community, the information is primarily aimed at finding places in the learning program that should be improved.

A Common Thread for Different Purposes Despite the many different uses for assessment, there is a common thread. In order to provide feedback to learners based on a specific educational assessment, it is important to gather and interpret the evidence or results of the assessment in light of its relationship to learning. You may find it helpful to keep this common thread in mind as you explore the many different assessment methods and statistical approaches that are used today.

If you find yourself overwhelmed by the many ideas that surround assessment, ask yourself these questions:

1. What kind of evidence, data, or information do I need in order to accomplish my purpose?

2. How does this evidence, data, or information relate to the learning outcomes that I intended for my learners to master?

3. What context or setting shall I create so that learners are motivated to show me what they do or do not know or what they can or cannot do?

4. How can I interpret the findings to provide meaningful feedback to both learners and parents?

Resource for Your Assessment Toolkit

Two Assessments with Different Purposes

Assessments have different purposes, and these purposes influence the way an assessment looks and feels to learners. Sometimes an assessment is inviting and comfortable, and at other times an assessment can feel like a competition.

Here are two assessments focused on mathematics computation. The first is called a **criterion-referenced test,** and its purpose is to uncover what a learner knows about adding two-digit numbers with no regrouping. The second is called a **norm-referenced test,** and its purpose is to determine how much a learner knows about computation in comparison with other learners who are the same age and grade level. You may wish to keep these annotated examples in your assessment toolkit to provide you with templates for two types of assessment with different purposes.

Criterion-Referenced Assessment

Directions: Add the following numbers and place the correct answer after the equal sign. Take your time and hand in your work when finished.

$$12 + 16 =$$
$$34 + 35 =$$
$$81 + 17 =$$
$$46 + 52 =$$
$$73 + 24 =$$

Norm-Referenced Assessment

Directions: Compute the following numbers and place the correct answer after the equal sign. You have 3 minutes to complete your work. I will tell you when to begin and when to stop.

$$12 + 16 =$$
$$134 - 99 =$$
$$801 \times 193 =$$
$$46 / 15 =$$

These two assessments differ in a number of ways that may not be immediately obvious. First, examine the directions because the directions can change the assessment significantly. In the first assessment, learners are allowed to take as much time as they wish. The reason for this latitude is that the purpose of the assessment is *to find out if learners really know how to add two-digit numbers with no regrouping.* There is no interest in comparing learners to others just to see who can calculate the most correct answers in the shortest time. Rather, learners are compared to a single criterion: adding two-digit numbers with no regrouping.

In the second assessment learners are given a precise time limit. This time limit can change learners' performance. Learners may know how to answer the question, but they may not be able to compute fast enough to display their knowledge, or their anxiety may slow them down. However, the purpose of the second assessment is comparative and competitive. The second assessment is written in such a way so as *to determine how well a learner performs compared to other learners of a similar age.* At the end of this assessment, you cannot determine whether a learner knows how to add, subtract, multiply or divide because there is only one opportunity for learners to show their knowledge of any one type of computation.

Another difference in the two tests rests in the questions themselves. Notice that in the first assessment all the questions are based on the same learning task. In the second assessment, the questions involve increasingly difficult learning tasks. Once again, this difference relates to the different purposes of the two assessments. In the first assessment, precision is important. Does the learner really know this learning task? In the second assessment, learners answer a range of questions drawn from a similar area so as to determine what this learner knows across the range of tasks, compared to other learners of the same age.

?Ask Yourself

Recall a time when as a learner you actually enjoyed participating in an assessment. What aspects of the assessment contributed to your enjoyment? Was the assessment competitive, or was it an opportunity to show what you knew and could do?

Recall a time when you as a learner felt uncomfortable or anxious during an assessment. What aspects of the assessment contributed to your anxiety? Was the assessment about ideas or skills that you had studied but had not mastered, or was the assessment about ideas or skills that you do not even remember being taught? Or were there other reasons for your anxiety?

Principles of Good Educational Assessment

We have shown that at the heart of any educational assessment is the gathering and interpretation of evidence that clearly relates to learning. A good assessment focuses on these three dimensions:

- Gathering good evidence that relates to teaching and learning
- Interpreting the evidence properly
- Clearly understanding the key dimensions of learning

How we know things and how we learn are at the center of what it is we want to measure. For this reason, before we can consider what constitutes good educational evidence, we have to answer these fundamental questions: What learning is most valuable? What is important enough that we would teach it to learners and then assess it?

Clarifying Your Assumptions about What Counts in Learning

Assessment in education always relates to learning that is valuable. A crucial aspect of assessment, then, is to clarify what learning looks like and what counts as valuable learning. Most national learning standards and educational theorists (Darling-Hammond, 1993; Gardner, 1993; NCSS, 1998; NCTM, 2001) contend that valuable knowledge has three dimensions:

- Understanding of content
- Skills or strategies
- Dispositions or values

Although there is general agreement about the importance of these three dimensions of learning, most state and national tests tend to evaluate only one of them: the mastery of content. It may not be surprising that there is a

Resource for Your Assessment Toolkit
Standards for Teacher Competence in Educational Assessment

The following standards are drawn from the American Federation of Teachers (AFT), the National Council on Measurement in Education (NCME), and the National Education Association (NEA). Keep these standards in mind as you work through the ideas of this text; consider your progress in meeting these important skills.

Teachers should be skilled in choosing assessment methods appropriate for instructional decisions.

Teachers should be skilled in developing assessment methods appropriate for instructional decisions.

Teachers should be skilled in administering, scoring, and interpreting the results of both externally produced and teacher-produced assessment methods.

Teachers should be skilled in using assessment results when making decisions about individual learners, planning teaching, developing curriculum, and school improvement.

Teachers should be skilled in developing valid pupil grading procedures that include pupil assessments.

Teachers should be skilled in communicating assessment results to learners, parents, other lay audiences, and other educators.

Teachers should be skilled in recognizing unethical, illegal, and otherwise inappropriate assessment methods and uses of assessment information.

Source: American Federation of Teachers, National Council on Measurement in Education & National Education Association, 1990.

disconnect between what we say is important and what we assess, because the assessment of skills and dispositions is difficult and rarely possible in a standardized context like that used in national and state testing programs.

Some of our metaphors for assessment are the most effective ones to use when trying to assess skills and dispositions. For example, we can assess skills and strategies by observing and questioning the learner. By placing learners in a context that requires the use of thinking and other skills, the assessor can simply sit beside learners as they perform some important learning task. Taking notes and asking questions as a learner performs the learning task provides valuable information about what the learner can do.

Dispositions, that is, patterns of behavior that are valued by our society, can also be assessed in this naturalistic, task-oriented context. For example, the national science standards state that perseverance is an important disposition to nurture. By placing learners in a situation that requires their perseverance (such as making daily observations on a science project and taking notes), the teacher can collect evidence by noting the care and constancy of the daily notes that learners keep. This evidence provides data to assess perseverance.

What Counts as Important Content Knowledge? Most national standards (for example, American Association for the Advancement of Science [AAAS],

1992, 1993; National Council for the Social Studies [NCSS], 1998; National Council of Teachers of Mathematics [NCTM], 2001) emphasize concepts or big ideas as the important knowledge content that learners should learn over time. **Big ideas or themes** are large concepts that cut across many different areas and can be taught across a variety of grades. Big ideas provide a way to categorically organize information from science and other disciplines and to make sense of concepts and events. The emphasis or focus on big ideas allows teachers to integrate instruction and show the interdisciplinary nature of knowledge.

What are some examples of big ideas? Figure 1.1 displays some big ideas from science. In mathematics, the knowledge standards are organized by conceptual strands: number systems, computation and estimation, probability and statistics, measurement, geometry, patterns, and relationships. Once again, the emphasis is on large concepts that are developed gradually across all grade levels. Social studies standards emphasize the big ideas of culture, change over time, space, and place; groups and institutions; community; and multiculturalism.

What Counts as Important Skills and Strategies?

What Counts as Important Skills and Strategies? Standards also focus on valued skills and strategies that learners should master. Most skill standards focus on thinking and problem-solving tactics and strategies. Note that thinking tactics and strategies are not separate thinking skills like observation, elaboration, application, analysis, synthesis, or evaluation. (Barry Beyer, 1994, has identified as many as 144 separate thinking skills.) Instead, thinking tactics and strategies are *sets* of thinking skills used together. In general, *thinking tactics* are smaller collections of related skills, and *thinking strategies* are more complex collections of thinking skills.

What are some contemporary examples of thinking tactics and thinking strategies from education? Thinking tactics include the use of a logical sequence of tasks for experimentation, the use of a set of steps to write a paragraph, and the use of the proper method for solving an ill-structured problem. Thinking strategies are more complex and include clarifying multifaceted problems in an attempt to uncover the key underlying difficulty that needs to be answered first and determining how to find an answer to a question when there are insufficient data. Because these thinking tactics and strategies are so important, it is critical for educators to be aware of the rich variety of such tactics and strategies available to them. This awareness also enables teachers to be more specific in assisting learners to develop these strategies and, more important, to assess them. Furthermore, when teachers name and describe these thinking skills and tactics, learners are enabled to self-assess, reflect, and clarify their own evaluations about specific thinking abilities and weaknesses.

In science the important tactics and strategies are called *process skills*. Within the process skills are individual thinking skills such as observation, inference, drawing conclusions, extrapolation, graphing, predicting,

Figure 1.1 *Big Idea Examples*

cause–effect: Those situations where one particular observation or event is always followed by another specific observation or event.

communication: Imparting or exchanging of ideas, points of view, or information through speech, signs, or symbols.

conflict: Collision, disagreement, contradiction, or opposition; understanding how groups and nations attempt to resolve conflicts and seek to establish order and security.

culture: Common, identifiable characteristics that characterize a group of people over time.

cycle: Series of events or changing states that form an identifiable pattern that upon completion produces a final state identical to the original one.

energy: That which can bring about change or that which enables a material system to bring about change in itself and other systems when interacting with them.

force: A push or a pull that can be physical or psychological.

fundamental entities: Basic units of structure and function.

interaction: Reciprocal or mutual action or influence between two or more objects or things.

matter: Anything that has weight and takes up space.

model: Tentative, human-made schemes or structures that correspond to physical things or phenomena.

perception: The detection of input signals by the senses, transmission of these signals or messages to the brain, and the interpretation of these signals by the mind.

population: Groups of things that are similar in one or more ways.

power and authority: Possession of control or command over others; study of how groups affect the dynamic relationships among individual rights and responsibilities.

probability: Likelihood, chance, or possibility that some event will occur.

quantification: Assignment of numbers or measurements to phenomena.

symmetry: Broadly, harmony, balance, similarity, proportion, and arrangement.

system: Collection of related objects that collectively represent a whole.

theory: A set of interconnected statements relating to a certain aspect of the natural world.

time continuity and change: Recognition that past events account for change that is evident in the present; understanding that the present is connected to the past.

Source: Definitions are extracted from lengthy explanations in the National Science Standards and the 1995–1997 work of David Cox at Portland State University.

hypothesizing, and others. In mathematics, tactics and strategies are called *problem-solving skills*, within which are estimating, measuring, logic, drawing a conclusion, and so on. In social science they are labeled *critical thinking skills* and include interpreting, analyzing, evaluating, and explaining.

The important thing to remember about these diverse tactics and strategies is that teaching and assessing them is just as important as assessing content knowledge.

What Counts as Important Dispositions? National standards also focus on dispositions—ways of acting that are valued by our society. Dispositions are labeled differently by the different disciplines. For example, in science the national standards include such dispositions as perseverance, curiosity, open-mindedness, respect for life, and willingness to suspend judgment, while in social studies the dispositions include civic duty, loyalty, and concern for the poor. Mathematical dispositions include precision, accuracy, logical reasoning, and the capacity to see number and form in the real world. Dispositions drawn from literature and the arts include the capacity to see line, form, and function within the world, to view alternative perspectives, and to feel empathy for others.

Because the development of dispositions is so difficult, a group of experts met to call attention to the importance of dispositions across all types of thinking. After much debate these experts developed a consensus statement listing critical thinking dispositions. By providing a consensus list of key dispositions, they hoped to energize educators to go beyond assessing content and skills and ultimately to teach and assess dispositions. Figure 1.2 lists a part of the dispositions—the ones focused on critical thinking—that were developed by these experts.

Figure 1.2 *Consensus Statement of Critical Thinking Dispositions*

- Inquisitiveness with regard to a wide range of issues
- Concern to remain well-informed
- Trust in the processes of reasoned inquiry
- Self-confidence in one's own ability to reason
- Open-mindedness regarding divergent worldviews
- Flexibility in considering alternatives and opinions
- Understanding of the opinions of other people
- Fair-mindedness in appraising reasoning
- Honesty in facing one's own biases, prejudices, stereotypes, egocentric or sociocentric tendencies
- Prudence in suspending, making, or altering judgments
- Willingness to reconsider and revise views where honest reflection suggests that change is warranted

Source: Facione, 1990, p. 25.

Figure 1.3 *Putting the Pieces Together: How the Assessment Purpose Drives the Choice of Assessment Type*

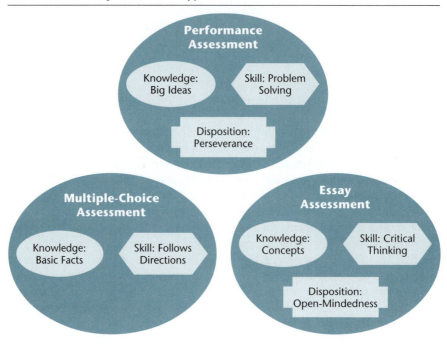

Teachers are challenged to teach learners to adopt these dispositions. It is a difficult task, and there are no easy methods to help learners develop valued dispositions. To date, the main instructional approaches that seem to encourage the development of dispositions center on real-world applications, problem-based learning, and cooperative learning approaches. Even though the assessment of such dispositions is equally difficult, throughout this text we will describe several methods that can be used.

In fact, as you think about the concepts, skills and strategies, and dispositions that you wish students to master, the type of assessment that is appropriate will often emerge. For example, if you are focused on teaching some basic, important facts that need to be mastered and if there is one correct answer and a need to follow directions, it is logical that a simple multiple-choice or short-answer assessment is useful. On the other hand, if you are interested in assessing problem-solving skills in a cooperative learning environment, a performance assessment is appropriate. Figure 1.3 displays how different types of assessments come together in different ways based on the specific purposes and types of skills, concepts, and dispositions that you wish to assess.

Gathering Good Evidence: Validity and Reliability

Since educational assessment involves gathering and interpreting evidence that clearly relates to learning, it is logical that its principles should be drawn from three areas: principles of good evidence, principles of good interpretation, and principles that show that the evidence and interpretation relate to an appropriate learning theory. Having considered what counts as valuable learning, we now turn to what makes evidence acceptable and useful and how to interpret the evidence we collect.

People reason from evidence every day to make any number of decisions, small and large. What shall I wear today? is a typical question posed by many of us as we get ready for school or work. Often we gather evidence by peering out the window to see if it is raining or bright and sunny. We may gather more evidence by listening to the morning weather report, and finally we may venture outside for first-hand experience. In a sense, we gather a stream of evidence, and with each piece we reason to a decision.

To some degree, good assessment is similar. In a good assessment procedure, you have some question about what a learner knows or can do. You need to gather appropriate evidence about that learner from a variety of different sources, such as classroom quizzes, standardized achievement tests, computerized tutoring programs, and conversations with the learner as she works through an experiment or some other learning project. As you think about each piece of evidence and go through a chain of reasoning, you gradually draw conclusions about what your learner still needs to learn.

The heart of an assessment is the gathering of evidence, but good evidence needs to be *valid* and *reliable*. What does this mean? We begin now to explore the key concepts of validity and reliability, and because they are so important, we will return to them again and again throughout the book.

Assessment Validity Good evidence is first of all valid. **Validity** means that the evidence clearly relates to and measures what it is that we are trying to assess. For example, if you wish to assess a learner's ability to comprehend reading passages in short stories written on a seventh-grade reading level, you would begin by selecting several reading passages from several short stories at the seventh-grade level. You would ask the learner to read each passage and then tell you what the passage means. The learner's answers are the evidence, and the evidence is valid to the degree to which it truly measures the learner's ability to comprehend the passages from the short stories (rather than something else like the learner's ability to understand metaphors or parts of speech).

But if you had only selected a single passage drawn from a single short story, and you asked the learner to tell you what it says, the validity of your assessment is considerably weakened. This is so because when you only give the learner one passage from one story, by chance that passage could be especially easy or especially hard. A learner who normally can read and comprehend seventh-grade stories might fail to comprehend one that is especially difficult, while a learner who cannot normally read at that level might be able to comprehend an especially easy example. As you can see, validity relates to how carefully you choose evidence. Your evidence is strongest or most valid when it closely matches the intentions of the assessment.

Evidence is not totally valid or totally invalid. Rather, there are degrees of validity for the evidence you collect. The closer the evidence is to the actual thing you are assessing, the more valid it becomes. For example, are you assessing a learner's ability to comprehend certain paragraphs in a story or the learner's ability to follow written directions? Here are some questions that will help you determine the validity of the evidence provided by your assessment.

- Does the assessment focus on important ideas and skills that I wish to assess?
- Are the directions and wording of the questions clear, concise, and easy to understand so that they do not stand in the way of the learners showing what they know and can do?
- Is the assessment focused on concepts and skills that were taught?
- Is the assessment one in which learners will feel comfortable showing what they know and do?
- Are the scoring directions clear, and do the directions specify the key components of the concepts and skills that are my focus?

Assessment Reliability Another standard for evidence is its reliability, the consistency of assessment results. **Reliability** is the degree to which assessment results are consistent across repeated administrations (*test-retest reliability*) or consistent no matter who collects the evidence (*inter-rater reliability*). For example, if you develop an assessment for learners to show their understanding of some concept, it is reasonable to expect that whatever evidence you uncover would be the same if you assessed the learner a second time on the same day or a day later. If you find that your assessment results differ, then you have a reliability problem, and you will need to rethink your assessment. A reliable assessment produces consistent results time after time as long as no new learning has occurred.

Here are some questions that will help you determine the reliability of your assessment.

- How typical are the results of this assessment compared to the performance of learners at other times and places?

- If the assessment were conducted by another assessor, would the results be similar?

- If learners were asked to complete the assessment at another time of day, would the results be similar?

Interpreting Results Accurately

The standards for good interpretation are difficult to describe because these standards depend on the quality of the evidence that was collected. The standards for interpretation are also connected to what you believe about the nature of learning because your belief influences the kind of evidence you choose to collect and interpret. A good interpretation is also connected to your awareness of possible biases that you may have introduced either in the types of evidence you have collected or in a narrow view about the nature of knowledge. In the end, a good interpretation is one that is clearly connected to your assumptions about the nature of knowledge and learning and one that is free of bias.

Here are some practical questions to help you interpret assessment results accurately.

- What do I mean by understanding, and how does this look in my classroom?

- Do my assessments match my view of understanding and skills?

- Do my assessments favor any one ethnic group?

- Do I have sufficient evidence to draw a conclusion about a learner?

- Did I provide the learner with different types of assessments in an effort to uncover what he or she knows?

Ask Yourself

Recall a time when as a learner you felt that an assessment was unfair. Examine the questions in the previous sections that relate to the validity, reliability, and interpretation of assessment results. Consider each question as it relates to the unfair assessment. Then determine if the assessment was unfair primarily because of the validity, reliability, or interpretation of assessment results. As a teacher, how would you change the unfair assessment in an effort to make it fair?

Ethical Issues and Professional Responsibilities in Assessment

Teachers are granted a profound trust by society. They are charged with the development of future citizens and are also given the right to assess that development. This means that teachers have a grave responsibility to develop assessments that are just and equitable and that enhance learning. This responsibility is particularly important for the teaching profession because learners have no choice about school attendance. They are required to attend school and are by law under the control of teachers. Learners are also more vulnerable than adults in a situation in which they will be judged, because they are less experienced and more impressionable than adults.

Such a responsibility requires teachers to be vigilant and self-reflective because fairness, justice, and equity are difficult to evaluate in the middle of a teacher's daily pressures. Throughout this text, we will return to issues of fair, just, and equitable assessments as these issues relate to the different components of assessment. However, for now, a simple review of the underlying characteristics of these terms is helpful.

Fairness in assessment means that the teacher is free from bias, and judgments are made carefully and impartially. The National Education Association (1975) reminds us of the many types of bias that teachers must control. Their ethical standards for teachers' relations with pupils state that teachers "shall not on the basis of race, color, creed, sex, national origin, marital status, political or religious beliefs, family, social or cultural background or sexual orientation exclude any learner from participation in any program, deny any benefits or grant any advantage."

Justice implies that teachers act in a morally upright manner and conform to high standards of conduct. Plato contends that a just person is one who works for the good of others. Justice requires that those in authority work to benefit, not to harm, others. When it comes to assessment, justice requires teachers to use their power to develop, not harm, students.

Equity requires teachers to consider the unique characteristics of each child and carefully incorporate these differences so as to achieve a proper balance among conflicting needs and rights of learners. For example, if learners in a single classroom live in both urban and rural areas, it is important to select examples that come from experiences that both learner groups will understand.

Needless to say, the requirements of fair, just, and equitable assessment can be daunting. In an effort to respond to this challenge, one of the best things you can do as a teacher is develop a beginning list of positive behaviors or other proactive actions for yourself that set the stage for fair, just, and equitable assessment in your classroom. Then, regularly return to this list of proactive practices and update them in light of life's complex demands. Here are a few such proactive practices.

- Inform learners about specific learning expectations.
- Describe for your pupils the characteristics of assessments that you will use to meet these learning expectations.
- Describe how the characteristics of assessments match the learning expectations and provide the students with concrete examples or practice assessments.
- Be sure that your evaluations of learners are based on more than a single assessment.
- Carefully guard against snap judgments.
- Do not use emotion-laden labels for learners such as "disinterested," "slow," "sloppy," and so forth. Discuss possible stereotypes with your learners.
- Avoid terms and examples that may be offensive to learners of different genders, races, religions, and ethnicities.
- Recognize the positives of cultural differences.
- Respect pupils' diversities and disabilities and ensure that pupil participation and interactions are not limited.

Another way to help you work toward fair, just, and equitable assessment is to read publications and actively participate in workshops and conferences provided by professional organizations dedicated to this important goal. Organizations such as the National Council on Measurement in Education (www.ncme.org), the American Psychological Association's Joint Committee on Testing Practices (www.apa.org), and the National Academies' National Research Council (www.nationalacademies.org) provide workshops, conferences, and publications. In addition, the American Federation of Teachers (www.aft.org) and the National Education Association (www.nea.org) have subcommittees and special interest groups dedicated to the development of fair, just, and equitable assessment practices. The importance of participating in the national conversation about assessment cannot be overstated because the way that we assess learners is as important as the way we teach them.

?Ask Yourself

Remember a time when you made a snap judgment and later discovered that you were in error. What did you fail to recognize? Were you influenced by some underlying bias? Did you react because of emotion rather than reason? Did you find that your expectations were unreasonable in the first place?

Summary

- There are different metaphors for assessment, and each implies different environments, methods, and purposes: assessment as sitting beside, judging, and coaching.

- There are a variety of reasons for assessment, and these reasons determine the type of setting or context for the assessment:

  - Assessment as instruction and providing feedback

  - Assessment as determining what learners need to learn next

  - Assessment as diagnosing learner difficulties or misconceptions

  - Assessment as determining progress along a developmental continuum

  - Assessment as program evaluation or accountability

- Despite the many different uses for assessment, there is a common thread. At the heart of any educational assessment is the gathering and interpretation of evidence that clearly relates to learning.

A crucial aspect of assessment is to clarify what learning looks like and what counts as valuable learning. National learning standards state that valuable learning has three dimensions: understanding of content, skills or strategies, and dispositions.

- At the heart of an assessment is the gathering and accurate interpretation of valid and reliable evidence. Valid evidence is evidence that closely matches the type of learning that you are trying to assess, and reliable evidence is evidence that is consistent. A good interpretation is one that is clearly connected to your assumptions about the nature of learning and is free of bias.

- Teachers are granted a profound trust by society in that they are not only charged with the development of future citizens but also are given the right to assess that development. Teachers have a grave responsibility to develop fair, just, and equitable assessments that enhance learning.

Key Terms

assessment (6)

big ideas or themes (13)

criterion-referenced test (10)

feedback (8)

formative assessment (7)

foundational approach (4)

norm-referenced test (10)

reliability (18)

summative assessment (7)

validity (17)

For Further Discussion

1. Provide a metaphor for assessment that matches your personal point of view and explain why the metaphor is consistent with your view of teaching and learning.

2. Although there are different purposes for assessment, describe what these purposes have in common.

3. Recall an assessment from your personal experience that was especially meaningful to you and describe why it was so meaningful.

4. How would you respond to a parent who asks you to describe the validity and reliability of a classroom assessment you constructed?

5. Develop a coat of arms that represents your code of ethics and responsibilities as an assessor of student learning. Share the symbolism that underlies your coat of arms.

Comprehension Quiz

In each chapter, we provide a short review of some key ideas in the form of an assessment. The use of these formats can remind you of the way that the format of an assessment changes your response to the experience. For Chapter 1, we have chosen to provide you with a selected-response, forced-choice assessment experience.

Part One

Select the appropriate purpose or purposes for each of the assessment settings listed below. Use the following list of purposes.

    a. Assessment as instruction and providing feedback

    b. Assessment as determining what learners need to learn next

    c. Assessment as diagnosing learner difficulties or misconceptions

    d. Assessment as determining progress along a developmental continuum

    e. Assessment as program evaluation or accountability

1. Chantelle is given a set of reading passages followed by comprehension questions for each passage. The reading passages range from easy to difficult, and she is told that she must complete the assessment within 15 minutes.

2. Mr. Jacobs, high school history teacher, is about to discuss the Revolutionary War with his freshman students. He interviews several of his students, asks open-ended questions about the Revolutionary War, and records what they say.

3. Every year all fifth-grade pupils are required to complete a nationally normed assessment in mathematics and reading.

4. Every 15 minutes Juan is asked to read the temperature of a cup of water that has been placed in the sun and to record the temperature readings in a data table that he creates.

Part Two

What type of learning is the major focus for each of the following assessment contexts?

    a. Understanding of content

    b. Development of skills or strategies

    c. Development of dispositions or values

1. Ralph is asked to define a life cycle and then provide an example of a specific organism's life cycle.

2. Karen is asked to solve a mathematics word problem and describe her thinking along the way.

3. Amy Lou is asked to observe, measure, and record the growth of a plant each day for 3 months.

Relevant Website Resources

Authentic Education

(www.grantwiggins.org

This website focuses on resources for teaching and assessing understanding. It provides *Big Ideas*, a monthly online journal showcasing best practices and insights for fostering authentic learning in the classroom. The Good Ideas Database and Good Idea of the Week offer learning activities, thought-provoking questions, and in-service exercises. All these resources relate to the Understanding by Design framework.

Print resources, websites, and the Understanding by Design framework.

Digital Edge Learning Interchange

http://ali.apple.com/ali_sites/deli/nav1.shtml

This website is a partnership of the National Board for Professional Teaching Standards (NBPTS), the International Society for Technology in Education (ISTE), Apple Computer, and AT&T, which promotes accomplished teaching and technology.

In "Exhibits" one can find Opening Classroom Doors presented by the NBPTS. Video clips of national board certified teachers' classrooms provide insights into teaching and assessment. In addition to content standards and the assessment cycle, the website also highlights authentic assessment, alternative assessment, informal assessment, and online assessment. Of particular interest to teachers is material on peer evaluation and self-evaluation.

References

American Association for the Advancement of Science (AAAS). (1992). *Science for all Americans*. Washington, DC: Author.

American Association for the Advancement of Science (AAAS). (1993). *Benchmarks for science literacy*. Washington, DC: Author.

American Federation of Teachers, National Council on Measurement in Education & National Education Association. (1990). *Standards for teacher competence in educational assessment of students*. ERIC document ED323186. From http://www.ode.state.or.us/teachlearn/real/documents/buros-standardsforteachers.pdf. Accessed December 18, 2007.

Beyer, B. (1994). *Teaching for thinking*. New York: Allyn and Bacon.

Cox, D. C. (1989). *Science Concept Working Papers 1–20*. Portland, OR : Portland State *University*.

Darling-Hammond, L. (1993). *Authentic assessment in practice: A collection of portfolios, performance tasks, exhibitions and documentation*. New York: Center on Restructuring Education, Schools, and Teaching.

Dewey, J. (1916). *Democracy and education: Introduction to the philosophy of education*. New York: Macmillan.

Facione, P. A. (1990). *Critical thinking: A statement of expert consensus for purposes of educational assessment and instruction*. ERIC Document ED315423.

Gardner, H. (1993). *Frames of mind: The theory of multiple intelligences*. New York: Basic Books.

Marzano, R. J., Pickering, D., & McTigue, J. (1993). *Assessing learner outcomes*. Alexandria, VA: Association for Supervision and Curriculum Development.

National Council for the Social Studies (NCSS). (1998). *National standards for the social studies*. Washington, DC: Author.

National Council for Teachers of Mathematics (NCTM). (2001). *National standards for mathematics*. Washington, DC: Author.

National Education Association (NEA). (1975). *Code of ethics for the education profession*. Adopted by the NEA Representative Assembly, 1975. http://www.nea.org/aboutnea/code.html. Accessed September 2, 2007.

Stiggins, R. J. (2005). *Learner-involved assessment for learning*. Upper Saddle River, NJ: Pearson Prentice-Hall.

Wiggins, G. (1998). *Educative assessment*. San Francisco: Jossey-Bass.

CHAPTER 2

The Psychological Foundations of Assessment

Chapter Objectives

After reading and thinking about this chapter, you will be able to:

- **Explain the difference between assessment and testing.**
- **Explain the importance of using multiple sources of data in assessment.**
- **Distinguish among several learning theories by explaining their implications for assessment.**

- **Describe the implications of motivation theory for classroom assessment.**
- **Describe the importance of differentiated teaching and assessment.**

The purpose of this chapter is to present assessment from the psychological and social foundations perspectives. Here we describe the theories developed by important thinkers and researchers in the field of learning, and we explain the implications that these theories have in creating effective classroom assessments so that you can appreciate the differences among your students. We ask you to think more broadly about assessment by posing the question, How do multiple assessment methods come together to present a truly authentic picture of student learning?

In foundations textbooks, students most often examine the historical, social, and philosophical foundations of education. The psychological perspective is often referred to as the fourth foundation. The **psychological foundations** perspective is no less important than the first three. As you will see in this chapter, a deeper understanding of how students learn forces us to think critically about how we plan, how we teach, and how we assess our students.

We understand that all students are different—they have different personal histories, they have different abilities, they have encountered teachers with different approaches to learning, and they have access to different resources. At the same time, there are characteristics that students share in how they learn that allow us to teach and assess appropriately. This chapter presents several ways of looking at learning and motivation—the psychological foundations perspective. By understanding this more thoroughly, we can improve our teaching and assessment of students.

Foundational Questions for Your Consideration

- What factors motivate students and what factors inhibit students in showing what they know and can do?
- What implicit cues do students interpret from school life that might make them unable or unwilling to show what they know and can do?
- How do relationships and other affiliations influence a student's willingness to take part in assessments?
- When students develop misconceptions about an area of study, how can you help them correct these misconceptions without decreasing their motivation and willingness to try again?

What Can Assessment Tell Us?

Before we can effectively answer the question of what assessment can tell us, it is important to make a critical distinction between *assessment* and *testing*, two related but not synonymous terms. Teachers, students, administrators, parents, and others recognize that testing has become a priority, indeed a legal mandate, in American public schools today. In many ways, the language and practice of education have made this important distinction somewhat less clear.

Testing is the means by which educators evaluate students' knowledge or skills by their performance on a particular instrument or task. Tests may take a number of forms, but in general they are intended to serve as an **objective** measure of learning. Test results may also be used in a variety of ways. For example, one tenth-grade student's test score may provide an indicator of how well that student understands the causes of the American Civil War. That same score might also indicate how well that student scored relative to the rest of the class or to the student's own performance on prior tests in the same class. And taken together, the performance of all the tenth-grade students on that same test can provide evidence of the district's standing in terms of knowledge of the Civil War when compared to districts across the state or nation.

Teachers and students are probably most familiar with the classroom-based paper-and-pencil variety of test, but in any school setting, other testing forms may be used. Physical education classes, for example, may require that students demonstrate proficiency in particular skills, such as the time it takes them to run a mile. Regardless of the form, context, or academic discipline in which the testing occurs, however, tests are intended to evaluate something. The results of tests can be used in your teaching practice to:

- Determine your students' ability relative to other students on a similar task.
- Demonstrate the degree of students' growth over time in a particular area of knowledge or skill.
- Provide evidence of depth of understanding of an idea or content area.
- Predict students' future performance.

Assessment, as you recall from Chapter 1, is a much broader term that includes the practice of testing but also includes a variety of formal and informal methods of gathering information. Assessment focuses not only on student performance and potential but also on the factors that influence students' learning—personality, level and style of motivation, home environment, and perhaps areas of exceptionality, for example. Assessment tells us both what our students have learned and what they have the capacity to learn. Assessment provides us with evidence for reflection about our own teaching and learning. Assessment is the basis for all critical decisions about our students. Regardless of the form and purpose of a particular assessment, the most critical consideration that educators must keep in mind is that all assessment should be conducted with the student at the center.

Testing most often occurs in a structured setting (like an in-class final exam in geometry), but assessment can take many forms. Although assessment may involve structured tests, it also can be less formal but equally meaningful observations of student behaviors, conversations with students and with colleagues, collected samples of student work, or interviews with parents or family members.

As a teacher, you want to come to know and understand your students deeply—in what areas do they excel, in what areas are they struggling, in what subjects are they particularly motivated to learn, and in what ways do they most effectively communicate their learning? If assessment included, for example, only weekly content-area paper-and-pencil tests, your understanding of your students would be limited. The purpose of this book is to assist you in the development of tests and other formal assessments that show how much students have learned but also to help you increase your ability to effectively capture and communicate less formal indicators of student learning. And when you attempt to create and use your assessments, we want you to take into account a variety of learner characteristics.

Ask Yourself

As a college student, you probably receive a syllabus for each of your classes on the first day of the semester. What is often the first thing students do when they receive a syllabus? Turn to the course calendar to determine when tests will be administered and when papers or major assignments are due. Take some time to review your syllabi for this current semester or year. How many forms of assessment have your instructors implemented? Do the assessments seem to differ by subject? Do your instructors rely on multiple ways for you to demonstrate understanding?

Assessment and Different Ways of Learning

Why are the psychological foundations so important to assessment? You already realize that students will arrive in your classroom with a variety of abilities, a broad range of experiences, and unique ways of communicating. And, as you will discover as you move through your studies, differentiation of instruction attempts to meet the needs of learners based on an understanding of specific characteristics, such as learning disabilities or exceptional talents. The psychological and social foundations of education tell us that before we can assess a student's competence in a content area, we need to "size up" the student.

To do this, we need to understand the characteristics that research has shown to be important to successful learning. These include the personal attributes and traits that make a student more interested in learning and more likely to be successful and those principles identified by researchers that will make teaching and assessment more successful.

This chapter will first introduce you to two key theories or models in the field of psychology that discuss how children learn. The first is the developmental perspective, which suggests that learning is a process that occurs in interaction between the person and the environment; the second is a social approach, which focuses on learning that occurs through our interactions with the people around us. No one perspective is the right or correct theory, but each helps us understand learning and how to effectively use assessment.

Students' Developmental Differences

You are a fifth-grade teacher, and it is your first day of teaching at a new school. What could you know about your students? They are all fifth-graders, so they must all be about 11 years old. Many of them probably went to the same school and had the same teacher in fourth grade, so they have had comparable educational experiences. Many live in the same neighborhood, and you may even have siblings in the class. Therefore, you can safely conclude that they are all pretty much the same and that you do not have to change your teaching for any of the students, right?

Of course not. We could not draw the same conclusion about any class-room, no matter how similar the students appear. Not only do they bring different experiences to the classroom, they are probably different developmentally. **Developmental learning theories** focus on the change and development of individuals over time—from infancy to adulthood. That we would not teach sixth-graders in the same ways that we would teach second-graders is obvious. It is not just that sixth-graders are more experienced and have learned more, but we know that sixth-graders are developmentally different in the ways that they make sense of and apply information they have learned. Learners faced with a particular situation will react differently and gain differently from that situation, depending on their developmental level.

But go back to your fifth-grade classroom. Do you think that even within one grade level developmental levels are similar? In fact, at certain ages and in certain grades, there may be significant differences among your students in certain abilities. In your fifth-grade class, many of your students may still require manipulatives or visual representations of objects to help them solve problems, while a handful of students in the same class may be developmentally ready to think abstractly and handle more complex math or logic problems without assistance. If you teach in a multi-grade or multi-age classroom, you can see much more clearly how students in different developmental stages (not necessarily ages) address problems.

You have probably encountered in other classes the work of Jean Piaget (1896–1980), a Swiss psychologist. According to Piaget, children learn by discovery, but what they are able to learn is limited by their level of development. Piaget's theories of learning are beyond the scope and intent of this chapter, but they provide a picture of the characteristics of children at different ages that may help us think about differentiating our assessment practices. According to Piaget, cognitive development proceeds through four stages. In each of these stages, the child constructs new ways of understanding the world through maturation and interaction with the environment. The stages are summarized in Figure 2.1 (Ormrod, 2008).

Piaget recognized, of course, that the age levels within each of his proposed stages were fluid and approximate. That is, children do not wake up on their twelfth birthdays with the capacity to think abstractly. Instead, the process is one of transition that roughly coincides with chronological age. This overview is admittedly brief and does not sufficiently capture the richness of Piaget's understanding of development, but it points us toward a critical consideration as we look at methods to assess students' understanding.

Figure 2.1 *Piaget's Stages of Cognitive Development*

1. *Sensorimotor (birth to about age 2):* In this developmental stage, learning is characterized by the coordination of sensory input and physical actions. Infants learn through these actions that there is a difference between themselves and the physical world.

2. *Preoperational (approximately ages 2 through 7):* In the preoperational stage, children begin to assign names and meaning to their physical environment, and they develop the capacity to represent their world through fanciful drawings and symbols.

3. *Concrete operational (approximately ages 7 through 11):* An important evelopmental trait during this stage is children's ability to apply increasingly sophisticated logical reasoning, as opposed to intuition, to their lives. They are, however, unable to think in abstractions and, in solving problems, must still have images or objects in front of them that represent the problem or situation on which they are working.

4. *Formal operations (beyond approximately age 11):* Formal operations represent the highest developmental level of thinking according to Piaget's scheme. The formal operations stage is characterized by the ability to think in the abstract, no longer requiring the presence of objects to manipulate in order to figure out how to solve a problem. In formal operations, hypotheses can be developed and tested and conclusions drawn based on different results.

Source: Omrod, 2008.

Two of the authors of this text collaborated in the development of a system of assessment at an institution for students gifted in mathematics and science. Gifted populations often have an average age somewhat younger than other students at their grade level because many of the gifted students will have skipped a grade during their elementary education. At one point in the development of our school's curriculum, a decision was made to restructure the science course offerings so that all sophomore students would be required to take both physics and chemistry. This decision was grounded in current research in science education, but it did not take into account that a number of these gifted high school sophomores—having skipped one or two grades—were only 11 or 12 years old. Given what we know about Piaget's developmental scheme, might we expect that our younger sophomores, despite their academic talent, would struggle to understand the abstractions inherent in an upper-level physics course?

To find out if this was the case, we administered several instruments that were designed to assess students' development on a Piagetian scale. The results showed that our 11- and 12-year-old sophomores were slightly developmentally behind their older classmates, which could explain some of their initial difficulties in grasping high-level physics concepts. So, armed with new information about students' learning, the science faculty reconsidered the ways in which they presented concepts and, just as important, the way they assessed learning.

What Developmental Differences Say about Learning and Assessment

In what ways can developmental theory inform assessment? First, an understanding of developmental theory should become part of your assessments, especially at critical developmental ages. Careful observations, conversations with colleagues and parents, and patterns of classroom performance can provide you with multiple indicators of your students' readiness for more complex concepts and areas of difficulty. For example, when asked to orally answer a question about the earth's rotation, does your fifth-grade student require manipulatives, such as marbles or tennis balls, to help her communicate her understanding, or is she able to satisfactorily explain the motions of the planets without such assistance? While this is only a single data point, if you know also that this student becomes frustrated and stops trying when confronted with problems that are equally abstract, it may suggest that she is not developmentally ready for such material.

Consequently, to administer a class-wide paper-and-pencil test may not be the most appropriate measure for all of your students. While all of your students may fully understand planetary motion, a few may not be able to communicate the principle effectively on paper. As you come to know your students, you will soon recognize that, despite their ages or grades, they represent different levels of developmental ability and thus may need to be assessed differently.

Differences in Students' Social Experiences

Social learning theories focus on the interaction between learners and their social environments—the other people around them. Which of the following scenarios is more helpful to a student?

Situation 1: You are in a calculus class and your teacher permits you a half hour at the end of class to work alone on tomorrow's assignment. You answer the first two questions, but the third problem is exceptionally difficult. You take the question to the professor and tell him that it is too hard for you; so he takes your homework from you, jots down the correct answer, and hands it back.

Situation 2: Same class, same homework, same teacher. But instead of doing the problem for you, he sits you down beside him and says, "Let's see if we can work this out together." You try method A, and when A does not work, he asks if you have tried method B. By supporting you by tapping

Gathering Information Through Careful Observation

What can mollusks teach us about assessment? It depends, perhaps, on how closely we observe them. Although most teachers appreciate Piaget for what he contributed to our understanding of how children learn and develop systems of logic and understanding, what is often overlooked is that he was trained as a biologist. His experiences as a scientist shaped the methods by which he arrived at many of his important ideas of psychological development. For example, in one study, Piaget observed the physical changes that occur when a mollusk is transported from the still water of a lake to the swiftly moving water of a river. Mollusks adhere to solid surfaces by means of appendages called *feet*, and when they are moved to faster-moving water, they will develop extra feet that will allow them to adhere more firmly.

By observing mollusks in various settings, Piaget provided not only scientific data but also demonstrated the importance of careful observations of living things in their natural settings.

Indeed, this naturalistic observation characterized Piaget's study of children. By watching them, conversing with them, and playing with them in their own settings (parks, schools, playgrounds), Piaget was able to capture the cognitive development of children in an authentic, real-world way.

As a teacher, you will find it helpful to keep Piaget's methods in mind. Often, teachers are concerned with whether their students arrive at the right answer. But if we borrow Piaget's observational skills and ask a student *how* he arrived at an *incorrect* answer, the student's logic and reasoning can also be assessed. You may find that the reasoning was logical, despite the wrong answer.

So, while we know that Piaget offers useful insights about how children learn and develop, we can also learn a great deal by applying Piaget's methods and by attempting to see the world through our students' eyes.

into what you already know and building on that understanding, the teacher creates an opportunity for you to solve the problem.

Either of these scenarios could have changed your understanding of calculus, but the second scenario, we hope you will agree, represents the more meaningful exchange between teacher and student. Social learning theories suggest that it is the development and exchange of language and symbols that define learning.

As children develop, they acquire different means of communication. By pointing and gesturing, by making certain noises or using different inflections, and eventually by using formal language, children are able to communicate ideas and to refine their understanding of the world. And all of these forms of communication require the interaction among the developing individual, the environment, and other people.

Why are social contexts important to understanding differences among students and properly assessing them with respect to those differences? A large body of research suggests a strong correlation between socioeconomic status and academic achievement. This, of course, does not mean that poverty causes low achievement. In fact, there are many remarkable examples of high-achieving students in schools in impoverished areas.

But think for a moment about how children's social context might differ along economic lines and how that could influence academic performance. Parents' level of education or literacy, single-parent homes, access to remedial services, access to enriched preschool experiences, the amount and quality of television watched in the home, and even the number of books in children's homes have been related to student achievement. None of these alone would predict low achievement, but these factors often occur in combination, and therefore development and achievement often lag behind for students because they do not have enriched exchanges with others who can enhance and broaden their learning outside of school.

Russian psychologist Lev Vygotsky (1896–1934) studied children's learning extensively during his short life. Like Piaget, Vygotsky asserted that learners actively construct their own meaning and their own understanding of the world, but Vygotsky's theory focuses on social interaction. Vygotsky's theory of learning, *social constructivism*, relies on the belief that learning occurs through the interactions of people using language and symbols. While cognitive development is limited to a certain range at any given age, it is the development of language and our interactions with others that allow us to understand and explain the world in new ways that are meaningful to us.

But what can Vygotsky tell us about assessment? The answer lies in his most widely recognized concept, the **zone of proximal development.** The idea is illustrated in the following example. Suppose you have two 10-year-old students who performed at the 8-year-old level in standardized testing. Is this sufficient information with which to begin planning instruction? Vygotsky would argue that it is not because this initial assessment does not present a full picture of the developmental levels of the students.

A formal test can show you what a student does in a particular instance on his own. Vygotsky suggests that you can learn much more about a student if you sit beside that student, as we described in Chapter 1, continuing to assess as you provide assistance and support. For example, you might re-administer part of the test, giving the student more time to respond. You might give hints when the student struggles with an item. You might state a question differently for the student. Having provided this extra support, you discover that one of the students can now solve problems at the 10-year-old level, while the other student solves problems at the 12-year-old level. According to Vygotsky, you have used these students' zones of proximal development, which he defines as

> the difference between the *actual developmental level* as determined by independent problem solving and the *level of potential development* as determined through problem solving under adult guidance or in collaboration with more capable peers. (Vygotsky, 1978, p. 86)

To fully assess a student's development, then, it is not sufficient to rely on a standardized measure of achievement. The formal test can tell us the student's actual developmental level, but it should also be a departure point from which the teacher can use observation, interaction, and interpretation of students' unique understanding to fully assess both ability and potential.

Social Constructivism and Differentiated Teaching and Assessment

Educational philosophy and practice have long recognized the value of social interaction in the learning process—interaction between teacher and student, between the student and classmates, and between students and their families. There is a significant body of research demonstrating how each of these relationships influences learning.

How can social constructivism inform assessment? According to Vygotsky, for instance, since language mediates learning and understanding, it may be instructive for you to observe carefully just how your students communicate their answers. Deep understanding is reflected not by your students' ability to recite an answer but rather by the degree to which they communicate their understanding in a new way.

For example, it is common for some students to study for a test by memorizing all of a chapter's key terms, usually those terms that appear in bold or italic type. Most teachers would agree that this strategy does not lead to deep conceptual understanding, but many classroom tests contain a significant number of items that can be answered by students who study and recognize only the bold and italicized terms. Again, through observation, conversation, and other interaction, the assessment-minded teacher will use a wide variety of language to define, explain, and illustrate an idea to students. Most important, assessment-minded teachers will create opportunities for students to communicate their understanding in a variety of ways *prior to* a formal test of the material.

Social theorists raise considerations that help us see the importance of going beyond simple, formal testing when we assess our students. We should, of course, be sensitive to where our students are developmentally. And social theorists emphasize that a math placement test might tell us what students are capable of doing without assistance in the classroom. But only through more careful observation and less formal assessment are we able to determine our students' potential.

?Ask Yourself

Think of a time when a fellow student attempted to respond to a question and answered inaccurately. Did you feel embarrassed for the student? Did the student seem to withdraw from the interaction? How did the teacher respond to the incorrect or inarticulate answer? What can you learn from this experience that will help you to encourage students to take risks and yet maintain the respect of others? Do you think teachers need to teach students to respect different approaches to understanding? Do you think you should encourage students to take risks and look at errors as opportunities to learn?

Are Students Differently Motivated?

Motivation is a complex and often-misunderstood dimension of teaching and learning. Most teachers approach motivation as if it were something that we can do to our students, as in, "What can I do to motivate my students?" And many teachers will describe their students as somewhere between "unmotivated" and "highly motivated."

While both of these notions are legitimate, psychological motivation theories can give us insights through the eyes of the learner. They can explain what students are interested in, why they are interested in it, and what we can do to keep that interest going. Three models that have been developed to explain motivation are presented here. Each model provides a different dimension of motivation, and each has important implications for your use of assessment as a teacher.

Motivation as Achievement Goal Orientation

Motivation can be defined as the "process whereby goal-directed activity is instigated and sustained" (Pintrich & Schunk, 2002, p. 5). There are several key points in this definition. First, motivation is a process, not necessarily a single, observable action, like starting a car. Second, there are goals involved. Those goals may be very apparent (such as earning a gold star for a perfect score on a vocabulary test) or intangible (such as the feeling of accomplishment for successfully solving a difficult physics problem). And third, motivation leads to some degree of extended engagement.

Since the notion of "goal-directed activity" is a part of a generally accepted definition of motivation, it should not be surprising that a significant body of educational research explores the relationship between goals and student learning. So how does this relationship influence our assessment of student learning? The answer is in two important ideas that come out of the research on goal orientation: performance and mastery.

Performance goal orientation represents a learner's inclination to learn and demonstrate a new skill in comparison to others' skills. For example, knowing that class rank will be an important criterion for the National Honor Society, a student seeks to earn nothing less than an A in all classes during junior year. For this student, the opportunity for learning and growth is less important than the recognition or reward of honor society membership.

Performance goal orientation can be further divided into avoidance and approach performance goals. Avoidance suggests that students will not attempt certain activities in order to avoid the appearance of incompetence. They may avoid asking questions when they need help or give up easily when they cannot understand the task. An honor student may enroll in less challenging classes in order to avoid appearing a less capable student or to avoid getting a lower grade. An approach orientation, on the other hand, might lead a student to spend every evening and weekend studying for the SAT, either to ensure college admission or to boast the highest score in the school.

Mastery goal orientation, in contrast, is characterized by a desire to learn for the sake of learning, to develop new skills, to meet personally established goals, and to monitor one's learning. When we use language such as "lifelong learning" to describe our hopes for our students, it is likely that we want students to become mastery oriented—that is, students who learn for the inherent satisfaction of learning.

What do these concepts mean in terms of assessment? On the one hand, most teachers would prefer to have their students move from a performance orientation toward a mastery orientation. Indeed, there is significant research suggesting that mastery orientation is related to feelings of success and accomplishment (Ames, 1992) and effective cognitive and self-regulatory learning habits (Pintrich & Schunk, 2002; p. 225). On the other hand, performance orientation is not without some motivational benefits. For example, approach performance goals have been demonstrated to relate to high and sustained levels of engagement. Avoidance goals, however, are more likely to be negatively related to the use of higher-order cognitive strategies. And most important, the classroom environment—especially the way students are evaluated—has a major effect on students' goal orientations (Ames, 1992).

So, as teachers, it might first be instructive to think about how our classrooms could effectively support mastery orientation. However, we might also want to assess our students' individual goal orientations. Such an insight would inform our interactions with individual students and make us much more effective teachers.

Motivation as Self-Efficacy

Closely related to the concept of mastery orientation is another theory of motivation called **self-efficacy,** which can be defined as one's feeling of competence to achieve a desired outcome. According to psychologist Albert

Bandura, our sense of self-efficacy has a deep influence on how we feel, think, and act. *Self-efficacy* is not synonymous with *self-esteem*, which is an overall, global sense of self-worth. Instead, self-efficacy is context and task specific, and it has little generalizability across academic areas (Bandura, 1994).

Here is an example: Suppose that in the first few weeks of school you recognize that one of your seventh-graders makes many negative statements about his performance in your math class. Such a feeling of low self-efficacy in mathematics may have many causes—poor prior performance, siblings or friends who have had similar experiences in mathematics, or improper placement in a prior math class—but the student's low self-efficacy may translate into problematic behaviors in class, such as low engagement or lack of persistence in facing difficult problems.

According to Dale Schunk (1991), self-efficacy not only characterizes the manner in which students approach a task or a problem, but it also plays a significant role in which tasks students *choose* to engage in. Students with high self-efficacy tend to be more engaged, persistent, and resilient in certain areas, and they expect to perform well in those areas.

How do issues of self-efficacy relate to classroom assessment? As with students' goal orientation, self-efficacy can in many ways define and predict student performance and behavior. Not all students are forthcoming about their feelings of competence in school, or at least not publicly. So while some students may approach you and state emphatically, "I have never been good in math," other students may hide this feeling and require specific attention from you to uncover it. Even students who tend to perform well in a discipline may not have high self-efficacy in certain tasks, such as timed tests. While it is appropriate to administer a pretest to determine students' relative level of ability or skill, it would be worthwhile for you to dig a little deeper and assess students' sense of efficacy along with their skills. High performance may not necessarily reflect high efficacy and vice versa.

The Concept of Flow and Motivation

As we suggested at the beginning of this section, teachers often ask themselves what they might do or do differently in order to "motivate their students." And by looking at goal orientation and self-efficacy, we can see that there are characteristics in the typical school or classroom that can influence student motivation. For example, a math classroom that relies on frequent quizzes and tests may negatively influence the feelings of competence that some students have in mathematics. And the same practice may create a competitive environment in the classroom in which high grades, rather than an interest in math, may direct students' attention.

But what about those interests and passions that students bring to the classroom with them—those classroom experiences for which we do not have to motivate our students? Why is it that the same student, day after

Resource for Your Assessment Toolkit
Assessment of Self-Efficacy

Psychologists have studied self-efficacy for several decades, and their research has provided a variety of measures that shed insight on the concept. Let's examine some of these assessments of self-efficacy so that you will know how to recognize these dimensions with your students.

Teachers' Self-Efficacy

Here are sample items for the Teachers' Sense of Efficacy Scale developed at Ohio State University.

Directions: This questionnaire is designed to help you gain a better understanding of the kinds of things that create difficulties for teachers in their school activities. Please indicate your opinion about each of the statements below.

Use the following scale to respond to each question.

1	2	3	4	5
Nothing	Very little	Some influence	Quite a bit	A great deal

a. How much can you do to get through to the most difficult students?
b. How much can you do to help your students think critically?
c. How much can you do to control disruptive behavior in the classroom?
d. How much can you do to motivate students who show low interest in school work?
e. To what extent can you make your expectations clear about student behavior?
f. To what extent can you craft good questions for your students?
g. How much can you use a variety of assessment strategies?
h. How well can you keep a few problem students from ruining an entire lesson?
i. How much can you assist families in helping their children do well in school?
j. How well can you provide appropriate challenges for very capable students?

Students' Self-Efficacy

This measure of self-efficacy is designed for students. Although it relates to a career choice, the scale also assesses students' confidence in their ability to perform different learning activities. Here are sample items from the Multiple Intelligences Self-Efficacy Inventory.

Directions: Please use the following scale to rate how confident you are that you can perform each of the activities identified below.

1 2 3	4 5 6 7	8 9 10
Cannot do it	Moderately certain can do	Certain can do

a. Analyze literary pieces such as novels, stories, essays, or poems.
b. Get the main idea from a text.
c. Write with grammatical accuracy.
d. Write formal papers or compositions.
e. Interpret survey or census statistics.
f. Solve geometric problems.
g. Use perspective in drawing.
h. Design scale models.
i. Play a musical instrument as a soloist.
j. Read musical scores.
k. Quickly recognize other peoples' wishes.
l. Engage in public speaking.
m. Promote a product or service.
n. Do physical exercises or compete in sports.
o. Understand your own personality.
p. Analyze the causes of your emotions.

Sources: Tschannen-Moran & Woolfolk Hoy, 2001; Perez & Baltramino, 2001.

day, is the first student to arrive and the last to leave your astronomy class? What drives this student to study astronomy on her own time and bring new and insightful questions to class every day? Most teachers would describe this student as highly motivated—and accurately so. But, more important, what can this student's passion for studying the stars tell you about motivation and how can you effectively channel and maintain a student's interest?

Mihalyi Csikszentmihalyi (1990) characterizes such motivation as **flow,** or moments of optimal experience. We have all had these moments: It might be a game of golf or an afternoon in the garden or writing poetry in the evenings. Whatever the task may be, we find ourselves lost in the activity, and we glance at the clock to realize that we have lost track of time. Such an experience produces not only enjoyment but feelings of satisfaction and accomplishment. And for teachers, it might provide more insight and another strategy for motivating students.

As suggested above, motivation is a process, and the process begins with engagement—interest in a task or topic. And flow begins with the understanding that learners must be initially engaged, that they must find something interesting enough to invest their time and energy. According to Csikszentmihalyi, you might first engage your students by authentically demonstrating that you are interested in the subject, that you the teacher are intrinsically motivated. This can be a challenge in some areas; we do not love every subject. But we can challenge ourselves to find interesting aspects in each subject and interesting ways of thinking and talking about them, because if it is not interesting to us, why should it be interesting to our students?

There also must be a balance between the student's level of skill and the challenge of the task. Think of it in terms of tennis: If you are a beginning player, you recognize the limitation in your skill, and you improve your game by playing opponents who are at or slightly above your skill level. If your opponent is too advanced a player, you will grow frustrated, and because of the mismatch, your game probably will not improve. And as you advance as a player, you will become bored and unmotivated if your opponents are too far beneath your ability. But if your opponent's skill matches yours, the challenge is not too great, and you receive feedback on your performance, which leads to sustained engagement.

Think about how flow might be apparent in your astronomy class and how it might provide a source of formative assessment. You know that your top student brings a deep interest in astronomy to your class, and because most of your students seem not to have the same high level of interest or the same deep understanding, your top student can easily become bored with the daily classroom activities. And even though your student appears self-directed, it is important that you offer challenge and appropriate goals in the types of exercises you provide.

Resource for Your Assessment Toolkit
Using Assessment as a Motivator to Learn

One way of thinking about assessment is as a motivation technique. Teachers have developed all sorts of ways to use assessment as a motivator to learn rather than as a deterrent to learning. You will need to use this list wisely because some tips will motivate some students and discourage others. The key is to use assessment as a set of tools and select the right tool for the right person.

- *Encourage students to make up questions and answers about the content they are studying.* You can then take all the questions and create a practice quiz. By using questions created by students, you create a sense of ownership and importance for the quiz. You can also include some of these student-developed questions on the actual examination.
- *Mix practice quizzes and tests with instruction.* Using practice quizzes gives students the opportunity to analyze their responses and uncover their thinking in light of the correct answers. They can also be motivating to some of your students if you put these quizzes in the form of puzzles or contests.
- *Use a final project or final test to promote learning.* Teachers often use this approach to encourage students to learn. By making a direct connection to an upcoming examination question, those students who care to perform well take note and attend to the content with greater interest. As you might suspect, students who do

not care about grades will not respond to this approach.
- *Allow students to use their notes on examinations.* This technique allows students to use any handwritten notes that they have developed along the way. Students tend to take better notes as they are studying because they know that these notes can be used to help them answer questions on the final assessment. Students may also tap into outside resources so that they can improve their notes and enhance their understanding.
- *Encourage students to work together to create their notes for the final examination.* Allowing students to build on one another's work enhances the social aspects of student learning, but, more important, it permits students who excel to help others and students who have difficulty to learn from peers. What about the concern that students are simply copying someone else's work and not really learning? Although at first glance this possibility may seem problematic, students who have to write out the information in their own handwriting will at least begin to learn the material from this exercise alone. And students who do not understand the written material will still be unable to answer assessment questions that require understanding rather than simple recognition of the correct answer.

Sources: Smith, 2004; Stiggins, 1999.

Where and how should you begin to implement the principles of flow in your assessment and classroom practice? Observe your students thoughtfully. Look for moments when they seem to be deeply engaged. What kinds of classroom activities captivate your students? Ask them about their interests and look for ways to integrate their diverse interests into your classroom. Answers to these questions can help you find those activities that seem to engage your students most deeply. Your creativity as a teacher can provide meaningful ways to challenge your students' skills and sustain their interest.

?Ask Yourself

Have you ever felt overwhelmed by a task that others thought you could easily perform? What did you do to deal with this problem? Did you seek help from a friend, parent, or teacher? In the end, were you able to perform the task? If yes, why did you feel overwhelmed in the first place? If no, what could you or others have done to bring about success? Does the research about flow and learning provide you with any further insights?

Differentiated Instruction and Assessment

You will enter your first classroom with an understanding that learning is influenced by a complex interaction of developmental, social, familial, and educational factors. All students are unique, and throughout this text we will be addressing issues related to those students who are exceptional in one way or another—in the form of some learning disability, or high aptitude in mathematics, or not yet having learned English, or a combination of characteristics.

This chapter points out that your day-to-day instruction should be attentive to the differing needs and capacities of the students in your class. Piaget's developmental theory provides a good example of such a consideration. We often associate Piaget's developmental levels with certain chronological ages (birth to 2, 2 to 7), but Piaget's understanding of learning was a generalized scale based on observations. In other words, it would be a misapplication of his ideas to suggest that all 11-year-old fifth-graders would be at the same developmental level.

Within the group of fifth-graders we used as an example earlier in the chapter, we may find that many of them are at roughly the same developmental level. There are probably a few lagging behind and a few ready for high school math. Understanding developmental differences requires that we both instruct and assess with students' developmental levels in mind, which suggests, of course, that the teaching profession that you have chosen requires a very deliberate and intentional attention to individual students.

?Ask Yourself

To some degree, each of us is exceptional. You might be an excellent organizer or have a gift for helping others resolve a problem. You also might have a weakness in your ability to quickly respond to new situations or to communicate in a public forum. When you notice students in a classroom setting who have been identified as exceptional, do you tend to think of them as fellow students or do you treat them differently?

How might your reaction to students who are different from you in some way affect your role as a future teacher? What can you do to recognize more fully that all of us are a mixture of talents and weaknesses?

Summary

- Properly administered and interpreted, assessment can assist teachers in:
  - Determining students' ability relative to other students on a similar task.
  - Determining the degree of students' growth over time in a particular area of knowledge or skill.
  - Providing evidence of depth of understanding of an idea or content area.
  - Predicting students' future performance.
- To truly enhance student learning, it is as important for teachers to understand *how* a student has learned as *what* a student has learned.
- According to Piaget, children develop increasingly complex and abstract reasoning skills from birth through about age 11. Within a single classroom, students may represent different developmental levels, so assessment should be appropriate for and sensitive to students' different levels.
- Vygotsky asserts that learning is the product of social interaction. We can determine a student's actual developmental level: a level of problem solving that a student is able to achieve without outside help. We should also be able to determine the level of problem solving that a student is able to achieve with the support of a teacher

or peer. The difference between these two levels is known as the zone of proximal development.

- Motivation is a process involving engagement, goals, and directed activity.
- Performance goal orientation represents a learner's inclination to learn and demonstrate a new skill in comparison to others' skills.
- Mastery goal orientation is characterized by a desire to learn for the sake of learning, to develop new skills, meet goals, and monitor one's learning. Mastery orientation, in general, leads to deeper conceptual learning and greater persistence and resilience than performance orientation.
- Self-efficacy is one's feeling of competence to achieve a desired outcome and has a deep influence on how we feel, think, and act. Self-efficacy is not synonymous with self-esteem, which is an overall, global sense of self-worth. Self-efficacy is context and task specific, and it has little generalizability across academic areas. For example, high self-efficacy in English does not necessarily lead to high self-efficacy in mathematics.
- Flow represents feelings of deep engagement created through interest, appropriate challenge, and timely feedback on performance. Flow experiences may lead to higher levels of efficacy and self-sustaining interest and performance.

Key Terms

developmental learning theories (31)

flow (41)

mastery goal orientation (38)

objective (28)

performance goal orientation (38)

psychological foundations (27)

self-efficacy (38)

social learning theories (33)

testing (28)

zone of proximal development (35)

For Further Discussion

1. Think about a time in your education when an effective teacher recognized your skills in the zone of proximal development and appropriately challenged you.

2. List ways in which a teacher could identify a student's performance goal orientation and mastery goal orientation to better enhance the learning process.

3. What relationships might exist among self-efficacy, interest, and achievement?

4. Describe how theories of learning and motivation in the classroom can be used to honor and respect the range of abilities of students.

Comprehension Quiz

In this chapter, we provide a short comprehension review in an essay format. In contrast to a forced-choice format, this type of review permits you to construct a response using your own words.

1. What is the difference between testing and assessment in an educational context? What implications does each have for your teaching?

2. How does Piaget's developmental theory of cognitive constructivism inform assessment?

3. What implications for assessment come from Vygotsky's writings?

4. Briefly describe three theories of motivation.

5. Why is it important to assess student motivation?

Relevant Website Resources

Edutopia, the New World of Learning

www.edutopia.org

This is an assessment portal covering standardized testing, performance assessment, project-oriented assessment, and technology and assessment. The site explores multiple intelligences and assessment and media literacy. A "Take Action" section supports educator, parent, and stakeholder advocacy. Interviews with assessment experts and a complete library on assessment are featured.

ETS, Educational Testing Service

www.ets.org

The "Assessments" section provides a wealth of up-to-date news, information, and research on assessment and testing. The site offers "A Guide to Testing for Parents," "Professional Development Solutions," teaching in at-risk schools, NCLB, and the National Report Card.

Scholastic

http://teacher.scholastic.com/professional/assessment/indexbk.htm

Scholastic's "Assessment" section spotlights Assessment ABC's, a checklist pertaining to learning environments and assessment. Examples of learning strategies, rubrics, and portfolios are offered in addition to resources for assessing writing, student self-evaluation, and a test for teachers on attitudes toward standardized testing and how they affect student performance.

4Teachers

http://www.4teachers.org/profdev/as.php

The site provides models for using learning indicators, portfolios, and rubrics; assessment tools and resources; and special needs assessment. It also includes the *Handbook for Project Evaluation* and a listing of conferences.

References

Ames, C. (1992). Classrooms: Goals, structures and student motivation. *Journal of Educational Psychology*, 84, 261–271.

Bandura, A. (1994). Self-efficacy. In V. S. Ramachaudran (Ed.), *Encyclopedia of human behavior* (Vol. 4, pp. 71–81). New York: Academic Press. Reprinted in H. Friedman (Ed.), *Encyclopedia of mental health*. San Diego: Academic Press, 1998.

Csikszentmihalyi, M. (1990). *Flow*. New York: HarperCollins.

Ormrod, J. E. (2008). *Human learning*. Upper Saddle River, NJ: Pearson Prentice-Hall.

Pintrich, P. R., & Schunk, D. H. (2002). Motivation in education theory, research, and application. Upper Saddle River, NJ: Prentice-Hall.

Schunk, D. H. (1991). Self-efficacy and academic motivation. *Educational Psychologist*, 25, 71–86.

Smith, I. *Motivating students through group projects and open-notes examinations*. Paper presented at the 2004 Enhancement Themes Conference sponsored by the Scottish Higher Education Enhancement Committee. From http://www.enhancementthemes.ac.uk/documents/events/20040205/smithpaperrevised.pdf. Accessed December 18, 2007.

Stiggins, R. J. (1999). "Assessment, Student Confidence and School Success." *Phi Delta Kappan*. November, pp. 191–198.

Vygotsky, L. S. (1978). *Mind in society*. Cambridge: Harvard University Press.

CHAPTER 3

The Social Foundations of Assessment

Chapter Objectives

After reading and thinking about this chapter, you will be able to:

- **Identify major social, political, and cultural trends in standardized assessments.**
- **Connect current assessment practices to historical practices.**
- **Explain the achievement gap and its causes.**

- **Detail major criticisms of standardized assessments, including issues that relate to test design and bias.**
- **Detail uses of assessment for accountability purposes.**
- **Explain the criticism of accountability systems that focus on test scores.**

The first two decades of the twentieth century marked an important point in the evolution of educational assessment. That time could be called the years of psychometrics, because that period saw refinement of psychometric instruments (intelligence tests), the application of test scores to a variety of settings (such as the sorting of military personnel), and changes to educational practice based on test scores. But with new insights about certain intellectual abilities and traits came many implications for how we characterize individuals and groups and how we educate them.

Today, large-scale assessments are used in a variety of ways in education—to measure what students know and can do, which teachers have been successful, and which schools are meeting their obligation to improve the academic achievement of students. They play an important role in American education. Such assessments are often said to be objective (fair to all students), valid (they measure what they say they measure), and reliable (scores represent consistent measures). This chapter focuses on the social foundations of educational assessment, which includes the historical, social, political, and economic background of large-scale testing, as well as current debates regarding the appropriate purpose and place of such assessments in American schooling.

Foundational Questions for Your Consideration

- What is the appropriate role of large-scale standardized tests in American schooling?
- What do large-scale educational assessments tell us about students and about schools?
- To what extent are the scores on educational assessments (when compared on the basis of race, ethnicity, gender, and socioeconomic status) a reflection of inequalities in society?
- Is it possible to develop assessments that are without bias?

Major Historical Trends in Standardized Assessment

One way to understand the concept of assessment is to examine the recent history of educational assessment in the United States. This history reflects the thinking of the Greek philosopher Pythagoras. Writing in the sixth century BCE, Pythagoras said that to really know the world we must learn how to measure it. For Pythagoras, the use of numbers was a key way to uncover the nature of people and things. This Pythagorean point of view provided one rationale for much of the thinking about assessment in American education throughout the twentieth century.

Alfred Binet and the Beginning of Mental Testing

Modern educational assessment, particularly the assessment of intelligence using standardized tests, began in France. French psychologist Alfred Binet and his colleague Theodore Simon created the first test of intelligence in 1905. France, in the late nineteenth century, had mandated compulsory education for all children. Binet and Simon worked on behalf of the French Ministry of Public Instruction, which wanted to find an objective way to identify children with learning problems who might have difficulty with formal education. Binet and Simon developed an intelligence test that was designed to identify "slow" and potentially mentally retarded students. The test included items related to memory, vocabulary, general knowledge, and problem solving.

Binet was the first to use higher-order cognitive skills such as reasoning, judgment, and comprehension as measures of intelligence. He developed the idea of IQ or intelligence quotient, which he defined as a comparison between the person's chronological age and his or her "mental" age. The idea that intelligence is a general ability that a person is born with, that it can be objectively measured, and that the measurements can be used to predict future learning potential continue to provide the framework for many standardized tests today.

Large-Scale Testing Begins in the United States

During the early part of the twentieth century, the United States was undergoing significant societal changes involving industrialization, specialization, and efficiency reforms. The conviction that we could master the earth through the use of science, technology, and measurement spread through all institutions—including schools.

Then came World War I (1914–1918), which significantly impacted educational assessment because it legitimized the concept of mental testing. Learning of the U.S. Army's need to identify officer candidates quickly, the psychologist Robert M. Yerkes offered to create a test for the purpose of sorting recruits to determine who was officer material. With his colleagues, he developed a written exam called the Army Alpha test. The Army Beta, a pictorial test, was also developed for recruits who failed the Alpha test or who could not read. Yerkes's assistants managed to test large numbers of recruits throughout U.S. Army bases during the war. The tests were developed using true-false, short-answer, and multiple-choice items so that they could be easily and inexpensively scored. The scores were interpreted based on how well the recruits, when compared to one another, performed on the tests.

The Army made little use of the test scores, but Yerkes's publications of his results during the 1920s created a flurry of interest and began a century of psychometric assessment activity. Assessment became associated with assigning a number to a student's achievement, and statistics were developed and used in an effort to sort both adults and children according to different levels of ability.

Testing in Mid-Twentieth Century America

By the 1950s, as the testing industry in the United States became established, **standardized tests** were increasingly used by school districts to help sort students into different educational tracks. As students moved through school, high performers were tracked into courses designed to prepare students for college, others were tracked into non-college prep courses, and low performers were often tracked into vocational education courses. Student scores on standardized tests were an important component of this system of sorting and selecting. Tests were seen as objective measures of intelligence that fairly determined students' IQ and their potential for learning. This view of the role of schools and assessments would later be strongly challenged. But the belief in test scores as a fair and impartial way of understanding student abilities and determining educational opportunities remains a cornerstone of American education. It is part of the American belief in meritocracy, a system whereby the talented are selected and moved ahead based on achievement.

The Changing Face of Testing

During the 1960s and 1970s, social activism such as the civil rights movement and the War on Poverty brought new voices into the testing arena. Many citizens and parents, particularly African American parents, were disappointed with the quality of schooling provided to poor children and children of color. They viewed the results of standardized tests as evidence of the extent to which schools continued to be separate and unequal. Looking at the test results from a new perspective, these parents questioned the meaning of the test scores for their children.

The 1980s and 1990s brought a new era of testing to the nation's public schools. Tests were to be used to *improve* the quality of American education. In 1983, a report entitled *A Nation at Risk* highlighted the mediocrity of American students when their test scores were compared with the scores of students from other industrialized nations. The report encouraged more rigorous academic standards and ushered in a wave of **high-stakes testing** for students, as well as for teachers and schools. In response, states adopted new and tougher policies in which grade level promotion and high school graduation were more closely tied to standardized test scores. State-level expectations for schools in terms of the percentages of students passing annual tests rose significantly. These changes were a precursor to the No Child Left Behind Act of 2001, a bill that reauthorized the Elementary and Secondary Education Act of 1965 and mandated improved academic achievement for all students as indicated by improved test scores. A stated goal of this legislation is to close the achievement gap among students in U.S. schools by 2014.

Ask Yourself

Recall a time when you took a standardized test. Do you think that the test measured what you had learned in school, your potential for future learning, or both? Did your scores provide you with information about what you know or about how you measure up when compared to other students, or both? Which type of information is most helpful? Under what circumstances?

The Achievement Gap

The **achievement gap** refers to differences in school grades, graduation rates, and test scores among racial, ethnic, gender, and socioeconomic groups. The achievement gap also refers to differences among students from diverse backgrounds in rates of college attendance and rates of college graduation. Though the gap is narrowing, females score lower on math and science indicators than males. African American, Latino, and Native American students score lower on all of these indicators than their White and Asian/Pacific Islander peers. And students from lower socioeconomic backgrounds score lower on all of these indicators than do their peers from middle and upper socioeconomic backgrounds.

A good way to understand the achievement gap is to look at scores from the **National Assessment of Educational Progress (NAEP)**. NAEP is a standardized test that is designed to assess the academic performance of children in public and private schools over time. NAEP has assessed fourth- and eighth-grade student reading and mathematics performance since the early 1990s. The scores can be compared based on the students' race and ethnicity, gender, and poverty level. A ten-point difference in NAEP scores translates to about a year's worth of learning (EdTrust, 2003). In the following sections we describe differences in NAEP scores between groups and identify some of the proposed causes of the differences.

Achievement Differences Based on Gender

The achievement gap between females and males is a complicated picture. Figure 3.1 shows some of the NAEP scores for 2005. As you can see, females scored higher than males in reading and scored about the same as males

Figure 3.1 *Differences in 2005 NAEP Reading and Math Scores by Gender*

	Reading		Mathematics	
	4th Grade	**8th Grade**	**4th Grade**	**8th Grade**
Males	216	257	239	280
Females	222	267	237	278

Ten points correspond to one year of achievement.

Source: Compilation of scores from USDE, *Condition of Education*, 2006.

in math. In reading, females scored higher than males in both fourth and eighth grades.

On some other NAEP assessments, males have higher average scores than females. The NAEP science tests reveal differences in male and female scores for White and Latino students, with males outperforming females. The gap in scores widens as the test takers get older, with the largest difference in scores occurring in twelfth grade and measuring between 10 and 15 points.

Differences in achievement based on gender are also demonstrated in SAT scores and in scores on Advanced Placement (AP) tests. On the SAT verbal tests, females scored lower than males, the only exception being African American college-bound females, who scored higher than their male counterparts. On the SAT math test, females on average scored about 40 points lower than males in all racial/ethnic groups. Finally, while females are more likely than males to take an AP exam, males are more likely to score high on AP calculus and AP biology exams (Coley, 2001).

Causes of Achievement Differences Based on Gender

Though females have made gains to close the achievement gap with males, there are ongoing inequities in society and schooling that negatively affect learning and reinforce the gender gap in academic achievement. For example, in a large-scale report commissioned by the American Association of University Women (AAUW, 1998), 20 percent of girls reported that they have been sexually abused, and 25 percent reported signs of depression. In addition, 25 percent of girls did not have access to appropriate health care when they needed it. The report concluded, among other things, that the prevalence of sexual abuse, depression, and lack of appropriate health care negatively affects girls' ability to learn. These problems may hinder some female students' ability to perform at their fullest potential on **achievement tests**.

Teacher behaviors and expectations also contribute to differences in achievement between males and females in math and science. David Sadker (1999) identifies several types of societal and in-school biases that may cause a difference in achievement between males and females. Most notably, he identifies classroom climates in which teachers interact with boys more frequently and more precisely, providing boys with increased attention, both positive and negative, and girls with less. According to Sadker, increased teacher attention translates into increased student achievement. One study found that boys are five times more likely to receive attention from teachers than girls are (AAUW, 1992). Another study found that boys are more likely to be encouraged to solve problems while girls are more likely to be told the answer to problems (Jewell, 1996). Some teachers, conditioned by stereotypes in society, have lower expectations for girls than for boys in math and science. These expectations contribute to lower achievement rates. Because some teachers have lower expectations for girls in math and science, they may be less encouraging to girls than boys, and they may not recommend that

Figure 3.2 *Differences in 2005 NAEP Reading and Math Scores by Race/Ethnicity*

	Reading		Mathematics	
	4th Grade	**8th Grade**	**4th Grade**	**8th Grade**
African American	200	243	220	255
American Indian	204	249	226	264
Hispanic	203	246	226	262
Asian/Pacific Islander	229	271	251	295
White	229	271	246	289

Ten points correspond to one year of achievement.

Source: Compilation of scores from USDE, *Condition of Education*, 2006.

girls take AP and honors level courses in math and science (Catsambis, 1994; Jewell, 1996; Shakeshift, 1995). Similarly girls may self-select out of these courses to conform to the behaviors and expectations of their peers.

Course enrollment is another factor that adversely affects girls. While female enrollment has increased in AP and honors courses, males are still more likely to enroll in and complete physics, and are still more likely to complete three high school sciences—biology, chemistry, and physics—than females. Similarly, females are less likely to be enrolled in advanced computer science and computer design classes. These course-taking patterns adhere to the stereotype that females are less inclined toward math and science than males. These patterns limit female exposure to rich and rigorous learning experiences in science when compared to boys. A lack of exposure to a rigorous curriculum has been linked to lower test scores on standardized exams (Chubb & Moe, 1990).

Achievement Differences Across Race and Ethnicity

African American, Latino, and Native American students scored below the national average and below the scores of their Asian/Pacific Island peers on NAEP reading assessments. As you can see in Figure 3.2, African American fourth-graders scored lower than Asian/Pacific Islander and White fourth-graders; Latino fourth-graders scored lower than Asian/Pacific Islander and White fourth-graders, and Native American students scored lower than their Asian/Pacific Islander and White peers. At the eighth-grade level, African American students scored lower than Asian/Pacific Islander and White eighth-graders; Latino eighth-graders scored lower than Asian/Pacific Islander and White eighth-graders; Native American eighth-graders scored lower than Asian/Pacific Islander and White eighth-graders (USDE, 2006). The gaps in 2005 were the about the same as they were in 1992 (USDE, 2006).

A similar pattern can be seen in math scores, both for fourth- and eighth-grade students. Among fourth-graders, African American students scored lower than White students. Latino and Native American fourth-graders scored lower than White students. And African American, Latino, and Native American eighth-graders scored lower than White students.

An analysis of the size of the differences in test scores between African American and White students over time indicates that, in math, the gap narrows during elementary school, widens during junior high school, and stays constant in high school. The size of the difference is more difficult to characterize for reading (USDE, 2001).

Causes of Achievement Differences Across Race and Ethnicity

Social scientists have suggested many causes for the achievement gap between African American, Latino, and Native American children and their more successful peers. Because a large percentage of the children from these communities are also poor, many of the causes of the gap are discussed in relation to environmental factors, such as socioeconomic background and cultural influences. We will discuss those issues in the following section.

However, even when socioeconomic status is taken into account, differences still persist between groups. Arthur Jensen (1969) and Richard Herrnstein and Charles Murray (1994) contend that the differences in IQ scores between Whites and African Americans can be explained by the genetic superiority of one group over the other. However, in a review of the major studies on heritability, Richard Nisbett (1998) found no evidence that differences in IQ are caused by ancestry. In fact, the studies found strong evidence that environmental factors play a large role in the differences.

Many researchers and commentators agree that environmental factors affect student achievement (Jencks, 1998). Some contend that the achievement gap exists because of cultural conflict between home and school. According to these researchers and commentators, school culture is steeped in White middle-class norms. When children from communities with large percentages of students of color and students from lower socioeconomic backgrounds enter into the school environment, their cultural norms are different from the norms of the teachers and administrators who manage the schools. These differences lead to misunderstandings that can escalate into conflicts. Conflicts about issues of dress, language, attitudes, behaviors, and learning styles can negatively affect the teacher–student relationship and interfere with the teaching and learning processes (Erickson, 1984; Heath, 1983; Irvine, 1990).

Another proposed cause of low achievement among racially and ethnically diverse students is low teacher expectations (Ferguson, 1998; Weinstein, 2002). Teachers may have low expectations for student learning because they see differences in dress, attitudes, language, and behaviors as deficits. They may not respect the children as learners with skills and talents that should be built on. They may believe that children are less intelligent if they use different dialects of English or they do not yet speak English. They may be critical of parents and may not work to engage them in the life of the school.

Achievement Differences Based on Socioeconomic Status

NAEP measures the poverty levels of schools based on the percentage of children in the schools who are eligible for free or reduced-price lunch. Schools are divided into five categories, ranging from less than 10 percent of students who are eligible to more than 75 percent of students who are eligible. The 2005 NAEP scores show a negative relationship between test scores and the poverty levels of schools. That is, the higher the poverty level of the schools, the lower the test scores. In the highest poverty-level schools, the average math score for fourth-graders was 219. In the lowest poverty-level schools, the average math score for fourth-graders was 239 (USDE, 2006). The differences in scores link poverty to low achievement.

NAEP scores have also been analyzed based on whether schools are located in central-city, urban fringe, or rural areas. Central-city areas have a higher percentage of high-poverty schools than other areas. In addition, schools in central-city areas are more likely than schools in other areas to have high percentages of African American and Latino students. Students in central-city schools scored lower in math and reading at both grade levels than did students in rural and urban fringe schools, as you can see in Figure 3.3. The gap in scores between students attending central-city schools and students attending urban fringe and rural schools demonstrates the way that race/ethnicity and socioeconomic status interact and affect students' success in schools and performance on tests.

Some researchers go beyond traditional measures of socioeconomic status that focus on parental income and education or on whether the students receive free or reduced-cost school lunch. They look to indicators such as accumulated wealth, the types of schools attended by mothers, and parental

Figure 3.3 *Differences in 2005 NAEP Reading and Math Scores by Location of School*

	8th Grade Reading	8th Grade Mathematics
Central-city schools	253	267
Urban fringe schools	265	280
Rural schools	264	279

Ten points correspond to one year of achievement.

Source: Compilation of scores from USDE, *Condition of Education*, 2006.

family background, such as the socioeconomic status of grandparents. Parental family background is an important indicator because it suggests a generational effect on student achievement. When these indicators are added together, a large proportion of the variance in test scores between students can be explained (Phillips, Brooks-Gunn, Duncan, Klebanov, & Crane, 1998).

Causes of Achievement Differences Based on Socioeconomic Status

Most researchers believe the gap is caused by a combination of nature (natural ability) and nurture (the home, school, and community environments) and is the result of both in-school and out-of-school factors. Paul Barton (2003) reviewed the research on the achievement gap and identified the 14 most significant factors that affect student achievement. The factors are listed in Figure 3.4. He then determined the extent to which these factors are present in poor communities and communities of color.

In-School Factors Barton identified six in-school factors that affect academic achievement and contribute to the achievement gap. The first factor is *rigor of the curriculum* or the extent to which students take challenging, often higher-level, courses in core academic areas. Research consistently shows that exposure to a rigorous curriculum promotes higher academic achievement (Chubb & Moe, 1990). While exposure to these types of courses has increased since the early 1980s for all students, the percentages of Asian American students with substantial credits in academic courses is significantly higher than that of White, African American, Latino, and Native American/Alaskan Native students, respectively.

Figure 3.4 *Factors That Affect School Achievement, Identified by Research*

In-School Factors
- Rigor of the curriculum
- Teacher knowledge and skills
- Teacher experience and attendance
- Class size
- Availability of appropriate technology-assisted instruction
- School safety

Out-of-School Factors
- Low birth weight
- Lead poisoning
- Hunger and poor nutrition
- Reading to young children
- Amount of TV watching
- Parent availability and participation
- Student mobility

A second indicator of the rigor of the curriculum is exposure to Advanced Placement exams. African American and Latino students take fewer AP courses and exams than do their White counterparts. In some high schools, AP courses are a mainstay of the curriculum; in other high schools, AP courses are the exception and not the rule.

Another in-school factor that affects academic achievement is the *academic knowledge and skills of teachers* (Mayer, Mullins, & Moore, 2000). Eighth-grade students who are poor and from racially and ethnically diverse backgrounds are more likely than non-poor White students to be taught by a math teacher who does not have a major or minor in mathematics. In addition, while one-third of the core academic courses in high-poverty schools (that is, schools with 50 percent or more of poor students) are taught by teachers without at least a college minor in the subject, only 15 percent of the courses in more affluent schools are taught by such teachers (Jerald, 2002). When taking achievement tests, students who are poor and from minority backgrounds are disadvantaged because their teachers are more likely to have less academic knowledge and skills than the teachers of students from other backgrounds.

Teacher experience and attendance are additional factors that disadvantage poor and minority students and contribute to the achievement gap. Research demonstrates that students learn more from teachers with experience than they do from novice teachers (Mayer, Mullins, & Moore, 2000). Schools with high levels of low-income and minority student enrollment are twice as likely to have teachers with three years or less of experience. These schools are also twice as likely as other schools to have 6 to 10 percent of teachers absent on an average day. The students in low-income schools score lower on achievement tests in part because of a lack in teacher experience and attendance (Jerald, 2002).

Class size is also a factor in student achievement. Research has found that smaller class sizes (20 students or less) yield greater academic achievement, especially at the elementary level and especially for students from low-income and diverse backgrounds (Glass & Smith, 1978; Mishel & Rothstein, 2002). While research does not reveal class-size differences between students based on poverty status, students from racially and ethnically diverse backgrounds are more likely to be in classes with larger class size than their White peers. This is ironic because these are the students who benefit the most from class-size reductions. Many schools and school districts serving poor and minority students have policies in place to decrease class size. Administrators in these districts and schools view smaller class size as a way of increasing academic achievement and decreasing the achievement gap.

Another in-school factor affecting the achievement gap is *access to technology-assisted instruction*. Studies show that the use of computers for drill and practice activities increases achievement in those areas. Studies also show that the increases are greatest for students from low-income and diverse backgrounds. Schools with high percentages of students from low-income and diverse backgrounds have roughly the same access to computers in classrooms as do other students. However, students from low-income and racially and ethnically diverse backgrounds do not have as much access to the Internet and are only half as likely to be assigned research on the Internet as are other students. The uneven access to computers and other technologies in schools places ethnically and racially diverse students and students from low-income backgrounds at a disadvantage relative to academic achievement (Mayer, Mullins, & Moore, 2000).

The final in-school factor identified by Barton as having an effect on academic achievement is *school safety*. A synthesis of research demonstrates positive connections between school safety and academic achievement (Mayer, Mullins, & Moore, 2000). One measure of school safety is the presence of gangs in schools. Students from minority and low-income backgrounds report the presence of gangs in their schools at higher percentages than do their White and higher-income peers. One-tenth of African American and Latino students reported fear of an attack at school or on the way to school. Because feeling safe is a prerequisite to learning, academic achievement is threatened when school safety is not assured. This too contributes to the achievement gap.

Out-of-School Factors According to the research reviewed by Barton, out-of-school factors also contribute to the achievement gap. The out-of-school factors can be grouped into three categories: physical factors, factors associated with parenting, and factors associated with mobility.

The *physical factors* that contribute to the achievement gap include low birth weight, hunger and poor nutrition, and lead poisoning. Clearly, these factors play a role in how children from low income and diverse backgrounds perform on standardized tests.

- Birth weight affects development and can cause learning disabilities (Child Trends Data Bank, 2002). The percentage of African American infants born with low birth weight (13%) is almost double that of White infants (7%).

- Hunger and nutrition affect the development of the mind and body and the ability to concentrate and behave (Rothstein, 2002). Thirteen percent of children who live in poverty do not get enough to eat on a regular basis and have experienced hunger.

- Lead poisoning can cause learning disabilities, delayed development, and behavior problems (Rothstein, 2002). Children from low-income and minority backgrounds are more likely to be exposed to lead and more likely to have lead poisoning than other children. Twelve percent of children from households below the poverty level under age 6 have unhealthy levels of lead in their blood compared to 4 percent of children from households at or above poverty level.

Parenting factors have also been linked to achievement on standardized tests. These include time spent reading to children and parental involvement in school.

- Reading to young children supports early literacy development. It is positively linked to strong reading comprehension skills and general school success. White parents and parents at or above the poverty level read to their young children at a higher rate than do African American and Latino parents and parents with income below the poverty level.

- Parental involvement is positively linked to better student behavior and higher academic achievement. Research shows that parents from lower-income backgrounds are less likely to be involved in schools in traditional ways and often feel less than welcome in schools. Forty-four percent of urban parents feel unwelcome in schools while 20 percent of suburban parents feel unwelcome (Child Trends Data Bank, 2002).

- Though there is no conclusive research, watching 5 or 6 hours of TV each day may also contribute to differences in achievement. Some research indicates that children watching 6 hours of TV per day are less likely to be engaged in intellectually stimulating activities. African American and Latino fourth-graders are more likely to watch 6 hours or more of TV per day than their White peers.

The final out-of-school factor is related to *mobility*—that is, *changing schools frequently*. Research confirms that mobility affects academic achievement and high school graduation rates (U.S. General Accounting Office, 1994). Thirty percent of third-graders from households with an income of $10,000 or less moved three times or more since first grade as compared to 10 percent of households with incomes of $50,000 or more. One-fourth of African American and Latino third-graders changed schools three times or more since the first grade. This instability affects student performance and contributes to the achievement gap.

For each of the factors presented, poor communities and communities with large percentages of racially and ethnically diverse students fared worse than communities that were wealthier and Whiter. According to Barton, "The gaps in school achievement mirror inequalities in those aspects of schooling, early life and home circumstances that research has linked to school achievement" (2003, p. 7). Given this finding, it is not surprising that some researchers contend that socioeconomic status accounts for at least two-thirds of the differences highlighted in the achievement gap.

Classroom Implications

Understanding some of the causes of the achievement gap is important for teachers. Teachers are often asked to review and analyze school, district, state, and national test scores. They are also asked to analyze data from assessments that they develop themselves. Sometimes teachers form negative judgments about students based on these analyses. Knowledge of the broader social and economic forces that surround the lives of students and how these forces affect learning will help teachers see that assessments may not accurately reflect the real abilities of students. Rather, assessments reflect what students have learned in the context of their in-school and out-of-school experiences.

It is helpful to understand that assessments reflect these learning experiences and not the innate ability of children to learn. All children can learn, regardless of previous test scores. Teachers who truly believe that all students can learn maintain high expectations for student learning. They are clear about their learning objectives and teach students techniques so that the students can monitor their own learning. These teachers use informal classroom assessments to clarify what students know and to find out how students are processing what they are learning. And these teachers use multiple assessments to give students different types of opportunities to demonstrate what they know and can do.

In addition, understanding the context of student test scores will highlight for teachers how out-of-school factors can affect learning and assessment. To help students learn more and perform better on assessments, teachers should be able to interact successfully with families from different socioeconomic backgrounds. Teachers should also be prepared to draw on the expertise and resources of school counselors, social workers, and

Digging Deeper
Reducing the Achievement Gap

James P. Comer is a psychiatrist and a professor of child psychology at the Child Study Center, a part of the School of Medicine at Yale University. He works to create positive school climates in settings where there are large percentages of poor and minority students.

Comer's School Development Program aims to create a school climate that ensures that students' social and psychological needs are being met. This climate is created through positive relationships among principals, teachers, school and district support personnel, families, and students. Three important components of the School Development Program are that

- Problems are discussed in a no-fault atmosphere
- All stakeholders (that is, parents, teachers, businesses, community organizations) are involved in collaborative working relationships
- All decisions are made based on consensus

According to Comer,

In 1968 we set out to demonstrate that children from all backgrounds could achieve adequately in school if the setting supported their overall development. We applied the principles of the social and behavioral sciences to every aspect of elementary school programs, first locally and now nationwide, and in doing so, we changed attitudes and behaviors of staff, parents, and students, and often enabled them to perform in ways that brought student social and academic achievement to acceptable levels. (Comer, 1993, p. 297)

The School Development Program is operating in over 250 schools in 19 states. It has been successful in raising students' academic achievement, increasing their attendance, and improving social skills.

Go to this website for more information: http://www.ed.gov/pubs/OR/ConsumerGuides/comer.html.

psychologists, when available, to help build the networks of support that promote student learning and achievement (Comer, 1993; Sanders, 2000).

Ask Yourself

Did you ever change schools when you were growing up? Was it difficult for you to adjust to a new school? How do you think moving several times within a few years might affect a student's achievement?

Criticisms of Standardized Achievement Tests

Some researchers question whether standardized tests are fair and valid measurements of academic achievement. Specific criticisms include confusion about what the tests are actually measuring and the extent to which culture affects test content and unfairly penalizes students from a culture different from that of the test developer.

Bias in Standardized Tests

There are different types of bias. Christopher Jencks (1998) writes that *labeling bias* exists when tests claim to measure one thing but actually measure something else. Tests that are labeled "intelligence tests" or tests of **aptitude** are popularly interpreted as tests that measure both developed (learned) *and* **innate** (inborn) abilities. Most psychologists agree that a great deal of what is measured on IQ and aptitude tests is not innate. Instead, the tests are actually measuring developed abilities, some developed in school and some developed in home environments. Instead of being fixed and unchangeable, these test scores can be changed through exposure to new learning and environments that support or transmit the tested information. Understanding what is actually being measured is important for interpreting test scores.

Another type of bias in standardized assessments has to do with *culture*. Deborah Meier (2002) contends that all tests come with implicit and sometimes explicit cultural assumptions. She writes, "Any choice of subject matter, vocabulary, syntax, metaphors, word associations and values presupposes a certain social and personal history" (p. 111). In subtle and not so subtle ways, background, experience, exposure, and socioeconomic status impact how students interpret, approach, and answer test questions. Students may select some answers that are not "correct" because they are interpreting the questions differently or using logic and reasoning that make sense from the perspective of their experiences but are different from the perspective of the experiences of the test maker.

Because of this difference in perspective, these critics believe that students who are outside of the dominant, White, middle-class culture are disadvantaged when taking such tests. There is, according to these critics, inherent unfairness in the system when scores from these tests are used to determine which students gain access to a rich curriculum, which students learn from the most qualified teachers, which students are promoted, and which students receive a diploma.

Standardized Tests and Accountability: No Child Left Behind

Standardized tests scores are often used as a way of holding schools accountable for the academic achievement of students at the school, district, and state levels. In some **accountability** systems, academic achievement is defined only in terms of scores on a standardized test, and schools face rewards and penalties based on their ability to improve the test scores. The No Child Left Behind (NCLB) Act of 2001 contains this kind of accountability system.

The Purpose of the No Child Left Behind Act The NCLB Act is designed to increase funding for schools that serve the poor, to ensure that each child is taught by a highly qualified teacher, and to hold accountable schools that receive federal funds for increasing the academic achievement of all students.

The law holds schools accountable by requiring that they

- Test students in grades 3–8 annually in math and reading/language arts
- Meet annual yearly progress (AYP) targets for subcategories of students

The subcategories include students living in poverty, students of color, students with limited English proficiency, and students with special needs. The schools are to disaggregate their test scores, rather than reporting all of the scores together for a particular grade level. **Disaggregation** means that the school must report scores separately for each subcategory. Requiring schools to disaggregate the scores by these subcategories ensures that the scores of vulnerable groups of students are not hidden inside the averages for each grade level.

When schools do not meet AYP targets for each subcategory, they are labeled "in need of improvement" and later "failing." Failing schools face a series of sanctions, including reconstitution, closure, paying transportation costs for students who must be allowed to transfer out, paying for the costs of outside tutors for students, and possibly losing federal funds for the school district and/or state. Within this accountability context, standardized test scores become high stakes.

Supporters of the law praise its four pillars (USDE, 2007). These pillars include: accountability for results, more freedom for states and communities, proven education methods, and more choice for parents. The law encourages states to close the achievement gap by making student achievement public. The public reporting to parents and communities is an accountability mechanism, which is strengthened by the threat of significant changes in school management if student test scores do not improve. Accountability for results also includes ensuring that there is a highly qualified teacher in every classroom.

The law also gives states flexibility in how they spend the money they receive from the federal government for educational purposes. Before NCLB, states and districts received federal funds that had to be spent on specific programs. With NCLB, states and districts are free to spend up to 50 percent of their federal funds in ways that fit their particular needs.

The law also promotes the use of designated education programs. These programs must be highly effective based on "rigorous scientific research." Reading First is one such program that many contend is helping to raise student scores in reading.

Finally, the law promotes giving parents greater choice in determining where their children go to school. Under NCLB, parents who have children in low-performing schools have the right to transfer their children to schools

Resource for Your Assessment Toolkit
Understanding Educational Policies

Teachers work in the context of district, state, and federal policies. No Child Left Behind is an example of a federal policy that led to additional state and district policies. You will need to be able to understand and judge the merit of educational policies, especially policies related to accountability and assessment. Here are a few questions that will help you in this endeavor.

- What does the policy aim to do?
- What are the policy's purposes and goals?
- What is the likelihood that the policy will achieve its goals?

- What does the research say?
- How will the policy be implemented? What is the time frame?
- Who will implement the policy?
- Who will be affected?
- How will the policy affect students and classrooms?
- What are the possible and real unintended consequences?

within their districts that have higher test scores. Parents whose children go to schools plagued by violence can also transfer their children to safer public schools within the district.

Supporters say that the law is working. According to the Department of Education,

- More reading progress was made by 9-year-olds in 5 years than in the previous 28 years.
- Reading and math scores for 9-year-olds and fourth-graders have reached all-time highs.
- Between 2003 and 2005, an additional 235,000 fourth-graders learned their fundamental math skills.
- Forty-six states and the District of Columbia improved or held steady in all categories of students tested in reading and math (USDE, 2007).

Criticisms of NCLB Critics of the law have identified significant technical problems related to its implementation. First, some contend that the law is underfunded by up to $12 billion. They cite inequity in school funding, with some wealthy school districts spending as much as three times as much money per pupil as some poor districts. Others argue that the law holds everyone accountable for school improvement except the federal government, which has fallen short on its financial obligations and turned the bipartisan law into an unfunded mandate. The results of unequal funding are larger class sizes, fewer qualified teachers, and less adequate supplies and services in schools that serve poor students and students of color.

The second problem with the law, from the critics' perspective, is that its restrictive definition of highly qualified teachers focuses almost exclusively on content knowledge. Students in the most socioeconomically challenged schools are taught by teachers with little to no experience or preparation in how to teach. Rural areas find it difficult to find teachers who have the necessary qualifications to teach multiple subjects (Wood, 2004).

Beyond these technical problems of implementation, some interested parties have identified a host of criticisms of the law itself, many of them related to the law's use or misuse of standardized tests. According to Linda Darling-Hammond (2004), NCLB's most significant problem is that it mistakes measuring schools for fixing them and ultimately does more harm than good to the students it is designed to help. The law requires that all students meet increasingly higher levels of proficiency within the next several years, but the use of norm-referenced tests makes it impossible for all students to perform at high levels. A norm-referenced test by definition means that 50 percent of the test takers are expected to score below the norm. The majority of states have adopted norm-referenced tests to meet the reporting requirements of NCLB without addressing this inconsistency.

As noted earlier, schools must meet the annual yearly progress (AYP) targets in every student subcategory. But this requirement does not take into account the difficulties that a school with a high percentage of students with disabilities or a high percentage of **English language learners** (ELLs) will face in trying to meet the yearly targets. Many special education students have learning disabilities that prevent them from meeting the targets on a set timetable and sometimes from meeting the targets at all. English language learners may not be proficient in English. Even with accommodations, language often poses a barrier to meeting the requirements for improved test scores. According to these critics, requiring annual progress from schools with high percentages of these populations is unfair. And because students with disabilities and students with limited English proficiency are often poor, this unfairness falls disproportionately on schools that serve students from low-income backgrounds, one of the targeted groups that the law was supposed to help. For this reason, the law's requirements actually cause more harm than good for these students. The critics suggest that instead of relying on a single test score to measure learning the requirement should be broadened to include improvement on other indicators, such as graduation rates, and on indicators that are more closely matched to the curriculum, such as classroom tests and performance-based assessments.

Another criticism of the law's accountability requirements is that the almost exclusive focus on test scores has the unintended effect of narrowing the curriculum. When teachers are under pressure to ensure that students pass the exams, they may feel forced to limit time teaching other subjects so that they can focus on the subjects to be tested. As drilling in test-related content and test-taking skills occupy more of the school day, other subjects such as science, social studies, music, and art are eliminated or pushed to the margins. Teachers, rather than concentrating on teaching higher-order skills such as reasoning, analyzing, communicating, and problem solving, are focusing on the lower-level skills covered by the tests. This reduces students' access to a rich and meaningful curriculum and limits creativity in the teaching and learning processes.

A final criticism is that the law's accountability requirements are actually pushing students out of school and contributing to higher dropout rates. When schools, districts, and states feel pressure to make annual yearly progress, they may look for ways to maximize their schools' scores. One way to maximize scores is to avoid testing students who will score poorly. Through expulsion, grade retention, counseling, and transferring policies, vulnerable students are encouraged to leave.

Overall, critics often agree with the intent of accountability systems dependent on test scores as indicators of student achievement. But many have pointed out the unintended consequences that may harm the children the systems are designed to help.

Ask Yourself

How would you feel if the school in which you worked was labeled "failing"? What would be your response to such a label? What types of conversations would you have with peers, parents, and students?

Avoiding Bias in Assessment

So far, much of our discussion about the relationship of social and cultural factors to assessment has been focused on standardized tests. You might wonder what teachers can do to make their assessments fair and sensitive to cultural differences in their classrooms. This section describes some areas that may help you.

Assessments are biased when scores have different meanings for different groups or individuals because of problems in the tests themselves or because of problems in the way the tests are administered (Helms, 2003). When writing items for standardized tests, test developers use sophisticated methods and statistical techniques to avoid bias and to try to ensure that the tests are fair to all students. Classroom teachers should also take precautions to ensure that the assessments they develop are fair and valid measures of student knowledge. Specifically, when developing assessments, teachers should be aware of and avoid the use of stereotypes, offensiveness, and unfair penalization.

Awareness of Stereotypes

Stereotypes are images of a group that conform to a fixed or general pattern. These images represent an oversimplified opinion, prejudiced attitude, or uncritical judgment, usually about another group. Stereotypes do not allow for individual characteristics or differences. For example, females are often stereotyped as being passive and demure. Assessment items that portray individuals in stereotypical roles are insensitive and can adversely affect student performance.

Avoiding Offensiveness

Offensiveness occurs if the content of the assessment upsets, distresses, angers, or otherwise creates a negative feeling or atmosphere for particular students or a subgroup of students. Offensiveness happens when assessments are written in poorly conceived language and are based on task situations that are insulting or that make students feel uncomfortable. For example, assessments that use racially charged words, stereotypical situations, or other cultural insensitivities will interfere with student performance. Although most offensiveness in assessment is unintentional, simply being aware of the possibility may prompt reevaluation and elimination of this kind of bias.

Reducing Unfair Penalization

Unfair penalization is a bias that disadvantages a student because of content that makes it difficult for students in some groups to do well. For example, if a group of students have not had the opportunity to learn a given concept, then it is not fair to test the students on that concept. The students would be unfairly penalized. Similarly, if English language learners are taking a mathematics test, the language on the test should not be unduly complicated. If the language is complex, then the test will be measuring, in part, the extent to which students understand English. This problem weakens the validity of the math assessment in that the test no longer measures mathematics in the English language learners. Instead, it measures a nonspecific interaction between language and mathematics. The test scores will have different meanings across groups, and the English language learners will have been unfairly penalized.

Resource for Your Assessment Toolkit
Reducing Bias in Classroom Assessment

Working to reduce bias in assessment is an important responsibility of all teachers. Here are some questions that you as a teacher can ask yourself to help reduce bias.

- *Am I using multiple types of assessment that address different learning styles?* Students may not be able to really demonstrate what they know if teachers only use one type of assessment. Different types of assessment include performance assessments, portfolios, journals, oral reports, and artwork.
- *Am I including content that will be engaging to students from different gender, socioeconomic, and racial/ethnic backgrounds?* Assessments that are connected to real-world activities and issues may create more meaning for students and increase their motivation.

- *Am I encouraging all students to do their best as I assess them orally and provide written feedback?* Teacher expectations can play a large role in student success.
- *Am I using formative assessments (assessments that focus on helping students learn rather than evaluating how well they performed compared to others) to better understand what students know and how they are processing new information?*
- *Am I sure that students understand the learning objectives and how they will be assessed?*
- *Am I sure that there is a clear connection between learning objectives and assessments?*
- *Am I sure that assessments are not offensive and do not reinforce stereotypes?*

Ask Yourself

Most discussions of the achievement gap focus on differences in test scores among racial and ethnic groups. Researchers note that the differences *within* groups are greater than the differences *between* groups. They also note that much of the difference in scores between groups relates to socioeconomic status. How does this finding dispel stereotypes about some groups being smarter than other groups?

Summary

- The ideas that intelligence is global in nature, that it can be objectively measured, and that the measurements can predict future learning were developed in the early twentieth century by French psychologist Alfred Binet.
- As the industry was established, standardized tests came to be viewed as fair and impartial as-

sessments of what students know and are able to do, and educators used them to sort students into various vocational and academic tracks.

- The scores from standardized assessments reveal significant differences in the academic achievement of students from different groups. These differences—along with differences in grades, in course enrollment, and in college attendance—are often referred to as the achievement gap.

- Based on assessments from the National Assessment of Educational Progress (NAEP), most males score higher than their female peers in science; Asian/Pacific Islander and White students score higher than African American, Latino, and Native American students in reading and math; students from higher socioeconomic backgrounds score higher than students from lower socioeconomic backgrounds in reading and math.

- The achievement gap has many causes. They involve gender bias, cultural differences, and in-school and out-of-school factors that disadvantage particular groups of students.

- Major criticisms of standardized tests are that (1) they do not measure innate intelligence (although the public believes that they do, because of how they are labeled), and (2) the content includes cultural assumptions that unfairly penalize students from diverse backgrounds.

- *A Nation at Risk* (1983), an influential report on American schooling, ushered in an era of high-stakes standardized testing and was a precursor of the No Child Left Behind (NCLB) Act of 2001.

- The No Child Left Behind Act was designed to improve the academic achievement of all students, especially students from diverse backgrounds, and aims to close the achievement gap by 2014.

- Critics of NCLB say that the act has not been sufficiently funded and that the definition of a highly qualified teacher is inadequate. Critics also state that the accountability system required by NCLB unfairly labels schools that face great educational challenges as "failures," narrows the curriculum in many schools to what will be assessed on standardized tests, and provides incentives to push students who do not perform well on standardized tests out of school.

- In developing classroom assessments, teachers should avoid the use of stereotypes, offensiveness, and unfair penalization.

Key Terms

accountability (64)

achievement gap (53)

achievement test (54)

aptitude test (64)

disaggregation (65)

English language learner (ELL) (67)

high-stakes testing (52)

innate (64)

National Assessment of Educational Progress (NAEP) (53)

offensiveness (69)

standardized test (51)

stereotypes (69)

unfair penalization (69)

For Further Discussion

1. Chapter 3 identifies several trends in assessment that have roots in the early twentieth century. What are some of these trends? How do these trends affect the students in classrooms today?

2. What skills do you think teachers need to help reduce the achievement gap?

3. What changes, if any, would you make to high-stakes accountability systems like No Child Left Behind?

Comprehension Quiz

This chapter emphasizes the influence of students' environment and culture on learning. To that end, we have chosen a set of essay questions that allow you to respond in your own words, to develop answers using your own experiences, and to communicate your personal point of view.

1. What aspects of assessment today have roots in the first half of the twentieth century?

2. Why are there differences in test scores between males and females in areas such as science and technology?

3. Identify three of the in-school factors that are linked to differences in test scores between students from different socioeconomic backgrounds. How are these factors associated with the achievement gap?

4. How can classroom teachers avoid bias as they develop assessments?

5. What are the pros and cons of high-stakes accountability systems such as the one associated with NCLB?

Relevant Website Resources

U.S. Department of Education

http://nces.ed.gov/nationsreportcard/lttnde/

This website of the U.S. Department of Education provides information on student outcomes from the National Assessment of Educational Progress (NAEP).

Gender Bias

http://www.american.edu/sadker/genderequity.htm

David Sadker, prominent scholar of gender bias, developed this website. It provides information on gender bias, how to recognize, and how to avoid it.

No Child Left Behind

http://www.ed.gov/nclb/landing.jhtml

U.S. Department of Education website for the No Child Left Behind Act of 2001.

References

American Association of University Women, Education Foundation. (1992). *How schools shortchange girls: The AAUW report.* New York: Marlowe & Company.

American Association of University Women, Education Foundation. (1998). *Gender gaps: Where schools still fail our children.* New York: Marlowe & Company.

Barton, P. (2003). *Parsing the achievement gap: Baselines for tracking progress.* Princeton, NJ: Educational Testing Service.

Catsambis, S. (1994). The path to math: Gender and racial-ethnic differences in mathematics participation from middle school to high school. *Sociology of Education, 67,* 199–215.

Child Trends Data Bank. (2002). http://www.childtrendsdatabank.org/indicators/39parentalinvolvementinschools.cfm.

Chubb, J. E., & Moe, T. M. (1990). *Politics, markets, and America's schools.* Washington, DC: Brookings Institution.

Coley, R. J. (2001). *Differences in the gender gap: Comparisons across racial/ethnic groups in education and work.* Princeton, NJ: Educational Testing Service.

Comer, J. (1993). *School power: Implications of an intervention project.* New York: Free Press.

Darling-Hammond, L. (2004). From "separate but equal" to "no child left behind": The collision of new standards and old inequalities. In D. Meier & G. Woods (Eds.), *Many children left behind: How the No Child Left Behind Act is damaging our children and our schools* (pp. 3–32). Boston: Beacon Press.

Donovan, M. S., Bransford, J. D., & Pellegrino, J. W. (Eds.). (1999). *How people learn: Bridging research and practice.* Washington, DC: National Academy Press.

EdTrust. (2003). *African American achievement in America.* www.edtrust.org.

Erickson, F. (1984). School literacy, reasoning, and civility: An anthropologist's perspective. *Review of Educational Research, 54*(4), 525–546.

Ferguson, R. (1998). Teachers' perceptions and expectations and the Black–White test score gap. In C. Jencks & M. Phillips (Eds.), *The African American–White test score gap* (pp. 273–319). Washington, DC: Brookings Institution.

Glass, G., & Smith, M. (1978). Meta-analysis of research on the relationship of class size and achievement. *Educational Evaluation and Policy Analysis, 1*(1), 2–16.

Heath, S. B. (1983). *Ways with words, language, life, and work in communities and classrooms.* New York: Cambridge University Press.

Helms, J. E. (2003). Fair and valid use of educational testing in grades K–12. In J. Walls & G. Walz (Eds.), *Measuring up: Assessment issues for teachers, counselors, and administrators* (pp. 81–88). Washington, DC: ERIC Clearing House on Counseling and Student Services.

Herrnstein, R., & Murray, C. (1994). *The bell curve: Intelligence and class structure in American life.* New York: Free Press.

Irvine, J. J. (1990). *Black students and school failure: Policies, practices, and prescriptions.* New York. Greenwood Press.

Jencks, C., & Phillips, M. (1998). Racial bias in testing. In C. Jencks & M. Phillips (Eds.), *The African American–White test score gap* (pp. 55–85). Washington, DC: Brookings Institution.

Jensen, A. (1969). How much can we boost IQ and scholastic achievement? *Harvard Educational Review, 39,* 1–123.

Jerald, C. D. (2002). *All talk, no action: Putting an end to out-of-field teaching.* Washington, DC: EdTrust.

Jewell, T. O. (1996). "And they is us": Gender issues in the instruction of science. ERIC Document 402202.

Mishel, L., & Rothstein, R. (Eds.). (2002). *The class size debate.* Washington, DC: Economic Policy Institute.

Mayer, D. P., Mullins, J. E., Moore, M. T. (2000). *Monitoring school quality: An indicators report.* Washington, DC: U.S. Department of Education, NCES 2001-030.

Meier, D. (2002). *In schools we trust: Creating communities of learning in an era of testing and standardization.* Boston: Beacon Press.

National Commission for Excellence in Education. (1983). *A nation at risk.* Washington, DC: U.S. Department of Education. Available from www.ed.gov/pubs/NatAtRisk/risk.html.

Nisbett, R. (1998). Racial bias in testing. In C. Jencks & M. Phillips (Eds.), *The African American–White test score gap* (pp. 55–85). Washington, DC: Brookings Institution.

No Child Left Behind Act of 2001, P.L. 107-110, 115 Stat. 1425 (2002).

Phillips, M., Brooks-Gunn, G., Duncan, G. J., Klebanov, P., & Crane, J. (1998). Family background, parenting practices, and the African American–White test score gap. In C. Jencks & M. Phillips (Eds.), *The African American–White test score gap* (pp. 103–148). Washington, DC: Brookings Institution.

Rothstein, R. (2002). *Out of balance: Our understanding of how schools affect society and how society affects our schools.* Chicago: Spencer Foundation.

Sadker, D. (1999). Gender equity: Still knocking at the classroom door. *Educational Leadership, 56* http://www.american.edu/sadker/stillknocking.htm.

Sanders, M. (Ed.). (2000). *Schooling students placed at-risk: Research, policy, and practice in the education of poor and minority adolescents.* Mahwah, NJ: Erlbaum.

Shakeshift, C. (1995). Reforming science education to include girls. *Theory in Practice, 34*(1), 74–79.

U.S. Department of Education (USDE), National Center for Education Statistics. (2001). *Educational achievement and black-white inequality.* http://nces.ed.gov/pubs2001/inequality/. Washington, DC: U.S. Government Printing Office.

U.S. Department of Education (USDE), National Center for Education Statistics. (2006). *The condition of education 2006.* Washington, DC: U.S. Government Printing Office.

U.S. Department of Education (USDE), Promoting Education Excellence for All Americans. (2007). http://www.ed.gov/NCLB/overview/intro/4 pillars.html.

U.S. General Accounting Office. (1994). *Elementary school children: Many change schools frequently, harming their education.* Washington DC: Author.

Weinstein, R. S. (2002). *Reaching higher: The power of expectations in schooling.* Cambridge, MA: Harvard University Press.

Wood, G. (2004). Introduction. In D. Meier & G. Wood (Eds.), *Many children left behind: How the No Child Left Behind Act is damaging our children and our schools* (pp. vii–xv). Boston: Beacon Press.

CHAPTER 4

Assessment: The Link Between Standards and Learning

Chapter Objectives

After reading and thinking about this chapter, you will be able to:

- **Describe the relationship between assessment and the development of understanding.**
- **Examine findings from cognitive science about the nature of understanding and how it relates to assessment.**
- **Compare different types of standards.**

- **Connect standards to the development of knowledge, skills, and dispositions.**
- **Clarify the learning and assessment implications for these different types of standards.**
- **Use learning outcomes to determine appropriate assessments.**

The first critical question for any teacher is, What do my students need to achieve? You might think that this is an easy question to answer, but it is not. There are many factors that make this question challenging. First, because the world is always changing, it can be difficult to determine what a student will need to be successful. Also, students develop differently, and their interests and abilities make a single instructional focus problematic. Also there are a variety of expectations from different groups, some of which conflict. These conflicting demands can overwhelm educators, a challenge that will be the focus of this chapter.

Teachers and administrators are asked to respond to a wide variety of demands, such as responsibility for developing knowledgeable learners, ethical citizens, caring human beings, and competitive performers. Because all of these demands are worthy, the task of educators is to carefully determine how they will be met or modified within the environment in which they work.

This chapter shows how important it is to consider how students learn, how they come to understand important concepts, and how they develop valued skills and dispositions. This knowledge is critical in developing good assessments.

The chapter also lays out the different types of content and instructional standards developed by different groups of professionals. It describes the basis for these different types of standards and clarifies what the standards imply for instruction and assessments.

Foundational Questions for Your Consideration

- What does it mean to understand something well?
  - Is understanding the mastery of a lot of facts?
  - Is understanding the ability to perform tasks quickly and accurately?
  - Is understanding the ability to learn quickly?
- What does it mean to think well? Is thinking a matter of logic or creativity?
- How can understanding and thinking be assessed?
- Should parents, expert professionals, politicians, or other groups determine what standards students should achieve?
- For what standards should teachers be held accountable?

The Critical Connection Between Assessment and the Nature of Learning

In Chapter 1, we showed how assessment could be thought of as placing learners in a situation that enables them to show what they know and can do. To be successful at this, you need to grasp the process by which students come to understand new ideas and skills. In fact, the National Research Council's Committee on the Foundations of Assessment states that good educational assessment is primarily based on a set of scientific principles and philosophical assumptions about how knowledge and understanding take place over time (National Research Council, 2001).

For that reason we must first clarify our assumptions about the nature of cognition or what it means for learners to understand and what it means to think. Then, we may design tasks that are compatible with our view of understanding that are most likely to bring out what learners know and can do.

Ask Yourself

Identify something that you really understand. List some reasons why you believe that you really understand it. The reasons you have identified may help you figure out what understanding means to you. For example, if you stated that you believe you understand something because you know so much about it, this would indicate that you think understanding something means that you know its many dimensions or pieces. Use your reasons and try to list the characteristics that indicate your view of understanding. Think back to the experiences or activities that helped you develop your understanding. Examples may be that you read a great deal, you practiced over and over again or in many different contexts, you observed others closely, you talked to others and they explained things to you, you asked questions along the way and tried to answer them yourself, and so on. Whatever you believe has helped you develop your understanding, these same things might help your students develop an understanding about new concepts. Describe what you would do if you wanted to teach another what you understand.

What Is Understanding?

What does it mean to understand something? What does good thinking look like? What thinking skills are important for today's society? Answers to these questions over the past hundred years have moved us from a rather simple model of understanding to a more complex model. Thanks to recent decades of research in the cognitive sciences, we now have a better sense of how to answer these questions. In fact, we now know more about how children develop understanding, how people reason and build structures of knowledge, which thinking processes are associated with competent performance, and how knowledge is shaped by social context. In the following section we describe some of these ongoing findings about understanding and thinking. We believe that these findings will help you clarify your notions about understanding and thinking so that you can apply them as you teach and assess your students.

Understanding Involves Multiple Pathways to Learning

First, we know that students arrive in the classroom with different ideas of the world and different levels of readiness. The work of Howard Gardner (1993) has brought into focus the idea that there are sets of intellectual strengths that can be considered "ways of knowing." According to Gardner, learners tend to use several of these intellectual sets with greater agility than other sets, and he contends that educators need to honor these different ways of looking at the world. Figure 4.1 illustrates what Gardner terms *multiple intelligences.*

While these specific individual intelligences have not yet been supported by research, they reflect in part the common observations of teachers

Figure 4.1 *Gardner's Multiple Intelligences*

- *Linguistic:* This understanding consists of the ability to think in words and to use language to express and appreciate complex meaning. Authors, journalists, public speakers, and newscasters often exhibit high degrees of linguistic intelligence.
- *Logical/mathematical:* This type of intelligence makes it possible to calculate, quantify, consider propositions and hypotheses, and carry out complex mathematical operations. Scientists, mathematicians, accountants, engineers, and computer programmers all demonstrate especially strong logical/mathematical intelligence.
- *Spatial:* This intelligence instills the capacity to think in three-dimensional terms, as do sailors, pilots, sculptors, painters, and architects. Spatial intelligence enables one to perceive external and internal imagery; to re-create, transform, or modify images; to navigate oneself through space; and to produce or decode graphic information.
- *Bodily/kinesthetic:* This intelligence enables one to manipulate objects and fine-tune physical skills. It is evident in athletes, dancers, and surgeons, for example.
- *Musical:* This intelligence is evident in those with sensitively to pitch, melody, rhythm, and tone. Those demonstrating this intelligence include composers, conductors, musicians, critics, and instrument makers, as well as sensitive listeners.
- *Interpersonal:* This type of intelligence refers to the ability to interact effectively with others. It is evident in those who are successful teachers, social workers, actors, salespersons, consultants, or politicians.
- *Intrapersonal:* This type of intelligence refers to the ability to perceive an accurate model of oneself and use such knowledge in planning and directing one's life. Some individuals with strong intrapersonal intelligence work as theologians, psychologists, or philosophers.
- *Naturalistic:* This intelligence refers to the ability to perceive details in the natural, physical world with great clarity. This ability is evident in many biologists, anthropologists, and engineers.
- *Spiritual:* This type of intelligence refers to the ability to perceive underlying meanings and symbols within the human context. This ability is evident in successful religious leaders, writers, politicians, and reformers.

Source: Gardner, 1993.

that students can differ from one another in their learning strengths and weaknesses when they first enter the classroom. They are a reminder that you must teach broadly and assess broadly to allow students different forms of expression.

In this book we encourage you to use many different ways and many different intellectual tools to present and examine concepts. You will also need to use a variety of assessment techniques that lend themselves to different ways of expressing understanding. To fully assess students' learning, you would not always limit them to writing, for example. At various times you would allow them to make oral presentations, group presentations, and visual or artistic presentations.

Understanding Involves Personal Meaning Making

Other psychological and social scientists approach understanding from a **meaning-making** perspective. According to several researchers (Caine & Caine, 1994; O'Keefe & Nadel, 1978), the search for meaning and the need to act on our environment are automatic and basic to the human brain; the mind/brain innately seeks to make connections. According to David Ausubel (1975), the search for meaning is at the heart of learning, and much of the energy and drive to pursue goals and engage in essential tasks come from this search. The central thrust of Ausubel's work is that children are always engaged in the process of making sense of things.

How do people make sense of the unfamiliar? In this view of learning, ideas are understood through the lens of culture and from the society that surrounds the individual. Ultimately, this view goes back to Lev Vygotsky (1962), who described understanding as a process involving persons in conversation. From his perspective, understanding is constructed when individuals talk about and work together on shared problems and tasks. For example, in discussion two individuals can express their unique understandings of an idea or method. In the act of sharing their understandings, the individuals may dynamically modify their perspectives by accepting or rejecting others' ideas. Through discussion with others our own ideas become clearer.

Some of what children learn comes from being introduced into their culture by its more skilled members. This means that valued learning is knowledge that encompasses the richness of a person's context, and knowledge is subject to the values that surround the learner. So, for example, how parents introduce children to reading, or the extent to which the language of the home matches the language in the books used in school, can play an important role in helping children view reading as a form of communication and help them in understanding the world.

This personal meaning perspective implies that every assessment method is at least in part a measure of the degree to which a student's home environment does or does not support a particular assessment method. For example, some students will be better prepared than others to participate in formal assessments like multiple-choice tests, due to their histories. One way to make assessment methods or practices fairer, regardless of students' past experiences, is to ask students to explain what a particular concept means to them in relation to their unique environment. Asking students to "give an example from your own life" or "show how this might affect you" would be useful in this way.

Understanding Requires a Large Knowledge Base

Cognitive science has gathered a large body of data about the development of expertise in various disciplines, including those we address in our classrooms. These studies have shown what learning looks like as a person moves from novice to expert in a particular area, and they demonstrate that experts become experts by amassing a large body of knowledge and skill and by organizing that body of knowledge into useful categories.

Although these descriptions of expertise are interesting, what can be done to develop knowledge and skill? Cognitive scientists have uncovered some very specific suggestions.

Opportunities for Practice and Feedback As you have found as a learner yourself, acquiring deep knowledge and skill is long-term and labor-intensive work. A great deal of practice is necessary, but for the practice to result in real understanding, learners must have careful feedback. Learners need to know what they are doing correctly and what they are misunderstanding. They need to avoid practicing their errors and to be encouraged to acquire a needed skill correctly.

Learning from Errors The feedback you give your students must have certain characteristics so they can learn what they need to know. First, the feedback must have specific information about what the student can do to improve (Fuchs & Fuchs, 1986). Second, the feedback must focus on mastery of learning goals rather than on giving grades or improving self-esteem. In fact, feedback to make students feel better, irrespective of the quality of their work, may be ineffective and even harmful (Kluger & DeNisi, 1996).

Understanding Involves the Organization of Schemas or Categories of Knowledge and Skills

Research has found that experts organize their information and skills in **schemas**, that is, meaningful units that allow them to quickly retrieve and use their large body of knowledge. As students develop their understandings, they will be engaged in this process of creating schemas. Schemas organize information on the basis of common functions or underlying features. For example, the mathematical researcher Richard C. Anderson notes that "people acquire most new mathematical knowledge by constructing for themselves new organizations of concepts and new procedures for performing mathematical operations" (1977, pp. 213–214).

Jerome Bruner (1956) has also focused on the mental structures within a person's thinking, which he calls **cognitive maps.** Bruner contends that all of knowledge can be collapsed into a set of abstract structures, or big ideas (such as interaction, cause–effect, equilibrium, dissonance), that should spiral throughout the school curriculum. Bruner calls these "structures" because they connect and organize all conceptual information into clearly linked maps of information.

Artificial intelligence (AI) researchers agree with Bruner that all knowing is a complex mapping process (Caine & Caine, 1994). We create mental maps by processing new experiences and placing these experiences into a maplike mental structure. Learning becomes the art of connecting bits of information in a logical way and ultimately using these connections to retrieve information about a concept whenever necessary.

The fact that learners develop schemas or cognitive maps of knowledge and skills on the way to becoming expert has important implications for assessment. Most important, you will want to ask your students to explain their thinking as they solve new problems. Their explanations will give you insight into the way in which they are organizing their knowledge and where they need help in recognizing underlying patterns or similarities.

The Importance of Metacognition

As students gain knowledge and understanding, their learning will be enhanced if they also acquire metacognitive skills. **Metacognition,** or thinking about thinking, includes the skills of reflecting on one's thought processes. If learners think about their own thinking as they develop answers to questions, complete learning tasks, or examine their completed works, they can develop important insights and understandings.

Although students can improve somewhat in metacognition on their own, these skills can also be taught, just like other skills. You can teach your students to monitor their understanding as they learn so that they can self-correct. You can help them figure out which strategies to use to solve a problem and why that will make future problems easier to solve. And you can help them take ownership of their learning.

Implications for Assessment

If our goal is to develop students from novices to experts, assessment must be anchored in regular, helpful feedback. Coaching students in the process of thinking and acting, conversing with students before and after a learning task, and providing guidance as they progress through a task are important

Resource for Your Assessment Toolkit
National Recommendations for Developing Assessments

The National Research Council's Committee on the Foundations of Assessment (2001) was established to review and synthesize advances in the cognitive sciences and measurement and to explore their implications for improving educational assessment. The committee contended that it was of critical importance that educators develop new kinds of assessment that better serve the goals of equity. After much deliberation, the committee determined that it was critical for teachers to study contemporary theories of learning and knowing and that teachers should explore the many different ways that knowledge is represented, organized, and processed in the mind. The committee also developed the following recommendations for *assessment practice.*

- *Developers of assessment instruments for classroom or large-scale use should pay explicit attention to all three elements of the assessment triangle—cognition, observation (or testing), and interpretation—as well as their coordination.* All three elements should be based on modern knowledge of how students learn and how such learning is best measured. Considerable time and effort should be devoted to a theory-driven design and validation process before assessments are put into use.

- *Developers of educational curricula and classroom assessments should create tools that will enable teachers to implement high-quality instructional and assessment practices, consistent with modern understanding of how students learn and how such learning can be measured.* Assessments and supporting instructional materials should interpret the findings from cognitive research in ways

that are useful for teachers. Developers are urged to take advantage of technology to assess what students are learning at fine levels of detail, with appropriate frequency, and in ways that are tightly integrated with instruction.

- *Policymakers are urged to reconsider the limitation of current assessments and to support the development of new systems of multiple assessments that would improve their ability to make decisions about education programs and the allocation of resources.* Important decisions about individuals should not be based on a single test score. Policymakers should instead invest in the development of assessment systems that use multiple measures of student performance, particularly when high stakes are attached to the results. Assessments at the classroom and large-scale levels should grow out of a shared knowledge base about the nature of learning.

- *The balance of mandates and resources should be shifted from an emphasis on external forms of assessment to an increased emphasis on classroom formative assessment designed to assist learning.*

You may not be in a position to make assessment policy or implement assessment systems that match these noble intentions, but this resource may be valuable when you are teaching in a district that lacks some of the coherence demanded by this committee. Use this resource as evidence to support encouraging assessments that relate to a consistent view of cognition and teaching.

Source: Committee on the Foundations of Assessment, 2001.

assessment methods. Interestingly, we often think of such activities as teaching, not assessment.

Providing time for students to reflect on their work is also important. Regularly asking students to describe how they developed a solution to a problem rather than simply assessing whether an answer is correct or incorrect helps students develop a vocabulary to describe their thinking. Encouraging students to share different approaches to a problem with each other is another effective way to help students learn from their errors and from the work of others.

Ask Yourself

Think again about something that you understand clearly. What was done in school that helped you develop understanding? What got in the way of developing understanding?

What Does Thinking Mean?

According to the Committee on the Foundations of Assessment (National Research Council, 2001), it is equally important for educators to clarify both what they mean by *understanding* and what they mean by *thinking*. Just as with theories of understanding, there are many ways to consider what it means to think well.

One way to consider the meaning of good thinking is to consider thinking as a set of tools or strategies much like the tools of an artist or a carpenter. If the proper tools are not available, it will be difficult to complete the work. If the tools of thinking are imprecise or poorly developed, the final product will suffer.

Like quality tools, if thinking strategies are finely tuned, the products of thinking will benefit. For example, expert artists not only recognize the different brushes and strokes available to them but also know which brush and stroke are needed to achieve a specific effect. The same is true for thinkers using thinking tools. In addition to recognizing the variety of thinking tools available, it is equally important for thinkers to recognize that the type of thinking skill or strategy influences and determines the structure of the understanding that the learner will achieve.

To understand thinking as tools or tactics, let's first note what they are not. Thinking tactics are not simply separate thinking skills like observation, elaboration, application, analysis, synthesis, or evaluation. (Barry Beyer [1994] has identified as many as 144 separate thinking skills.) **Thinking strategies or tactics** are sets of thinking skills that are used together. Contemporary examples of thinking tactics include the use of a logical sequence of steps for experimentation, the use of a set of steps to write a paragraph, or the proper method for solving an ill-structured problem.

Because these thinking tactics are so important, educators must be aware of the rich variety of thinking tactics available to them. Such awareness enables teachers to be more deliberate when planning instruction and assessment.

Thinking Strategies Drawn from Dimensions of Learning

Robert Marzano provides a set of thinking strategies in his model called Dimensions of Learning (1993). Marzano contends that there is a set of thinking strategies that support the learning process. These strategies include comparison, classification, and abstraction; induction and deduction; error analysis, support construction, and perception analysis; decision making, problem solving, and invention.

Thinking Strategies Drawn from Benjamin Bloom

Benjamin Bloom (1956) provides another well-known way of thinking about thinking. Bloom proposed a taxonomy for thinking based on increasingly complex or higher-order categories. This taxonomy has been extremely influential in education for the past 50 years.

Bloom's first level, *knowledge,* is the underpinning of five higher levels. Bloom called the higher levels "skills." These are *comprehension, application, analysis, synthesis,* and *evaluation.*

Recently, other educators in collaboration with Bloom and some of his co-authors have revised this taxonomy based on recent research in cognitive science (Anderson & Krathwohl, 2001). The revised model breaks the content of the knowledge category into four types: *factual, conceptual, procedural,* and *metacognitive.* The six categories are reworded with verbs to represent what a thinker is doing within that category (for instance, *comprehension* becomes *understand*). In addition, the final two categories are reversed in the revised taxonomy. You can compare the two taxonomies side by side in Figure 4.2.

Ask Yourself

Think back to a specific grade in your life as a student. What type of thinking was your teacher emphasizing in that grade? Can you recall a time when your teacher explicitly taught you any of the thinking strategies cited in this chapter? Did the assessments match the type of thinking that your teacher emphasized during instruction?

Resource for Your Assessment Toolkit
Marzano's Thinking Strategies

The following types of thinking strategies were developed by Robert Marzano to help teachers relate specific questions to a specific strategy. This resource can assist you in the development of assessment questions. By considering the questions that relate to each thinking strategy, you will be clear about the type of thinking you are assessing. In fact, you could use these sample questions as they are written to inform many of your assessments.

Comparing

These questions help describe how things are the same and different.

What things do I want to compare?

What is it about them that I want to compare?

How are they the same? How are they different?

Classifying

These questions help group things that are alike into categories.

What things do I want to classify?

What things share a common likeness and could be put into a group?

What other groups can I make?

Would it be better to split up any of the groups or put any groups together?

Inductive Reasoning

These questions help make general conclusions from specific information or observations.

What do I know about this one thing?

What do I know about this other thing?

What connections or pattern can I find that they share?

What general conclusions can I make?

As I get more information, what do I need to change about my general conclusions?

Deductive Reasoning

These questions help use general statements to draw conclusions about specific information or situations.

What general information do I already know that helps me understand this topic?

In what ways does the general information apply or not apply to this topic?

What do I know better about my topic?

Error Analysis

These questions help find and describe errors in your own or others' thinking.

What exactly is being communicated?

Does something seem incorrect or inconsistent? Why?

Does something need more clarity?

What might be added or deleted?

How can I get more or better information?

Constructing Support

These questions help provide details or elaboration for statements.

Am I stating information or a point of view?

If I am stating an opinion or point of view, do I need to offer further support?

What can I add (information, examples, evidence, appeals)?

(continued)

Resource for Your Assessment Toolkit
Marzano's Thinking Strategies (continued)

Abstracting

These questions help find and explain general patterns in specific information or situations.

What are the important characteristics or pieces of this thing, situation, idea?

How can I say these important characteristics in a more general way?

What other things have the same general pattern?

Analyzing Perspectives

These questions help describe reasons for your own point of view and for different points of view.

What is my point of view?

What are the reasons for my point of view?

What is another point of view?

What might be some reasons for this other point of view?

Decision Making

These questions help develop and use criteria to select from among choices that seem to be equal.

What is the focus of my decision?

What are my choices?

What are the important criteria for choosing?

How important is each criterion?

What choice best matches the criteria?

Experimental Inquiry

These questions help develop and test explanations for things we observe.

What do I observe (see, touch, feel, hear)?

How can I explain it?

Based on my explanation, what can I hypothesize?

How can I test my hypothesis?

After testing, what happened? Do I need to modify my hypothesis?

Investigation

These questions help suggest and defend ways to clear up confusion about ideas or events.

What idea or event do I want to better understand?

What do I already know about this idea?

What questions do I have about this idea?

What suggestions do I have for clarifying any confusion I might have?

Invention

These questions help develop original products or processes that meet specific needs.

What do I want to make or improve?

What standards do I want to set for my invention?

What pieces make up my invention?

How do the pieces fit together? How does a rough draft look?

Does my invention meet the standards I set?

What do I need to do differently?

Problem Solving

These questions help overcome limits or barriers that are obstacles.

What is the real problem?

What are the obstacles or barriers to the problem?

What are some ways of overcoming the limits or barriers?

Which solution seems best? Why?

Comparison, classification, and *abstraction* are thinking strategies that examine similarities and differences among ideas, objects, and events. The focus of these thinking strategies is to identify the degree to which items reflect common characteristics. *Induction* and *deduction* are thinking strategies that are used to make conclusions and to link generalizations to specifics and vice versa. *Error analysis, support construction,* and *perception analysis* are thinking strategies that deal with the reasons for a conclusion or point of view. These thinking strategies help thinkers take a position and construct support for the position. *Decision making, problem solving,* and *invention* focus on establishing criteria, dealing with constraints and limiting conditions, and revising and meeting standards.

Source: Adapted from handout by McRel Institute, 1995.

Figure 4.2 *Revision of Bloom's Taxonomy*

Original Taxonomy	Revised Taxonomy
Knowledge ⟶	**Remember**—retrieve relevant knowledge from long-term memory (recognize, recall).
Comprehension ⟶	**Understand**—determine the meaning of instructional messages (interpret, exemplify, classify, summarize, infer, compare, explain).
Application ⟶	**Apply**—use a procedure in a given situation (execute, implement).
Analysis ⟶	**Analyze**—break material into parts and see how they related (differentiate, organize, attribute).
Synthesis	**Evaluate**—make judgments based on criteria and standards (check, critique).
Evaluation	**Create**—put elements together to form a novel, coherent whole or make an original product (generate, plan, produce).

Source: Adapted from Anderson & Krathwohl, 2001.

Resource for Your Assessment Toolkit
Thinking Questions Spanning Bloom's Revised Taxonomy

The following examples drawn from simple mathematics computation may help you differentiate the types of thinking that relate to Bloom's revised taxonomy. Each question relates to the addition of one- or two-digit integers, but the type of thinking required to solve each question is quite different.

Remember

7 + 9 =   (requires recall)

Understand

To find the difference   (requires understanding
between 7 and 9,   of the operation)
you must _____.

a. add   c. multiply
b. subtract   d. divide

Apply

17
+9   (requires application of
                           regrouping algorithm)

Analyze

7 + 9 = __ + 8   (requires analysis of relationship
                           of left to right side in equation)

Evaluate

Here is Susan's   (requires judgment according to
work. What can   criteria and analysis of errors)
you say about
her subtracting?

31	76	45	71
− 9	−17	−25	−35
38	61	20	44

Create

Write four sub-   (requires an original
traction prob-   production for a purpose)
lems to give to
Susan that will
test whether she
can borrow.

Standards, Standards, and More Standards: The Content Focus for Assessment

There are many, many standards in the world of education. Since the mid-1980s, educational standards have been disseminated, celebrated, debated, and revised. To make sense of the content focus that may be required in your future classroom assessments, you will find it useful to examine the many different definitions for standards as well as the sources for them. In this section we describe different ways of thinking about standards, different groups that have developed standards, and the different learning dimensions that make up educational standards. An examination of these fundamental ideas about standards and their origins will help you determine which standards best fit the needs of your students. It will also help you balance calls for accountability with your responsibility to connect your instruction to your students' needs.

What Exactly Is a Standard?

Is a standard a goal? An objective? How big is it? Should it be achievable by all? For over 20 years Grant Wiggins (1989, 1991, 1998) has asked us to consider the different meanings and implications of the term **standard** before rushing into the standards-based education arena.

Vision of Excellence Wiggins and others (e.g., Hammerman & Musial, 1995) have suggested that a standard should first and foremost represent a *vision of excellence*. Such a notion calls for a reflective process wherein experts clarify what is of most worth to a society. It implies that standards are *noble goals that motivate educators* to make decisions about what they emphasize in their classrooms.

At a glance, this is precisely what standards-based education has done. Teachers across the country are given lists of standards and directed to teach them and then show that students have mastered the standards. However, if standards are translated into reasonable competencies that all students should achieve by a certain grade level, they become nothing more than the behavioral objectives of old.

This does not imply that we should dismiss the importance of developing reasonable objectives to guide our daily routine, but we should realize that such objectives stand in sharp contrast to a noble goal that calls us to action. It ultimately becomes the responsibility of teachers to keep students focused on the larger goals or standards and to let these standards guide them as they help students achieve the smaller competencies that are connected to the standard.

World-Class Performance Another meaning for standard is a *world-class performance* or worthy achievement. In this definition, the worthy goal is not simply an idea that motivates. Rather, the standard is encased in an empirical, real-world, expert, and summative performance that has, in fact, been achieved. Examining Olympic champions or the works of great authors, musicians, dancers, scientists, and mathematicians evokes these standards.

Once again this meaning for standard implies a noble but possibly achievable goal that motivates all of us to learn and practice and develop. Generally, when standards are based on the achievements of experts, they remain broad goals that provide an invitation to move students along a continuum. The teacher again faces the problem of determining what specific performances along this continuum are reasonable for students to achieve in their classrooms. When translated into a classroom context, we use the terminology *summative performances* as they would represent the culmination of a particular course of learning.

Benchmarks and Performance Competencies A benchmark or performance competency is not a standard itself, but is a part of a standard. A **benchmark or performance competency** *is usually defined as a discrete competency or accomplishment that shows progress toward a larger standard or goal.* For example, a standard could be stated as "Students will demonstrate the ability to critically analyze competing arguments." A *benchmark* of progress toward meeting this important standard might be stated as the following sixth-grade-level performance: "Sixth-grade students will compare the messages implied by two opposing political cartoons."

Clearly this smaller, more focused, benchmark, or *competency,* that requests students to do a comparison relates to the larger standard that calls for critical thinking. However, the competency is smaller than the standard and represents progress toward the larger goal. The key to the proper use of benchmarks rests on the legitimate and clear connection of benchmarks to the larger standard or goal. Unless such connections are carefully developed, the benchmarks can become ends in themselves without necessarily leading to the broader standard.

How Do Expectations Influence Standards?

Standards develop from expectations that different vested interest groups have for education. For example, policymakers usually focus on the larger long-term needs of society. They tend to want more rigorous academic standards so as to maintain world-class status for this country. They want students to know more science, history, mathematics, literature, and geography than students in other countries. They expect schools to graduate students who have high-level, discipline-specific achievement and can demonstrate world-class performances. Such a view tends to emphasize standards as noble goals or worthy performances in a competitive environment.

Business leaders tend to want high school graduates ready for work—able to read, write, and compute. They expect schools to prepare a supply of future workers. Businesses are willing to provide specific job training, but they do not want to teach what they consider basic skills. The underlying conception of a standard implied by this expectation is focused on competencies or benchmarks.

Parents tend to choose standards based on their personal goals and family histories. Some parents want their children to go to prestigious colleges, and others want their children to obtain a good job immediately after high school. Still others want their children to join a particular profession. These expectations tend to focus on summative performances that relate to specific careers.

Digging Deeper
The NEA Committee of Ten

In the late 1800s, the high school was added to American educational institutions. The high school was a controversial concept in U.S. culture, and the society struggled to define its purpose. Traditional educators wanted high school to be a college preparatory institution, while others wanted high school to offer practical courses for the common student. To help pave the way for high school, a curriculum standard was needed, so the National Education Association (NEA) appointed a Committee of Ten in 1892. Charles Eliot, president of Harvard, was appointed as the leader of the committee.

After much debate (similar to the debates that surround contemporary standards), a curriculum emerged that had four strands. All of the strands began with the first year covering the same five subject areas: foreign language, English, history, algebra, and what was called "physical geography," which included geography, geology, and meteorology. Other sciences were introduced in the second year, while the other four subjects were continued.

To the modern eye, three of the strands appear to differ very little beyond the number of foreign languages learned and how many were to be ancient versus modern. For example, the Classical strand focused on Greek and Latin, with one modern language, and also differed from the other strands in its smaller number of science courses. The Latin-Scientific and Modern Language strands both emphasized sciences in addition to the basic curriculum, but no Latin or Greek was taught in the Modern Language strand.

The fourth or English strand contained only one foreign language, which could be ancient or modern, and also allowed flexibility to add more practical courses. Beginning in the second year, for example, the mathematics class could be bookkeeping and commercial arithmetic, and the sciences beginning in the third year could be replaced with "practical subjects in trade or the useful arts."

The committee strongly recommended a common curriculum for the first two years that would introduce all students to the subjects that were seen as most beneficial in developing the student's mind and interests. As the committee explained, they wished to "give time enough to each subject to win from it the kind of mental training it is fitted to supply."

Further, they recognized that many students might only attend the first two years of high school, so it was important to expose students to all important subjects during those two years. As they pointed out, a student needs to

> discover his tastes by making excursions into all the principal fields of knowledge. The youth who has never studied any but his native language cannot know his own capacity for linguistic acquisition, and the youth who has never made a chemical or physical experiment cannot know whether or not he has a taste for exact science. The wisest teacher, or the most observant parent, can hardly predict with confidence a boy's gift for a subject which he has never touched.

Of course, it was not thought at the time that a girl would have this same focus and deliberate thought about education.

The Committee of Ten determined that "the goal of high school was to prepare all students to do well in life, contributing to their own well-being and society's good, and to prepare some students for college."

The Committee of Ten made two important recommendations that affect schools today. First, they made high school a learning place for college-bound students and non-college-bound students alike. Second, they set the criteria concerning how many years it should take for students to complete elementary and high school educations.

Source: "The N.E.A Committee of Ten" at http://www.nd.edu/~rbarger/www7/neacom10.html. Accessed September 15, 2006.

In the end, these competing, although related, interests of different groups give rise to competing definitions for standards. This competition accounts for much of the confusion surrounding the standards-based education movement. Your mission as a teacher is to show how your students are meeting the standards by developing reasonable expectations that students can achieve at your specific grade level. As you do so, you will be working to develop a clear understanding of how the specific assessment task you use relates to other tasks that ultimately make up the larger standard.

Where Do Standards Reside?

In education, *content standards* reside in written documents produced by national professional organizations. Many educators and national associations think of standards as discipline based and, therefore, the property of professional, discipline-specific organizations. These subject-matter standards are statements concerning what teachers and students should know and be able to do in various disciplines: science, mathematics, history, geography, social studies, physical education, and the arts. Usually these discipline-based standards emphasize content acquisition and skill mastery; teachers are encouraged to cover subject matter and make certain that students master specific knowledge and skills.

The first group to claim that standards reside in their documents was the National Council of Teachers of Mathematics in 1989 (most recent version is 2001). Their initiative set a precedent for other standard-setting projects. During the 1990s the U.S. Department of Education funded subject-area groups and coalitions to prepare similar standards in disciplines such as science, history, civics, language arts, geography, the fine arts, and foreign language.

Standards continue to be developed and published by many groups. For example, the American Association for the Advancement of Science (1993), the National Council for the Social Studies (1994), and the National Association for Sport and Physical Education (2004) have all published sets of standards that represent what they believe students should know and be able to do throughout primary, elementary, middle, and secondary school.

These national subject-area standards have been used by most states and translated into sets of state educational standards. Individual school districts have also developed district learning standards based on their unique interpretations of state standards. You can find a list of national standards publications developed by different subject-matter groups in Appendix A.

In addition to the work of discipline-specific groups, professional educator organizations have developed standards for teachers, information specialists, school counselors, and so on. These standards articulate what educators should know and be able to do within each profession. There is no single set of teaching standards. Rather, different professional agencies have adopted their own sets. Some of these professional standards are mathematics teaching standards from the National Council for Teachers of Mathematics, science teaching standards from the National Research Council, as well as general teaching standards from the National Board for Professional Teaching Standards.

Although all of these professional teaching standards are worth examining, it is not easy for teachers to determine which set best suits their individual contexts, philosophies, and teaching styles. To do so, teachers need a clear understanding of each group's rationale for developing standards and professional reasons for endorsing one set of standards over another.

Who Sets Standards?

Conflict surrounds the question of who is setting the standards: subject-matter professionals, politicians, parents, business leaders, school districts, teachers, or students? There is also conflict concerning which of these groups should make the final decision about the standards.

As an example of this dissension, the National Council for Teachers of English, the International Reading Association, and the Center for the Study of Reading at the University of Illinois received funding from the U.S. Department of Education to draft curriculum standards in English. However, the Department of Education rejected the standards that this group proposed and terminated funding, claiming that the standards were excessively concerned with process and insufficiently concerned with products or outcomes.

Conflict over standards may also occur when two professional groups attempt to develop standards for the same area. The *National Science Education Standards* (NAS, 1996) was developed through federal funds by the National Academies of Science and *Benchmarks for Science Literacy* (1993) was developed by the Association for the Advancement of Science. Both exist as independent sources for science teaching.

Some educators argue that different sets of national standards are useful because they lead to a critical discussion that will help in selecting standards. Healthy conflict allows for change and guards against developing an inflexible set of standards. Others note that in the absence of a single set of national standards, schools are left in the precarious position of choosing their own sets of standards that will impact what their students will know and be able to do at the end of their public schooling experience.

How Do States Interpret and Use the Standards?

In addition to conflicts among professional groups, conflicts arise about the uses of the standards across different states. Each of the 50 states has developed a standards framework that interprets the national standards for use within that state's schools. These state standards provide the key content that is the focus of every school district within that state. Recently, with the passage of No Child Left Behind, as we explained in Chapter 3, these standards are also used to develop large-scale assessments that are administered annually to provide accountability information to the public.

A **standards framework** is a structured description of how standards fit both larger learning goals and smaller benchmarks or performance competencies. An example of one state's standards framework in the area of science standards is illustrated in Figure 4.3. Science Standard 1 is broad, encompassing virtually all of the fundamentals of life sciences: "Students will understand the fundamental concepts, principles and interconnections of the life sciences." Next, this state's Board of Education took a smaller part of that standard and termed it Science Goal 1: "Know and apply concepts that explain how and why living things function, adapt, and change." This is one of a number of goals that would be needed to encompass the breadth of Science Standard 1.

As the next step, the state Board of Education created a series of benchmarks within the goal, describing how the goal might look at each level of development—from early and later elementary perspectives, a middle school perspective, and early and later high school perspectives. Two benchmarks for each of these five levels are shown in Figure 4.3. And finally, a state test was developed and administered to all students at certain grade levels to see how well they perform on this standard.

Figure 4.3 provides a very neat-looking summary of Science Standard 1 and one of the state's science goals that flows from Science Standard 1. But how well do the ten benchmarks really cover the goal? The benchmarks mention life cycles of plants and animals, but what about other kinds of cycles? Genetic variation is covered, but what about the relationship among DNA/RNA, genes, chromosomes, and ultimately the cell? The component parts of cells and the requirements for cells to live are covered but what about the death of cells and how the death–life cycle forms systems? This analysis is not intended to criticize a particular state but to illustrate the narrowing process that takes place as states attempt to translate broad standards into tests to determine if students are meeting those standards.

Furthermore, looking at the state test items, we can see that what was once a broad standard is now reduced to something much smaller. For practical reasons, a statewide test will naturally have to be made up of objective questions, similar to the way standardized tests are given in schools across the country. How well can these small, focused test questions truly assess students' mastery of the standard in all its breadth? When you compare the breadth of the standard ("Understand the fundamental concepts, principles, and interconnections of the life sciences") to the small-focus questions that supposedly test it, you find that fundamental concepts have come down to questions about skin and the parts of the cell.

Figure 4.3 *Science Standard 1*

Students will understand the fundamental concepts, principles, and interconnections of the life sciences. As a result of their schooling students will be able to:

Science Goal 1	Early Elementary Benchmark	Late Elementary Benchmark	Middle School Benchmark	Early High School Benchmark	Late High School Benchmark
Know and apply concepts that explain how and why living things function, adapt, and change.	Identify and explain the component parts of living things (e.g., birds have feathers, people have bones, hair, skin) and their major functions.	Describe simple life cycles of plants and animals and the similarities and differences in their offspring.	Explain how cells function as building blocks of organisms and describe the requirements for cells to live.	Explain how genetic combinations produce visible effects, variations among physical features and cellular functions of organisms.	Explain changes within cells and organisms in response to stimuli and changing environmental conditions (e.g., homeostasis, dormancy).
	Categorize living organisms using a variety of observable features (e.g., size, color, shape, backbone).	Categorize features as either inherited or learned (e.g., flower color or eye color is inherited; language is learned).	Compare characteristics of organisms produced from a single parent with those organisms produced by two parents.	Describe the organization of cells and tissues that underlie basic life functions including nutrition, cellular transport, biosynthesis, and reproduction.	Analyze the transmission of genetic disease traits and effects.
Sample state test items (all are multiple choice or matching).	Mammals need skin because it a. protects them from the outside world. b. makes them easy to recognize. c. helps their bones develop.	Which of the following features are inherited in humans? a. the language the individual speaks b. the color of the person's eyes c. the person's favorite color	(Diagram of a cell). Match the list of cell parts to the letters shown in the diagram. 1. nucleus 2. cytoplasm 3. vacuole 4. ribosomes 5. cell membrane	Basic cell functions include: a. learning. b. reproduction. c. variation.	A state of equilibrium produced by a balance of functions and of chemical composition within an organism is: a. homeostasis. b. dormancy. c. biosynthesis.

Not surprisingly, what happens over time is that teachers, while using these standards frameworks, begin to concentrate more and more on the tiny parts of each benchmark that match the state tests. Rather than expanding their curriculum to broaden the coverage in science beyond the small objectives listed for them, they are pressured to make sure their students pass the state tests. And the people who now set the standards are not the politicians or the professionals of various disciplines, but rather the state test writers (in some cases, a for-profit corporation). In a sense, the testing company, rather than the standard, is determining the curriculum.

The key response by teachers should be to interpret benchmarks and performances on tests in light of the larger standards that give rise to the benchmarks. There is much that surrounds these benchmarks and it is a challenge for teachers to determine all the related content so that the overall standard is being met rather than a limited number of objectives. This means that teachers must constantly return to and reflect on the larger learning standard, continue to read about the standard, and view it from the position of national standards documents—the position of working scientists and other experts as they develop new knowledge.

It is important for teachers to understand the standards framework for their state as well as the district curriculum that supports this framework. You can access your state's standards framework through a helpful service link provided by Education World at http://www .education-world.com/standards. Your state's standards framework will show you how national standards are interpreted by your state. Even if the terminology is different than that used in this book, you will find that the structure generally goes from standards, large learning goals, or outcome statements, to smaller benchmarks, performance competencies, or objectives.

What Unintended Consequences Have Come from Standards-Based Education?

The national movement toward standards is having both positive and negative effects on schools. On the positive side, the standards education movement provides a vocabulary and more precise information about what different school districts and states value. Standards also have the potential to make learning expectations clearer and more consistent across state lines. Standards aid students in understanding what is most important to learn, and they help teachers, schools, school districts, and states in determining the learning outcomes that should be assessed.

Still, as with any education initiative, there are a number of unfortunate, unintended consequences. We highlight below several of the more important consequences that have direct impact on teachers and students in classrooms.

High-Stakes Testing As the focus on student performance has increased, policymakers, especially at the state level, have mandated that students be tested regularly. Federally mandated annual testing of students under NCLB is now in place. Student test results are regularly compiled by schools and reported to the public. Schools are often named and ranked in newspapers, which raises sharp questions about the "low-performing" status of certain schools. In a few states, "high-performing" schools receive additional funds.

Much more frequent than rewarding schools is some sort of sanctioning of low-performing schools. In some states, schools that are designated "in crisis" are assigned an experienced master teacher or principal who is responsible for helping the school improve. Principals can be reassigned and school staffs replaced. In other states, entire school districts designated "low performing" can be taken over by the state.

Tests can be high stakes for students as well. Twenty-eight states now use standardized exams to determine graduation from high school, and 19 states use tests to decide student promotions.

Teaching for the Test A related unintended outcome has to do with the time teachers spend on topics "likely to be on the test" rather than addressing the specific instructional needs of their students. *Any single test samples only a very limited part of what students need to learn.* Some state tests have little overlap with what is specified in various sets of content standards and what is emphasized in the district curriculum materials. Time spent preparing for high-stakes tests reduces the time available to teach related material and other subjects, such as art and music, which are often not tested (National Education Commission on Time and Learning, 1994).

One Size Fits All Another critical issue related to the heavy focus on testing is the assumption that the same test is appropriate for all students and schools. In 1980 just about half of the states had mandatory testing programs. By 1998 all but two states had some type of mandatory state assessment. Historically, in the American system of education, heavy emphasis has been placed on the importance of attending to individual and developmental differences. As noted above, some states mandate that one test be given to all students at a certain grade level at a specified time; in other words, one size fits all. All students are required to take the same relatively narrow test, and major decisions about individual students and/or schools are often based on the test results.

A National Exam Some educators are concerned that the adoption of national curriculum standards and state tests will lead to a national exam and subsequent national curriculum (Pipho, 2000). This is the one-size-fits-all concept taken to the extreme.

It is interesting to note that at present there exists a sort of national exam that is given strictly for statistical purposes, not to grade individual schools, school districts, or states. This is the National Assessment for Educational Progress (NAEP), discussed in Chapter 3, which is administered each year to students in a representative sample of schools in each state. The test makes it possible for policymakers and educators to view how well students are doing across the nation as a whole and to make comparisons with student achievement in other countries. Also, because of the way the data are gathered, NAEP results can be used to make inferences about student achievement within states and thus to compare one state with another. Ironically, although NAEP has existed for several decades and its findings have been useful to educational planners because they are strictly anonymous, school districts are increasingly unwilling to participate in the testing due to the mounting pressure and time demands of the many other required tests.

What Do Standards Imply for Assessment?

Finally, let's consider the question of how assessment relates to standards. In many states it is assumed that once a standard is officially selected, teachers should be held accountable for students' achievement of the standard. This assumption is seriously flawed. World-class standards or standards as noble concepts are meant to lead students and teachers to higher and higher levels. Focusing on the mastery of small competencies without making an effort to fulfill more of the broad standard makes for piecemeal development rather than reaching deeper levels of knowledge and understanding.

For this reason, accountability itself needs to be debated and better understood. To whom or to what should teachers and students be accountable? Are standardized multiple-choice tests appropriate assessments for standards? How can we be sure that the competencies we are assessing are big enough pieces of the standards and important enough to assess?

Despite all of these difficulties concerning the proper way to assess standards, teachers can still make a difference for their students by developing clear, classroom-based assessments that are closely linked to standards. The key is that teachers need to be well-informed about standards. They need to access the different sources for standards and not rely simply on statements provided by state standards frameworks. Teachers need to study the connections between the goals and standards and the concrete benchmarks that relate to the larger standards.

In addition, rather than simply relying on multiple-choice tests (which are generally used in state and national assessments), teachers can develop a variety of classroom assessments to measure the knowledge, thinking strategies, and dispositions that are implicit in the standards. Portfolio development, performance assessments, authentic assessment projects, interviews, and observations are just a few of the types of assessments that may be able to focus on the broad standard rather than on limited answers to smaller questions. Assessing students through a variety of assessment methods that complement one another enables both students and parents to know more clearly what students know and can do. The next section of this chapter will help you better understand how to keep your focus on the larger standards of instruction while concentrating on the specific developmental levels of your students.

Ask Yourself

Take a look at a standard from one of the published national standards documents. Then consider how a world-class professional might perform the standard you selected. Compare a published standard with your understanding of the world-class version. What insights does each description provide? Does either the written version or the world-class performance version seem more useful to you as a teacher, or do you find unique insights from both versions? How might students at a particular classroom grade level display the same standard in a performance task? In what ways does the classroom task relate to the written and world-class versions? In what ways does the classroom task differ from the written and world-class versions?

Three Dimensions of the Instructional Process: Standards, Learning, and Assessment

The instructional process involves three basic components: standards, learning, and assessment. In other words, it involves clarifying students' learning outcomes (linked to important standards), providing learning activities that help students master the intended outcomes (linked to the teacher's views about understanding and thinking), and, finally, assessing students to determine if they have achieved the learning outcomes. You might think that these three steps are linear with step one preceding step two, and step two preceding step three. But this is not the case. In fact, the instructional process requires you to carefully consider all three steps simultaneously because each of these components influences the others (Figure 4.4).

The figure displays the dynamic relationship among the development of learning outcomes, the selection and implementation of learning activities, and the design of assessments that match both the learning outcomes and the learning activities. However, Figure 4.4 also shows how each of these activities is linked to larger foundational considerations, indicated in the colored ovals.

Figure 4.4 *Three Dimensions of the Instructional Process*

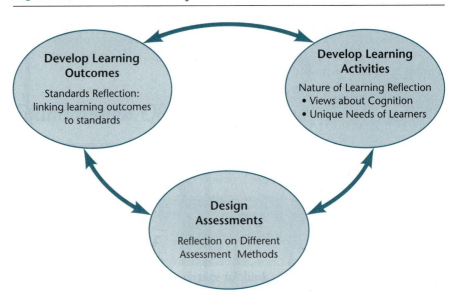

For example, it is not enough to simply take a learning objective and teach it in isolation; it must be connected to its corresponding standard. It is not enough to simply develop a teaching activity; it must be connected to the specific learning needs of the students and to the larger view of understanding that the teacher holds. Finally, it is not enough to purchase a commercially developed assessment tool or to write a test without considering the many ways students might know and be able to communicate their understanding.

Because the process shown in Figure 4.4 is cyclical, you can theoretically start anywhere. Let's start with developing the learning outcomes or objectives. As you work on this task, you will use the curriculum goals adopted by your school board, but you will also reflect on the broad standards that the goals are part of, asking yourself, "Is part of the standard missing from our written goals? What and how can I teach so that I meet the goals and at the same time deepen my students' understanding of the larger standard?"

After clarifying the learning outcomes, you develop learning activities that will accomplish your learning outcomes. Again, you will find yourself reflecting on some important issues: your understanding of the nature of learning, your personal views about cognition, and the unique needs of the learners in your classroom.

And having administered your assessments and evaluated your students' performance, you are in a position to modify or extend your learning objectives. You may broaden your learning activities to address areas of misunderstanding, and you may broaden your learning activities to deepen your students' understanding or to include activities that relate to students' interests.

Constructing Learning Outcomes that Match Standards

In order to design appropriate assessments, teachers need to state learning outcomes or objectives that clearly convey the focus, that is, what it is that students are to learn. Only when you have developed learning outcomes that clearly connect to the standards and also fit the unique needs of your students can you develop clear assessments. Assessments should always relate to the intended standards and to the specific ways that your students learn.

Specifically, how can you clarify a learning outcome and be certain it matches the larger standard? An initial important step to accomplish this is **unpacking the standard:** breaking the larger goals and standards of your curriculum into the key ideas and skills stated in the standard. Focus on the vocabulary of the standard and examine the terms and concepts. Consider how this vocabulary connects to the content of your grade and other grade levels. Talk to teachers about the concepts and terms of the standard and find out how they introduce these terms to students. What learning tasks are student provided that link to the standards? By analyzing these tasks, you can develop similar tasks that connect to those learning tasks that students have or will have experienced in other grade levels (Burke, 2006).

Another key step that you can use to determine if a learning outcome matches the larger standard is to *determine the big ideas or essential questions* that are often embedded across related standards. Susan Drake and Rebecca Burns (2004) believe that teachers can find these big ideas and questions by using an integrated approach to the study of their curriculum. Teachers often start a unit of learning by focusing on a topic like dinosaurs, medieval times, butterflies, or the Civil War. It is important for teachers to see the big ideas or concepts that relate to these topics and focus the learning on the related ideas. For example, dinosaurs include the concept of extinction, medieval times includes culture, butterflies include life cycles, and the Civil War is permeated by the big idea of conflict. It is the big ideas that need to be the focus of standards-based learning, rather than the specific topics.

?Ask Yourself

Recall a teacher that you believe really helped you learn. What types of instruction did the teacher use that seemed especially effective? Why do you think these instructional methods were so effective? What types of assessments did the teacher use? Did these assessments match the types of instruction that were employed?

Summary

- Every assessment is grounded in assumptions about the nature of cognition or what it means to understand and what it means to think. It is imperative for teachers to clarify what they mean by understanding and thinking.

- Understanding is a complex concept that includes multiple pathways to learning, personal meaning, the development of schemas, and cognitive maps.

- Allowing students to learn from error—providing opportunities for practice and feedback—helps develop understanding.

- Providing time for students to reflect on their learning is important for understanding.

- There are different views about the nature of thinking, including Marzano's dimensions of learning and Bloom's taxonomy of thinking.

- Standards can be thought of as a vision of excellence, a world-class performance, or a benchmark.

- Standards reside in the ongoing excellent work of professionals, in national documents developed by professional organizations, and in state and local school district documents.

- Some unintended consequences that surround teaching for standards are high-stakes testing, teaching for the test, and the threat of a national examination.

- Assessments need to match the intentions of standards and should not simply measure the test items of high-stakes testing.

Key Terms

benchmark or performance competency (90)

cognitive map (81)

meaning making (79)

metacognition (81)

schemas (80)

standard (89)

standards framework (94)

thinking strategies or tactics (83)

unpacking the standard (101)

For Further Discussion

1. What types of school experiences really helped you understand a concept or a skill?

2. What types of assessment really made you think?

3. What types of feedback did you receive in school that helped you correct a misconcep-

tion or provided you with information about what you needed to learn next?

4. Share an example of a learning benchmark that your teacher emphasized. Did your teacher clarify how this benchmark or learning objective matched a standard?

Comprehension Quiz

In each chapter, we provide a short review of some key ideas in the form of an assessment. The use of these formats can remind you of the way that the format of an assessment changes your response to the experience. For this chapter, we have chosen a multiple-choice assessment. We hope you enjoy the review.

Part One

Select what type of standard matches each example.

> a. Vision of excellence
> b. Benchmark
> c. Summative performance

1. Martell has completed her student teaching semester at a rural high school. She receives high ratings on her student teaching competency checklist.

2. Ricardo correctly answers all questions about adding two-digit numbers with no regrouping.

3. Karen receives a letter from the Westinghouse Foundation that her research on the character-istics of a specific protein and its effects on tumors has been selected as an example of outstanding research.

4. All 17 students from first grade can recite the alphabet without error.

Part Two

What type of assessment closely fits the following learning objectives?

> a. Multiple-choice or short-answer test
> b. Essay question
> c. Performance assessment

1. Learners will be able to analyze the causes of the Revolutionary War.

2. Learners will be able to list the three components of the instructional process.

3. Learners will be able to collect firsthand data, develop a data table, and infer a conclusion from the data they collected.

Relevant Website Resources

American Alliance for Health, Physical Education, Recreation & Dance

http://www.aahperd.org

Formed in 1885, the American Alliance for Health, Physical Education, Recreation & Dance (AAHPERD) comprises five national associations and six district associations promoting a healthy lifestyle through physical activity. The AAHPERD developed standards for physical education and related areas, and the site provides material for lesson plans, professional development, and publications.

American Association for the Advancement of Science

http://www.aaas.org

The American Association for the Advancement of Science (AAAS) was founded in 1848 and is dedicated to advancing science around the world through education and leadership. One of its projects is Project 2061 that sets out recommendations for what all students should know and be able to do in science, mathematics, and technology by the time they graduate from high school.

International Reading Association

http://www.reading.org

The main goal of the International Reading Association (IRA) is to advance the literacy movement for people of all ages locally, nationally, and worldwide. For more than 50 years, IRA has provided research, publications, advice, and lesson plans to educators of all types, including professors, teachers, and parents. The IRA also posts news articles regarding literacy and related issues. Grants and award opportunities are available for qualifying teachers, programs, and educational institutions.

National Academies and the National Research Council

http://www.nationalacademies.org/nrc

Founded in 1916 by the National Academies, an umbrella organization for the National Academies of Sciences, National Academy of Engineering, and Institute of Medicine, the National Research Council (NRC) provides services to government entities and to public, scientific, and engineering communities. The NRC developed the national standards for science education and many other publications about the science of instruction and assessment. The site offers access to these resources.

National Arts Education Network (ArtsEdge)

http://artsedge.kennedy-center.org/teach/standards.cfm

ArtsEdge is a National Arts Education Network that supports the placement of the arts at the center of the curriculum and advocates creative use of technology to enhance the K–12 educational experience. ArtsEdge offers free, standards-based teach-ing materials for use in and out of the classroom as well as professional development resources, student materials, and guidelines for arts-based instruction and assessment. The site provides access to the national standards for arts education developed by the Consortium of National Arts Education Associations.

National Council for Teachers of English

http://www.ncte.org

Founded in 1911, the National Council for Teachers of English (NCTE) provides a website full of information and resources on the subject matter of English. There are state standards listed, along with professional standards. NCTE also offers professional growth through local and national conferences.

National Council for Teachers of Mathematics

http://www.nctm.org

The National Council for Teachers of Mathematics (NCTM) offers a website with access to national standards in mathematics instruction and teaching, instructional resources, and professional development opportunities.

National Council for the Social Studies

http://www.socialstudies.org

The mission of the National Council for the Social Studies (NCSS) is to provide leadership, service, and support for social studies educators. The site offers resources for lesson plans, teaching activities, and professional development. Membership is needed to access full benefits for the NCSS website.

References

American Association for the Advancement of Science. (1993). *Benchmarks for science literacy*. New York: Oxford University Press.

Anderson, R. C. (1977). "The notion of schemata and the educational enterprises: General discussion of the conference." *Schooling and the acquisiton of knowledge*. Hillsdale, NJ: Erlbaum.

Anderson, L. W., & Krathwohl, D. R. (Eds.). (2001). *A taxonomy for learning, teaching and assessing: A revision of Bloom's taxonomy of educational objectives*. New York: Longman.

Ausubel, D. P. (1975). *Educational psychology: A cognitive view*. New York: HoltRinehart & Winston.

Beyer, B. (1994). *Teaching for thinking*. New York: Allyn and Bacon.

Bloom, B. (Ed.). (1956). *Taxonomy of educational objectives.* New York: McKay.

Bruner, J. S. (1956). *A study of thinking.* New York: John Wiley.

Burke, K. (2006). *From standards to rubrics in six steps: Tools for assessing student learning, K-8.* Thousand Oaks, CA: Corwin Press.

Caine, R. N., & Caine, G. (1994). *Making connections: Teaching and the human brain.* New York: Addison Wesley.

Committee on the Foundations of Assessment. (2001). *Knowing what students know: The science and design of educational assessment.* Washington, DC: National Academy Press, pp. 13–14.

Drake, S. M., & Burns, R. C. (2004). *Meeting standards through integrated curriculum.* Alexandria, VA: Association for Supervision and Curriculum Development.

Fuchs, L. S., & Fuchs, D. (1986). Effects of systemic formative evaluation: A meta-analysis. *Exceptional Children, 53*(3), 199–208.

Gardner, H. (1993). *Frames of mind: The theory of multiple intelligences.* New York: Basic Books.

Hammerman, E., & Musial, D. (1995). *Classroom 2061: Activity-based assessments in science.* Arlington Heights, IL: IRI Skylight Training and Publishing.

Kluger, A. N., & DeNisi, A. (1996). The effects of feedback interventions on performance: A historical review, a meta-analysis, and a preliminary feedback intervention theory. *Psychological Bulletin, 119,* 254–284.

Marzano, R. J., Pickering, D., & McTigue, J. (1993). *Assessing student outcomes.* Alexandria, VA: Association for Supervision and Curriculum Development.

National Academy of Sciences (NAS), Committee on Science Education and Assessment. (1996). *National science education standards.* Washington, DC: National Academy Press.

National Association for Sport and Physical Education. (2004*). Moving into the future: National standards for physical education,* 2nd ed. Washington, DC: Author.

National Council for the Social Studies. (1994). *Curriculum standards: Expectations of excellence.* Silver Spring, MA: Author. www.socialstudies.org.

National Council of Teachers of Mathematics. (2001). *Principles and standards for school mathematics.* Reston, VA: National Council of Teachers of Mathematics.

National Education Commission on Time and Learning. (1994). *Prisoners of time.* Washington, DC: Government Printing Office.

National Research Council, Committee on the Foundations of Assessment. (2001). *Knowing what students know: The science and design of educational assessment.* M. Pelligrino, H. Chudowsky, & R. Glaser (Eds.). Board on Testing and Assessment, Center for Education, Division of Behavioral and Social Sciences and Education. Washington, DC: National Academy Press.

O'Keefe, J., & Nadel, L. (1978). *The hippocampus as a cognitive map.* Boston: Oxford University Press.

Pipho, C. (2000). The sting of high stakes testing and accountability. *Phi Delta Kappan, 31,* 645–646.

Vygotsky, L. S. (1962). *Thought and language.* Cambridge, MA: MIT Press.

Wiggins, G. (1989). A true test: Toward more authentic and equitable assessment. *Phi Delta Kappan, 20,* 703–713.

Wiggins, G. (1991). Standards not standardization: Evoking quality student work. *Educational Leadership, 48*(5), 18–25.

Wiggins, G. (1998). *Educative assessment.* San Francisco: Jossey Bass.

CHAPTER 5

Selected-Response Assessments

Chapter Objectives

After reading and thinking about this chapter, you will be able to:

- **Understand why reliability and validity are essential characteristics of an effective test.**
- **Describe the relationship between testing and assessment.**
- **Explain where selected-response tests fit into assessment.**

- **Describe the essential characteristics and assess varied examples of**
  - **Multiple-choice items**
  - **True-false or alternative response items**
  - **Matching items**
- **Construct items that assess student understanding at multiple levels, from factual recall to understanding of principles and concepts.**

Throughout this text, we have anchored our discussion of assessment with the image of a teacher sitting beside a learner, trying to understand what that learner knows or can do. The teacher may be asking the learner a set of questions on a specific topic or may be asking the learner to perform a task that will demonstrate mastery of a particular skill. This technique of using a set of focused questions or focused observations leads us to the concept of testing. Tests are part of the assessment process, and they can provide valuable information about the learner.

In this chapter we describe forms of tests and test items that require the learner to select an answer that has been predetermined by the teacher. We present procedures for developing, interpreting, and refining multiple-choice, matching, and true-false test items.

What are the foundational questions and issues underlying such forms of assessment? Think for a moment about the last test in which you invested quite a bit of study time. Now recall the test itself. How much of what you knew about the subject was actually covered on the test? When you create a test for your students, you have identified those ideas and skills that you deem most important, but can any test fully capture the breadth or uniqueness of your students' understanding?

Foundational Questions for Your Consideration

- Is an objective test (such as multiple choice, true-false, or matching) truly "objective"?
- Since many of our schools' standardized tests rely heavily on true-false and multiple-choice items, is it proper to develop such instruments for classroom use for the purpose of preparing and familiarizing students with the format?

Testing and Assessment

As discussed in Chapter 2, *testing* is the process of evaluating students' knowledge or skills by their performance on a particular instrument or task that is presented in a controlled manner. Tests may take a number of forms, but in general they are intended to serve as an objective measure of learning. The type of questions that are used can vary widely in their formats (for example, true-false, essay, multiple choice). The environment can also vary (paper and pencil, oral, computer; timed or untimed; open notes or no notes). In addition, the number of questions in a single test can range from a small number of items focused on a single concept to multiple groups of items with each group leading more deeply into a concept. The type, precision, and depth of information obtained through a test depend on the question format, the number of questions per concept or skill, and the type of environment in which the test takes place.

Test results may also be used in a variety of ways. For example, a student's score on a test could tell us how well that student understands the causes of the American Civil War. We could also use that same score to measure how much the student has learned since he or she took an earlier test on the same subject. Or we could compare a student's knowledge to that of the rest of the class. And, taken together, the scores of all the students in the class on that same test can tell us something about the class's standing in their knowledge of the Civil War when compared to students across the state or nation.

Teachers and students are probably most familiar with the classroom-based selected-response variety of test, but in any school setting, many different types of tests are used. Physical education classes, for example, may require that students demonstrate proficiency in particular skills, such as the time it takes them to run a mile. In a history class, students may be asked to recite the preamble to the Constitution.

Testing is one form of assessment, which we defined in Chapter 1 as the art of placing learners in a context that clarifies what it is a learner knows and can do, as well as what a learner may not know or be able to do. But assessment encompasses many more ways of evaluating students, both formally and informally, than testing alone. In addition to testing, assessment includes methods for evaluating student products, work habits, complex behavioral skills, abilities, dispositions, attitudes, and interests. Further, assessment focuses not only on student performance and potential but also on the factors that influence a student's learning—personality, motivation, home environment, and areas of exceptionality, for example. Assessment tells us what our students have learned and their capacity to learn. Assessment gives us evidence for reflection about our own learning and teaching. Assessment is the basis for all critical decisions about our students.

The purpose of this book, then, is to help you learn to create tests and other formal assessments that show how much students have learned and also to help you capture and communicate less formal indicators of student learning and development.

In summary, testing can be used to:

- Show the depth of understanding of an idea or mastery of a skill.
- Show a student's growth over time in a particular area of knowledge or skill.
- Compare one student's or one group's achievement to another's on the same task.
- Predict students' future performance.

Ask Yourself

Think about some of the tests you have taken in the past—math tests, driver's license tests, hearing and vision tests. Each of those tests measures or assesses a particular skill—your understanding of algebra, your ability to safely operate a car, the acuity of your eyesight. But in what ways might such tests be limited? Are they truly the most accurate means to assess such skills? Can you think of a more comprehensive way to assess those skills or characteristics?

Validity and Reliabity in Testing

Before considering how to construct sound test items, try to answer the following question: What is a good test? You might answer this in many different ways, but from teacher-made midterms to international tests of mathematics, we strive to develop tests that are both consistent in the way they measure learning and accurate in what they measure.

Good tests—tests that are *reliable* and *valid*—give us results that we can use to make decisions about students. Recall from Chapter 1 that validity is what we have in mind when we ask the question, "Am I testing what I think I'm testing?" And reliability refers to the stability or consistency of the test results. Let's consider reliability first.

Test Reliability

When you give a test to your students, you would like to think that their responses are stable. That is, you would hope that their scores would be basically the same if you had given the same test at another time or place (assuming the students had the same amount of instruction and practice). As a teacher, you want to avoid introducing error into the testing situation. You want the students' scores to reflect what they know—to be as close as possible to their true level of knowledge and skill, with as little error as possible.

At the same time, it is important to realize that there is always error in any kind of testing or measurement. In fact, it can be helpful to think of a student's test score as a combination of two factors: the true score and some error. Some of the error comes from the student. If the student is tired, ill, or bored, these factors can have the effect of lowering the true score. We say that the student "didn't do her best." Or if the student is guessing at the answers, his test score will also contain error that raises or lowers his score. On the other hand, some error is external to the student, and most of this is under the teacher's control. Factors such as poorly worded test items, confusing directions, and classroom interruptions during the test can also lower a student's true score. Of course, the true score is an abstraction, a hypothesis about what the student is truly capable of.

Reliability is important both to teacher-made classroom tests and to standardized, norm-referenced tests such as the SAT. We will discuss standardized tests in Chapter 12 and will describe how to statistically determine a test's reliability. In the classroom, however, you will most often be using your professional judgment rather than statistical calculations to determine if your students' scores are reliable.

Types of Reliability

There are several ways to determine a test's reliability, each of which has a different purpose and focus. **Test-retest reliability** is a means of determining reliability that is easy to understand and apply in a classroom setting. Test-retest determines a test's reliability by administering the same test to the same group of students at two different times and then comparing the scores on the first and second testing. Comparable scores between the two testings indicate stability or consistency over time.

There are several cautions with test-retest reliability, however. First, if the students have had the opportunity to learn some additional information that is relevant to the test contents, then you would not expect stability in the test scores. Second, the time between administrations can also influence the test's reliability. If the testings are too close together, then familiarity with specific items can influence the score on the second administration.

Another type of reliability is important when a tester uses two different forms of a test and wants to be certain that they are equivalent. **Equivalent forms reliability** determines if two forms or versions of the same test contain items that are comparable in form, length, and difficulty. Equivalent forms reliability is more common in standardized testing, where tests often have two or more forms. In the classroom, you might create a second test similar to one that you have already given in order to allow a group of students who missed the first test to make it up.

Internal consistency reliability is relevant when you are creating a test that is focused entirely on one concept or specific area. In this case, you are interested in making sure that all of your test items are aimed only at that concept or specific area and that there are no unrelated items within the test.

Finally, **inter-rater reliability** refers to the degree of consistency of scoring when student responses (usually an essay or constructed-response item) are assessed by more than one scorer. Tests that use selected-response items (multiple choice, true-false, for example) require little judgment in scoring—all you need is an accurate scoring key. But essay items may elicit opinions or guesses from the person doing the scoring. We will discuss how to minimize error due to lack of agreement between raters in Chapter 6.

Validity

As we suggested, reliability can be determined with reasonable confidence using various strategies and statistics. But is a test that is reliable also valid? Not necessarily. In fact, a test can be very reliable and not at all valid. What might happen if, in a psychology class, the teacher administered a 50-item, multiple-choice biology test? Some students would do quite well, others would do not as well, and some would do a lot of guessing. If the teacher administered the same test (test-retest reliability), individual students' scores probably would not differ by much. So this test is reliable, but it in no way measures what the teacher intended to measure.

This is an absurd example, but it points to ways to think about validity in classroom tests. **Content validity** refers to the degree to which your test aligns with what you intend to measure, which would usually be your teaching objectives. For example, if you administer a test intended to cover the first 8 weeks of mathematics instruction, but the items only address concepts covered in the first 4 weeks, it does not have strong content validity.

Criterion validity asks how a particular assessment aligns or correlates with another measure. Does your classroom-level third-grade reading test, for example, correlate with districtwide assessments of third-grade reading?

Validity should be considered as you construct or select your classroom assessments. Careful planning of the test, consideration of individual test items, and a determination of exactly what it will cover are essential to developing a valid test. The planning involves comparing the list of learning objectives you intend for students to master to the list of test items you have constructed.

Validity becomes especially important when considering state-level learning standards. And state standards should provide a meaningful framework in the construction of such items. Ask yourself, as you construct an item or test, "Does this item indicate understanding relative to the state standard in this content area?"

Validity is not a precise practice but consider the implications of administering and then interpreting an invalid test. In the previous example, we thought we created a test that covered 8 weeks of math concepts but somehow we only included items from the first 4 weeks. When we interpret the scores on this test, we are going to make serious mistakes about our understanding of students' progress. Figure 5.1 summarizes ways to increase a test's reliability and validity.

Figure 5.1 *How Can You Increase Reliability and Validity in Classroom Tests?*

- **Use longer tests,** within reason. The more items, the more chances the students have to show what they know.
- **Create good test items.** Make sure they match what you have taught, make them understandable and easy to read, and remove extraneous material.
- **Give good directions.** Make them short and clear.
- **Use objective scoring,** where appropriate.

?Ask Yourself

Recall a time when you took an unscheduled test and received a poor score. Did you feel that the score was a true measure of your knowledge? Why or why not? Did the test results help you study further so that you could do better the next time? What could have been done differently to make the experience more effective?

Where Do Selected-Response Tests Fit into Assessment?

A selected-response test is one tool that allows teachers to tap certain kinds of student achievement with accuracy and efficiency. Because of the level of detailed planning they require in order to be valid, selected-response tests also challenge teachers to clearly specify the important content and skills that they have been teaching and that they want to include in a test.

Selected-Response Tests

Chapters 5 and 6 each focus on one category of paper-and-pencil assessment. In this chapter, we will be presenting **selected-response items.** These are items in which students are not asked to produce an original answer because the answer to each question appears in some place on the test. In **multiple-choice, matching,** and **true-false** tests, the teacher has predetermined the correct answer; and, while students may need to perform a simple calculation for a math problem, for example, they are not expected to produce an answer that is not already shown on the test itself. In Chapter 6, we will present another type of paper-and-pencil assessment in which the responses are *student-produced*. These assessments include simple items like fill-ins and short answers as well as more complex essay items, all of which require students to generate an answer that is not supplied by the test.

One note: We use the term "paper-and-pencil test" in this text knowing that, in many academic settings, such assessments are often carried out using classroom computers. We use the term more generally, however, to describe an assessment that includes teacher-made items as described in this and the next chapter, regardless of how the test is administered.

Advantages of Selected-Response Tests

There are plenty of reasons that teachers would want to use selected-response tests. Good selected-response tests

- Provide formative feedback about particular strengths or areas needing improvement.

- Provide diagnostic information about student errors and misunderstandings.
- Yield scores that are easily summarized for parents or administrators.
- Allow for reasonable comparison among students and between classes.
- Are relatively easy to grade.
- Prepare students for some of the context and format of the standardized testing that they will encounter throughout their schooling.

Meaningful selected-response items can assess low-level knowledge through higher-order cognitive skills. Different item types offer different strengths in assessing learning. The construction of such items demands attention and deliberate thought.

Disadvantages of Selected-Response Tests

Selected-response items alone do not offer insight into students' reasoning. Good multiple-choice items have one right answer, and that is how the students' scores are determined by how many right answers they choose. But it may be just as revealing for you as a teacher to know why your students chose a particular answer as it is to know their test score. One way to achieve this is to allow students an opportunity to explain their incorrect answers to you after they have seen their scores.

The most frequent criticism of selected-response test items is the possibility of students guessing the correct answer. This is a valid criticism, although it only applies to lucky guesses. Students who correctly guess some answers will receive a test score that does not accurately reflect their level of understanding.

Ask Yourself

Recall an instance when you were proud of your performance on a test. What type of test was it? Objective? Constructed response/essay? Why were you particularly proud of your performance on that test?

True-False or Alternative-Response Items

For many students and teachers alike, true-false items (also called *alternative-response* or *binary-choice* items) seem not to be the most effective way to assess or demonstrate understanding—and certainly not the kind of deep understanding that we hope to develop in students. Further, isn't it true

Digging Deeper
What Did the First Standardized Test Items Look Like?

How far have we come in the development of ways of assessing student learning in an objective manner? Alfred Binet was commissioned by the French Ministry of Education to develop a test that would identify students who needed remedial attention in school. The result was one of the first tests of intelligence, and Binet's influence is still recognized in the form of a widely used intelligence test that bears his name: the Stanford-Binet.

The following task is taken from Binet's "New Methods for the Diagnosis of the Intellectual Level of Subnormals" (1905), which was intended to identify degrees of impairment and levels of ability. As you read through this task, ask yourself these questions: How objective were these original tests? Do the instructions to the test administrator allow for too much interpretation of the child's answer? What might be the consequence of such testing practices? Do you think a more objective test item type could give us a more realistic picture of a student's true ability?

Comparison of Known Objects from Memory
This is an exercise in ideation, in the notion of differences, and somewhat in powers of observation. *Procedure.* One asks what difference there is between paper and cardboard, between a fly and a butterfly, between a piece of wood and a piece of glass. First be sure that the subject knows these objects. Ask him, "Have you seen paper?" "Do you know what cardboard is?" Thus ask him about all the objects before drawing his attention to the difference between them. It may happen that little Parisians, even though normal, and eight or nine years old, have never seen a butterfly. These are examples of astounding ignorance, but we have found, what is still more extraordinary, Parisians of ten years who have never seen the Seine.

After being assured that the two objects to be compared are known, demand their difference. If the word is not understood, take notice and afterward choose more familiar language. "In what are they not alike? How are they not alike?" Three classes of replies may be expected. First, that of the children who have no comprehension of what is desired of them. When asked the difference between cardboard and paper, they reply, "The cardboard." When one has provoked replies of this kind, the explanation must be renewed with patience to see if there is not some means of making oneself understood. Second, the absurd replies, such as, "The fly is larger than the butterfly," "The wood is thicker than the glass," or "The butterfly flies and so does the fly." Third, the correct reply.

Sources: Binet, 1905; Plucker, 2007.

that students can simply guess on true-false items? Both of these criticisms may be valid, but as you will see, true-false items can, in fact, assess learning in a meaningful way.

Compared to other types of selected-response items, true-false items are fairly easy to write and are also easy for teachers to score—the answer can be only correct or incorrect. It is this apparent simplicity of construction and scoring that has probably led us to believe that true-false items cannot be powerful, discriminating questions. But they can be if they are properly written. Figure 5.2 presents some of the advantages of true-false tests.

Figure 5.2 *What Are the Advantages of True-False Items?*

- True-false items are relatively easy for teachers to write and to score.
- Compared to multiple-choice and short-answer items, true-false items can be answered quickly, so teachers can present approximately one-third more questions on a timed test than when using multiple-choice items.
- True-false items are presented in a format that is similar to typical classroom dialogue.

What Does a Good True-False Item Look Like?

A true-false item begins with a *proposition*—a statement that asserts a particular truth about an idea, relationship, or concept. Think about the following:

1. The earth experiences four different seasons. (T)
2. The earth travels in a highly elliptical orbit around the sun. (F)
3. The earth's seasons are caused by changes in the distance of the earth from the sun. (F)
4. The earth's seasons are caused by changes in the earth's tilt, which changes the directness of the sun's rays. (T)

The items are stated as propositions—statements of fact that require recall of a fact ("The earth has four seasons") or a relationship (such as between the changing distance from the earth to the sun and its effect on the seasons).

These examples demonstrate several important principles about true-false items:

- First, they can test student learning from simple recall to higher-order understanding of principles.

- Second, these items are short statements from which a variety of items can be developed from a single idea or concept.

- Third, statements two and three are presented as false statements that are actually typical of misconceptions often held by students (and teachers, too), another way in which true-false items can assess meaningful learning and lead to better teaching.

These items respond to a common criticism of true-false items: that they typically only assess students' recall of facts and encourage rote memorization as a learning strategy. As a teacher, there will be times that you will want to assess simple recall, such as on a quiz that is intended to determine whether students have completed their assigned reading. But if you have identified clear objectives and learning targets for your students, true-false items can also be an effective way for you to assess understanding of important propositions.

Guidelines for Effective True-False Items

What makes an effective true-false item? As you develop your true-false items, keep the following guidelines in mind.

1. *True-false items should focus on an important idea rather than a trivial fact.*

Look at the following two items and ask yourself which contains the more important idea:

- Jean Piaget's theory of development has four stages. (T)
- A child in Piaget's concrete operational stage is able to think inductively. (F)

The first of these two questions is really only important in that students should probably be expected to be able to name and describe the stages, and recalling that there are four may help in remembering the stages themselves. But the second question gets at several important ideas that are essential to understanding Piaget's developmental theory. Whether a student can simply recall that Piaget's theory has four stages is less likely to be worth a test item than whether the student has an understanding of the cognitive characteristics of each stage.

Students can also, through their answers to well-written true-false items, demonstrate understanding of important ideas through application of that idea. Consider the next two true-false questions.

- Vygotsky believes that cognitive development occurs in age-related stages. (F)
- A biology teacher who administers a pretest on the first day of class to determine students' knowledge of biology is assessing his students' zone of proximal development. (F)

The first question may be somewhat important in that it makes a critical distinction between Vygotsky and other theorists, but the second question is more meaningful for two reasons. First, it assesses students' understanding of a central concept in development, and, second, it expects students to apply their understanding to a real-world context, in this case, a classroom.

2. *Answers to true-false items must be either true or false.*

This seems self-evident, but think back on tests you have taken. How often have you or a classmate argued with a teacher about a true-false item that might have been correctly answered as either true or false? Another charge against true-false items is that they are inherently ambiguous, when, in fact, the right answer should always be defensible. Read the following items:

- Students' self-efficacy in mathematics is positively correlated with persistence in mathematical problem solving. (T)
- Self-esteem is related to higher academic achievement. (F)

The first of these questions points to a clear relationship between two different variables—self-efficacy and problem solving. It is clearly worded, and, although it is not stated in absolute terms, the question is much more true than false. The second question could be argued either way. On the one hand, higher self-esteem may be slightly positively correlated with achievement, suggesting that the item should be marked true. At the same time, there are many factors that are more strongly related to achievement, suggesting that the item should be marked false. An item like this opens the door to arguments between students and the teacher.

3. *A good true-false item avoids the quotation of phrases from the textbook.*

It is sometimes tempting for teachers to create test items by repeating statements from the textbook after changing a word or two. This practice has perhaps led to some of the criticism about true-false items. For example, compare these two items:

- A person's score on an intelligence test was originally calculated as a ratio of mental age to chronological age and termed the Intelligence Quotient. (T)
- Children with a high IQ typically perform better on standardized tests than children with a lower IQ. (T)

The first question may initially seem useful in assessing students' understanding of intelligence, but it has several problems. The question is written using language that sounds very much like textbook phrasing. In other words, students may recognize that the question is not asking for understanding but rather recall from their reading. The second question, however, expects students to understand the relationship between IQ and other important skills.

4. *A good true-false item does not contain inadvertent clues.*

Teachers sometimes will insert a word or two into a true-false item in order to throw off the test taker. Very often, this is done by making a positive statement into a negative statement as in these two items:

- B. F. Skinner argued that learning is characterized by a response followed by a reinforcing stimulus. (T)
- B. F. Skinner argued that learning is *not* characterized by a response followed by a reinforcing stimulus. (F)

The false statement is not only false, but it will immediately appear to students as false because of the unnatural placement of the word *not* in the middle of the statement. Such a practice is a form of laziness or lack of attention to creating a good test item. It is quickly recognized by students, who are then given the opportunity to be lazy themselves and use otherwise irrelevant cues in the item rather than depending on their understanding to figure out the correct answer.

?Ask Yourself

Get a copy of a test that has a number of true-false items. Examine the characteristics of a good true-false question and determine which of the items has all of these characteristics. What do you conclude about the relative merit of these true-false items in assessing your understanding about the topic?

Multiple-Choice Items

Multiple-choice items are perhaps the most widely used type of test item in schools, for several reasons. Although they are not as easily constructed as true-false items, they are easy to score, and they can be written to assess various levels of understanding. Also, multiple-choice tests are less susceptible than true-false tests to the effects of guessing. Multiple-choice items are the type students are most likely to encounter on standardized tests, so they have come to expect the familiar multiple-choice format. Figure 5.3 summarizes the advantages of multiple-choice items.

The construction of an effective multiple-choice item appears simple but requires care and precision on the part of the teacher who uses it. A multiple-choice item has three components:

Figure 5.3 *What Are the Advantages of Multiple-Choice Items?*

- They are easy to score.
- They can be written to assess various levels of understanding.
- They are less susceptible than true-false tests to the effects of guessing.
- They are the type of item that students are most likely to encounter on standardized tests.

- The stem, which presents a question or an incomplete statement to the student
- A single correct or best answer
- **Distracters**, usually three or four per question, which present plausible, alternative answers to the correct answer

You will find as you begin writing multiple-choice items that it is relatively easy to develop a meaningful question, a right answer, and one or two plausible distracters. The difficulty often comes in trying to develop enough meaningful distracters to assure that the item truly tests what you intend.

The Stem

Let's begin with the stem. The two most common ways to present a multiple-choice question to a student are a direct question that the student must answer or an incomplete sentence, as illustrated in these two examples:

- What is the capital of Alaska?
- Alaska's capital is named _____.

Either of these common stem formats is acceptable, although some texts recommend that you write the stem in the form of a direct question because it can present the student with a clearer task. Regardless of the form of stem, it is important to keep the wording as succinct and clear as possible. *All of the words in the stem should be relevant to the task.*

At the same time that you are writing a stem that is short and to the point, you also must *be sure that your stem presents the question fully and completely.* One useful way to think about your stem construction is to ask yourself if you could answer the question even without looking at the answer and distracters. Consider this stem:

- Chicago is _____.

Without an answer or distracters, there are quite a few ways you could answer it: Chicago is a city, it is the largest city in Illinois, it was the site of a great fire in 1871, it was the subject of a Carl Sandburg poem, and there are many other possible answers. Each of these answers is correct, but the test writer probably had only one of these answers in mind when writing the test. A better way to pose the stem would be:

- Which Illinois city has the largest population?
  or
- The Illinois city destroyed by a great fire in 1871 was named _____.

As you construct your multiple-choice items, consider carefully *the relationship between the stem and the answers.* Grammar and punctuation are important in creating a good test item, one that is understandable and at the same time gives no accidental hints to the student. Take a look at the following items.

- Which of the following is a mammal?
    a. cat
    b. fish
    c. turtle
    d. bird

Notice that in this example, the item is expressed as a *direct question*. The stem begins with a capital letter and ends in a question mark. The answers do not need to complete a sentence and are not proper nouns. Therefore, the correct answer and the distracters begin with lowercase letters and have no punctuation following.

Now consider another type of item.

- A portion of land nearly surrounded by water and connected with a larger body is called
    a. an island.
    b. a peninsula.
    c. an isthmus.
    d. a land bridge.

This item is stated as an *incomplete sentence*, so in this instance the stem ends without punctuation. (You may also complete the stem with a colon.) Notice, though, that the answer and distracters, which serve to complete the sentence, begin with lowercase letters and have terminal punctuation (a period).

The stem should also *ask a question for which there is either one correct or best answer*. What is the difference in the following two items?

- Which U.S. city has the highest literacy rate?
    a. New York
    b. Seattle
    c. Los Angeles
    d. Baton Rouge

- Which of the following U.S. cities is most important to international trade?
    a. New York
    b. Seattle
    c. Los Angeles
    d. Baton Rouge

The first question can have only one correct answer. Even if the student does not know whether the answer is New York, Seattle, Los Angeles, or

Baton Rouge, there is only one, single best answer. The second question, however, does not have an obvious best answer. You would probably find that experts on the topic would differ in their answers to the second question. This kind of item is asking the student to respond with an opinion. While interesting, such questions are not suited to a multiple-choice format. They are better suited to a constructed-response or essay test. Here is another example:

- The most significant maritime event of the twentieth century was
  a. the sinking of the *Titanic*.
  b. the sinking of the *Eastland*.
  c. the grounding and oil spill of the *Exxon Valdez*.
  d. the attack on Pearl Harbor.

Again, this question is more appropriate to a discussion or an essay question.

Presenting a direct or indirect question is not the only way to create the stem for a multiple-choice test item. *An effective way to vary the complexity of the task represented by the multiple-choice item is to vary the format of the stem.* For example, for younger students, the teacher may read the stem aloud, while the students look at the answers and mark one of them. Or a series of questions could be focused on a passage, read by the student, that states a problem. Or the stem could include graphics that require the student to interpret them in order to answer the question. You will find it helpful to consider the possible array of stems when you begin to design a multiple-choice test.

Distracters

Distracters are the feature of multiple-choice items that allow teachers to make generalizations about student learning. Therefore, the distracters must be constructed so that they require understanding and careful thought but are sufficiently wrong that students who are prepared for the test can identify which is the correct answer. On the other hand, well-written distracters should all appear plausible to students who are not prepared. As you write your multiple-choice test, there are a few important considerations in developing your distracters.

Plausibility First, distracters should be plausible but incorrect. Consider the following:

- Which of the following is the best predictor of college grade point average?
  a. a student's performance on the SAT
  b. a student's performance on the Presidential Physical Fitness Test
  c. a student's height
  d. a student's weight

Resource for Your Assessment Toolkit
Formatting Options for Multiple-Choice Items

Multiple-choice items have a variety of formats. The stem, the distractors, and the correct answer can have different forms, and these differences can enhance the effectiveness of an item to assess student learning. It is important to examine the structure of your items in light of the type of instruction you have given your students. For example, it would be inappropriate to test students using a multiple-choice stem that contained a long example of a concept when all you have taught students is the definition of the concept.

This list provides specific names for the different formats of multiple-choice items. You may find it useful to review these examples when you are developing a multiple-choice assessment for your students. (The correct answer is starred.)

Stem Variations for Multiple-Choice Items

Oral Stimulus   Teacher says, "Which is the number four hundred and three?" The student sees only choices, not stems.

a. 34
b. 43
c. 304
***d.** 403

Passage Related   Kim has a 5-dollar bill and wants to buy as many 41-cent stamps as she can. How many will that be and what change will she get?

1. To solve this problem, what would be the best operation to use?

a. addition
b. subtraction
c. multiplication
***d.** division

2. How can you find out how much change Kim will get?

a. Subtract the number of stamps from $5.00.
b. Add the cost of the stamps to $5.00.
***c.** Find the remainder after dividing $5.00 by 41 cents.
d. Multiply the number of stamps by 41 and add that to $5.00.

Graphic Related

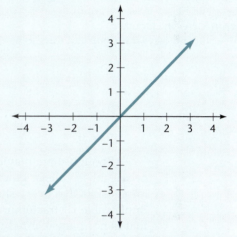

The above is a graph of the solution set of

a. $y = x + 2$
b. $y = x - 1$
***c.** $y = x$
d. $y = 2x$

Answer Variations for Multiple-Choice Items

Five students have the following scores:

Kelsey   15
Jason   10
Jennifer 18
Greg   13
Yasmin   14

(continued)

Resource for Your Assessment Toolkit
Formatting Options for Multiple-Choice Items (continued)

For each of the situations below, tell whether the change would cause the mean to . . .

List Reference
    a. increase
    b. decrease
    c. stay the same
    d. can't tell

1. A new student, Tammie, with a score of 16, joins the group.
2. Two new students, Chris and Cary, with scores of 14 and 15, join the group.
3. Greg and Kelsey leave the group.
4. Jason leaves the group.
5. Two students leave the group and three join.

Answers That Are Not Words or Numbers

Which number line shows the right way to solve $2 + (-2) = ?$

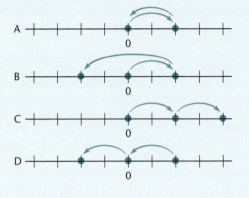

Although there may be research out there that somehow relates height or weight to college grade point average, answers b, c, and d are really so implausible that every student should answer this question correctly. Three implausible distracters make for a poor test item, but even one distracter that is not plausible reduces an item's ability to discriminate between students who know the material and those who do not.

All of the Above, None of the Above It is also tempting to include one or two distracters that imply that none, two, or more answers are possible. Items that offer "all of the above," "none of the above," or other similar choices as answers have several potential drawbacks. First, some students will recognize the first answer as correct and fail to read the other possible answers, never getting to the "all of the above" choice. Second, some teachers will only use "all of the above" or "none of the above" when they are unable to come up with a reasonable third or fourth distracter, and students will come to recognize this pattern and discount those choices as possible correct answers. Or, conversely, students might recognize that teachers only use such distracters when they are in fact the right answer. If you decide to use these, do so both as correct and as incorrect answers. Further, when using "all of the above" as an answer, it is important to ensure that all answers are entirely correct.

Indirect Clues Another common error in writing multiple-choice items is that teachers sometimes provide indirect clues to an answer in either the stem or among the answers. What clues does the stem give you about the answer to this multiple-choice question?

- Sternberg's three-part model of intelligence is known as the
    a. triarchic model.
    b. multiple intelligence theory.
    c. information processing model.
    d. IQ.

Even students not familiar with Sternberg or his theory of intelligence could guess that "a" is the correct answer to the question, due to a linguistic clue. Since his theory has three parts and answer "a" has the prefix *tri* in the first word, students might reasonably guess the answer to this question.

Students are also aware that answers that are longer or constructed differently from the other answers often represent the correct response. As you write your test, it is important to ensure that the correct answer does not appear to be written with greater precision or clarity than the distracters. Often such attention to detail results in the correct answer being much longer than the distracters. Here is an example:

- What is the most widely accepted definition of intelligence?
    a. IQ
    b. a source of human difference
    c. the level of mental development
    d. the combination of verbal ability, problem-solving skills, and the ability to adapt to and learn from life's everyday experiences

To write good multiple-choice items, you will need practice. You will also need to review your items for possible faults that might give away the answer or make the item impossible for students to answer correctly.

The Correct Answer

It probably seems obvious that a right answer is a correct answer. However, it is useful to reflect on the precise characteristics of a correct answer. One characteristic of the correct answer relates to the concept of "best." *An answer is correct when it is the best choice from a list.* "Best" implies that there are other choices that have a reasonable connection to the question, but one

Resource for Your Assessment Toolkit
Common Errors in Constructing Multiple-Choice Items

Here are some examples of multiple-choice question errors that are often made by practicing teachers. Each error has a specific phrase that will help you remember to avoid the error when you're developing multiple-choice questions. Review this list when you write a multiple-choice item and check your item against these common errors. (The correct answer is starred.)

Item with Vague Stem

- George Washington
*a. was a great general.
b. was born in 1776.
c. wrote the Declaration of Independence.
d. abolished slavery.

Double-Barreled Item

- In the past, whaling and cotton growing were important industries in

a. the Northeast and the West.
b. the Middle West and the Southeast.
*c. the Northeast and the Southeast.
d. the West and the Middle West.

Item with Multiple Correct Answers

- Two of the most important characteristics of a good test are validity and

*a. reliability.
b. accuracy.
*c. consistency.
d. logic.

Grammatically Non-Parallel Item

- The correct way to find the area of a triangle is to
*a. multiply the length of the base by the height and take half.
b. add the lengths of the sides.
c. area = base × height.
d. 1/2 (side 1 + side 2 + side 3).

Inconsistent Alternatives

- The difference between an achievement test and an aptitude test is

a. the test is objectively scored.
*b. that one measures what a person has already learned and one measures the person's ability to learn new material or skills.
c. between power and speed.
d. between personality and cognition.

Implausible Distracters

- What is a denominator?

a. the top number of a fraction
*b. the bottom number of a fraction
c. a kind of church
d. all of the above

Trick Alternatives

- What is 3/4 + 3/8?

*a. 9/8
b. 6/12
c. 6/8
*d. 1 1/8

choice has the most important or appropriate connection. For example, you may wish to assess if a student understands the concept of a conflict. The question might be worded as follows:

- Which of the following characteristics *best* defines the concept of conflict?
  - a. a disagreement between two people
  - *b. a struggle between opposing interests
  - c. competitive sports like football
  - d. mediation between parties

In this example all of the answers relate in some way to the concept of conflict, but "b" is the best answer. Choice "b" states the underlying characteristics that could relate to many types of conflict, while "a" and "c" illustrate the concept rather than defining it. Choice "d" is only slightly related.

Another way to think of the correct answer is that it is the choice from among other choices that most closely *matches the objectives and content* of the instructional unit. If you, as teacher, choose to emphasize a specific aspect of some content, then the correct answer will include that emphasis. For example, if you developed an instructional unit that emphasizes that all life cycles have distinct, developmental phases in the life span of an organism, then the correct answer for a question about the key characteristic of a life cycle would be the response that includes distinct developmental phases.

Finally, when considering the characteristics of the correct answer, caution is in order. It is important to examine the distracters for a test item and *eliminate possible overlap* with the correct answer. A distracter should relate to the question in some way to truly test the student's knowledge. But you must make sure that the distracter's relationship to the question is distinct from the correct answer's relationship to the question. Again, be aware that the wording, the emphasis, and the relationship between the correct answer and the distracters is a complex task that requires a good deal of reflection.

The Added Value of Multiple-Choice Items

As we have suggested, multiple-choice items are of practical value to teachers and students for several reasons. First, they are relatively easy to construct and very easy to score. They also represent the most common item type on standardized tests such as the ACT and SAT. Now let's look at a third advantage: their ability to assess a variety of learning outcomes and levels of understanding.

For example, you may want to assess students' recognition of characters in a novel, ability to define vocabulary terms, or recall of state capitals. Or you may want to dig deeper and assess whether students understand the effects of the jet stream on weather patterns. Multiple-choice items can be constructed to assess a range of learning, from recall to understanding of processes and principles. The following sections provide some examples of such purposes for multiple-choice items.

Recognition of Terms and Vocabulary One of the simplest learning outcomes is the recognition of specific terms and vocabulary that provide the basis for further understanding. For example, your sixth-grade class is studying a new science unit, and, to ensure that they are able to recognize and define key terms, you develop the following items.

- The study of the interrelationships of living organisms and their environment is

  a. ecology.

  b. astronomy.

  c. physiology.

  d. biology.

- An organism living in or on another organism is

  a. a predator.

  b. prey.

  c. a parasite.

  d. a host.

Factual Knowledge Factual knowledge is essential to the development of deeper conceptual understanding. People who are experts in their fields demonstrate an ability to look at a problem from many perspectives, but their understanding is based on extensive factual knowledge. Multiple-choice items can be written to assess students' grasp of discipline-based factual knowledge, such as the following geography questions.

- Which of the following states does *not* border Oklahoma?

  a. Colorado

  b. Missouri

  c. Nebraska

  d. New Mexico

- Which is the smallest of the Great Lakes?

  a. Lake Erie

  b. Lake Huron

  c. Lake Michigan

  d. Lake Ontario

  e. Lake Superior

Procedural Knowledge Factual knowledge provides evidence that students know *who, what, where,* and *when.* Procedural knowledge, however, provides evidence that students know *how*—how something works or how one should approach a problem or situation. Before we allow students to use an expensive or potentially dangerous piece of laboratory equipment, for example, we might develop multiple-choice items that assess procedural knowledge.

- The correct procedure for combining acid and water is to
  a. add acid to large amounts of water.
  b. add water to large amounts of acid.
  c. add acid to water, cool, and swirl.
  d. add water to acid, cool, and swirl.

- If you are the first person on the scene at a car accident, what should you do first?
  a. Call 911.
  b. Assess the scene to see if it is safe.
  c. Check victims for signs of pulse and breathing.
  d. Move the victims away from the site of the accident.

Higher-Order Thinking When presented with propositions, conditional information, or hypothetical situations, students can be assessed on the degree to which they can apply their learning or transfer understanding to new situations. Multiple-choice items dealing with cause-and-effect relationships, for example, can assess students' understanding of the relationship between facts.

Consider how the following examples move students beyond simple recall.

- Your students take a quiz every Monday over an assigned reading. The results of your students' first several quizzes were very low, so you begin praising students who scored well on the quizzes, and over time your class's quiz performance began to improve. This is an example of
  a. operant conditioning.
  b. observational learning.
  c. information processing.
  d. social constructivism.

- Which of the following is the best example of the principle of surface tension?
  a. a windshield wiper wiping away rainwater
  b. a baseball leaving the barrel of a bat

 c. an insect walking on water

 d. a braking car's tires leaving tread marks

- You fire a gun straight ahead of you and drop a ball at the same time and from the same height as the barrel of the gun. Which object will hit the ground first?

 a. the bullet from the gun

 b. the ball

 c. neither—they will land at the same time

Multiple-choice tests are versatile and valuable indicators of student learning, but effective multiple-choice items require planning and thought in their construction. As with any skill, you will refine your ability to write effective items over time. Just as important, you will begin to recognize characteristics of effective items on multiple-choice items constructed by others.

Ask Yourself

When you are a teacher, your students will probably ask you what kinds of items they can expect to see on an upcoming test. Now that you have had a chance to explore common item types in some depth, how would you answer your students? Do you think it is useful to let them know the purpose of the assessment (for example, will they be expected to remember names and dates rather than understand principles)? Do you think that knowing what types of items will be on a test leads students to study differently?

Matching

Matching items ask students to identify an item in one column with a closely associated item in a second column. In other words, in matching items students are not expected to create new information in order to answer correctly but rather to be able to identify common characteristics between two sets of items similar in nature.

Advantages and Disadvantages of Matching Items

Like multiple-choice and true-false items, matching items are relatively easy to construct and to score. One limitation of matching items is that they cannot reasonably assess learning beyond factual recall. Although they are not as discriminating as true-false or multiple-choice tests, they can assess a broad array of factual learning relatively quickly.

Creating Good Matching Items

There are steps you can take to ensure that the matching items you develop are meaningful for the kinds of factual recall you intend to assess.

Consider this question. If you have a list of four facts about U.S. presidents in one column, do you have four names of presidents in the second column? Not necessarily.

Which president was associated with each event?	*Presidents*
1. inaugurated as president in New York City	**a.** John Adams
2. established the U.S. Forest Service	**b.** Thomas Jefferson
3. president during the ratification of the Fourteenth Amendment	**c.** Abraham Lincoln
	d. Franklin D. Roosevelt
4. elected to four terms as U.S. president	**e.** Theodore Roosevelt
	f. George Washington

Offering an unequal number of items in your two columns is an effective way to reduce the possibility of answering correctly through the process of elimination. For this reason, it can be useful to qualify your instructions with the statement that items may be used more than once or not at all. In the example above, if only four presidents had been listed for four events, students who could make three correct matches would know the fourth match was the only combination left.

Another important consideration in the development of matching items is that the items in your columns be grouped homogeneously. For example, think about the homogeneity of the following matching exercise regarding famous artists.

Artist	*Work of Art*
1. Leonardo DaVinci	**a.** *American Gothic*
2. Edward Hopper	**b.** *The Thinker*
3. Michelangelo	**c.** *Mona Lisa*
4. Auguste Rodin	**d.** *The Last Supper*
5. Grant Wood	

The column at left seems rather diverse with artists from very different times and places. Perhaps the teacher's purpose is to assess general knowledge of art as a pretest. Or she may be working with younger students who may only have familiarity with a limited number of major works of art covered in a textbook. But, for older students or students with a deeper understanding and familiarity with art history, the above matching exercise would not be appropriate. For these students, it may be more appropriate, for example, to match a particular artist or work of art with a period in art history, such as impressionism or the Renaissance.

You might also incorporate images or pictures into a matching exercise, for example, by having students match the outline of a U.S. state with the state's name. Also, since we read in English from left to right, matching items should be written with the longer phrases in the left-hand column and the shorter responses (names, dates) in the right-hand column.

Finally, for ease of administering the test as well as scoring, you can make the task of matching much less cumbersome by keeping all of your pairs of items on one page and by keeping your pairs of items in a logical order. For example, if one of your columns includes a list of important dates in U.S. history, the dates should be arranged chronologically. If the column is a list of names, you may want to put them in alphabetical order.

?Ask Yourself

Now that you have had a chance to think about the potential value of selected-response items, do you believe that the tests you have taken as a student used such items to assess deeper levels of learning? Do you believe that students and teachers recognize that true-false items are effective in assessing higher-order thinking? Next time you take a test or see sample items in a textbook, try to evaluate the items using the criteria presented in this chapter.

Recommendations for Developing Selected-Response Items

The development of good selected-response assessments is a skill that requires careful attention to item construction. Improvement in item construction comes with experience, practice, and reflection. Over time, you will become more adept at writing items and aligning items with student ability and learning targets, and you will also become more critical readers and consumers of items developed by others, such as those found in test banks and teachers' manuals. With that in mind, we conclude this chapter with two additional strategies that will aid you in the development of selected-response assessments, regardless of item type.

- *Share your tests with colleagues.* Regardless of your skill in constructing selected-response assessments, the eyes of a colleague can give you an indispensable perspective. Have you taken tests during which several students raise their hands to ask the teacher to clarify a question? Keep in mind that you want all of the students to read each question the same way, and the best way to make sure of this is to ask a colleague—preferably one teaching the same subject—to read the test items carefully for clarity.

- *Watch spelling and punctuation.* Tests can engender anxiety among some students. For some, the appearance of a misspelled word may trigger thoughts that the teacher is intentionally misleading students. Also, students should expect to encounter items without distraction, and spelling and punctuation can sidetrack students' focus. Proofread your items carefully.

?Ask Yourself

Sharing your work with others is a powerful way to self-assess. It can be difficult to receive constructive criticism from colleagues or classmates and to critically appraise a friend's work. But, as we suggest above, sharing test items with colleagues for review can enhance your assessments. As a pre-service teacher, how might you begin to incorporate such a practice into your coursework? Could you begin writing sample test items for content in your classes and share them with your colleagues?

Summary

Selected-response assessments are useful classroom assessments for a number of reasons.

- They provide quick feedback about strengths or areas of improvement in student understanding.
- Compared to constructed-response items, they are relatively easy to grade.
- They allow for reasonable comparisons among students or classes.
- They result in scores that can be easily summarized and presented to parents or administrators.
- They prepare students for the context and format of the types of standardized testing that they will encounter throughout their academic careers.

Well-constructed test items have characteristics specific to the type of item.

- True-false items should examine an important idea rather than a trivial fact.
- Answers to true-false items *must* be either true or false.
- Multiple-choice items can be used to assess thinking at various levels, such as factual knowledge, procedural knowledge, and cause and effect.
- Matching items are used to assess students' understanding of the relationship between ideas.
- Matching items should include short, homogeneous lists.
- Matching items should avoid having the same number of items in each column.

Key Terms

content validity (112)

criterion validity (112)

distracter (120)

equivalent forms reliability (111)

internal consistency reliability (111)

inter-rater reliability (111)

matching test (113)

multiple-choice test (113)

selected-response items (113)

test-retest reliability (110)

true-false test (113)

For Further Discussion

1. How would you respond to a teacher who states that she only uses essay tests because selected-response tests only assess surface knowledge or recall?

2. Student guessing on true-false and multiple-choice items is a persistent criticism of such item types. Number a piece of paper from 1 to 25. Now, next to each number, write down either a, b, c, or d. This represents an answer key to a 25-item quiz. Now turn to a partner and ask him to try to guess the letter you wrote next to each number. How many did your partner answer correctly?

3. Think about your experiences as a student. Do you prefer selected-response items on assessments that you have taken, or do you prefer constructed responses, such as in-class essays? Why do you prefer this type?

Comprehension Quiz

Below are examples of selected-response items designed for an undergraduate psychology course. Your task is to critique the questions with respect to the criteria presented in this chapter. Read each item and rewrite it so that it conforms to all criteria of a well-written selected-response item. There may be more than one error in each item.

1. There are two major viewpoints about children's cognitive development embraced by educators today, who are the psychologists?

   a. Vygotsky and Piaget
   b. Piaget and Freud
   c. Vygotsky and Freud
   d. Freud and Erickson

2. What is temperament?

   a. Is a person behavioral style and characteristics ways of responding.
   b. Is distinctive thoughts.
   c. Is how individuals adapt to the world.
   d. Is problem solving and decision makeing.

3. Which of the following is not something that early maturing girls are more likely to do than late maturing girls?

   a. Have an eating disorder.
   b. Go through depression.
   c. Hold back in the classroom.
   d. Date

4. True or False:

B. F. Skinner is the Russian psychologist who is famous for classical conditioning.

5. True or False:

Everything we know is learned.

References

Binet, A. (1905). New methods for the diagnosis of the intellectual level of subnormals. *L'Année Psychologique, 12,* 191–244.

Marsh, H. W., Ellis, L. A., & Craven, R. G. (2002). How do preschool children feel about themselves? Unraveling measurement and multidimensional self-concept structure. *Developmental Psychology, 38*(3), 376–393.

Plucker, J. "Human Intelligence. Alfred Binet." From http://www.indiana.edu/~intell/binet/shtml.

Relevant Website Resources

University of Minnesota—Office of Measurement Services

http://oms.umn.edu/oms/index.php

This website provides a broad array of measurement and assessment resources. Under the "Classroom Resources" link on the main page, you will find useful reminders and pointers on the development of multiple-choice and true-false items. Bookmark this page for its user-friendly recommendations for assessment in multiple educational contexts.

University of Oregon—Teaching Effectiveness Program

http://tep.uoregon.edu

Under the "Resources" tab, this useful teachers' website presents sound recommendations for the development of multiple-choice items that assess higher-order critical thinking skills. Specifically, this website succinctly summarizes Bloom's taxonomy of cognitive development and then provides sample items and design considerations. Techniques, such as case study items and incomplete scenario items, are provided as examples of items that assess critical thinking.

CHAPTER 6

Constructed-Response Assessments

Chapter Objectives

After reading and thinking about this chapter, you will be able to:

- **Articulate the advantages and disadvantages of constructed-response items.**
- **Describe the essential characteristics and evaluate varied examples of short-answer items and essay questions.**
- **Construct items that assess students' ability to articulate their unique understanding of concepts and relationships.**
- **State the considerations teachers must make to ensure that students' constructed responses are assessed fairly and reliably.**

In 2005, the College Board, an organization that publishes and scores many widely used educational assessments, added a third component to the familiar SAT. The new SAT writing test provides students with a topic, and students' responses are scored by experienced teachers. They assign scores between 1 and 6, with 6 being the highest score. The criteria for grading students' writing include development of a point of view and evidence of critical thinking, use of appropriate examples and evidence, coherence and progression of ideas, skillful use of language and vocabulary, and proper use of grammar.

Not long after the College Board announced its writing test, some people began asking critical questions: How important is writing style? Does the assessment of this writing task demonstrate reliability? Does a timed test of writing authentically measure the skills that go into effective writing? One of the more humorous responses to the SAT writing addition was an article entitled "Would Shakespeare Get into Swarthmore?" (Katzman, Lutz, & Olson, 2004). This clearly rhetorical question about assessing student writing can lead to deeper questions about how and why we should use constructed-response/essay items as a means of assessing learning.

In Chapter 5, we identified the relative strengths and advantages of multiple-choice, true-false, and matching items, which provide a means of assessing student learning at a variety of levels. This chapter describes forms of assessment that require students to construct a response in order to demonstrate meaningful understanding. In other words, students use their own words to express their understanding at different levels of complexity. Both short-answer items and essay questions require a constructed response.

Foundational Questions for Your Consideration

- In what ways might essay questions provide authentic evidence that students have learned?
- A number of standardized tests (the SAT, for example) now include a writing component. Can such administration and scoring of writing samples adequately capture students' writing ability?

Constructing Responses to Test Items

In this chapter, we look at **constructed-response assessments,** items that teachers might present to see whether learners are able to construct a proper response. We first examine short-answer items, and we conclude with essay or extended-response items.

It may seem unorthodox to study short-answer and essay items in the same chapter, but they are similar in several important ways. First, as we have mentioned, although these items can be written to test recall, they do not rely on a student's recognition of a term or word. Second, both short-answer and essay items are open-ended, but to different degrees. If we think of open-endedness as a continuum from very open to very restricted, short-answer items are at the very restricted end. Short-answer items are written with a single, brief, correct answer in mind, and, to be counted correct, the students must restrict their responses to that answer. Essay items, however, can be written in such a way that they fall at all parts of the continuum. At the more restricted end, essay items might ask students to produce a short list in response, while at the unrestricted end they might ask students to produce a unique analysis of a concept or theme.

?Ask Yourself

Various technologies have been developed to assess student writing. So, instead of having a teacher or expert read your essay for content, clarity, organization, and understanding of concepts, you might, during your academic or professional career, have your writing analyzed and scored by a computer that recognizes key words, phrases, and structures in composition. How might the use of such innovation influence the way you or your students write? Do you believe that removing the human perspective from scoring undermines writers' creativity or divergent thinking?

Short-Answer Items

Short-answer items are assessments that ask students to supply a focused answer using their own constructed response. Such items differ from true-false and multiple-choice questions in that they ask the student to supply an answer rather than to select the correct answer from several possible answers. Also known as fill-in-the-blank items, short-answer items assess primarily factual recall—names, dates, places, or specific persons.

What Are the Advantages and Disadvantages of Short-Answer Items?

Compared to true-false or multiple-choice items, students are less likely to guess correctly on short-answer items. In both true-false and multiple-choice items, the answers are provided for the test taker. That is, the answers may be only true or false or one of several possible answers in a multiple-choice item. Not only are short-answer items less subject to blind guessing, but correct responses cannot be identified by simple recognition, as they can for multiple choice.

On the other hand, short-answer items focus only on recall of information and not on higher-level thinking. They require careful attention to clarity in the stem to avoid ambiguity. The scoring also may be more subjective than with other simple types of assessment items, and for this reason would be more time-consuming.

Format Options for Short-Answer Items

There are two major format options for short-answer questions: (1) completion or fill in the blank and (2) question or command.

Completion or **fill-in-the-blank items** are constructed of a sentence from which one or more words are missing. A blank line is inserted in the sentence, and the student is to write in the missing words at that point. The first option is illustrated below.

- Dividing a baseball player's number of base hits by his or her total number of official at-bats yields a statistic known as the player's <u>batting average.</u>
- Abraham Lincoln was born in the state of <u>Kentucky</u>.

The first example shows a typical formatting in which a definition or description is written, with a blank at the end in which the student is to write the name of the item being described or defined. The second is a simpler item, asking for the name of a state. Note that the stem *specifies* "state" to assure that students are directed toward the required answer. Suppose that was left out and the item read,

- Abraham Lincoln was born in _____.

Now the item is ambiguous, and students will not know what sort of response the teacher has in mind. Is "a log cabin" a correct response? What about "1809"? If you want the students to respond with the name of a state, be sure you have written the stem clearly to ask for it.

Here are some more examples.

- Written during the reign of King John, <u>the Magna Carta</u> was the document that has had the greatest impact on our modern democracy.
- The vernal equinox is the point at which the sun appears to cross <u>the celestial equator</u> from south to north.
- Our earth is a part of <u>the solar system,</u> which also includes seven other planets.

In these examples, the blanks are inserted somewhere *within the sentence* rather than at the end. Again, it is important to remember when using this formatting option to give a clear and complete statement in the item. Do not simply lift a sentence from the text and insert a blank for a key term. Further, you must include enough of the context to direct the student toward the correct answer and away from irrelevant alternatives.

Because it can be difficult to write a natural-sounding sentence while leaving out a word or two that can be readily recalled by a student who has studied the material, teachers often lean toward the second format option, the **question** or **command**. This option tends to be easier to write clearly, as no blank space is used that might add ambiguity. Here are two examples, one written as a question and the other as a command.

- What are the two prime movers of soil that cause erosion?
- List the two prime movers of soil that cause erosion.

The format is simple in this option, and the task is clear to the students. In order to be graded as correct, they must list two things, which are well-defined by the stem. At the same time, this format can place some restrictions on the complexity of the thinking that the student will do in order to answer. Compare these two examples:

- When you divide a baseball player's number of base hits by his or her total number of official at-bats, what statistic do you obtain? (batting average)

- A baseball player's batting average is calculated by dividing a player's <u>base hits</u> by his or her number of <u>at-bats</u>.

The first item, in the form of a question, only asks the student to recall the name of a baseball statistic after reading its definition. The second item requires a more complete understanding of the statistic, in that the student must supply the two components of the formula that define it.

The preceding examples demonstrate levels of recall or understanding for students who are able to read, but how might you assess a kindergartner who has not developed effective reading skills? After a unit on farm animals, you might read questions aloud to the entire class and ask them to draw pictures instead of writing answers:

- What kind of farm animal gives us milk?
- What kind of farm animal gives us eggs?

Understanding can be communicated through various symbols (remember Vygotsky?). Allow students to express their understanding at a level that is consistent with their developmental abilities by adapting a variety of ways of expression.

What Characteristics Make Short-Answer Items Effective?

Effective short-answer items are written clearly and unambiguously. A good place to start in writing an item is with the response you are looking for. *What is it that you want students to recall, and in what context should they recall it?* Answering these questions will help you determine how best to approach writing the question.

You will also need to consider the ramifications of poorly written items. As we mentioned earlier, to reduce the possibility that students are reading their texts only to memorize the textbook definitions, you should avoid creating short-answer items by copying the textbook definition and then simply leaving out a key word to be filled in by the student.

Another common mistake in writing these items is the unintentional insertion of clues to the question's correct answer. Although such clues often find their way into multiple-choice or true-false items, they are perhaps most prevalent in short-answer items. Take a look at the following short-answer items:

- Intelligence quotient, or IQ, is a standardized measurement of _____.

- One of the oldest and most commonly used intelligence tests is known as the _____-_____.

In the first question, the test writer likely copied a textbook definition of IQ and added a space at the end of the statement for student recall. Of course, using the word *intelligence* in the stem of the question unintentionally supplies the test taker with the correct term. The second question, however, might have been somewhat less obvious except that the test writer inserted a hyphen in the answer blank, suggesting that the answer is compound or hyphenated. Many psychology students could recognize this as a clue that the teacher is looking for the Stanford-Binet as the correct answer.

Another possible clue is the length of the blank. Instead of drawing short blanks for short answers and long blanks for long answers, make all blanks the same size. The Stanford-Binet example above also illustrates this unintended clue, with the first blank obviously longer than the second, suggesting a longer word followed by a shorter word.

The most important factor, though, in creating a good short-answer item is *clarity*. It is all too easy for ambiguity to surface in your short-answer items. When you write a short-answer item than can be correctly answered in more than one way, you will find yourself arguing with the students who have picked the "wrong" way and seek to justify their often-plausible answers. Here are a few more examples:

- Psychology is _____.

The teacher who wrote this item wanted the students to write a short definition as learned in class ("the science of mind and behavior"). But the lack of direction provided for the students allows other options—some plausible, some not so—for example, "a division of the social sciences," "a complex field of study," and so on. A clearer presentation of this same question is the following:

- The science of mind and behavior is called _____.

Here is another way that ambiguity can arise:

- The two most desired characteristics in a test are _____ and _____.

The teacher writing this item is expecting the responses "reliability" and "validity" and will be dismayed to read "clarity" and "precision." Here is a better way to write this item:

- The two most desired characteristics in a test are reliability and _____.

By providing one of the two important characteristics of a test, the teacher directs the students to recall the other.

When Are Short-Answer Items Useful?

When would you choose short-answer items over other item types in developing a test? You might consider writing a short-answer test when students are just beginning to build a vocabulary in a particular area, such as in an introductory biology course. Or perhaps you would use them as part of a course's pretest, to determine how familiar your students are with the terms they will encounter in your course. Short answers are widely used to get a quick assessment of students' knowledge (recall) of a recently studied topic.

Ask Yourself

Compare a time that you took a multiple-choice assessment with a time that you took a short-answer assessment. Which type of assessment better represented what you knew about a subject area? Why did one type of assessment provide a better representation of your knowledge?

Essay Items

Essay items, as we have suggested, allow students to communicate a unique, constructed answer to a question. The major difference between essay items and short-answer items is that a short-answer item focuses on a highly specific response and greatly limits the degree of student construction. There is little room for individuality, nor is it expected or desired. Essay items allow students more choice in constructing their answer and consequently permit greater individuality in their responses.

There are different types of choices that students can be allowed to make when developing a personalized response. For example, in some essay questions, learners are allowed to select their vocabulary, use their own style of writing, or employ graphics and other visuals to provide a response. Another choice in essay questions is that learners sometimes are permitted to select the precise content or the examples that they wish to use to support an answer. Given these possibilities, an important consideration for you as a teacher when constructing an open-ended item is the degree to which you intend to narrow or broaden your students' responses.

Resource for Your Assessment Toolkit

Constructing Short-Answer Items

One way of approaching a short-answer item is to think of it as a multiple-choice item that is open-ended and without distracters. Recall that one difficulty in writing multiple-choice items is in developing plausible distracters. In addition to the correct answer, each multiple-choice item must have three or four alternate answers that are either incorrect or less plausible than the correct answer.

Consider the following multiple-choice item:

- Which of the following U.S. holidays originally celebrated the end of World War I?
  a. Flag Day
  b. Labor Day
  c. Memorial Day
  d. Veterans' Day

This question meets the criteria for a well-constructed multiple-choice item. All of the information needed to answer the question is contained in the stem of the question, and each of the distracters is a plausible alternative to the correct answer (d). Its limitation, of course, is that, in terms of factual memory, it asks students only to *recognize* the correct answer. It does not ask them to recall and produce the name of the holiday.

As a short-answer question, a similar item might read:

- Which U.S. holiday originally celebrated the end of World War I?

This question now assesses students' ability not only to recall but also to write the name of the holiday. It does not offer the students any inappropriate clues to help them eliminate possible wrong answers, nor does it allow them to guess the right answer.

Guidelines to Writing Good Short-Answer Items

1. Construct the stem so that the answer is definite and brief.
2. Make sure that there is only one correct answer.
3. Avoid lifting sentences from the students' textbook.
4. For completion and fill-in-the-blank formatting:
   - Make the response blanks equal length.
   - Avoid grammatical clues preceding the blank.
   - Do not use too many blanks in one item—usually no more than two.
   - Include enough information in the stem to ensure the desired response.

The Continuum of Restrictiveness of Constructed-Response Items

The category of test items covered in this chapter can run the gamut from a tightly restricted response to a broad and unrestricted response, depending on what you want to assess. We have examined short-answer items at the restricted end of the continuum. Essay items are by nature broader than short-answer items. But essay items themselves can also be structured along a continuum from more restricted response to more extended response.

At the *restricted-response* end of the essay continuum are essay questions that intentionally limit students' answers. While these questions rely more heavily on recall of information, rather like short-answer items, they go beyond such items by requiring students to recall and organize information, to structure a personal response, or to briefly defend a conclusion. The following are examples of restricted-response items:

- List each of Howard Gardner's intelligences and describe a brief (1–2 sentence) classroom activity you might use to develop each of the intelligences.

- Name each of Piaget's developmental stages, and in a sentence or two, explain the cognitive abilities that children display during each stage.

- List three advantages and three disadvantages of using multiple-choice items in classroom assessments.

- What are the three branches of the U.S. government? For each branch, write a 1–2 sentence summary of its function as defined in the U.S. Constitution.

Each of the above examples demonstrates students' ability to recall important concepts, such as each of Gardner's multiple intelligences. But the task for students goes beyond recall because they are asked to apply their understanding to the use of multiple intelligences in the classroom. These items go beyond a simple one- or two-word response and require more time to score, but they are still easier to evaluate than the more open-ended essay questions. They also lie somewhere between short-answer items and broader essay items in the extent to which they allow students to construct unique responses that give more insight into their thinking and learning.

As essay questions become more open-ended, they can be considered *extended-response* items. At the extended-response end of the continuum, we are not limiting students' responses and are intending to assess higher-order outcomes such as evaluation, organization, analytical reasoning, or originality. Extended-response items, however, do not simply ask students to relate everything they know or can recall about a topic. Instead, the question or prompt itself directs students toward the type of information or skill the teacher is trying to assess. Consider the following:

- Describe the influence of Darwin's theory of natural selection on scientific research conducted in psychology before 1920.

- Critically evaluate behaviorism as a theory of human learning. Indicate strengths and weaknesses, supporting your claims with research. (You need not give exact citations.)

- Analyze the evolution of special education in American public schools since 1920, focusing on the factors that have driven the changes and on the consequences of the changes for the schools, for the students themselves, and for teacher training.

These items are more open-ended and less restrictive than the sample essay items given above, but they do provide students with enough direction to fully understand the task. In other words, these questions ask students to demonstrate their understanding of the relationship between a theory and other academic disciplines (evolutionary biology and psychology), to evaluate a theory (behaviorism), or to narrate an idea and its causes and consequences within a certain time period (special education in the twentieth century). Students are given considerable latitude in how they develop their responses, but the task is more specific than simply asking students to "Describe behaviorism." As you construct essay items, use language that captures your intent: evaluate, describe, analyze, critique, defend.

Varied Degrees of Student-Constructed Responses for Essay Questions

The following examples provide a range of student-constructed responses as they relate to essay questions. The categories may help you clarify the specific types of student construction you are permitting when you write essay questions. To get us started, we will take a single question from biology and demonstrate how you can effectively assess students' recall at one end of the continuum and students' elaboration of understanding at the other end. Then we will consider how to extend the degree and type of student response even further.

The life cycle of the darkling beetle (remember mealworms?) is a very common unit of study in the classroom. So how does it lend itself to multiple levels of assessment of student understanding?

Singly Focused Constructed-Response Questions Students can use their own vocabulary when answering **singly focused constructed-response items,** but there will be a narrow range of acceptable responses. That is, there is one correct answer, but students may use different wording. For example,

- Describe the stages of the life cycle of the darkling beetle.
- What are the stages of the life cycle of the darkling beetle?

These two questions about the life cycle of the darkling beetle ask for specific and narrow information. In other words, the teacher is looking for evidence that the student knows and can articulate the life cycle—egg, larva (the infamous mealworm), pupa, adult (the infamous beetle). There are four distinct stages to the cycle. Students may describe or identify the stages differently (for example, they may identify the larval stage as the mealworm stage), but the question calls for no elaboration and expects an answer within a narrow range of vocabulary.

Multiply Focused Constructed-Response Questions This type of essay question allows students not only to use their own wording but also to choose their own example, adding another layer of individuality to the response. In the singly focused items, the teacher expects students to identify and describe the characteristics of the life cycle of a particular organism. In the multiply focused question, however, the teacher expects students to reveal a conceptual understanding of life cycles—not just the life cycle of the darkling beetle. The multiply focused item, then, allows students to articulate their understanding of a life cycle in their own words rather than in the anticipated words of the teacher.

- List the underlying characteristics of all life cycles. Then select one example of a life cycle and describe the characteristics that make it a life cycle.

In this example, students must first abstract and describe the factors that define life cycle. Beyond understanding how darkling beetles move through four separate stages, students are expected to demonstrate what life cycles look like in other species. Then they can use the darkling beetle life cycle, if that is the one they have selected, to show the specific stages that make it a life cycle.

Multiply Focused and Extended Constructed-Response Questions This type of question allows students to show their understanding of a concept, use their own wording, make some choices about how they will approach the response, and then elaborate on their understanding in a way that demonstrates how they think about something. As teachers, we expect students to demonstrate creativity in their thinking by developing an idea or understanding that is new. But, at the same time, students can demonstrate creativity and unique understanding by *elaborating* on important concepts or ideas as we demonstrate below.

Multiply focused and extended constructed-response items allow students to demonstrate their unique understanding in several ways:

1. *Showing their work.* "Show your work" is a common refrain from teachers, but why exactly are we so insistent on it? From a foundational perspective, the logic that students use to arrive at a solution to a problem is just as important as the answer itself.

2. *Connections to real life.* Students' understanding of an idea or concept may often be more clearly articulated if they are allowed to use real-life issues or examples.

Figure 6.1 *Example of a "Show Your Work" Essay Item.* Calculate the area for the following figure. Show how you went about solving this problem.

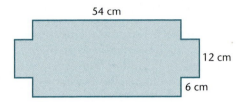

3. *Connections across disciplines.* When students articulate how a key principle or concept from one discipline applies to another (say, from math to physics), they demonstrate an integration of knowledge that is a form of higher-order cognition.

Questions like these are helpful for both teachers and students. They enable students to clarify their approaches to problems, and they provide insight to the teacher concerning the way a student understands a concept. Consider the example shown in Figure 6.1 of an extended-response essay question (drawn from mathematics) that asks students to show their work.

Requiring students to show their work gives the teacher insight into the approaches that students use to solve a problem concerning the area of an irregular geometric figure. You will be able to see different levels of sophistication in students' thinking and you will also be able to find errors in their thinking. The errors students reveal here will be especially valuable to you in improving your teaching of this type of problem. Figure 6.2 shows an essay question that connects the students to a real-life situation and asks them to solve a geometry problem and interpret the answer.

Think about what these different types of essay questions are asking students to perform. Notice how the different questions provide students with more freedom to respond in unique ways. Each question requires students to go beyond the task of simply calculating area or perimeter.

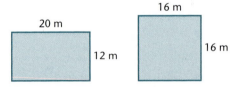

Figure 6.2 *Example of a "Connections to Real Life" Essay Item.* You have been asked by a friend to help build a fenced area for her new dog Gunnar. She has 64 meters of fencing and wants it to provide as large a usable space as possible.

The two rectangles shown below are the two possibilities allowed by the current house and its lot. Which of the two rectangles would you recommend to your friend? What would you say to your friend to explain the reasons why that rectangle is a better choice than the other?

Rather, these questions ask learners to explain a principle of geometry, not to just solve the problem.

A third type of extended-response essay question allows students to support an answer by making connections drawn from other theories, disciplines of study, or research findings that they have uncovered themselves. Such a question fits an interdisciplinary instructional approach (often employed in social studies) in which students are explicitly taught to analyze arguments from different disciplines of study. Here is an example of an extended-response essay question that builds on students' interdisciplinary instruction:

- Drawing from at least two perspectives (e.g., sociological, economic, philosophic, etc.), analyze the causes of the American Civil War.

In this extended-response question, the learners are free to select and make connections drawn from various disciplines. There is a requirement that they employ at least two distinct disciplinary perspectives, but they are free to select the perspectives they wish, depending on their unique interests and backgrounds of study.

In conclusion, note that there are many different ways to allow students to elaborate and provide an extended response. The key for you as the teacher is to be clear in the stem of the question about the content and thinking that is required and the type of constructed response that students are allowed to provide. The examples and the categories we have demonstrated will help you to determine the degree of openness or restriction appropriate to the learning outcomes you need to assess.

What Are the Advantages of Essay/Constructed-Response Items?

Essay questions are most effective at assessing complex learning and higher-order skills. When well written, they require students to organize, integrate, and apply their knowledge in a unique way. They ask student to evaluate ideas, provide arguments and justifications, and analyze outcomes. It is important to keep this in mind as teachers develop essay items, because reducing an essay item to a task of simple factual recall in an extended format is a poor use of this item type.

Essays can enhance students' study habits. Test taking is a skill for which students must prepare and rehearse. Just as teachers sometimes develop objective test items by pulling a definition straight from the text and changing a word or two, students often use a similar habit in studying—memorizing bold terms and developing mnemonic aids to remember them. Effective essays, however, require that students demonstrate a deeper conceptual understanding by analyzing information or by organizing information in new ways. If students know that their assessment will include essay questions, they are prompted to go beyond simply memorizing a few key points from a chapter.

Digging Deeper
What Might Vygotsky Say?

From a psychological foundations perspective, how do constructed-response items effectively capture student learning? Lev Vygotsky and other social constructivist psychologists argue that allowing students to construct and convey understanding in their own words is the clearest evidence that a student has learned something. For example, if we assess students' ability to define key terms in a chapter, a word-for-word presentation of the definition does not necessarily demonstrate learning or understanding. But if we observe one student explaining the concept to another student in a clear, coherent, and unique way, we have more direct insight into our student's understanding. It is important, Vygotsky would say, for us to observe the many and varied ways that our students communicate understanding—ways that go beyond paper and pencil.

Essay questions are relatively easy and time efficient to construct. Of course, you would not want ease of development to be the major rationale for using a particular item type, but well-developed and purposeful questions that are clearly linked to learning targets can be written and refined in much less time than a multiple-choice test, for example.

What Are the Disadvantages of Essay/Constructed-Response Items?

Scoring essays is quite time-consuming. Students are interested in the grade attached to the essay test, but to respond to students with meaningful comments about the content—as well as style, grammar, or other elements of the essay— can demand as much time as your students took to compose their responses.

Because essay responses are often fairly long, essay tests give a deeper but narrower picture of a student's mastery of content. This mastery of the material is in comparison to a 30-item multiple-choice test, which may take the same amount of time to administer to your students.

Subjectivity in scoring can be a problem. This is a question of *reliability,* or consistency of assessment results (remember that reliability refers to the likelihood of a similar score on a particular assessment administered to the same student over time). Unlike an effective and well-written multiple-choice item, for example, students and teachers are certainly aware of the possibility of two teachers scoring an essay differently.

Unintentional bias in scoring is possible. Expectations about student work, and even teacher mood, may influence grades.

These last two points are important considerations to address as you prepare to grade your students' papers. We will respond to these points later in the chapter, when we discuss scoring.

Guidelines for Meaningful Essay Items

1. *Identify your purpose.* One of the most important guidelines to keep in mind is the appropriateness of essay questions to the concept or outcome you are trying to test. What are the learning outcomes that you are assessing? Essay questions are only appropriate if you want to measure complex learning outcomes and higher-order skills. If your learning outcome is one for which you can use objective questions, then it is inappropriate for an essay question. Once you have chosen essay questions as appropriate, your specific purpose will direct you to the type of essay item to prepare, either a restricted-response item or a more open-ended and extended-response item.

The following stems illustrate learning outcomes that assess higher-order thinking skills, such as analyzing or critiquing, that are appropriate to essay questions.

- Compare the following two methods . . .
- Present arguments for and against . . .
- Analyze the strengths and weaknesses of . . .
- Critique the following argument in favor of . . .
- Using evidence from your reading, explain why you agree or disagree with . . .
- Describe a situation that illustrates the principle of . . .
- Describe and analyze the factors that . . .

2. *Be specific and thorough.* Use the stem of the question to define the problem completely and identify the specific skills to be demonstrated. Use as much detail in the question stem as necessary. You will find that it is not a waste of time for your students to read longer directions because this will help them write a to-the-point answer. A good essay question specifies *how* students are to present their understanding, rather than leaving them to write everything they know about the topic. How might good and poor questions differ? Consider the examples in Figure 6.3.

3. *Prepare to score the responses.* Write your scoring plan or rubric at the same time that you write the question. This takes time, but, by having your scoring criteria clearly in mind, you will write a clearer question, and your students will be more likely to write meaningful answers. We will discuss how to develop your scoring guide in the next section.

4. *Give every student the same test.* Avoid offering students a choice about which essay item they address. When students respond to different

Figure 6.3 *Problems Often Found in Essay Questions with Suggested Revisions*

Problem: Unclear stem.

- What causes economic depressions?

Revision: Better and clearer question.

- Identify three major causes of the Great Depression of the 1920s and 1930s.

Problem: Ambiguous stem that invites students to give too wide a variety of responses, only some of which would be relevant.

- What is meant by "triarchic theory of intelligence?"

Revision: The question is stated more precisely and includes a higher-level skill requirement—the application of the student's knowledge.

- Define the three dimensions of Sternberg's model of intelligence and briefly describe the classroom characteristics of a student demonstrating each form of intelligence.

Problem: A selected-response item would be more appropriate to ask this question:

- Explain what is meant by Jefferson's concept of democracy.

Revision: A selected-response item is used instead.

- Which of these statements is most consistent with Jefferson's concept of democracy?
    a. Democracy is part of the divine plan for mankind.
    b. Democracy requires a strong national government.
    c. The purpose of government is to promote the welfare of the people.
    d. The purpose of government is to protect the people from radical or subversive minorities.

Problem: Poorly defined task as stated. A selected-response item could get at the answer.

- Who was John Dewey and why is he important to us?

Revision: The item is rewritten to focus on a higher-level task—the student's ability to evaluate what was read, to apply it to current conditions, and to take a position while presenting arguments supporting the position.

From your reading of *Democracy and Education,* enumerate what you believe to be Dewey's three most important principles. In what ways do you believe each of these three to be relevant to education today?

questions, they are in essence taking different tests. This is a concern for two reasons. First, since your assessments are linked to the learning targets that you believe to be important, you will want to know how each of your students has developed his or her understanding of those targets. Second, students will most likely respond to the items that they feel most comfortable and confident in answering, and you will not know how well students understand the material in the questions they chose not to answer. That content is equally important or you would not be writing an essay question about it.

5. *Time the test properly for your students.* As part of the test instructions, indicate the approximate time to be spent on each question. This will help the students to pace themselves. And be sure to allow for thinking time. You are expecting your students to construct a thoughtful and meaningful essay, so be sure to allow them time to think through their response.

?*Ask Yourself*

In the first meeting of your history class, your professor tells you that he will administer paper-and-pencil assessments every Friday, but he will be alternating formats. One week he will present a 20-point objective test, and the next week he will administer an assessment of two short essay questions. As you leave class that first day, do you think that the different test formats would cause you to study differently? How might the type of assessment influence your preparation for the weekly test?

Scoring Essays

Your class has finished its hour-long, in-class, constructed-response assessment, and you sit down at your desk to review their responses. It has been a long week, and as you scan the papers, you notice that some of the handwriting is sloppy, almost illegible. Several students have obvious spelling and grammatical errors throughout. The length of responses varies from two to five handwritten pages. How will these factors influence your assessment of the students' responses to your carefully crafted questions?

The Issue of Subjectivity and the Halo Effect

Students and teachers alike should be aware of the subjectivity of scoring essays and essay items on tests. Your students should, of course, recognize that the grade or score that an essay receives represents your appraisal of their work relative to the criteria that you have established and presented to the students through your learning targets and your expectations for the particular assessment. And you, as the teacher, should make every effort to ensure that your assessment of student essays is as objective as possible and not arbitrary or related to your knowledge of individual students.

What can you do to ensure that your assessment of written work is reliable and objective? First, it helps to consider a factor that has been shown to undermine teachers' ability to evaluate essays fairly and reliably: the **halo effect.**

We have had extensive experience in working with gifted and high-achieving high school students. One of the characteristics of many such students is that they demonstrate tremendous verbal facility at a young age. By the time these students have reached junior high and are required to write in more complex and analytical forms, their papers are often easily distinguished from their classmates' by the rich and varied vocabulary. Use of such a vocabulary, however, does not guarantee that the students have mastered the skills of developing their ideas, marshaling their evidence, setting forth a meaningful argument, and so on. But their papers often sound so much better than their peers' papers that they receive high grades simply on the basis of the vocabulary used. This is an example of the halo effect, meaning that *an irrelevant factor can act as a "halo" around the essay, making it appear better than it really is.*

The opposite can happen as well. If teachers know the identity of an essay's author, their attitude toward the student may be reflected in comments to the student or even in the final grade. When a teacher dislikes a student for any reason—say inappropriate classroom behavior—the teacher may find himself grading that student's essay more harshly than it deserves.

We offer two suggestions to offset possible bias in scoring:

1. *Establish criteria for grading that focus specifically on the skills that students are supposed to be demonstrating in their writing.* Communicate specifically beforehand what elements of students' responses will be taken into account in the assessment of their work.

2. *If possible, try not to identify the student when reading an essay response.* This can be difficult, especially when you read a series of drafts from each student before they hand in a final version of a paper. But every effort that you make will be a step toward a more objective scoring of student-constructed responses.

Developing an Effective Scoring Guide

In order to rate essay responses appropriately and fairly, it is necessary to develop an objective system of scoring in a situation that, by its nature, is subjective. How can we assess the elements of students' written work and still allow them the freedom and creativity that distinguish effective verbal communication? The answer is a **scoring guide** (sometimes called a **rubric**).

Because it is critical that both you and your students understand what will constitute an effective and appropriate essay, your scoring guide must give students a clear set of expectations for their responses. The scoring guide does this by identifying a number of key elements in the expected answer and specifying how the instructor will assign numerical ratings to students' written answers. (Scoring guides or rubrics may also be developed for assessment of other forms of student performances or demonstration of processes. In this chapter, we focus on scoring guides for the assessment of written work. We will return to the subject of rubrics for all sorts of assessments in Chapter 9.)

But what constitutes an effective scoring guide? At a minimum, scoring guides list the key components in the essay that will be graded as well as the levels of performance that will receive points. A short description defines each level of performance along with the number of points that level will receive.

Figure 6.4 is an example of a basic scoring guide designed to score essay responses to an extended-response item at the high school level. This scoring guide identifies four elements that will be assessed: development of a thesis, the use of appropriate language, the presentation of appropriate sources, and conventional spelling. Each of these elements is assessed along a 4-point scale. Such a scoring guide answers two questions: What specific elements or characteristics in this essay will be assessed, and by what criteria will those same elements be assessed? It is important to note to students, for example, that you will be assessing them on spelling. It is equally important to note that you will *not* be assessing their formatting of citations, length of paper, or grammar.

For this essay, the teacher will be assessing the student on four elements, but you can see how this scoring guide might be used again in a slightly different context. Perhaps in a subsequent essay in the same history course, you would include these same elements and add elements that assess students' ability to compare causes of other conflicts, examine the advances in military technology, or properly format their paper for publication.

What is most important, though, is that you communicate to your students exactly what you will be assessing in their written work. Discuss the purpose behind each component of the scoring guide and be certain that they understand the way in which it will be applied. Not only should you share your scoring guide with students beforehand, as you administer the assignment, but you should invite suggestions about how the scoring guide might further be developed or refined.

Now let's look at Figure 6.5, which is a scoring guide for an essay question at the early elementary level. This essay question might follow a unit on community helpers (such as police, firefighters, librarians, mayors,

Figure 6.4 *Example of a Scoring Guide for a High School Level Extended-Response Item*

Test item: Identify three major causes of the American Civil War, and, for each cause, provide evidence from at least one primary source that supports the idea that this was a justifiable cause of the conflict from either the northern or southern perspective.

	1 point	2 points	3 points	4 points
Thesis	Does not identify causes of the conflict.	Identifies fewer than three causes.	Clearly identifies three causes of conflict.	Clearly identifies three causes of conflict and justifies thesis with sound argumentation.
Language/ vocabulary	Uses language that does not convey understanding of concepts.	Uses language that demonstrates familiarity with concepts.	Uses language appropriate for general readers.	Uses specific language that is appropriate for scholarship in this field.
Sources	No citations evident.	Uses only secondary sources.	Uses appropriate number of sources, but uses both primary and secondary.	Uses appropriate number and type of sources.
Spelling	10+ errors	6–10 errors	1–5 errors	No errors

mail carriers, and so on), in which young students learned the title and function of these people in their community. This simple scoring guide focuses only on the presence or absence of the four elements, rather than on rating the elements.

Developing a scoring guide that assesses clearly articulated learning targets and that presents objective and balanced criteria will demand a significant investment of time prior to administering the test, but there are several ideas to bear in mind. First, there will likely be a number of elements that will be common across several assessments, so the scoring guide,

Figure 6.5 *Example of a Scoring Guide for an Early Elementary Level Extended-Response Item*

Test item: Write the name of one community helper. Write the ways that the person helps us. Remember to use your best writing.

	Present	Not Present
Accurate title of community helper.		
Accurate statement of the way the community helper helps others.		
First word of sentence capitalized.		
Sentence ends with a period.		
Sentence contains subject and verb.		

or rubric, once developed, will be used in several contexts. For example, if you teach a junior year American literature course, you may assess students' spelling, grammar, syntax, and citations on each essay assessment. For this reason, you will not have to re-create those elements of a scoring guide for each assessment. Many teachers have a generic starting scoring guide or rubric that they modify, adapt, and add to from assessment to assessment.

It is also helpful to collaborate on the development of a scoring guide or rubric with colleagues in the same grade or discipline. This can enhance the quality and objectivity of your assessments, particularly if there are common assessments in your classes.

Other Considerations in Scoring Essays

In addition to creating a good scoring guide or rubric and preparing yourself to be objective by avoiding haloing factors, consider the following suggestions to help you to fairly assess constructed responses from your students.

1. *Decide how you will deal with factors that are irrelevant to your scoring guide.* For example, the scoring guide in Figure 6.4 includes points for spelling but not for grammar and usage. Poor grammar may be one of those factors that could lead you to downgrade a student's essay, even though it is not part of your scoring guide. It is helpful to think through such factors—another might be poor handwriting—to prepare yourself to be objective despite these potential issues in a given student's essay.

2. *In tests that contain more than one essay item, score all of one question at one time.* This strategy helps to maintain reliability in grading. If you grade all of one question before going on to the next one, you are more likely to follow your scoring guide carefully and evaluate each response from the same framework without being distracted by responses to other items.

3. *In tests with more than one essay item, shuffle the papers after grading all of one item and before going on to the next one.* This is another way of avoiding a potential halo effect, either positive or negative. A student's excellent answer to one question could affect your reading of that student's next response, for example. Or you might find that a particular response, which would sound acceptable when read in isolation, sounds either much better or worse when read following a poor or an outstanding answer. By shuffling the papers before reading the responses to the next question, you reduce this possibility for bias in scoring.

While we often think of tests as being either "objective" or "essay" format, it might be useful to consider how an understanding of essay—or constructed-response—tasks can inform other types of classroom assessment. Over the course of your career as a teacher, you will construct many and varied paper-and-pencil tests, comprising true-false, multiple-choice, matching, short-answer, and essay items. Well-constructed items of any format provide a particular insight into your students' understanding and give you a sense of how they have approached your learning targets. And in scoring objective items, you will arrive at a relatively precise score or percentage correct, because for each of the items, there is one right or best response.

But what about essay tests? Is there a right answer or a proper way for students to respond? What does a numeric or percentage score on a student's essay test communicate about the student's understanding? And what about reliability—a common and legitimate concern of students? That is, how is it that two teachers might score the same essay quite differently?

The reason that we do not refer to essay items as objective assessments is that, when grading students' written work, we always bring a certain amount of our own perspective to the process, so it is by nature a more subjective form of assessment. But your task as a teacher is to develop an objective means of assessing student work that reflects students' unique construction of knowledge and communication of ideas.

In a typical course on assessment, a common homework assignment is for students to develop a scoring method and attempt to score a sample essay. This is valuable practice for all, regardless of the age level or subject you will teach, because all teachers will be faced at some point with the need to assess student activities that do not have simple and obvious right answers. For example, how do music teachers assess original compositions? How should P.E. teachers assess swimmers? How can we fairly

Resource for Your Assessment Toolkit
Advice from a History Professor

Take a look around you the next time a professor returns a term paper or an essay. How many students turn directly to the last page of the paper to find out their grade and then turn to classmates to compare grades? Now, how many of those students do you think will consider deeply how much time the professor has spent reading and commenting directly on student work?

Our colleague—a historian and fine writer—recommends a highly effective way of allowing students to understand the assessment of their written work and improve their skills as writers. At the beginning of each semester he tells his students that if they intend to study history, they should be prepared to think and write like historians, who use a specialized form of communication (as do specialists in other areas, such as psychology, law, or education). Our colleague provides detailed writing assignments, both in his in-class essay exams and in his midterm and final research papers. He clearly articulates the learning targets, identifies specific considerations for each paper, provides clear purposeful questions, and shares his scoring guide or rubric with his students when distributing assignments for papers.

When he assesses the students' papers, he thoroughly reads each paper and comments throughout using his distinctive fountain pen. In this first reading, he comments only on those elements of the paper that directly influence students' recorded grades—proper citations, support from primary sources, grammar, and the like. Then, he reads each paper a second time and comments only in pencil. This second round of comments is more rhetorical in nature and leads students to be better writers of history; these comments do not influence the grade. For example, "Would a historian state this as you do?" Or, "You might want to read Livy's original text on this subject."

Do all of his students go on to become historians? Certainly not, but by the time they finish his course, they recognize that writing is a skill that requires deliberate attention to the ways in which ideas can be communicated.

appraise a student's performance in a class play? As you consider strategies for evaluating essays, note that essay questions represent one example of a larger class of assessments that require special attention to the scoring method. We will address this larger class in the next three chapters.

Ask Yourself

Students often ask whether any consideration of "effort" should be calculated into the final grade of an essay or research project. Can we as teachers ever fully discern how much effort a student has put into his or her paper? Think about the example of the gifted students. It is tempting to infer that a student who has provided good examples, used rich, descriptive language, and provided authoritative references in her paper has demonstrated significant effort. Can we as teachers be sure that she worked harder on her paper than the student whose vocabulary on the topic seems limited, whose references are from questionable sources, and whose arguments are weak and misinformed?

Summary

- Constructed-response assessments include both short-answer and essay items. They are intended to offer insights into student understanding that are not as readily gained using objective type items.
- Well-developed constructed-response items have several advantages:
  - They allow teachers to assess higher-order skills and complex learning outcomes.
  - They allow students to articulate their understanding of an idea in their own unique way.
  - They do not rely simply on factual recall (dates, places, events, definitions, and so on).
  - They enhance students' study habits.
  - For teachers, they are relatively easy to construct and link to specific learning targets.

- Essay items are subject to several disadvantages, in particular:
  - Scoring reliability is a problem for essay tests. In other words, how can we make sure that two readers of the same constructed response would grade it the same way? If scoring of essays is not done in a planned, objective manner, we run into the problem of poor reliability.
  - We need to eliminate such subjective influences as knowing the identity of the writer or the mood of the teacher during grading.
  - As teachers we need to ensure that students are responding to questions that present specific tasks and that are linked to clear learning targets.

Key Terms

completion item (139)

constructed-response assessment (138)

essay items (143)

fill-in-the-blank items (139)

halo effect (154)

multiply focused and extended constructed-response items (147)

question or command format (140)

scoring guide or rubric (155)

short-answer items (139)

singly focused constructed-response items (146)

For Further Discussion

1. Essay questions and short-answer questions allow students to communicate their understanding in ways that are not entirely prescribed by the teacher. How might such assessments effectively be used in courses such as mathematics? Music? Art?

2. How might you be able to rephrase the following questions so that they are appropriate essay items?

a. Discuss global warming.

b. Should gambling be legal?

c. What caused the Second World War?

Comprehension Quiz

Part One

Here are three examples of constructed-response items designed for different courses. Your task is to critique the questions with respect to the criteria presented in this chapter. Read each item and rewrite it so that it conforms to the criteria of a well-written essay item.

1. Discuss Vygotsky's theory of intellectual development.

2. Evaluate Darwin's theory of evolution.

3. Was the United States justified in entering the conflict in Vietnam?

Part Two

Choose one of your rewritten questions and devise a basic scoring guide that would assess what you believe to be the appropriate elements on which to assess students' responses.

Relevant Website Resources

The College Board

In this chapter we reference several times the writing assessment that has become part of the SAT. This website will provide you with an overview of the writing component, details of how the writing component is scored, and sample prompts.

http://www.collegeboard.com/student/testing/sat/about/sat/writing.html

ACT

ACT also offers an optional writing test. Like the College Board Site, the ACT site provides similar information and offers students strategies for test taking and sample student essays.

http://www.actstudent.org/writing/index.html

Brigham Young University testing handbooks

http://testing.byu.edu/info/handbooks/WritingEffectiveEssayQuestions.pdf

This online handbook has the subtitle, "A Self-Directed Workbook for Educators." It includes information on advantages and disadvantages of essay questions, guidelines for writing good questions, and a self-check set of review exercises.

Essay Scoring Manual for the Regents' Exam at Georgia Tech University

http://www.lcc.gatech.edu/regents/scoremanual.html

This site, while it addresses the assessment of standardized essay tests, provides useful resources for understanding the reliability issues associated with scoring essay items. It also gives examples of model essays and sample questions.

Reference

Katzman, J., Lutz, A., & Olson, E. (2004). Would Shakespeare get into Swarthmore? *Atlantic Monthly, 293*, 2.

CHAPTER 7

Assessment Through Observation and Interview

Chapter Objectives

After reading and thinking about this chapter, you will be able to:

- **Discuss the teacher's role in student observation.**
- **Identify observable behaviors and skills that match standards and desired outcomes.**
- **Construct observational checklists and rating scales.**

- **Develop checklists for students to self-assess their work.**
- **Describe how to use an anecdotal record or a student interview in assessment.**

If ten runners are competing in a mile-long run, and you stand at the finish line and record the times of the runners as they cross the finish line, you can draw several conclusions—the order of finish, the relative difference in time of completion for all of the runners, the margin of victory for the winner, and so on. But what do we *not* know from simply observing the runners as they cross the finish line? Had we carefully observed runners from start to finish, we might have a different perspective on our race. Maybe one runner was slightly hobbled by a nagging sprained ankle, and another runner lost a shoe in the last quarter mile. Or perhaps two runners collided, and one dropped out of the race altogether. How much richer will our understanding be if we observe and consider the circumstances of the runners and their performance throughout the race?

Teaching is driven by what you observe in your classroom. You note when students comprehend a topic quickly and require less direct instruction or when they have little or no prior knowledge and need instruction at the most basic level. You notice students behaving on and off task. Through simple observations, you can tell when students follow directions to complete an assigned project and when they do not.

In this chapter, we describe how to use your skills as an observer to reliably and validly assess your students. We will consider the kinds of skills and tasks that can be assessed by observation in formal and informal settings. We present procedures for individual and group observations and offer steps for creating anecdotal records, observation checklists, rating scales, interviews, and student self-assessments.

Foundational Questions for Your Consideration

- Can observations be entirely objective?
- In a sense, aren't all assessments observations? What distinguishes observational assessment from other assessments?
- How do you document observations without introducing your interpretation? Is it acceptable for teachers to interpret behaviors?

Observation: A Direct Means for Getting to Know Students

Observation is a direct means for learning about students, including what they do or do not know and can or cannot do. Students simply exhibit their natural behaviors as they move through the school day in the classroom, the lunchroom, and the playground. This type of assessment closely matches the metaphor of an assessor sitting next to the student. As described in Chapter 1, this metaphor relates to the Latin root *assidere* (meaning to "sit beside") and implies that assessment is a natural process of getting to know students by listening to them and observing their behavior. Observations involve an observer who notices when specific student actions or behaviors occur or when they do not. Researchers from Jean Piaget and Lev Vygotsky in the past to Thomas Guskey (2000), Robert Marzano (2000), Arthur Costa and Bena Kallick (2004), and Richard Stiggins (2004) today have promoted observation as one important method for examining how students think and learn.

Gathering observational information makes it possible for you to plan ways to encourage students' strengths and to improve their weaknesses. You can use data gathered through observation to make decisions about how best to differentiate teaching methods and motivational strategies. For example, sometimes we notice attention-grabbing situations such as students fighting or defying authority. In these conditions, teachers monitor behaviors and define skills that need to be learned or practiced. Sometimes we notice students struggling with a particular concept or process. In these situations, teachers try to identify the most effective approaches that will help the particular student understand the concept or apply the strategy. In all of these circumstances, you will find yourself assessing your students by watching them and then taking appropriate actions based on what you have observed.

> Several teachers were discussing the non-progress of a third-grade English language learner (ELL) student in reading comprehension. None of her written comprehension tests met grade-level expectations. The enrichment teacher had observed that the student had outstanding drawing skills and suggested that the student be allowed to answer comprehension questions through illustrations. Her reading teacher took her aside for private questioning/interview and encouraged her to answer the comprehension questions in pictures. Her visual responses showed that she did recognize the beginning, middle, and end of the story; she could identify the major characters and the setting of the story; and she could clearly distinguish the hero from the villain.

The enrichment teacher's informal observation, combined with a more formal interview, uncovered some important information about this ELL student that had not been revealed in other, more typical, assessments. A student who appeared to be failing was shown to meet all of the expected goals for the lesson when she was assessed in an individualized, adapted situation.

Advantages of Assessment Through Observation

Immediacy *Observation allows us to assess our students as we are teaching.* We can monitor progress and behavioral skills as part of the normal teaching process. *Observation of skills and knowledge can take place in the natural teaching and learning setting of the classroom without the need for a specific test or assignment.* For example, the physical education teacher watches students on the ball field as they play a baseball game. Even though students are intent on winning the game, the teacher gathers important insights about their abilities to hit or field the ball. Or the math teacher observes as students in a group create graphs on the computer to represent the data they collected for their research project. Both examples allow the teachers to observe students applying their knowledge of specific skills in lifelike, natural situations without the intervention of a specific test.

Unique Information *Observation allows you to discover skills and detect problems that would be difficult to uncover in any other way.* For example, a student who tests well on knowledge-based questions may show gaps in learning when placed in a natural context that requires the student to retrieve or apply that information. That gap in learning can be detected and then corrected by using observation in the natural context where a test would be inappropriate.

Differentiation *Observational methods can give us clues that permit us to adapt other assessments to student needs,* as in the case of the ELL student. The teacher's informal observation provided insight into a different way for that student to show what she could do.

Value Added *Observation can add a missing dimension to our assessment of students.* Information that you gain from observing a student can be used together with other, more formal, assessment methods, such as paper-and-pencil testing.

Disadvantages of Assessment Through Observation

Subjectivity There are several hurdles for a teacher to overcome when observing students, because *this form of assessment can be subjective.* We may form a faulty judgment based on a single instance of observation or from another teacher's report. We may set expectations that are unrealistic for our students. We can also be biased for or against a student due to prior positive or inappropriate interactions.

Time Factors Another hurdle for the classroom teacher is *the time needed to conduct observations.* You cannot do the work of observing your students from your home, as you do when you bring home a briefcase full of essays to grade. Observation notes taken in the classroom or elsewhere need to be recorded as soon as possible. If you observe a student on Monday and wait until Friday to complete an observation form or make notes, you are compromising the accuracy of the assessment.

Also, if you audiotape or videotape the student's behavior or performance in order to share with others, you will have to spend time replaying the tapes and recording the data. You will have a record of the student's behavior as documentation, but the act of taping and then replaying the tape to take notes is time-consuming.

Uncovering the Right Behaviors Other difficulties in observing students lie in *the reliability and validity of the observation.* If you do not specify the explicit skills to be observed and carefully plan your observations, you may end up observing unrelated behavior. For example, talking loudly is more noticeable than staying on task or being productive. You can become distracted from your target observation by extraneous behaviors or other irrelevant factors if you have not developed a clear and careful plan for the

Digging Deeper
Binet and Simon

Two French psychologists, Alfred Binet and Theodore Simon, are credited with the development of one of the first widely used intelligence tests for children. The Binet-Simon scale involved an assortment of tasks that Binet and Simon believed to be characteristics of children's abilities at different ages. In an effort to confirm their hypotheses about these tasks, both psychologists used extensive observation studies focused on children of different ages. Employing a variety of observation tools and examining data drawn from these tools, Binet and Simon developed a set of tasks ordered by difficulty and complexity level.

Once the tasks were developed, Binet and Simon tested them with 50 children—10 children each in five age groups. Teachers had identified these children as possessing average intelligence for their ages. Each child was then asked to tackle the Binet-Simon tasks ranging from simple to increased complexity. The test items ranged from very simple (shaking hands, pointing to parts of the body) to slightly harder (repeating three digits or simple sentences spoken by the examiner) to more challenging items (creating sentences from several words given by the examiners, describing differences between objects). "The hardest test items asked children to repeat back seven random digits, find three rhymes for the French word *obéisance,* and to answer questions such as 'My neighbor has been receiving strange visitors. He has received in turn a doctor, a lawyer, and then a priest. What is taking place?' (Fancher, 1985)"

Adaptations of the Binet-Simon scale continued to be used after Binet's death. The most famous, the Stanford-Binet scale, was adapted and named by Lewis Terman of Stanford University and covered both children and adults. The most recent version of the Stanford-Binet scale is used by psychologists to determine the aptitude of children and adults.

It is noteworthy that the work of Binet, Simon, Terman, and their successors is based on a careful series of observations. Observation remains a powerful assessment tool in that it provides a direct and often unobtrusive means for determining what children know and can do.

Source: Fancher (1985) quoted at "Human Intelligence": Alfred Binet, http://www.indiana.edu/~intell/binet.shtml). Accessed January 14, 2008.

observation. A written checklist targeting the explicit skills or behaviors will help the observer focus on the purpose of the observation.

Identifying Observable Behaviors That Match Standards and Desired Outcomes

Clearly, knowing what to look for is the key to sound observation. Are you observing a desirable behavior that you want to increase, or are you targeting an undesirable behavior that may be inappropriate or even harmful? Academic skills, psychomotor skills, and prosocial skills are behaviors that we want to increase or improve in our students. Obviously, inappropriate behaviors are those we want to decrease. Both appropriate and inappropriate behaviors can be the focus of an observation.

Academic Skills All of the academic subjects are included within the category of **academic skills:** reading, mathematics, science, social studies, language arts, foreign language. Each assessed cognitive skill area must be stated in observable, measurable terms. Moreover, the vocabulary for the observable and measurable terms should include the knowledge, skills, and concepts listed in each state's academic standards and benchmarks.

In general, you would develop a tool to observe academic skills that are displayed as part of some performance, like reading aloud, recording data, calibrating a balance, using technology or science equipment, participating in a dialogue in another language, or giving an oral report.

Psychomotor Skills The category of **psychomotor skills** includes gross motor and fine motor skills, physical movement as in various sports, dance, and physical exercise; the performing arts—singing, playing an instrument—as well as art and craft production, such as painting, drawing, and building a model. A flutist observed playing a specified piece of music might be assessed on pitch, tempo, tone, posture, and breath control. If one or more of these component skills is observed to be lacking, the teacher can target those areas for remediation.

Prosocial or Affective Skills Included here are the skills students need to work and interact with others appropriately. **Prosocial skills** involve student's attitudes, beliefs, feelings, or the dispositions they develop. These skills must be taught to students just as purposefully and precisely as academic skills.

Often the specific and more observable social skills are derived from the principles that set the climate for the class. Classroom principles are usually guiding precepts such as strive for excellence, respect yourself and the rights of others, accept responsibility for your actions, participate in your own learning, and cooperate with others.

It is difficult to assess these lofty goals without breaking them down into specific behaviors that students will understand. Figure 7.1 lists some observable social skills that are written in "kid language" so students understand the expectations.

We often place students in groups and tell them to "work together," "cooperate," or "be a team." We assume students know how to collaborate, and, when we do not get the behaviors we expect, we sometimes abandon cooperative group work and return to individual seat work in frustration. By breaking down the prosocial skills needed for individual or group work, selected skills can be taught and reinforced through the regular curriculum,

Figure 7.1 *Prosocial Learning Behaviors*

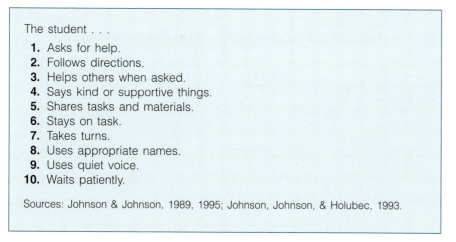

The student . . .

1. Asks for help.
2. Follows directions.
3. Helps others when asked.
4. Says kind or supportive things.
5. Shares tasks and materials.
6. Stays on task.
7. Takes turns.
8. Uses appropriate names.
9. Uses quiet voice.
10. Waits patiently.

Sources: Johnson & Johnson, 1989, 1995; Johnson, Johnson, & Holubec, 1993.

allowing you to observe your students and diagnose problems that the students may have, as well as offer interventions to increase achievement and prevent harm.

Adapting Your Vocabulary to Your State Standards

Each state has adopted its own standards and benchmarks (indicators, descriptors, elements, and proficiencies) that are assessed on the state's high-stakes standardized tests. Therefore, it is critically important that you create your academic skills checklists with the end in mind—and the end is the vocabulary, concepts, and principles of your state standards.

Another challenge involves implementing state standards while at the same time not allowing your textbook to dictate the vocabulary of knowledge and skills. The vocabulary in the textbooks may be different from the vocabulary used in the state standards and on the standardized tests that are aligned to those standards. Therefore, it is important to include the vocabulary from both sources—the textbook and the standards—in your instruction and assessments so students do not become confused. Figure 7.2 compares an example of textbook vocabulary to the vocabulary of a particular state's standards.

Building Reliability and Validity into Your Observations

Reliability In the context of observation, *reliability* refers to *consistency* and to *agreement among observers*. Suppose you and another teacher independently

Figure 7.2 *Textbook Versus State Standards Vocabulary*

Textbook Vocabulary	State Standards Vocabulary
Hook	Motivator
Closure	Clincher
Adjective/Adverbs	Modifiers
Paragraph	Passage
Main character	Protagonist
Greeting	Salutation
Summarize	Synthesize
Comparison	Similarities
Naming part	Noun
Base word	Root word
Circle graph	Pie graph
Types of literature	Genres

Source: Burke, 2006.

observed the same student at the same time, using the same method, and then compared notes. Would you come up with the same results? Would you agree on what you saw or would you disagree? You can see that reliability is closely connected to the issue of objectivity that we discussed earlier. Observers will be more likely to agree on what they see in an observation if they have *objectively defined the behaviors they are observing.*

Reliability in observation is also associated with *immediacy of recording.* Observations that are not recorded as you conduct them run the risk of being inaccurate or unsound. How much can you rely on notes that were taken after the observation, when time has passed and you have perhaps forgotten some important details?

In addition, reliability in observation is associated with *manageability.* If you are trying to observe a long list of behaviors and a number of students, you can easily find yourself overwhelmed by the experience. When there are many things to look for, it is easy to overlook one thing or another. In fact, you will miss some of what you intended to observe if you are trying to do too much.

Observation Validity **Observation validity** refers to *accuracy* and *completeness*. Are you really collecting information on the behavior or skill that you targeted? This is the accuracy component. Did you set out to observe cooperation in a group of students and then discover that your results relate to the one student who did all the talking during the group work? Defining behaviors and skills is not easy, as we discussed earlier. "Cooperation" is not an observable behavior but an *inference* drawn from the behavior in which you see your students engaged. You will need to determine what behaviors you can observe that will be indicators of cooperation. The specific behaviors you select will depend on the group's task, but they might include helping others when asked, saying supportive things to others, and taking turns. In this context you would probably also include such inappropriate behaviors as interrupting others, talking loudly, and refusing to share material. You would be collecting information on a series of behaviors that together could be a definition of cooperation in a particular situation.

Completeness in observation has to do with *collecting a representative sample*. When you observe your students, you must be sure that you have provided them with a reasonable *opportunity* to exhibit whatever it is you are observing. Otherwise, if they do not exhibit the skill, how will you know if it is because they cannot or because they did not have the chance? And one observation is never enough. If a student fails to perform the skill you are watching for, is it because you happened to observe her on the one occasion when she did not perform the skill? The only way to know is to observe more than once. This gives you a chance to get a better sense of the level at which the student is currently performing: Is this an emergent skill? Is it progressing? Or is the student showing mastery? These questions are answered through multiple observations.

How Do You Make Your Observations Reliable and Valid? First, be sure that you have carefully defined the behavior or skill you are going to observe and that you have a clear plan for when and under what circumstances you will observe. As a part of this process, you will plan the type of observation to conduct and will develop a form or checklist to use to collect your data. We will have a great deal to say later in this chapter about the various kinds of observations you can conduct and the formats that can be used.

Second, assure that your observations are reliable and valid by practicing observing your students and your planned behaviors and skills. Following the practice, you can revise your definitions and methods as needed. Often you will find that you have omitted a part of the behavior or skill that will be needed for an accurate observation or that some part of your planned definition is still unclear. Or you may find that the form you have prepared does not give enough room to collect the needed information or the format is awkward to use. Practicing allows you to correct any problems that come up and prepares you to be accurate and thorough in your observation.

Third, when possible, get expert help. Include another teacher in your observation so that the two of you can compare your findings. This gives you another opportunity to clarify your definitions or methods and a chance to get an outside opinion on any subjectivity that might be clouding your observation. Because it can be difficult for another teacher to set aside time for this, you may decide to save this step for the more significant or difficult observations—those that may have an especially large impact on a student or those where you find yourself struggling to define a behavior. And observations that are conducted across your entire grade level will require participation by your other grade-level teachers in this step.

Fourth, give sufficient opportunity for the observed students to show you the skill or behavior you are observing. This is an important issue that you must think through when you are planning the details of when and where to observe.

Fifth, record your observations immediately. This will happen automatically if you have prepared a specific form for the observation and have practiced with it so you can use it easily.

Sixth, review your data after the observation. Be sure that you have filled in all the spaces and notes as you planned and that it is readable so that at a later time you can interpret the data you collected.

You can create and use the tools yourself for your observations or develop them in your grade-level team and arrive at a group consensus of what behavior merits a particular interpretation or rating. The reliability of observation is improved when all teachers using the tools are trained and supervised during a practice session.

?Ask Yourself

Consider a student who often disrupts class, talks back, and causes the teacher to feel distressed. How might this inappropriate interaction affect the teacher's ability to fairly assess the student's participation in a co-operative group-work setting?

Systematic Approaches to Classroom Observation

Throughout the school day, teachers regularly observe students and make countless decisions concerning how to respond to students, what to teach next, and what behavior to encourage or discourage. This is part of daily

Resource for Your Assessment Toolkit
Observing Inappropriate Behaviors

A critical prerequisite of successful observation is to carefully determine (1) what behaviors you are looking for and (2) what specific questions you are trying to answer concerning those behaviors. For example, if you notice that a student exhibits off-task behaviors during sustained silent reading time, you could develop some specific questions that might guide some focused observations. Your objective for these additional observations might be to determine if the student has trouble staying on task in a variety of situations, in certain specific situations, or only during sustained silent reading.

Points to consider when observing inappropriate behavior include the following:

Setting: What was the situation in which the inappropriate behavior occurred? What was happening just before the student's behavior?

Behavior characteristics: What *exactly* did the student do? Was she off task by playing with a ruler at her desk, or was she off task by running around the room, knocking over other students' books?

Frequency: How many times was the child off task during 20 minutes of silent reading?

Length of time: How long did each off-task behavior or episode of the behavior last?

Latency: How long did it take before the student followed directions, took out a book, and began silent reading?

Consequences: What was the effect of the undesired behavior? For the off-task student who runs around the room, pushing books off desks may be reinforced by her classmates' laughter. This makes the behavior much more difficult to modify, and the teacher may need a completely new approach that involves the entire class, not just the off-task student.

classroom life. Some observations, however, can easily be forgotten in the midst of a busy day. Patterns of conduct may be overlooked because there are simply too many distractions and demands.

Observation tools are instruments and techniques that help teachers to focus and to record useful data about students' learning in a systematic way. The observation tools we will discuss are anecdotal notes, observation checklists for teachers, student checklists for self-assessment, rating scales, and interview guides. Each of these tools will help you record important observations. Together they provide a powerful source of assessment data that flows directly from the natural rhythm of the classroom.

Anecdotal Notes or Records

The least formal type of observation uses **anecdotal notes** or **records** as a means to document observations of significant skills, events, or behaviors of students. Anecdotal records are a quick, open-ended way to record observations, describing what happened in the teacher's own words. They are intended to record factual descriptions of meaningful incidents that the teacher has personally observed. Their purpose is to enable teachers to quickly note a behavior or concern or noteworthy event so that at the end of the school day, they can reflect on and better interpret patterns of conduct that need attention or deserve recognition.

Impromptu Anecdotal Records Even though you can plan in advance to use them, anecdotal records are often used spontaneously for unusual classroom incidents. You might find it most helpful to limit this kind of recording to capture instances of misbehavior or to focus on those students who need your help getting organized or completing academic tasks. Most likely, you will anecdotally record only exceptionally good or exceptionally troubling instances of student skills or behaviors, rather than every student in each skill or behavior. Your records can be used when writing report card comments or in parent or student conferences. They are also useful if another intervention, such as acceleration or specific subject tutoring, appears to be needed for the student.

Figure 7.3 is an example of an impromptu anecdotal record. It describes a behavioral incident and offers the teacher a record of her actions. The record notes only the facts of the incident, without an emotional accounting or evaluation.

The anecdote recorded in Figure 7.3 was spontaneous, but you can plan for such impromptu recording by designing a generic form to use whenever an unusual situation arises in the classroom. You might put the form on an index card, which would be easy to keep nearby and relatively unobtrusive to use. The card might have a few preplanned blanks (student's name, date, setting) followed by an area in which you can record whatever is needed. This format is designed to be nonspecific so that it can be used in a variety of situations.

There is no one right way of keeping anecdotal records. Some teachers keep an informal log in a notebook with information about all students. This is helpful when jotting down incidents after whole-class instruction.

Figure 7.3 *Anecdotal Notes for Gary M.*

Student Gary M   **Date** 10/18/2008

Setting Group poster project

WHAT HAPPENED

Today during a group poster project, Gary complained about the marker colors he was given. I reminded him of the rule, but he grabbed a marker and scribbled on the poster, ruining it.

Figure 7.4 *Anecdotal Record (A-B-C Recording) of Inappropriate Behavior in Context*

Date/ Time	Context/ Activity	Antecedent	Behavior	Consequence	Student Reaction
10/18/08 10:35	Students were working on a group poster project for their social studies unit.	Kim was the Materials Manager for Gary's group. She gave him 3 light-colored markers.	Gary said, "These colors stink!" He grabbed a black marker from Kim and scribbled all over the poster.	I stated the rule and sent him to the time-out section of the room.	Gary returned from time-out but refused to return to his work-group. He sat at his desk, facing away from the workgroup.

Or you might record anecdotal observations as running accounts, one for each student, on separate pages in a notebook. Some teachers use "sticky notes" and paste the notes into files in each child's portfolio. Another option is to use the computer to print general or subject-specific forms on adhesive labels. Then you can observe and record on the label, peel it off, and quickly attach it to a student's folder.

Figure 7.4 illustrates a more detailed anecdotal recording form to be used in an impromptu observation. Because it gathers information about what happened just before and after an incident, it can be used when the teacher suspects that an inappropriate behavior will require some kind of intervention. This is also called A-B-C recording because it includes the antecedent, the behavior, and the consequence.

The A-B-C recording provides a way to develop an understanding of a child's challenging behavior (Carr et al., 1994; O'Neill et al., 1997; Hieneman et al., 1999). The record allows the teacher to record certain unusual behaviors within their exact context. The form has a place to record the setting (*context*) of the event, what happened just before the behavior (*antecedent*), what the behavior looks like (*behavior*), and what happens after the challenging behavior occurs (*consequences*). The more detailed anecdotal record helps the teacher begin to uncover possible causes of the student's behavior and to predict what conditions could cause future behavior in order to develop a potentially useful intervention to decrease its frequency.

Figure 7.5 *Skill-Specific Anecdotal Record—Test Taking*

Student Sandor L._____   **Date** 10/25/08_____

Time/Period 3rd_____   **Subject** Algebra I_____

TEST-TAKING SKILLS: The student . . .

1. **Followed directions:** *Sandor was glancing out the window while I gave the directions.*
2. **Read or looked over entire test:** *Did not see him do this.*
3. **Attempted all problems:** *He did not finish—left 3 problems at end and also 1 earlier in the quiz.*
4. **Checked answers for accuracy:** *He went back and began checking some earlier answers part-way through. Then returned to end of the quiz. Then went back and checked some more in middle. Then time was up.*
5. **Watched time limitations:** *Did not appear to.*

Planned Anecdotal Records Anecdotal recording can also be used in a planned and systematic way by designing a tool that focuses on specific skills that are part of a larger task like problem solving or taking tests. You can use such a form in each subject area and for a variety of purposes. Figure 7.5 is an example of a skill-specific anecdotal record, focused on test-taking skills. In this case, the teacher is focusing on a student who is performing poorly on written classroom algebra quizzes. This is a student who seems to understand the concepts in class work and discussion but who scores poorly on quizzes. Could the problem be related to test-taking skills?

Note that in this anecdotal record the *number of behaviors to be observed is limited* so the teacher can avoid distraction, focus clearly, and use the time efficiently. Further, being clear on the overall skill and the behaviors you want to observe with planned anecdotal records will help to make this process more thorough and unbiased. Using this simple form, the observation can be recorded as the student is taking the test.

In any case, it is critical that you record your observation as soon as possible to maintain observation validity. Trying to recall the details of an observation and record them several days later will not result in valid data. Therefore, develop a method that accomplishes your purpose and is easy for you to use on the spot or immediately afterward.

Making Anecdotal Records Reliable and Valid By their nature, anecdotal records represent an informal method of observation. There are a few simple steps you should take to make your anecdotal records reliable and valid. If you are making planned observations, use the methods we discussed earlier to increase reliability and validity:

- Define the behavior.
- Create a form for recording.
- Practice.

If you are gathering data spontaneously, there are two critical factors:

- Record the incident as soon as possible.
- Keep it factual by avoiding interpretation or emotions.

For these spontaneous, or impromptu, records, having a generic form to use can help you get the observation down on paper without delay.

Observation Checklists

Observation checklists are clear and concise lists of behaviors that are used to assess a student's skills. The teacher observes the skills in a simple and straightforward manner, marking them as present or absent, correct or incorrect. Checklists are flexible options that can be used by the students themselves as well as the teacher.

Using a Checklist to Observe Academic Skills
Observation checklists can focus on the processes or tasks needed to demonstrate knowledge, abilities, or mastery of a skill. Each task must be written in a way that is observable and measurable. Such checklists can be used at specific intervals to ensure that a student moves forward with no gaps in his or her learning. Each component of the specific task is listed in order on the checklist.

The first step in preparing to observe an academic skill is to *identify the key dimensions of the overall skill*. For example, fluency is a common assessment focus in reading: A teacher observes as a student reads aloud and rates the student on fluency. But what exactly is a fluent reader? Fluency is made up of the separate skills of accuracy, decoding, phrasing, and expression. A student may be able to read accurately, decode new words, leave proper phrasing between sentences and characters, but still may read in a flat, expressionless tone. The teacher now has a skill area to target for that student in building full fluency.

For the skill of developing an orally presented argument, the dimensions can include stating a clear position, providing evidence to support the position, using precise vocabulary, exhibiting an awareness of counterarguments, and responding to critics who would not agree with the position. For the skill of presenting the oral argument, the dimensions can include speaking clearly, pausing to allow the audience sufficient time to process the information, and using inflections. These dimensions of the overall skill of developing and presenting an oral argument need to be considered carefully and translated into specific behaviors.

Next, you will need to *refine the precise behaviors that relate to the key dimensions in light of the students' grade level.* As noted above there are many different dimensions that relate to the skill of developing and presenting an oral argument. However, the precise behaviors that relate to these dimensions differ based on the maturity of the speaker. For example, when using precise vocabulary, you would expect that first-grade students' words choices would differ from sixth-grade students' choices. One way to specify this might be to expect first-graders' words to be drawn from level one of the Dolch Basic Word List.

A useful step in developing a thorough observation checklist is to *identify common errors that relate to the skill.* For example, as you observe your students informally, you might note that many students in the class forget to provide evidence that is based on empirical research. If this is the case, you would make certain to specify the presentation of empirical evidence as a specific behavior that deserves special attention and clarity in your checklist.

Figure 7.6 shows a checklist that focuses on the oral presentation skills that we have been discussing. Observations that result from the use of Figure 7.6 are useful for two reasons. First, the behaviors closely relate to a standard that has been selected as especially important. Second, the behaviors are specifically related to known weaknesses of students. By collecting data on these carefully selected behaviors, you can provide specific insights that will help students improve potential weaknesses.

Using a Checklist to Observe Psychomotor Skills Figure 7.7 is an observation checklist with specific behaviors that relate to physical education skills at the early elementary level.

How do you translate the information from the Figure 7.7 checklist into a meaningful description of proficiency? One way to use the same checklist to take account of growth over time is illustrated in Figure 7.8. It includes a proficiency criterion and is designed for use across multiple observations throughout the school year. Columns have been added to the left-hand side of the checklist to allow you to make observations at three points during the year. You then derive a score on each skill by summarizing. You would circle the YES (proficiency is achieved) if the student has displayed the skill more than half of the time (in this case at least two out of three times) or circle the NO if the student has not. The date at the top of the form would be the point at which you summarized your three sets of checkmarks.

Figure 7.6 *Middle School Oral Presentation Observation*

Name _____ Date _____

Standard: The student speaks effectively and utilizes appropriate organization, content, and delivery techniques.

Relevant Behaviors that Merit Observation	Observed	Not Observed
Organization of Speech: *Did the student . . .*		
Use a hook or grabber to engage the audience?		
Sequence the order of the speech appropriately?		
Use transitional words or phrases to connect the ideas coherently?		
Use a powerful closure to summarize the main ideas and/or initiate a call to action?		
Content of Speech: *Did the student . . .*		
Include facts and statistics that support the case?		
Include at least one quotation from an expert in the field?		
Delivery Techniques: *Did the student . . .*		
Establish eye contact with the audience?		
Speak loudly enough (volume) to be heard by the entire audience?		
Use appropriate facial expressions and hand gestures to convey the feelings?		
Enunciate clearly?		
Pronounce words correctly?		
Use appropriate gestures to reinforce the main points?		

Figure 7.7 *First-Grade Locomotion Skills Observation Checklist*

First-Grade Locomotion Skills

Name _____ Date _____

YES	NO	Skips width of gym in a straight route
YES	NO	Gallops width of gym in a straight route.
YES	NO	Walks in a straight route
YES	NO	Walks in a curved route
YES	NO	Walks in a zigzag route
YES	NO	Runs in a straight route
YES	NO	Runs in a curved route
YES	NO	Runs in a zigzag route

Figure 7.8 *First-Grade Locomotion Skills Observation Checklist, End-of-Year Summary*

Name _____ Date _____

Oct.	Jan.	Mar.	Skill: *The student . . .*	Proficiency	
			Skips width of gym in a straight route.	**YES**	**NO**
			Gallops width of gym in a straight route.	**YES**	**NO**
			Walks in a straight route.	**YES**	**NO**
			Walks in a curved route.	**YES**	**NO**
			Walks in a zigzag route.	**YES**	**NO**
			Runs in a straight route.	**YES**	**NO**
			Runs in a curved route.	**YES**	**NO**
			Runs in a zigzag route.	**YES**	**NO**

Proficiency Criteria:

YES—Demonstrated in <u>MORE</u> than half of the student's attempts in individual skill drill/task.

NO—Demonstrated in <u>FEWER</u> than half of the student's attempts in individual skill drill/task.

Using a Checklist to Observe Prosocial Behavior Checklists can easily be constructed to observe students as they work alone or in group settings. The steps for creating a checklist for observed behaviors are similar to creating an academic or psychomotor skill assessment checklist.

First, be sure to define the behaviors in observable, measurable terms on the checklist. "Listens to group members' ideas" or "Offers positive feedback to team members" are desired behaviors for a group interaction. "Raises hand when asking questions" may be a desirable behavior for an individual observation.

Second, establish a manageable period for observing. For example, if you are observing students as they work in groups, observe one group a day. If you are observing individual students, plan to monitor no more than four or five per day.

Third, give your students a copy of the checklist and explain why and when you will be using it. Make sure to inform students on the day you are observing them. And give them opportunities to grow comfortable with being observed.

Fourth, give the students feedback on what you have observed. Reinforce positive behavior and provide scaffolding and modeling for students who show harmful, inappropriate, or undesirable actions.

Figure 7.9 is a checklist that can be used when observing a cooperative group. Note that the behaviors are described explicitly in observable terms. The teacher should inform the group they are being assessed on their cooperative skills and place herself in close proximity to the group so she can watch all students. The students are given a check when the behavior is observed or NA when the behavior is not apparent. There is a place for comments or anecdotal notes. The group should be observed more than one time, especially if any of the group members did not have the opportunity to demonstrate all the skills. In fact, you may need to focus on one student at a time until that student has had sufficient opportunity to display each skill and only then focus on another student. No matter what approach you use, the key is to observe all students long enough to provide a valid observation. Information from the checklist should be shared with the group members after the observation.

Observation checklists provide a roadmap that helps teachers give students consistent feedback related to the task. But in addition to teachers using checklists to gather information about students, it is important to include students in the process so they can observe and self-assess their academic progress. This shift in focus from the teacher as third-person objective observer to the student as first-person stakeholder in the process can foster metacognition and self-assessment. These checklists are valuable tools in our assessment repertoire.

Figure 7.10 is a checklist designed for observing an individual student's behaviors. Observing one individual at a time is time-consuming for the

Figure 7.9 *Observation Checklist for Cooperative Group Work*

Group Project _____ **Date** _____

Group Members' Names and #s:

　1. _____　　4. _____

　2. _____　　5. _____

　3. _____

	Group Member #				
Behaviors: *The student . . .*	1	2	3	4	5
Helps the group to begin working promptly.					
Supports group in completing task by asking questions or contributing ideas.					
Displays positive group behaviors such as taking turns, encouraging others, helping others stay on task.					
Helps to problem-solve when difficulties arise.					
Responds to others with encouragement and tact.					
Speaks in a clear voice.					
Speaks with appropriate volume.					

Comments:

teacher, but it can offer specific information about a student's work and study habits. Furthermore, the cooperative group-work checklist in Figure 7.10 could be used by the group members themselves to rate their behavior and participation.

Using a Checklist to Assess Dispositions *Dispositions,* that is, patterns of behavior that are valued by our society, are included in all of the national standards. For example, the national science standards state that perse-

Figure 7.10 *Observation Checklist for Cooperative Group Work*

Group project _____   **Student name** _____

❑ **Teacher/Observer**   **Date** _____

❑ **Self**   **Date** _____

	Not Observed	Observed
Encouragement: *The student . . .*		
Restates (paraphrases) the ideas of others.		
Checks for understanding.		
Provides positive verbal feedback (encouraging words).		
Provides positive nonverbal reinforcement (facial expression, gestures, eye contact).		
Communication: *The student . . .*		
Speaks clearly.		
Speaks with appropriate volume (12-inch voices).		
Allows others to speak without interrupting.		
Listens attentively to other group members.		
Responds appropriately to comments.		
Problem solving: *The student . . .*		
Begins work promptly on the project.		
Brainstorms various ideas.		
Seeks input from all team members.		
Explores multiple solutions to problem.		
Encourages creative options.		
Helps build team consensus.		

What did the student do well?

What needs more work?

Source: Burke, 2008.

verance is an important disposition to nurture. By placing learners in a situation that requires their perseverance (such as making daily observations on a science project and taking notes), the teacher can collect evidence by noting the care and constancy of the daily notes that learners keep. This evidence provides data to assess perseverance.

The summary checklist in Figure 7.11 is based on multiple observations and focuses on four dispositions: work habits, study habits, persistence, and social skills. It can be used by the teacher, a peer, or the student, and it has a space for comments and future goals. Sometimes making the students aware of the behaviors to be observed will help them become more conscious of demonstrating those specific behaviors.

Making Your Observations Reliable and Valid In order to make your observations as reliable and valid as possible, consider the following suggestions.

First, think carefully about what it is that you are trying to observe so you can answer these questions:

- What behaviors will I look for?
- What is an appropriate number of behaviors to observe that will tell me what I need to know about the students without overwhelming me?
- What activity or context will give the students the best opportunity to show me those behaviors?

Second, having developed your definitions and formatted your checklist, practice observing several times to make sure your definitions hold up and your checklist is easy to use. Third, focus carefully when conducting the observations to avoid distractions. Fourth, when reviewing your data after the observation, be sure that you have completed everything in the checklist that you intended to and that you can clearly interpret what you wrote at a later time.

Rating Scales

A **rating scale** is another tool used to observe student skills and behaviors, in addition to anecdotal records and checklists. Rating scales are actually a form of checklist. In this case, the checklist has been modified by adding descriptive words, numbers, or both to rate the adequacy or appropriateness of a student's behavior. Typically a rating scale consists of a list of qualities that are judged according to a scale that indicates the degree to which each quality is present. The key that distinguishes the rating scale from other checklists is the assumption that each characteristic on the scale

Figure 7.11 *Checklist for One Student's Behaviors and Dispositions*

Student _____Denise_____ Class _____Science_____ Date _____12/5_____

Type of Assignment: _____Work Habits_____

	Not Yet	Sometimes	Frequently
Work Habits			
Gets work done on time.			✓
Asks for help when needed.		✓	
Takes initiative.		✓	
Study Habits			
Organizes work.			✓
Takes good notes.			✓
Uses time well.			✓
Persistence			
Shows patience.		✓	
Checks own work.	✓		
Revises work.		✓	
Does quality work.			✓
Social skills			
Works well with others.		✓	
Listens to others.		✓	
Helps others.		✓	

Comments: *I always get my work done on time and I am really organized. I just need to check my own work and help my group work.*

Future Goal: *I need to be more patient with my group and try to work with them more. I worry about my own grades, but I don't do enough to help group members achieve their goals.*

Source: Burke, 2005.

can be observed according to some underlying degree of accomplishment. Therefore, "more" accomplishment means the person will be rated higher on the rating scale.

Descriptive Rating Scales The basic rating scale is **descriptive** and is based on a series of adjectives or thumbnail sketches. The descriptions form a rising scale intended to describe different degrees of progress toward a desired learning outcome. They allow the teacher to rate the adequacy or appropriateness of a student's behavior along that scale. The "best," or most desired point, is last on the scale, and the other points along the scale are thumbnail sketches of how students' performances look along the continuum.

As with all forms of observation, you will construct a rating scale by first specifying the observable behaviors that are important in a particular context. Perhaps you have a short list of skills that a student is struggling with in a particular academic area. Having selected and defined those skills or behaviors, you will need to construct a rating scale. An easy method for writing the adjectives that will describe the points on the scale is to determine the best and worst likely performances and then choose in-between levels to create the full scale. Making the description as specific as possible enhances accuracy during the rating process.

Figure 7.12 displays a rating scale designed to be used when observing a student working math problems individually. It focuses on three math skills: working on problems, checking work, and correcting mistakes—generalized skills that could be contributing to the student's problems staying on task. This teacher has selected three levels or rating points for use in this rating scale, but the specific points differ for each skill. By creating specific points that are unique to each skill, the teacher has zeroed in as clearly as possible on the behaviors being observed. The result will be detailed information that can be used directly to remediate any problems that are uncovered during the observation.

Numerical Rating Scales The **numerical rating scale** associates numbers with descriptions along the scale. In most cases the higher the number the greater the accomplishment, and lower numbers imply lower accomplishment. Numerical scales are often used when summarizing observations across some period of time. You might use this type of scale after observing a series of discussions over time or after observing student behavior in a classroom over several weeks. For example, the numbered points within a rating scale could be based on the number of times a particular behavior has been noted. This kind of scale then could look as follows: 1 = never; 2 =

Figure 7.12 *Descriptive Rating Scale of Mathematic Skills*

Student _____ Date _____ Assignment: Math Skills

Working on problems	Doesn't start problems	Starts problems, abandons some without finishing	Works each problem until completed
Checking work	Doesn't check work	Checks some work	Checks all work
Correcting mistakes	Doesn't correct mistakes	Corrects some mistakes	Corrects all mistakes
Staying on task	Is distracted several times	Is distracted once	Stays on task during work time

Notes:

sometimes; 3 = usually; 4 = always. Clearly defined **descriptors** enhance the rating process as in the example here:

1 = **Never.** Behavior is not observed.
2 = **Occasionally.** Behavior has been performed, but repeated instances of nonperformances are observed.
3 = **Usually.** Behavior is performed, but a small number of instances of nonperformance are observed.
4 = **Always.** Behavior is consistently and regularly performed.

You should avoid using rating scales with numbers only—that is, without descriptive adjectives associated with each number—because without the adjectives there is no indication as to what differentiates a 3 rating from a 4 rating. It is sometimes recommended to have an even number of points to avoid clustering ratings in the middle.

You should keep one important caution in mind when using numerical rating scales. The numbers in the scale do not necessarily represent equal intervals. That is, it may not be the same distance in terms of skill development if a student moves from a rating of 1 to a rating of 2 as it would be to move from a 2 to a 3 or from a 3 to a 4. The numbers are used in a rating scale almost as if they were a different kind of descriptive adjective

Figure 7.13 *Rating Scale for Cooperative Group Projects*

Group Work Rating Scale

Project _____

Rating Scale

1 = Seldom or never

2 = Some/only part of the time

3 = Usually

4 = Always

	Group 1	**Group 2**	**Group 3**
Stays on task			
Makes progress			
Participates in group			
Respects other groups			
Cleans up			

Notes:

themselves. At the same time, the advantage of using numbers in the scale lies in the ease with which we think about and understand numbers. We are all thoroughly accustomed to recognizing that 4 is larger than 3, 3 is larger than 2, and so on. If the descriptive adjectives used in a particular rating scale are in any way unclear, the numbers remind us instantly which category is which and which direction is "up."

Figure 7.13 is a numerical rating scale for cooperative group work. As students work on the project, the observation focuses on the steps of group dynamics leading to the final project. When the entire class is working on a project or problem in cooperative groups, it is best to target only two or three groups at a time.

You can reuse this rating scale every time students work on projects cooperatively, keeping track of group members as groups rearrange. You will probably find that different mixes of students will show different observed behaviors. As in all group activities, the downside to this type of rating is that not all members may display the same behavior, yet you score the group as a whole.

Figure 7.14 notes how one student is observed performing in a group. This eliminates the problem of assessing the group as a whole. This type

Figure 7.14 *Rating Scale for Evaluating an Individual Group Member*

Group Members _____

Observed Student _____

Date _____ Activity _____

The student . . .	Never	Seldom	Often	Always
Works with a wide range of peers, not just with close friends.				
Shares materials and ideas with others.				
Shows respect for others by listening and considering other points of view.				
Follows group-work rules as established for the activity.				
Fulfills her/his responsibilities in the group.				
Participates in discussions.				
Contributes ideas to the group discussions.				

of single-student observation is time-consuming but provides more detailed information.

Cautions Regarding Interpretation of Observational Data

A basic feature of student observations is relying on personal opinion. Your conclusions are subject to all the characteristic errors of human judgment. By being alert to the following list of errors, you can avoid inadvertently making them during an observation:

- Scoring too leniently or too severely.
- Avoiding the extremes of the scale and scoring at the average.
- Allowing an outstanding or lesser feature of one performance to influence the scoring of other factors.
- Scoring a student lower than average if the previous student observation was outstanding or scoring a student higher than average if the previous student observation was not successful.
- Judging the student according to a personal stereotype or strongly held attitude.

- Judging the student by an initial impression rather than on the basis of multiple observed performances.
- Rating a student more favorably if the student is similar to you in respect to background, attitudes, or ethnicity.
- Forgetting observations if not systematically recorded.

Ask Yourself

Consider what it felt like when you were asked to perform a task in front of another person. Perhaps you had to take a driving test with an examiner sitting next to you. Perhaps you were asked to play a musical instrument in front of judges. Or perhaps you had an opportunity to audition for a play or some other performance. Did this observed experience enable you to perform better or did it cause you to make more errors? What does your experience tell you to do when you wish to observe students perform a task?

Interviews

Interviewing is an interaction in which the teacher presents a student with a planned sequence of questions, listens to the responses, asks further questions, and records data. Often interviews are associated with a particular problem with which the student is struggling. These exchanges can be an important source of information about how the student is forming concepts or using procedures.

Robert Marzano (2000) describes the informal interview as an opportunity for the teacher to probe the students' understanding of a topic in ways that cannot be used effectively with other forms of assessment. He says the informal interview "allows the teacher to pose questions like 'Tell me a little more about that' or 'Explain that to me again but in a different way.' This form of interaction is potentially the most valid type of assessment a classroom teacher can use" (p. 100). Additionally, interviewing students gives you data for modifying or enriching instruction and curriculum. Interviewing can be used with all levels of students, including those who are unable to take paper-and-pencil assessments or who have learning disabilities or disorders. It is especially appropriate with students who appear anxious when speaking in front of the class or who have trouble with writing.

Resource for Your Assessment Toolkit

Self-Assessment Checklist for Sentence-Writing Skills—First Grade

Here is a checklist that the students themselves can use. Even very young students can be encouraged to begin reflecting on their learning and to assess themselves. This kind of checklist will support that kind of reflection.

Name: Date:			
Capitalization	**Sept.**	**Oct.**	**Nov.**
I capitalized the first word of each sentence.			
I capitalized proper names. Ex. _____			
I capitalized proper nouns. Ex. _____			
Description			
I used descriptive words to describe people. Ex. _____			
I used descriptive words to describe things. Ex. _____			
Spelling			
I spelled short words correctly. Ex. _____			
I spelled word wall words correctly. Ex. _____			
Spacing			
I spaced short words correctly. Ex. _____			
I spaced word wall words correctly. Ex. _____			
Sentence Structure			
I had a beginning for all my sentences.			
I had a middle for all my sentences.			
I had an ending for all my sentences.			
I printed all my sentences neatly.			
Punctuation			
I used periods (.) to end my telling (declarative) sentences.			
I used question marks (?) to end my asking (interrogative) sentences.			
I used exclamation points (!) to end my exciting (exclamatory) sentences.			

Interviews provide opportunities to develop rapport with your students as you probe their thinking. As you question a student about how or why she came to a certain conclusion, you learn more about how she thinks, and you can ask follow-up questions to probe more deeply. Besides listening to a student's responses, you have the opportunity to observe him closely. Are there long pauses as he gathers his thoughts? Is he fidgeting in his seat or with a pencil? Does he make eye contact with you? These reactions may give you further insight into a student's abilities and provide you with data that you could not get in other ways.

Using Interviews in Your Classroom

Interviews can be structured or unstructured. In **unstructured interviews** the teacher asks developmentally appropriate questions that occur naturally in the conversation. These interviews evolve depending on the student's responses to questions. In **structured interviews** the teacher has prepared the questions in advance. Here are some tips for preparing questions:

- Word your questions so the students can easily comprehend what type of information is required.
- Do not deviate from standard classroom vocabulary.
- Let students know before the interview that they are free to ask for clarification of a question if they do not understand it.
- Use open-ended questions so the answers are not predetermined, and the students can respond in their own terms. Avoid questions that can be answered yes or no.

Begin all student interviews that have the same purpose by using the same directions and materials. This will help standardize the procedures and validate the data you gather from the interviews, even though you will modify your questions with each individual as you follow up on his or her responses.

Make sure to give the student enough time to formulate a response. Do not rush. If the student appears unable to reply to a question, wait several moments before you move on to the next question. Much of the value of the interview process comes from allowing the student to set the pace.

Decide how you will record the interview. You can use any of the observational methods we have discussed—anecdotal records, checklists, or rating scales—as a data collection tool for your interview. You may only be able to take brief notes during the interview to avoid interrupting the student's flow of thoughts. You can then transfer your notes from the interview to the tool you selected after the interview is completed. If your school permits, you might consider recording or videotaping the session. You will probably only want to record the most critical or difficult interviews, however, as every recording will have to be viewed or listened to again in order to gather your data, doubling the time you spend.

Some students may feel intimidated when you question them individually, but they usually enjoy sharing their experiences with each other. In this case, you may want to consider having students ask each other the questions while you listen to the responses. Students also enjoy sharing with their peers how they solved a problem or got an answer. Questions that ask students to describe how something they read in a story or studied in science or social studies relates to their lives can help students exhibit their learning. When teachers treat student-to-student interviews seriously, a spirit of cooperation and openness develops. Make sure students are comfortable with this arrangement and give classroom practice as needed.

Interviews also allow teachers to address higher-order thinking skills and essential questions that unlock understanding. Since time is limited, interviews could address the higher levels of comprehension, analysis, synthesis, and evaluation. Figure 7.15 gives a list of questions that encourage students to go beyond recall of facts.

Figure 7.16 gives a list of questions for a student interview about mathematics problem-solving skills. After giving the student a specific problem to solve, the teacher would use these questions to allow students to share their abilities, to explain what they are thinking, to clarify their approach, and to display creativity. Further probing questions would accommodate individual differences. This process can be repeated at

Figure 7.15 *Interview Questions Focused on a Book Report*

1. How do you *interpret* the protagonist's actions?
2. How would you *compare* the feelings of the protagonist and the antagonist?
3. How would you *explain* the major conflict in the story?
4. How did the author *relate* the theme of the novel to a current problem?
5. How would you *judge* the impact of this novel with the impact of the last novel we read?
6. *Analyze* the characters in the books and *explain* which one you admire most? Which one do you admire least?

Figure 7.16 *Interview Questions Focused on Problem Solving*

> 1. In your own words, state the problem that you are trying to solve.
> 2. What are you trying to find or do?
> 3. What information do you know from the problem?
> 4. What information, if any, is either missing or not needed?
> 5. Is there any kind of pattern? Describe it to me.
> 6. Are your calculations accurate? Explain how you computed.
> 7. Identify the strategy you used to solve the problem.
> 8. Did you check each step? Explain how you did that.
> 9. Is your answer reasonable? Why do you think so?
> 10. Is there another way you could have solved this problem? Explain it to me.

regular intervals as you introduce new problem-solving strategies in your instruction.

Again, you could record the student's responses on an anecdotal note card (Figure 7.17), an observation checklist (Figure 7.18), or an observation rating scale (Figure 7.19). You will notice that all three tools list the same skills, but the depth and breadth of the scoring differs for each tool. Each of the tools could also be used by the students to observe one another rehearse for the interview. This would give you an opportunity to make informal classroom observations and provide further learning opportunities for the students.

Figure 7.17 *Anecdotal Record as a Scoring Tool for a Mathematics Problem-Solving Interview*

> **Student** _____   **Date** _____
>
> **Observer** _____   **Time** _____
>
> **Mathematics Problem-Solving Interview** (attach copy of problem)
>
> Choice of Problem-Solving Strategy:
>
> Mathematics Concepts:
>
> Mathematical Reasoning:
>
> Explanation of Steps:
>
> Use of Mathematical Terminology:
>
> Other Notes or Comments:

Figure 7.18 *Checklist as a Scoring Tool for a Mathematics Problem-Solving Interview*

Mathematics Problem-Solving Interview (attach copy of problem)

Student _____   **Date** _____

Task/Activity _____

Interviewer _____

Check YES if skill is observed (✓): *The student . . .*

_____ Selects an efficient problem-solving strategy.

_____ Shows understanding of the mathematics concepts used to solve the problem.

_____ Uses skillful mathematical reasoning.

_____ Gives clear explanation of problem-solving method.

_____ Uses correct terminology to clarify explanations.

Notes:

The interview process can also be used informally with individual students or groups of students to review evaluations from other observation formats. Although interviews can be time-consuming, certain assessment objectives can be better achieved by student interview than by other techniques. Process objectives that focus on understanding the way students solved a problem lend themselves to interviews because the interview setting allows students to use words, drawings, and manipulatives to display their thinking. As the teacher listens and observes the child, misconceptions and erroneous strategies are uncovered and used to inform future teaching strategies. Moreover, when you have differentiated both your instruction and assessments, students will have selected product and performance options to meet their interests or abilities. Interviews allow teachers to ask specific questions to assess each student's level of understanding related to the tasks.

Processing questions require students to use metacognition as they reflect and adjust their thinking. Reflective questions listed in Figure 7.20 could be used as part of interviews to encourage students to transfer their learning beyond the academic content and make connections between their learned knowledge and their lives.

In addition, students with limited English skills or weak writing skills may not be able to explain their deep understanding of key concepts in a

Figure 7.19 *Rating Scale as a Scoring Tool for a Mathematics Problem-Solving Interview*

Mathematics Problem Solving Interview (attach copy of problem)

Student _____   Date _____

Observer _____   Time _____

Scoring Guide

B = Beginning learner

D = Developing learner

M = Meets expectations

E = Exceeds expectations

Skills: *The student . . .*	B	D	M	E
Selects an efficient problem-solving strategy.				
Shows understanding of the mathematics concepts used to solve the problem.				
Uses skillful mathematical reasoning.				
Gives clear explanation of problem-solving steps.				
Uses correct terminology to clarify explanations.				

Notes or comments:

Figure 7.20 *Reflective Questions for Interviews*

1. How would you change your project/performance if you did it over?
2. Compare this project or performance to another one you have done.
3. How does what you have learned connect to your learning in other subject areas?
4. What have you learned that has changed your thinking about this?
5. Explain what you feel is the big idea of this assignment.

written essay. Therefore, the interview allows them to express their ideas orally without being penalized for their language or writing weaknesses, organizational challenges, or time management skills. Interviews help balance the assessment opportunities for all students.

Conducting Reliable, Valid Interviews

The guidelines we have discussed earlier in this chapter are relevant here in making your interviews reliable and valid. Planning carefully, selecting a manageable chunk of material, and immediate recording of answers are all important. In the case of interviews, your planning will focus on the questions you want to ask, of course, but you also need to consider the context that will make the student most comfortable in responding to you. You need to think carefully about the way you set the context to elicit the student's best cooperation. You need to create a data collection tool that can be easily used while interviewing, and you need to practice with the tool you create. And, while interviewing, you need to focus carefully to avoid distractions. Review your notes as soon as possible and add to them where needed to make them as complete as you can. You need to be certain they will be fully understandable when you read them at a later time.

Ask Yourself

Interviews can be a powerful tool for uncovering what students know or do not know. However, the key to a successful interview is to enable the student to talk freely and without fear. How might you help students express their feelings and points of view freely? Think about your response to interviews. What things made you feel more at ease? What things made you hold back?

Summary

- Observation is the process of gaining information by watching and listening to students.
- Observation techniques can be used to evaluate students' knowledge, skills, dispositions, and behaviors.
- Observations based on standards can provide important insights into students' abilities.
- It takes time to fairly and equally observe all students and keep records of the data obtained.
- You can strengthen the reliability and validity of observations by using a clear, concise scoring tool that defines the desired performance criteria in observable, measurable terms.
- You can align your performance criteria to your state standards.

- Anecdotal notes, checklists, and rating scales are scoring tools that you can create, modify, and reuse to evaluate specific student skills and behaviors.
- Teachers can probe a student's thinking through interviews and record the observed data on a scoring tool that can be repeated at specific intervals to show growth.
- Data gained from observations should be combined with other forms of assessment to gain a clear picture of a student's abilities.
- Students can use the feedback from checklists and interviews to reflect on their learning and make appropriate adjustments to meet their goals and standards.

Key Terms

academic skills (168)

anecdotal notes or records (173)

descriptive rating scale (186)

descriptors (187)

interviewing (190)

numerical rating scale (186)

observation (164)

observation checklist (177)

observation validity (171)

rating scale (184)

prosocial skills (168)

psychomotor skills (168)

structured interviews (192)

unstructured interviews (192)

For Further Discussion

1. What do you see as the most important advantages and disadvantages of using observational methods compared to more traditional paper-and-pencil assessments?

2. Name three dimensions of an academic or physical skill of your choice and determine the specific behaviors that compose each skill.

3. List five prosocial behaviors that would be beneficial for you to record through direct observation. What problems might you encounter in defining these behaviors for observation?

4. Think of a task that your students perform on a regular basis, such as setting up a lab experiment or writing a journal entry. Create a checklist of all the steps the students need to carry out to complete the task.

5. How can self-assessment checklists help students take ownership of their learning?

Comprehension Quiz

Each observational scoring tool below has one or more design errors. Identify each flaw and correct it.

1. Anecdotal Record of Observed Student Behavior

Student _____Juanita_____ **Date** ___9/16/2005___

Observer ___Ms. Dayton___ **Grade** ____6th____

Juanita has not answered any math problems correctly. I am very upset that she doesn't respond to my help. I think she is pretending not to understand me so she can get out of doing her work. I am going to assign her more problems until she understands that she must do her work.

2. Checklist of Observed Student Reading Skills

Fifth-Grade Reading Comprehension Skills

Name _____ **Date** _____

Check YES if the learner can perform the step (✓)

_____ **1.** Likes to read.

_____ **2.** Reads at home.

_____ **3.** Identifies main characters.

_____ **4.** Identifies plot, setting, and conflict.

_____ **5.** Identifies genre.

_____ **6.** Reads for pleasure.

_____ **7.** Summarizes story events.

_____ **8.** Uses neat handwriting.

3. Rating Scale for Observing

Rating Scale for Observing Inappropriate Student Behavior

Name _____   **Date** _____

	1	2	3	4
1. Interrupts others.				
2. Argues with others.				
3. Talks too much.				
4. Is easily distracted.				
5. Fidgets with hands or feet or squirms in seat.				
6. Blames others for his/her mistakes or misbehavior.				
7. Refuses to comply with adults' requests or rules.				

	1	2	3	4
8. Does not listen.				
9. Blurts out answers before questions have been completed.				
10. Has difficulty playing quietly.				
11. Makes careless mistakes in schoolwork.				
12. Is angry or resentful.				
13. Leaves seat in classroom.				
14. Fails to finish schoolwork.				

Relevant Website Resources

Alaska Department of Education and Early Development

http://www.eed.state.ak.us/tls/frameworks/langarts/42tools.htm

The Alaska site includes examples of observation checklists for writing conferences, reading conferences, listening skills, anecdotal notes, six-trait writing, oral presentations, and group projects.

Center for Evidence-Based Practice: Young Children with Challenging Behavior

http://challengingbehavior.fmhi.usf.edu/fba.htm

This website from the University of South Florida contains information about Functional Behavior Assessment, a process that helps develop an understanding of children's misbehavior in specific situations. The process involves collecting information through interviews, using behavior rating scales, and recording setting, antecedents, behaviors, and consequences in order to determine what conditions reliably predict the occurrence of the child's challenging behavior.

Center for Information and Research on Civic Learning and Engagement (CIRCLE)

http://www.civicyouth.org/PopUps/Chi_checklist.doc

This site includes student observation checklists for civic skills and behaviors such as personal responsibility, caring for the community, leadership, and caring for others. The checklists are arranged by grade levels K–1, 2–3, and 4–5. The checklists are designed to help teachers document student civic development.

National Science Teachers Association

http://www.nsta.org/main/news/stories/science_and_children.php?news_story_ID=52414

The National Science Teachers Association (NSTA) site includes tools teachers can use to assess students in science. The article "Unlocking the Power of Observation" by Karen L. Anderson, Dean M. Martin, and Ellen E. Faszewski shows how to use checklists to help kindergarten through second-grade learners, particularly students with limited English language skills. It includes an assessment checklist and rubric to assess students' abilities to use their powers of observation.

TERC

http://www.terc.edu

The TERC website focuses on research-based materials based on national and state standards in mathematics and science. The performance tasks (some are in Spanish) target data literacy, scientific process, problem solving, evidence-based decision making, mathematical fluency, an understanding of the natural world, and student reflections on their own learning.

References

Burke, K. (2005). *How to assess authentic learning*, 4th ed. Thousand Oaks, CA: Corwin Press/Sage.

Burke, K. (2006). *From standards to rubrics in six steps: Tools for assessing student learning, K–8*. Thousand Oaks, CA: Corwin Press/Sage.

Burke. K. (2008). *What to do with the kid who . . . Developing cooperation, self-discipline, and responsibility in the classroom*, 3rd ed. Thousand Oaks, CA: Corwin Press/Sage.

Carr, E. G., Levin, L., McConnachie, G., Carlson, J. I., Kemp, D. C., & Smith, C. E. (1994). *Communication-based interventions for problem behavior: A user's guide for producing behavior change*. Baltimore: Paul H. Brookes.

Costa, A. L., & Kallick, B. (2004). *Assessment strategies for self-directed learning*. Thousand Oaks, CA: Corwin Press/Sage.

Fancher, R. E. (1985). *The intelligence men: Makers of the IQ controversy*. New York: Norton. Quoted at "Human Intelligence: Alfred Binet," http://www.indiana.edu/~intell/binet.shtml. Accessed June 5, 2007.

Guskey, T. R. (2000). *Evaluating professional development*. Thousand Oaks, CA: Corwin Press/Sage.

Hieneman, M., Nolan, M., Presley, J., De Turo, L., Robertson, W., & Dunlap, G. (1999). *Facilitator's Guide: Positive behavioral support*. Positive Behavioral Support Project, Florida Department of Education.

Johnson, D. W., & Johnson, R. T. (1989). *Cooperation and competition: Theory and research*. Edina, MN: Interaction Book Company.

Johnson, D. W., & Johnson, R. T. (1995). *Teaching students to be peacemakers*, 3rd ed. Edina, MN: Interaction Book Company.

Johnson, D. W., Johnson, R. T., & Holubec, E. J. (1993). *Cooperation in the classroom*, 6th ed. Edina, MN: Interaction Book Company.

Marzano, R. J., (2000). *Transforming classroom grading*. Alexandria, VA: Association for Supervision and Curriculum Development.

O'Neill, R. E., Horner, R. H., Albin, R. W., Sprague, J, R., Storey, K., & Newton, J. S. (1997). *Functional assessment and program development for problem behavior. A practical handbook*. Pacific Grove, CA: Brooks/Cole.

Stiggins, R. (2004). New assessment beliefs for a new school mission. *Phi Delta Kappan, 86*(1), 22–27.

CHAPTER 8

Performance-Based Assessment

Chapter Objectives

After reading and thinking about this chapter, you will be able to:

- **Define performance-based assessment.**
- **Describe what contributes to authenticity in performance tasks.**
- **Describe the many types of performance tasks.**
- **Discuss the strengths and limitations of performance assessments.**

- **Explain the steps in developing performance assessments.**
- **Construct a performance-assessment task and tools for scoring the task.**

John Dewey (1916) argued that "plays, games, and constructive occupations" are often a means of relieving students and teachers of the tedium and strain of regular schoolwork. Could this statement be applied to schools today? In *Democracy and Education,* Dewey contends that school should engage and sustain students' interests by opening up real-world opportunities for them. How much more motivated might our students be if their schoolwork allowed them to show skills directly related to their areas of deepest interest? In this chapter, we will consider performance assessment. As you think about this as a concept and practice, consider Dewey's recommendation from nearly a century ago.

The formal measurement of human accomplishment has had a lengthy history. Performance examinations date back at least to 2200 B.C.E. when they were used for entry into the Chinese civil service and involved demonstrations of skill in the arts of music, archery, horsemanship, writing, arithmetic, and rituals and ceremonies. Today, performance assessments are used to determine if an adult has achieved competence in a profession. For example, toward the end of their formal education, prospective teachers are evaluated on their student teaching, medical students are assessed during their hospital-based internship, and fine arts students are judged on their one-person show.

Having students perform tasks in an authentic setting provides evidence of what the students know and can do. In fact, in Chapter 1, assessment is described as the art of placing learners in a context that brings out or clarifies what it is a learner knows and can do, as well as what a learner may not know or be able to do. This underlying concept of assessment is especially true for performance assessment because the context is so close to the circumstances of real life. Also, since the context itself is so realistic, students recognize the relevance of their work. The assessor can sit beside, observe, interview, and gather evidence naturalistically as the student performs.

Foundational Questions for Your Consideration

- Do you believe that you display your abilities more fully in front of an audience or in the privacy of your own office or room?
- Why do schools spend so much time on drill and practice rather than allowing students to learn by playing the game or performing?
- When should students be permitted to investigate real multidimensional problems rather than simulations?

The Characteristics of Performance-Based Assessment

Performance-based assessments are at the heart of meaningful assessment because they require students to show what they know and can do through projects, performances, exhibits, or work samples. Students tend to be more motivated and involved when they are allowed to perform according to their own plan, collect data, infer a pattern, draw conclusions, take a stand, or deliver a presentation. Performance assessments motivate students to learn.

Matching performance assessments to classroom goals and learning objectives is challenging. This challenge stems from the increased freedom that performance assessments often provide students to display and communicate their understandings and skills. You will need to target your standards and curriculum goals, but you also will want to select topics that interest your students so they become active participants in their own learning. This section reviews the characteristics of a performance-based assessment and examines the strengths and weaknesses of such an approach.

What Is Performance-Based Assessment?

Any assessment can be considered a type of performance when a student is placed in some context and asked to show what they know or can do in that context. The performance assessment that you are very familiar with is the driving test that most of us took to get a driver's license. What does a performance assessment look like in a classroom? How would it differ from other kinds of tests or assessments?

Consider the situation in which students are given an essay test and asked to show what they know through a written response to a question. We call the final written response the **product**. Such written assessments give evidence of the student's thinking, knowledge, and expressive skills. But they do not tap the many related writing and thinking procedural skills such as choosing a topic, developing a plan, gathering information and evidence, preparing drafts, critiquing one's work, revising, and ultimately rewriting and rethinking. We use the term **process skills** to describe those skills and procedures that are used to create the final product.

Because paper-and-pencil tests limit the ways that students display the thinking processes and procedures that they use, we do not label such written tests performance assessments. Rather, we reserve the term *performance* for assessment tasks that allow students to show both the products and the processes behind them.

Performance-based assessments are tasks that permit students to show in front of an observer and/or an audience both the processes that they use and the products that they create. Types of activities that qualify as performance-based assessments include developing and writing a research report, solving a multi-step problem, conducting an experiment or investigation, preparing a demonstration, debating an issue, constructing a model, or creating a multimedia presentation. A performance assessment requires the student to "actively accomplish complex and significant tasks, while bringing to bear prior knowledge, recent learning, and relevant skills to solve realistic problems" (Herman, Aschbacher, & Winters, 1992, p. 2). These assessments challenge students to explore and solve open-ended, complex problems. They give teachers the opportunity to evaluate a cognitive skill while it is being performed.

Authenticity and Performance Assessment

Good performance assessments are characterized by tasks that are as authentic or natural as possible. **Authentic tasks** are similar to the activities that practicing professionals perform or that naturally relate to daily living. For example, an authentic **performance task** in science would generally include the development of some question or hypothesis, the selection of a set of observations that relate to the questions, the collection of carefully measured or described data, the interpretation of those data, and the determination of a conclusion or the development of another question. These are the steps similar to what a scientist does during research.

An authentic performance in music might include the writing of an original piece of music, the presentation of a musical piece in front of an audience, or the development of a musical score for a play or film. An authentic performance in writing might entail the writing of a letter to a real person, writing an article for a newspaper, creating a blog, writing a poem for a public reading, or writing an instruction manual for a product. An authentic performance in history might include examining and analyzing documents from a specific historical period, writing a paper that identifies cause-and-effect relationships or a set of reasons that account for actions or events, or developing and clarifying a position or argument that is presented to others for discussion.

Authentic tasks that relate to daily living include the development of a household budget, the completion of a mortgage application, planning the purchase and financing of a car, the preparation of a nutritious meal, the development of a plan to care for a new pet, or the planning of a travel route from home to a vacation spot.

The key to authenticity is that the performance task has a specific, meaningful purpose that relates to the activities of daily life or the daily world of work. This stands in contrast to a single-focused or restricted type of performance task that focuses on a single activity such as reciting the alphabet, naming state capitals, or drawing a graph. Although there is nothing wrong with such performances, they do not possess the added motivation that often accompanies a task that has a larger, more authentic, purpose. Figure 8.1 lists other examples of authentic performance tasks you could assign students.

The best performance assessment tasks are interesting, worthwhile activities that relate to instructional outcomes and allow students to

Figure 8.1 *Examples of Authentic Performance Tasks*

1. Prepare a marketing campaign for launching a new product.
2. Create a financial plan for 4 years of college that takes into account all expenses (tuition, room and board, books) and all sources of income (scholarship, loan, earnings from jobs).
3. Write a proposal to the city council advocating a new park in the downtown area.
4. Create a brochure that informs students about the symptoms and treatments for a specific disease.
5. Create a 30-second videotaped commercial for a political candidate that focuses on his or her platform.
6. Prepare a 5-day nutritious menu to share with the cafeteria manager.

demonstrate what they know and can do. Students will perform best when they can:

- Experience an interactive learning condition
- Talk with others about their understandings
- Monitor their own progress using scoring guides
- Have clear expectations for the quality of their work
- Learn that the knowledge can be transferred to other situations

Many complex learning targets require more than one task to demonstrate a student's skills and abilities. A complex, multiply focused, task needs to be subdivided into smaller tasks. For example, in order to organize material for the speech comparing two styles of art, the students might do research on the Internet, develop and implement a survey, and then fill in required information on a graphic organizer.

This complex performance would also require a variety of assessment tools to adequately collect the evidence that relates to the many different skills that students may demonstrate. For example, as students conduct Internet searches, you could require that they place their notes in a database and that they evaluate the validity of each citation. You could then review these citations and determine if students adequately critique sources drawn from the Internet. You could require students to document the steps that they employed to write a clear survey as well as the sampling technique they used to make certain that the sample is not biased. The student might practice her or his speech with partners or small groups who use peer evaluation checklists to offer feedback and reinforcement on the content and delivery of the talk. You could evaluate the graphic organizer for accuracy, and you could evaluate the speech for clarity, conciseness, accuracy, and organization.

Figure 8.2 is an example of an elementary-level performance assessment that is authentic to the lives of young students. The performance focuses on a variety of mathematical skills while authentically including the communication skill of letter writing.

If we advocate the use of more authentic performance assessments, teachers may need to change the way that they teach content and skills. If a teacher employs drill and practice of separate skills and content pieces, students will not necessarily be able to show what they have learned when asked to display these skills and content pieces in an authentic performance context.

To help make this clear, Figure 8.3 presents a continuum of context types ranging from simple to complex. These context types relate to different settings that occur throughout everyday life. For example, in everyday living, there are moments or contexts that are solitary, quiet, and allow for focused concentration (like cataloguing the wildflowers in a forest preserve). There are also moments that are just the opposite: filled with activity, noise, multiple demands, and a bit of chaos (like coaching a team of ballplayers

Figure 8.2 *Example of an Authentic Task: Selecting Fish for an Aquarium*

Your school principal sends you this letter that asks you to do a special job.

Dear Students,

Your class will be getting a 30-gallon aquarium. The class will have $25.00 to spend on fish. You will plan which fish to buy.

Use the *Choosing Fish for Your Aquarium* brochure to help you choose the fish. The brochure tells you things you must know about the size of the fish, how much they cost, and their special needs.

Choose as many different kinds of fish as you can. Then write a letter to me explaining which fish you have chosen. In your letter make certain that you do the following.

1. Tell me how many of each kind of fish to buy.

2. Give the reasons you chose those fish.

3. Show that you are not overspending.

4. Show that the fish will not be too crowded in the aquarium.

I hope to receive your letters by next week.

Sincerely,

Your Principal

Source: NCEE, 1997.

at a competitive game). Alongside these life contexts, we have identified learning approaches that match each context type in a classroom setting. Without context, students are often not able to apply what they learn in school to the authentic contexts of the world of work and daily living. If teachers restrict their students to assessments that require simple recall or are only in narrow and carefully structured academic contexts, they may not fully prepare their students for the authentic context of the world of practicing professionals and daily life.

Issues to Consider in Developing Performance Tasks

There are two issues in particular that affect the development of assessment tasks: complexity and focus. Some performances are singly focused and highly restricted while other performances are multiply focused and complex. Both

Figure 8.2A *Choosing Fish for Your Aquarium*

Choosing Fish for Your Aquarium

Planning Ahead

Use the information in this brochure to help you choose fish that will be happy and healthy in your aquarium. To choose your fish, you must know about the size of the fish, their cost, and their special needs.

Size of Fish

To be healthy, fish need enough room to swim and move around. A good rule is to have 1 inch of fish for each gallon of water in your aquarium. This means that in a 10-gallon aquarium, the lengths of all your fish added up can be 10 inches at the most.

Example:

With a 10-gallon aquarium, here are a few of your choices:

One 10-inch long fish, or   a 7-inch long fish   5 fish if each is and a 3-inch long fish, or   only 2 inches long.

10 inches   10 inches   10 inches

Cost of the fish

Some fish cost as little as $1, others cost much more. The prices of each kind of fish are listed in the chart.

Source: NCEE, 1997.

Special Needs

Use the chart to learn about the special needs of each kind of fish. Some fish need to live together in schools—a group of four or more of the same kind of fish—while other live in pairs or alone. A few kinds of fish have other special needs, which are listed in the chart.

Alone   Pair   School

---

the complexity of the task requirements and the focus of the performance interact and shape the final assessment context.

Singly focused tasks include tying a shoe, solving an equation, reading a story with expression, calibrating a piece of science equipment, measuring a distance, running a mile, or shooting a basket from the free-throw line. This single focus implies that the task is restricted in nature. The student is expected to focus on this single task and is restricted to that task alone.

Often singly focused tasks contain very clear, specific directions. There are usually few opportunities for the performer to make individual decisions concerning the process that is to be used or the product that is to be developed. In order to make sure that your singly focused task is truly a performance task, be certain that you are asking students to think for themselves,

Figure 8.2B *Freshwater Fish Chart*

Name	Cost	Length in Inches	Color	Special Needs, Facts
Zebra Danilo	$1	1 1/2 inches	Blue with gold lines	Lives in schools; gets along with other kinds of fish.
Marbled Hatchetfish	$1	2 inches	Yellow	Lives in schools; can leap 3–5 yards.
Guppy	2 for $3	2 inches	Red, blue, and green	Lives in schools.
Red-Tailed Black Shark	$5	4 1/2 inches	Black with red tail	Fights with other sharks, but gets along with other kinds of fish.
Cardinal Tetra	$5	1 1/2 inches	Red and green	Lives in schools.
Blind Cave Fish	$2	3 inches	Silvery rose	Lives in schools; uses its sense of smell and vibration to find food.
Ramirez' Dwarf Cichlid	$5	2 inches	Rainbow	Lives in pairs; rarely lives longer than 2 1/2 years; gets along with other fish.
Velvet Cichlid	$5	12 1/2 inches	Olive with stripes	Can be trained to take food from the hand and can be petted. Must be kept only with other Cichlids.

Source: NCEE, 1997.

not simply to follow a set of directions. Figure 8.4 is an example of a singly focused performance task to assess students' ability to calibrate a balance and determine the mass of several objects.

Multiply focused tasks encompass a variety of related tasks that work together to complete a larger action like solving a problem, making a decision, or developing a position about a complex issue. In such multiply focused tasks, students may have to decide what precise method needs to be employed, or what the final product should look like, or how they will get the necessary information to determine an answer. These multiply focused tasks are more likely to be authentic performances because they are closer to the working world of professionals and the complexities of daily life.

Figure 8.3 *Relationship Between Context Types and Learning Approaches*

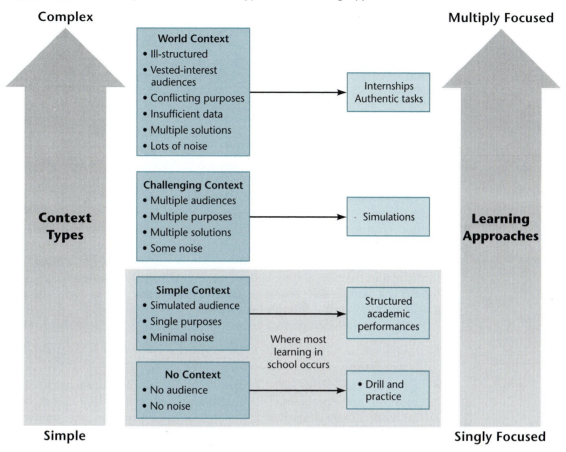

Source: Wiggins, 1995.

Types of Performance Assessment Tasks

The specific focus of a performance often relates to the final product that must be completed or developed. Is the product a solution to a problem? Is the final product a demonstration, a recital, a debate? In addition to the complexity of a performance, these different end products influence the types of thinking and procedures required by the performance task. So, it is worthwhile to consider each separately.

Tasks Focused on Solving a Problem Educators often mention the importance of teaching students to be critical thinkers and problem solvers. Instruction in these areas, however, is often limited to highly restricted problems with focused answers. Think of many word problems. Such problems ask students to focus on an artificial situation and then find a specific

Figure 8.4 *An Example of a Singly Focused Performance Assessment*

Task: The Student Council collected $100 to buy songs for the iPod in the cafeteria. Each homeroom will conduct a survey to find out what types of music (jazz, hip-hop, classical, R&B, country, rock, or Latin) students prefer. You will 1) plan and create a table to record all data you collect; 2) collect data in an organized format (table, frequency table); and 3) draw a bar graph to represent your data. The officers will compile the results and buy the songs you want to hear!

answer. Using this type of teaching approach does relate to problem solving and critical thinking, but it is limited.

Problem-based learning (PBL) was developed to provide a learning and assessment approach that requires students to do more than answer a focused question. In problem-based learning and assessment, students are asked to make sense of complex, ill-structured problems found within the curriculum (Barell, 2003; Sagor, 2003). The structure of a problem-based learning unit matches the structure of many performance assessments. Figure 8.5 is a sample PBL problem. The problem is relevant to students, and it asks them to craft a thoughtful solution.

In the school lunch problem scenario, students would follow these steps:

- *Clarify and identify the problem.* For example, "we need healthy food that tastes good."

- *Develop a plan.* They would plan a way to gather data to help find a solution to the problem. They might create a brochure that lists calorie, fat, and carbohydrate content for all foods and design other methods to involve the rest of the student body.

Figure 8.5 *PBL Scenario: The School Lunch Problem*

Problem Scenario

The principal has asked you to become a member of her new high school lunch task force. Parents were concerned about the media reports of teenage obesity, and they requested that the high school eliminate many foods from the cafeteria and substitute healthier choices.

Unfortunately, the students have refused to eat many of the new healthy items, and the cafeteria manager is losing revenue. Your job as a member of this task force is to investigate the problem and propose possible solutions to the Parent Teacher Organization at their next meeting.

- *Collect data.* Perhaps they would prepare a questionnaire about food choices to give to all students. Or they might interview students identified as taste testers, or interview students found eating in the cafeteria or leaving campus to eat elsewhere.

- *Analyze and synthesize the data.* They would decide on an appropriate way to summarize their findings. They would probably plan to identify some favorite tasty choices that are also healthy and would present the findings using charts or graphs.

- *Communicate a decision or result.* One option would be to prepare a Power-Point presentation for parents to show the results of their research.

Figure 8.6 illustrates key places where specific types of assessment could fit naturally. It displays how each of the five direction-setting events in solving

Figure 8.6 *Natural Assessment Opportunities in Solving a Problem*

PBL Event	Student Product	Assessment Opportunities	Assessment Criteria
Problem clarification and identification *Teacher role: Read and listen to students present individual problem statements*	Problem statement	Journal entry Problem map Oral presentation Poster abstract	Statement displays • Nature of problem • Problem complexity • Operational definition • Solvability
Plan development *Teacher role: Review tasks and listen to students clarifying plans*	Plan	Task analysis timeline GANT chart Flowchart Steps Proposal Budget	Tasks are • Comprehensive • Logical • Clear • Related to problem Extraneous variables are controlled
Data collection and inference testing *Teacher role: Observe, review notes and data, and read journals*	Data records Use of tools Practice of skills	Tables Charts Field notes Microscope use Balance use Instrumentation Interviews Observations Quizzes using notes	• Records data accurately • Uses tools correctly • Practices skills precisely

(Continued)

Figure 8.6 *Natural Assessment Opportunities in Solving a Problem (continued)*

PBL Event	Student Product	Assessment Opportunities	Assessment Criteria
Data analysis *Teacher role: Read and review tables*	Summary of findings Frequency tables Statistical tables	Summary statements with supporting data Compiled evidence	Statistical techniques are correct Interpretations are logical Presentation is collaborative
Synthesizing capstone performance *Teacher role: Develop a clear scoring guide Review final product*	Exhibition/Recital	News article Decision Recommendation Argument Speech Debate Invention Poem	Solution or decision relates to the problem definition Solution incorporates problem parameters

a problem can be developed into different assessment opportunities. Of course, these assessment opportunities are only available for students to receive feedback if the teacher has designed these assessments in advance. The chart shows how problem-solving events that naturally occur as a project progresses can be transformed into assessment opportunities or episodes by the teacher.

Tasks Focused on Completing an Inquiry Inquiry is a common theme for many authentic performances. An **inquiry task** is one in which students are asked to collect data in order to develop their understanding about a topic or issue. For example, an inquiry might focus on the causes of the Civil War or the relationship between sunlight and plant growth or graphing the performance of a set of stocks over time. Generally, an inquiry requires the development of an operational question, a prediction, or a hypothesis. Based on the operational question or prediction, students determine what data are needed and under what conditions that data should be collected. Students then collect firsthand data, develop data tables, infer patterns, and develop a conclusion. Examples of inquiries include science observations and investigations, social science surveys and interviews, history investigations, and research projects across a variety of disciplines.

Tasks Focused on Determining a Position Closely related to problem-solving performances are tasks that require students to make a decision or clarify a

Resource for Your Assessment Toolkit
Social Studies Performance Task

Standard: Understand the various roles and influences of interest groups in the political system. **Performance Task:** *Your Candidate Needs You!* This is an election year and our class has been asked to help one candidate analyze the opinions of the voters in our community. Because of your expertise in the political process, you have been asked to analyze the roles and influences of various individuals, groups, and media in shaping opinions. The candidate is interested in finding out how the general public, special interest groups, the media, and especially young people voting for the first time feel about the issues of: *immigration, healthcare, global warming, the war, and education.* You may select the issue that most concerns you and then work in teams to: 1) develop a questionnaire about the issue to distribute to members of the community; 2) prepare interview questions to use with people selected for a focus group on your issue; 3) interview reporters and political commentators from the local radio and television stations to find out how they shape public opinion; and 4) draft a political brief describing the perspectives of various socioeconomic, cultural, political, and age groups regarding your issue. Be prepared to present a 5-minute multimedia presentation recommending the stand the candidate should take on your controversial issue when the candidate and political advisors visit class.

You will be assessed on and provided with a detailed scoring procedure for the following:

Content Standards: Your understanding of how power and vested interest influence the type of argument and claims that are used to support arguments for or against a contested public issue.

Support: Your ability to provide sufficient and appropriate evidence for a claim.

Effective Communication: Your ability to effectively communicate through a variety of media.

position. This type of task often focuses on some urgent need to make a decision about an issue that is not fully understood. The key processes of such a task are gathering relevant information, evaluating different points of view, and determining a decision that is supported by evidence and logic. Examples of such tasks include selecting a candidate running for political office based on some platform, determining a course of action in response to a crisis, determining if it is wise to purchase a house or rent an apartment, developing a nutrition plan appropriate to your lifestyle, or constructing an argument on a controversial issue.

Demonstration Tasks Students explain or describe how something works or how to do something when they perform a **demonstration task**. The basic classroom task of coming up to the front board to demonstrate and explain the solution of a mathematics problem is a demonstration. Other applications include demonstrating the steps of CPR, or teaching others how to care for a pet, or explaining safety procedures prior to using a heat source. The focus of demonstration tasks is accuracy in clarifying the steps of a process as well as careful reasoning concerning the rationale for each step of the process.

Tasks Focused on Developing Exhibits **Exhibits** are visual presentations or displays that need little or no explanation from the creators. An exhibit is offered to explain, demonstrate, or show something. Classroom applications include a collage of words and pictures that represent an author's ideas from a given text, a bulletin board detailing the life of a famous athlete, a poster of the food guide pyramid, or a painting or set of drawings.

Presentation Tasks A **presentation task** is a work or task performed in front of an audience. Students make presentations when they act out a story, play a self-made instrument, give an oral book review, perform a cartwheel on the balance beam with a full turn dismount, or sing a theme song in the beginning chorus class.

Capstone Performances **Capstone performances** are those that most often occur at the end of a program of study and enable students to show knowledge and skills in a context that matches the world of practicing professionals. Capstone performances include science fair projects and participating in sports contests, as well as internships, student teaching, and one-person art shows.

Strengths and Limitations of Performance Assessment

We have explored the characteristics of performance assessment, and we have examined the impact that such assessments have on the very nature of teaching and learning. Such an examination gives a preview of the strengths of using performance assessments as well as the difficulties that such assessment imposes.

Strengths Performance assessments offer a clear and direct way to assess what students know and can do within a variety of realistic contexts. Authentic performance tasks are an opportunity for students to show integration of knowledge, skill, and abilities because they provide enough challenge and openness for students to construct their response and to draw from multiple disciplines. Performance assessments allow students to exhibit their ability to "do something on their own." They challenge students to use higher levels of thinking, and they prepare students to transfer those skills outside of the classroom. And, as a bonus for teachers, performance assessments measure multiple outcomes involving both knowledge and skills.

Limitations Performance assessments take a great deal of time to construct, complete, and score. The scores on one task provide little information about other tasks: A student who can competently compare and contrast two ani-

Figure 8.7 *Comparison of Selected-Response and Performance Assessments*

	Selected-Response Assessments	Performance-Based Assessments
Examples	Multiple-choice True-False Matching	Performance Product Essay
Major Uses	Assess knowledge	Assess skills Assess knowledge application Assess problem solving Assess higher-level thinking
Advantages	Efficient Reliable Broad in scope Objective	Meaningful Authentic In-depth Multidimensional
Cautions	Possibility for guessing correct answer Difficult to assess most thinking skills	Time-consuming Expensive

mals on a Venn diagram cannot necessarily write a paragraph doing the same. Students with lower learning levels or language differences may become discouraged when given a task that is a reach for them. If the teacher coaches them through the task, the validity is affected. Also, students will not be able to transfer what they know in a simple context to more challenging contexts if teachers do not teach students in challenging or authentic contexts. As a result, performance assessments may require major changes to instructional practice. Figure 8.7 provides a summary of some of the differences between performance assessments and selected-response assessments.

Ask Yourself

Think of times in your life as a student when you found yourself immersed in an interesting school assignment. What were the characteristics of the assignment? Which characteristics really motivated you to think and learn? What might a performance assessment that included these motivating characteristics look like?

Digging Deeper
Civil Service and Performance Assessment

Civil servants or public servants are civilian employees working for a government department or agency who have earned and maintain their employment through a performance-based merit system. One of the oldest examples of a merit-based civil service is the Chinese bureaucracy, which, during the T'ang dynasty, relied decreasingly on aristocratic recommendations and more on promotion based on assessments of merit. Over time, the Chinese civil service became a standard from which other nation-states adopted and adapted this principle of performance-based appointments. The significance of performance-based hiring and promotion practices is noteworthy because such a practice aims to prevent corruption and favoritism within public service.

In the British Civil Service, civil servants are career employees who are promoted on the basis of their administrative skill and technical expertise; as such, they are not appointed by elected officials or their political advisors. Civil servants are expected to be politically neutral and are prohibited from taking part in political campaigns or being members of Parliament.

In the United States, the Federal Civil Service is defined as "all appointed positions in the executive, judicial, and legislative branches of the Government of the United States, except positions in the uniformed services" (United States Code Title 5 2101). In the early nineteenth century, it was based on the so-called spoils system, in which government offices went to loyal members of the party in power. This changed after the Pendleton Civil Service Reform Act of 1883, which stated that U.S. federal civil servants were to be recruited and appointed based on merit.

Source: U.S. Office of Personnel Management.

Designing Meaningful Performance Assessments That Match Learning Goals

Once you have an understanding of the characteristics of a performance assessment, the next task is to design a performance assessment that matches students' learning goals. As you focus on the concepts and skills you have targeted, you will need to imagine a task that requires students to use the concepts and to display the skills that you have emphasized. It is easy to imagine a task that simply displays one skill or one topic; it is much more difficult to imagine a task that requires multiple skills and diverse content yet remains true to the knowledge and skills that students have mastered.

Clearly, designing performance assessments is both an art and a science. It is an art to create a context for your students. Once in this context, your students cannot help but display their knowledge, thinking, and habits of mind. For example, when future teachers begin their semester of student teaching, they work with real students in a real classroom. They respond to real problems, make real decisions, and use real teaching methods. It is natural for student teachers to "show what they know" in the context of doing their jobs. The task itself presents sufficient demands that the student teachers automatically demonstrate their skills.

Performance assessment is also like a science. As the teacher, you will need to meticulously identify and examine the important questions and other types of learning indicators that underlie the task. The following steps will guide you in developing motivating and rigorous performance assessments that match learning outcomes as well as students' interests and abilities.

Designing the Right Performance Task

There are several issues to consider when developing performance assessments. First, the proper context needs to be designed, one that permits students to show you what they have learned. Second, the context needs to be full of opportunities for the students to show what they know and can do in relation to your standards. Third, you will need to detail the performance indicators and criteria that allow you to judge the students' performance fairly and consistently.

Identifying a Proper Context for Performance Tasks The first and most important step in developing a performance assessment is to identify a task that permits students to show important learning, is motivating enough to encourage students to think, and is rich enough in offering opportunities for students to show what they know.

As with every assessment, selecting a performance task requires that you carefully consider the learning goals, state standards, and outcomes of current and past instruction as well as the relevance of the task to students' learning experiences.

To create a motivating context, teachers need to consider what the learning goals would look like in the lives and actions of scientists, writers, historians, mathematicians. Consider what professionals do and how they use their knowledge. Together, these considerations will often trigger ideas for the type of performance task that makes sense in this specific situation.

Here are some additional considerations:

- Is the task *practical*? Consider the classroom space and the time needed for the students to complete the task.

- Does the task appeal to the needs and interests of both boys and girls? Are there any elements of cultural bias?

- Does the task take into account *parental involvement* and *financial requirements*? A student from a lower-income background in a single-parent household is not going to have the same resources to complete tasks at home, especially if materials have to be purchased, as a student from a higher-income family with a stay-at-home parent.

As you think about these issues, you will begin to create the content of and context for a performance.

Stuffing the Performance with Multiple Opportunities to Show Learning

Once a context has been selected, it needs to be structured and filled with opportunities to show how and what students have learned. Asking students to display their cognitive abilities in as many ways as possible enhances the teacher's understanding of students' unique ways of knowing.

This is where it is helpful to use a variety of assessment tools. Observing students in action and recording these observations in a variety of ways is critical. You have already examined a number of ways to assess students. Performance assessments enable you to select many of these assessment methods and match them to a task. Here are some of these ways of assessing and documenting students' performance (Hammerman & Musial, 2008):

- *Anecdotal records:* Create a log in which you jot down relevant information about the students' learning progress.

- *Selected-response assessments:* Have students demonstrate their knowledge of specific information about key concepts under investigation by answering multiple-choice, short-answer, true-false, or matching questions about these concepts. The questions should be organized and administered in clusters so that students have sufficient opportunity to show their mastery, and the information that is assessed should relate specifically to the ideas implicit in the performance assessment.

- *Student-constructed responses:* Ask students to develop answers to various essay questions that require them to use their own language, clarify details, make connections, and elaborate on important concepts related to the performance task. Once again, the essay questions or open-ended prompts should relate to key ideas that are the focus of the performance assessment.

- *Graphic organizers:* Ask students to describe concepts and other information by graphically displaying the relationships that these concepts have with other ideas. Graphic organizers are visual representations of knowledge, concepts, or ideas. They assist in organizing thoughts and classifying information, thus helping to promote understanding. They take many forms, including Venn diagrams, story webs, concept maps, and sequence organizers. Students can use a concept map or a Venn diagram to classify animals, to diagram sentences by famous authors, or to plot plant growth stages on a sequence chart. The key to employing these graphic organizers is to embed them in places along the performance assessment that are logical and natural progressions of the task.

- *Interviews:* Interview students to assess their knowledge and understanding of a particular area. You can also conduct periodic interviews to determine a student's progress in completing the performance task.

- *Learning logs:* Ask students to keep an ongoing record of their observations, drawings, insights, charts, tables, and so on as they collect data during the performance assessment. A **learning log** is a detailed record of experiences or events that relate to some inquiry or learning event. Observations, insights about a recurring theme, and reflections about a topic can be captured in learning logs. Make certain that you ask students to record a variety of different types of information in their logs. You can add a metacognitive component by asking the students to specifically reflect on what they are learning. Ask them to respond to questions such as, "The thing that surprised me the most about my project was . . ." or "One thing I would like to learn more about is. . . ."

- *Direct observation using checklists:* Develop a list of important skills and content that you are emphasizing in the task. Use this checklist so that you can quickly note what skill or understanding students demonstrate as they actively participate in learning.

- *Audio- and videotapes:* Use audio- and videotapes to record a student's abilities in areas hard to document in any other way. You can also use video to record all of the products that students create. Then assess what you recorded with a checklist or rating scale.

- *Student products or projects:* Have students develop closure for their learning by completing a product or project, which is something that is made or created by the student. It is a task that requires time, organization, and planning. Evidence of achievement is found in the product itself, which can be assessed using a rating scale, for example.

Prior chapters have described how to develop these assessment tools. What makes performance assessment powerful is that you can choose from all of the available assessment methods and embed them in a performance task. That way you maximize the opportunities for students to display what they know and can do.

Include Different Types of Questions to Allow Students to Demonstrate Thinking When designing a performance assessment, it is important to carefully integrate specific questions that students are to answer throughout the performance itself. These questions may or may not look like essay questions. For example, as students are involved in a performance assessment that requires them to make a decision about some social issue, you can ask them to determine an answer to a variety of related, smaller, questions that are part of the decision that they must make. You can then assess their responses to these smaller questions, as part of the scoring tool for the decision-making performance.

Careful questioning is an important way to cue students to display their understanding. Research indicates that the academic culture of a classroom is determined by the types of questions that teachers ask. This is especially true during a complex performance assessment experience. Students should

Resource for Your Assessment Toolkit
Quest for the Best Banana

The following performance assessment relates to mathematics and science concepts and skills. The indicators would be modified to fit the specific concepts and skills that you have taught, and you would also need to develop specific criteria to measure each indicator.

Your marketing firm has been hired by Del Monte to assess how much of a banana is reasonably edible by humans. Your task is to determine a number and a formula that describes a legitimate, defensible answer to this question. You are also to present the strategy that you employed to answer this question and to defend this strategy should your suggested answer be questioned.

You are asked to present your answer and your strategy in the form of an oral presentation, with supporting visuals or handouts, to the executives of Del Monte on November 5.

Indicators that Could Be Observed During this Performance

- Approached the problem using nutritional constructs.
- Developed a reasonable operational definition for "edible."
- Identified a reasonable set of evidence to support an answer.
- Developed a clear data table for evidence.
- Developed a graph, histogram, and so on for describing data.
- Employed a central tendency technique (mean, median, mode).
- Recognized importance of variance (such as standard deviation).
- Analyzed the variable of ripeness and other intervening variables.
- Determined a strategy to incorporate ripeness and other variables in determining an answer.
- Developed a formula for edible proportion.
- Considered the social consequences of releasing a single number.
- Considered the competition.
- Communicated a clear argument in favor of the selected number to be used.

Source: Adapted from AIMS Education Foundation, 2007.

be asked many different types of questions within a rich, hands-on context. Figure 8.8 lists question types that give students the opportunity to show the multiplicity of their ways of knowing.

Organizing the pieces of a complex performance task is especially important because such tasks include multiple assessment opportunities while allowing students time and freedom to employ a variety of skills and approaches. In fact, planning a complex performance task can be compared to the task of writing a play that outlines the plot for students to perform. Figure 8.9, which lists the key components that could be considered in developing a complex performance assessment, is an example of a format you could use while planning your performance assessment.

In Figure 8.9, the *task description* provides the problem scenario that challenges the students and motivates them to engage in the performance task. The *whole-group instruction* reviews prior knowledge to activate what

Figure 8.8 *Types of Questions That Show Understanding*

- *Analysis questions:* What are the key parts? Which parts are essential and why?
- *Comparison questions:* How are these alike? What specific characteristics are similar? How are these different? In what way are they different?
- *Classification questions:* Into what groups could you organize these things? What are the rules for membership in each group? What are the defining characteristics of each group?
- *Connections clarification questions:* What does this remind you of in another context? To what is this connected?
- *Constructing support questions:* What data can you cite that supports this conclusion? What is an argument that would support this claim?
- *Deduction questions:* Based on this rule, what would you infer? What are the conditions that make this inevitable?
- *Inferring and concluding questions:* Based on these data, what would you conclude? How likely is it that this will occur?
- *Abstracting questions:* What pattern underlies all these situations? What are the essential characteristics of this thing?
- *Error analysis questions:* How is this conclusion misleading? What does not match?

students already know and introduces new knowledge and skills students will need to know to complete their group work and individual work.

When a task involves group work, most students select their group. They select the group based on either the topic that interests them or the mode of presentation. Sometimes you can assign the students if you want to differentiate the groups by ability levels in order to challenge some students and ensure success for others based on their skill levels.

Students tend to select the mode of presentation they prefer, so those who excel at technology might select a video presentation, and those who love to perform might choose to do an oral presentation. Carol Tomlinson and Jay McTighe (2006) believe assessment becomes responsive when students receive appropriate options for demonstrating their knowledge, skills, and understanding. They believe you should allow some choices, "but always with the intent of collecting *needed evidence based* on goals. Without a clear connection between the desired results and the required evidence, teachers will be stuck assessing apples, oranges, and grapes" (p. 73). In other words, students may enjoy creating the PowerPoint presentations, skits, posters, and poetry, but content must correlate to the objectives and standards in order to be valid products and projects.

The *individual work is the most important component* of the complex performance task. We know that in today's world of accountability, we need data to show *each* individual student meets the objectives and standards to

Figure 8.9 *Planning for a Multiply Focused, Complex Performance Assessment*

Title/Topic_____ Grade Level/Subject Area _____

Standards/Benchmarks

1. Select one or more key content standards from the relevant subject area (social studies, science, mathematics, language arts, foreign language, technology, etc).
2. Select process standards (such as writing, reading, problem solving, research, communication).

Task Description

Your task description would include such items as:

Hook/Motivator

Outside audience (You have been asked by . . .)

Problem scenario

Group work (four or five different performances)

Due date

Whole-Group Instruction

You would have already done some of these during the unit for which the performance task is the assessment:

- Direct instruction
- Readings
- Guest speakers
- Videos
- Internet research
- Class discussions

Small Groups: Selected by Students

Here are some examples you might consider:

Group One	**Group Two**	**Group Three**	**Group Four**	**Group Five**
Research	Presentation via artwork	Presentation via written material	Oral presentation	Multimedia presentation

Individual Work

Decide on what the students will do. This must match the target standards and outcomes and should be accompanied by scoring tools that list the criteria for judging student work.

Methods of Assessment

- Observations
- Checklists
- Rubrics
- Tests
- Interviews
- Logs

Source: Adapted from Burke, 2006.

demonstrate their knowledge and skills related to the topic in order to provide evidence they have met or exceeded the standards.

Because we need an objective method of assessing that performance, we should provide students with a scoring tool to give them the indicators (observable behaviors) and criteria that will provide them with feedback on how they are doing. The scoring tools will also help us grade the final product objectively and consistently.

The *methods of assessment* component includes the ways we can assess the students. You may find that a checklist or rating scale will give you the most critical information about each student's complex performance. But, as we said earlier, you can use a variety of ways such as anecdotal records, graphic organizer, interviews, selected response, and constructed response to provide additional feedback to students. Complex performance tasks include many simple performance tasks that may address standards from other subject areas. The integration of different subject areas is critical for most real-life tasks students will perform in life.

Figure 8.10 is an example of a performance assessment that was designed using the format shown above. In this assessment, students are to write a letter to the editor of a local newspaper. They are to state their case for either banning or allowing smoking in local businesses.

Identifying Performance Indicators

A rich context allows students to display many of the components of understanding as well as a variety of skills. The art of assessing well requires teachers to identify indicators of these important aspects of knowing and doing. An **indicator** is an observable behavior that is a sign that the student understands or knows something. Teachers need to determine how a successful way of doing and knowing something would look in the performance itself. When you know what "knowing this something" looks like, you have found an indicator.

To do this, teachers need to step back from the performance and identify those actions or behaviors that students need to do in the performance that indicate either knowledge, skills, or dispositions—valued ways of acting. This step is much like that of a physician who orders an x-ray in an effort to clearly see the bones of the body. The x-ray uncovers the skeletal structure that is hidden by the skin and organs of the individual. Finding the key indicators or behaviors that relate to learning that you wish to assess requires that you view the performance with x-ray vision in order to uncover places in the performance that indicate learning.

Uncovering key learning indicators or behaviors is not simple. It involves reviewing your own understanding of the concepts and skills that you are targeting. It may require reading professional publications and

Figure 8.10 *Middle School Language Arts/Science Performance Task*

Language Arts Standards: Letter writing; rearch; writing process; conventions; oral presentation techniques

Science Standards: Health, such as nutrition, exercise, and disease; effect of drugs and toxic substances

Math Standards: Statistics; graphing

Technology: Multimedia presentations

Task Description

As part of the school's "Health Fair Week," the Cancer Prevention Association has asked your class to develop a campaign for eliminating all smoking areas from local businesses. They are concerned about how the secondhand smoke is affecting the employees and the patrons. The project will include: (1) a summary of research data related to smoking; (2) a brochure depicting the health risks; (3) an informational poster that will be displayed in the downtown areas; and (4) a 3-minute video selling your ideas to business owners. Be prepared to present your anti-smoking campaign to members of the Cancer Association on November 18, at their monthly meeting at 7:00 in the Chamber of Commerce building.

Direct Instruction for the Whole Class

The whole class will be involved in the following learning experiences:

- Guest lecture from the school nurse on the effects of secondhand smoke
- Lectures and discussions on the health risks related to smoking
- Readings from articles and textbooks
- Review of oral presentation techniques and PowerPoint techniques
- Summary of research data

Group Work

Students select one group project.

Group One	Group Two	Group Three	Group Four
Prepare a summary using charts and graphs showing the effects of smoking on health.	Prepare a brochure that explains health risks related to smoking.	Prepare an antismoking poster to display in local stores.	Present a 3-minute video selling your idea to business owners.

Individual Work

In addition to the group project, each student will complete the following individual assignment: *Write a letter to the editor of our local newspaper stating your case either in favor of banning or in favor of allowing smoking in local businesses.*

Methods of Assessment

- Teacher-made test on the health risks related to smoking
- Criteria checklists to assess each of the four group projects
- Checklist and rubric to assess the individual letter to the editor

Source: Adapted from Burke, 2005.

other texts that describe the concepts and skills. Revisiting the state and national standards coverage of the concepts and skills is another valuable resource. Then, carefully examine the student activities that make up the performance assessment and determine where exactly the students will have an opportunity to show that they have mastered the skills and concepts you have identified. Asking for student input concerning the indicators of learning that they see in the performance helps students take ownership of the assessment. Students may also bring up indicators that the teacher would not have considered.

These indicators are only the first step in developing a scoring tool, but this first step is a very important one. The reason it is so important is that the identification of indicators needs to be carefully aligned to your learning outcomes that are connected to state standards. Since some state standards include indicators (also known as *descriptors*, *elements*, *proficiencies*, or *competencies*), it is critical to use the terminology of the standards in addition to synonyms from the textbook or class discussions that relate to the terminology. For example, if there is a state standard about critical thinking, the specific way that critical thinking is described may include terms like "analyze" or "recognize the arguments of an adversary" or "use logic." It is important to use the terms that match your state standard so that students learn the vocabulary as well as practice the skill.

Finally, set up a pilot test of the performance task and review it. Figure 8.11 suggests some indicators you can use to assess your performance task and scoring tools. Review your task to see if you have answered the ten questions in Figure 8.11.

Figure 8.11 *Ten Performance Task Self-Assessment Questions*

1. Does the task measure what it was designed to measure? Is it valid?
2. Does the scoring tool produce consistent results? Is it reliable?
3. What time and materials are needed for the task?
4. How much time is needed to score the task?
5. Is it practical?
6. Is it fair to all students?
7. Is it relevant?
8. Will the task be meaningful and challenging to the students?
9. Do the descriptors or criteria in the scoring tool correlate to vocabulary in your state standards?
10. Did you refine and improve the task and revise your list of indicators after you had the opportunity to pilot the task?

?Ask Yourself

Think of times in your life as a student when you were asked to perform a task in front of others. What did the performance require you to do that you would normally not do as part of other assignments? Did you find that the need to perform in front of others made you take the assignment more seriously? In what ways did the performance enable you to show what you know and can do? In what ways did the performance inhibit your ability to show what you know and can do?

Developing Criteria for Performance Assessments

Once you have designed a performance that matches your learning outcomes, it is important to identify the specific criteria that you will use to determine if the objectives of the performance assessment have been met. You already know that every performance contains important underlying features or indicators of the critical dimensions of learning. In order to assess what students know and can do, we need to transform these indicators of learning into performance criteria.

Performance criteria can be thought of as a set of rules that provide directions for determining a student's score. In their simplest form, performance criteria are answer keys. They provide teachers and students with a clear statement of the expected answers. For example, the answer key for a multiple-choice test is a list of correct choices. In this case, the rule for finding the student's score is to count the number of correct answers. The performance or scoring keys for multiple-choice tests are simple. Much more direction is required when developing criteria for a rich performance assessment. The performance criteria for more complex performances require a careful review of the indicators that were identified from the objectives and standards and a careful analysis of the criteria that you will use to determine if the indicator behavior is adequate.

Creating Scoring Tools Based on Performance Criteria

Unlike most conventional forms of testing, performance-based assessments often do not have clear-cut right or wrong answers. Rather, there are degrees to which students are successful or unsuccessful. The performance will need to be evaluated in a way that allows those varying degrees to be taken into consideration. This can be accomplished by constructing scoring tools that are matched to the complexity of each task the students complete.

For example, in a performance assessment in which students are to determine the relationship between sunlight and plant growth, you might ask students to make a prediction, to write down their predictions, and to give reasons for the predictions. You can then collect these predictions and score them on how logically their reasons and predictions are connected.

Later, you might ask students to set up a data table and collect data over 1 week. Simply collecting these data tables is an opportunity to assess the skills of data collection and data recording. You then might ask students to make an inference based on their data table. Once again, by examining the inferences, you can collect additional data. In the next section we present examples of scoring tools developed for particular performance assessments.

The letter to the editor checklist in Figure 8.12 is the individual assignment that each student completes during the performance task shown in Figure 8.10. The checklist includes both performance criteria and the key indicators that show how the criteria look in the letter to the editor. The criteria and indicators are written in student-oriented language and should be shared with students to help them become familiar with the vocabulary for the assignment as well as the vocabulary used in their state standards. *This checklist becomes the teacher's feedback* provided to the students as they plan, write, revise, and edit their letters to the editor. The "scaffolding" provided by the scoring tools provides specific and immediate feedback to each student as to how well he or she is meeting the goals and completing the task.

Guiding Principles for the Development of Valid and Reliable Performance Criteria

The most difficult aspect of developing performance criteria is the opportunity for unconscious bias and error to creep into the process. Therefore, a regular self-examination of the following principles is helpful. Although such reflection does not guarantee freedom from bias and error, it does help fight against it.

Performance Indicators and Criteria Are Educationally Important

Whenever students are asked to complete a performance task that has many components, you should focus the majority of your assessment on those components that are most important in your teaching. This may sound obvious, but many times performance assessment tasks display

Figure 8.12 *Letter to the Editor Checklist*

Language Arts Standards: *The student . . .*

- Practices process writing and, when applicable, uses the writing process to develop, revise, and evaluate writing.
- Acquires new vocabulary in each content area and uses it correctly.
- Practices the manuscript format and uses research and technology to support writing.

Science Standards: *The student . . .*

Researches smoking and evaluates health-related risks of secondhand smoke.

Task: *The student writes a letter to the editor of the city newspaper advocating a ban on smoking in all local businesses.*	**Not Yet 0**	**Some Evidence 1**
Criterion—Accuracy of Information: Did you include . . .		
Accurate facts and examples?		
Pertinent quotations from reliable sources?		
Valid statistics to support your opinion?		
Criterion—Persuasiveness: Did you use . . .		
Reasoned arguments to support an opinion?		
Reasoned arguments to refute an opinion?		
A call to action on an issue of local importance?		
Criterion—Organization: Did you . . .?		
Revise to improve the logic and coherence of the controlling perspective?		
Revise writing for specific audiences?		
Revise writing for specific purposes?		
Revise writing for the formality of the contexts?		
Revise writing to sharpen the precision of word choice?		
Revise writing to achieve desired tone?		
Criterion—Editing: Did you edit your writing to improve . . .		
Word choice?		
Grammar?		

Punctuation?		
Spelling?		
Criterion—Writing Process: Did you . . .		
Plan what you wanted to write?		
Plan your letter resourcefully (organization and time management)?		
Plan your letter independently?		
Write an outline for the letter?		
Write a rough draft?		
Revise your rough draft?		
Ask a peer to review your final draft?		
Criterion—Letter Format: Did you include . . .		
Date?		
Inside address?		
Salutation?		
Body (at least three paragraphs)?		
Appropriate closing?		
Signature?		
Criterion—Usage: Did you edit your letter for . . .		
Complete sentence structure?		
Correct subject/verb agreement?		
Correct pronoun/antecedent agreement?		
A variety of sentence structures?		

so many different skills that you can lose your focus on the essentials. For example, if students are asked to create a collage that expresses their understanding of the presence of prejudice in today's world, there is always the possibility that neatness and colorfulness can emerge as scoring criteria. While this is reasonable given that the mode of communication is a collage, these criteria should not overshadow the more important objectives of the task. The key learning that you might have taught about the nature of prejudice should be the main focus of your assessment tool.

Performance Indicators and Criteria Are Valid This means that they match learning outcomes with state standards. The intent of assessment is to determine if your learning outcomes are met. When developing performance assessments, you must fill the context of the performance with opportunities for students to show what they have learned, and you need to focus the performance in ways that match your learning goals. This match is key to establishing the validity of the performance assessment. Does the assessment measure what you intended?

As in the example cited above, if your teaching objectives focused on uncovering examples of prejudice in today's society, the use of the collage may be insufficient. In this case, you might add the requirement of writing a paper that explicates the different prejudicial instances cited in the pictorial collage. This added component to the performance makes the assessment more clearly match your teaching objectives and state standards that target informational writing.

Performance Indicators and Criteria Are Reliable This means that they are described in observable terms. It is important that any indicator of learning is one that you can personally observe in a school situation. Assuming that students displayed a task at home introduces all sorts of possible error. Most important, the characteristics of a behavior need to be clearly visible to the observer. Overt behaviors like clear enunciation, use of data to support a position statement, and participation in a discussion are readily observed. Less obvious factors include effort expended in an assignment, attitude toward science, or curiosity about a question. These dimensions tend to be rated unreliably because their presence must be inferred from indicators that are less precise. Whenever possible, confine assessments to those characteristics that can be observed and judged directly to avoid introducing bias based on inference.

Performance Indicators and Criteria Are Clearly Defined This applies to points on a scale as well. At times, you may use such a scale to indicate the degree to which an indicator is evident.

All Students Are Assessed on One Task Before Going on to Another Task The advantage of rating all students' performances on a task before starting another one is that it is easier to keep your scoring criteria clearly in mind. Also, when responses of a single student across several tasks are considered, there is a tendency for your evaluation of the student's performance on earlier tasks to create an expectation on your part. This expectation can result in more lenient or more stringent evaluations of the next performance.

When Feasible, Performances Are Assessed Without Knowledge of Students' Names This practice enhances fairness in your assessment. By keeping students' identities anonymous, you will not be biased by their prior performance or by other classroom behavior. This practice enhances fairness in your evaluation and reduces the chances that your evaluation will be influenced by a halo effect rather than by the actual performance of the student.

Ask Yourself

What would a performance assessment look like in the grade level that you wish to teach? What obstacles might you face in trying to implement the performance assessment that you have designed? How might you counteract the obstacle?

Summary

- The goal of performance assessment is to provide students with an opportunity to show what they know and can do within a meaningful context.

- Performance assessment evaluates student's knowledge and skills through tasks that are not measurable using paper-and-pencil tests alone.

- Performance assessment stresses the importance of the progression of learning and challenges students to use higher-order thinking skills.

- Performance assessments provide information on both the process and the product of student's work.

- Key steps in designing a performance assessment are to identify a context, provide a variety of opportunities for students to display their knowledge and skills, and include questions that relate to understanding.

- A crucial element of the performance assessment process is the design of a valid and reliable scoring tool.

- Scoring tools are created considering the multiply focused process of the performance task, and they include performance criteria that relate to important student outcomes linked to standards.

Key Terms

authentic task (205)

capstone performance (216)

demonstration task (215)

exhibit (216)

indicator (225)

inquiry task (214)

learning log (221)

multiply focused task (210)

performance-based assessment (205)

performance criteria (228)

performance task (205)

presentation task (216)

problem-based learning (PBL) (212)

process skill (205)

product (205)

singly focused task (209)

For Further Discussion

1. What are some advantages of using performance tasks instead of paper-and-pencil tests? What are some disadvantages?

2. With a specific teaching area (such as science, math, reading) in mind, what are three learning goals that the students need to master? Which goal is best measured with a performance task? Why?

3. Create a detailed task for discussion question 2. Include all directions, materials, and time constraints. Next list all the skills (criteria) the students need to demonstrate as they complete the process.

4. Finally, create a checklist or a rating scale to evaluate the students' progress. Will the tool be graded or ungraded? Are all the steps observable?

Comprehension Quiz

Performance Assessment Task

Find a performance assessment that is described either on the Internet, in a textbook, or is developed by a practicing teacher. Then, evaluate each of the following statements and determine if it is true or false. Provide a reason for each true or false response.

1. Performance assessments are easier to score than paper-and-pencil assessments.

2. Performance assessments target complex tasks that require higher-order thinking skills.

3. Checklists can be used at regular intervals to evaluate a student's progress toward completing a performance task.

4. Performance tasks simulate real-life experiences.

Finally, return to the performance assessment that you have identified and evaluate the assessment in light of your answers to the true or false questions.

Relevant Website Resources

Kathy Schrock's Guide for Educators

http://school.discovery.com/schrockguide/assess.html

This website has a collection of alternative and performance-based assessment links and subject-specific and general scoring guides to assess student performances. It includes tools to assess web pages, cooperative learning, graphs, oral presentations, posters, PowerPoint presentations, and other performance tasks and products.

Practical Assessment, Research, and Evaluation (PARE)

http://pareonline.net

PARE is a peer-reviewed electronic journal that provides effective methods, trends, and research developments. Type in "performance assessment" for the keyword to find articles about implementing performance assessment in the classroom. The articles from researchers in the field discuss formal and informal assessments, criteria, performance rubrics, and other current issues in assessment, research, and evaluation.

Performance Assessment Links in Science (PALS)

http://pals.sri.com

PALS in an online, standards-based, continually updated resource bank of science performance assessment tasks indexed via the National Science Education Standards (NSES) and various other standards frameworks. The site arranges the performance tasks by K–12 grade levels and major content areas. The tasks include administrative procedure, the task with student directions, a rubric, technical quality information, and examples of student work. The tasks are all correlated to national, state, or curriculum standards frameworks.

Arlington Central School District

http://www.arlingtonschools.org/Curriculum/Assesssment/mathassess.html

This site includes mathematics performance assessment tasks from K–8. Each assessment lists material, procedures, activities, and suggested time allotments. Most of the tasks also include rubrics for assessing the tasks.

North Central Regional Educational Laboratory (NCREL)

http://www.learningpt.org/page.php?pageID=243

This site features a series of articles about alternative assessments where students have to *create* a response to a question or task rather than *choose* a response from a given list.

Performance Assessment for Science Teachers

http:www.usoe.K12.ut.us/CURR/science/Perform/Past5.htm

This site provides guidelines for developing a performance test, reviewing a performance assessment, and developing a scoring guide. It also features sample science performance tasks that include the problem, materials needed, investigation, grading, and teacher notes.

References

Barell, J. (2003). *Developing curious minds.* Alexandria, VA: Association for Supervision and Curriculum Development.

Burke, K. (2005). *How to assess authentic learning,* 4th ed. Thousand Oaks, CA: Corwin Press.

Burke, K. (2006). *From standards to rubrics in six steps: Tools for assessing student learning, K–8.* Thousand Oaks, CA: Corwin Press/Sage.

Dewey, J. (1916). *Democracy and education.* New York: Macmillan.

Hammerman, E. & Musial, D. (2008). Integrating science with mathematics & literacy: New visions for learning and assessment. Thousand Oaks, CA: Corwin Press.

Herman, J., Aschbacher, P., & Winters, L. (1992). *A practical guide to alternative assessment.* Alexandria, VA: Association for Supervision and Curriculum Development.

Sagor, R. (2003). *Motivating students and teachers in an ear of standards.* Alexandria, VA: Association for Supervision and Curriculum Development.

Tomlinson, C. A., & McTighe, J. (2006). *Integrating differentiated instruction and understanding by design: Connecting content and kids.* Alexandria, VA: Association for Supervision and Curriculum Development.

U.S. Office of Personnel Management. Our history. http://www.opm.gov/about_opm/tr/history.asp. Accessed December 20, 2007.

CHAPTER 9

Portfolio Assessment and Rubric Development

Chapter Objectives

After reading and thinking about this chapter, you will be able to:

- **Identify different types and structures of portfolios.**
- **Compare portfolio types based on their purposes.**
- **List the steps in developing a portfolio that matches your educational setting.**

- **Identify the characteristics of generalized, holistic, and analytic rubrics.**
- **Compare rubric types based on their purposes.**

Think of movies you have enjoyed. Now choose your five favorite ones and rank them from 1 to 5, with 1 being your all-time favorite. Some people could do this quite easily, and others would want to qualify their rankings. If you were permitted to create criteria for selecting a favorite movie, would that be helpful? Quality of acting, character development, costumes, soundtrack, special effects—most of these elements would contribute to a quality movie, but problems arise: Is character development more important than the cinematography? Is the movie's music really important at all?

When we assess student learning, we must carefully consider a number of questions. What specific elements constitute the evidence of learning? What is the relative importance of each of those elements? And how do we provide evidence of growth—that is, where did the students begin, and where did they end up? Portfolios give a way for teachers—and students as well—to gather a variety of learning evidence that they believe shows growth. Through rubrics, both teachers and students communicate how these pieces of evidence show growth in an authentic, meaningful way.

In this chapter we describe the unique opportunity that portfolios provide to assess students' achievements. Portfolios are not a new concept in that they have been used for decades as a method for displaying a person's abilities in career settings. Visual artists, engineers, cosmetologists, and writers have consistently developed portfolios of their work as a quick, easy way to display to potential employers that they have what it takes. When portfolios are used in this manner, they tend to represent what a person has learned to do well.

Only recently have portfolios become useful tools while students are developing their talents. Portfolios are now found in classrooms across all grade levels. Their purposes differ based on the context of each classroom—sometimes they are used to display accomplishments, sometimes they are used to show growth, sometimes they are used as a reflective diary of work. No matter what the purpose, portfolios provide a tool that allows the learners to support the claim that they have achieved some success.

In previous chapters, we have described a variety of assessment approaches and have shown how you can use these different assessment approaches within a larger performance assessment. In this chapter, we will unravel the term *rubric* and show you how a rubric can assist you in the assessment of a portfolio or a complex performance. We define the concept of rubric, describe different types of rubrics, and finally show you how to develop rubrics for complex assessment situations.

A key foundational consideration for this chapter is that portfolios challenge us to reconsider what it means to be educated. Portfolios emphasize student reflection about their growth rather than their acquisition of specific knowledge and skills. Considering students' *reflection* as a key component of what it means to be educated is quite different from considering students' knowledge and skill acquisition as the key characteristic of an educated person.

Foundational Questions for Your Consideration

- How often were you asked to reflect on your learning and to make decisions about what you needed to do next?
- Did you ever have your grade determined by the way you were able to explain your progress and make personal learning goals?
- Did you ever receive more credit for providing an explanation of how you solved a problem than for getting the correct answer?
- Do you think that students' reflection should be a key focus of a school's curriculum? Why or why not?

The Unique Role of Portfolios in the Classroom

Portfolios have the potential to reveal a great deal about students. They allow students to assume ownership in ways that few other instructional approaches or assessments do. Portfolio development requires students to collect and reflect on examples of their work, providing a self-assessment component to the curriculum. Portfolios allow the teacher to assess students' thinking strategies more directly. They provide opportunities for teachers to better understand the educational process at the level of the individual and can give teachers a sense of how students are thinking.

While other forms of assessment offer specific insights into targeted instructional objectives, portfolio assessment provides a wider view. With portfolios, teachers can observe students taking risks, developing creative solutions, and using **self-reflection** to make judgments about their performances. A portfolio provides a complex and comprehensive view of student performance in which the student is a participant rather than solely the object of assessment. Above all, a portfolio provides a forum encouraging students to be independent, self-directed learners.

Portfolios Defined

In order to define a portfolio, we must first define *artifact*. An **artifact,** sometimes called a **folio,** is a piece of evidence that displays some valued skill, ability, knowledge, or approach. A **portfolio** is a purposeful, organized collection of evidence that demonstrates a person's knowledge, skills, abilities, or disposition. For this reason, the term *portfolio* implies that from a larger set of evidence or artifacts, a portable subset of these artifacts is collected and displayed to another because they tell a specific story.

Portfolios are used in a variety of professions including architecture, engineering, writing, education, and fashion. They also have a long history in the field of art. In general, a portfolio contains significant works or snapshots that display a person's ability or growth in a field of work. These artifacts complement one another to create an overall picture of a person's unique contribution within a career.

For example, a portfolio for a photographer might contain a series of photos along with an explanation of the significant or worthy characteristics of each photo. A portfolio for a musician might contain the musical score for a piece that was written by the musician as well as several audio discs that represent the musician's interpretation of different musical pieces. The portfolio for a teacher might include a philosophy of education, lesson plans, letters of support from parents, student evaluations, and student products. In conjunction with a résumé, the portfolio offers tangible evidence of the work that the résumé simply cites. As professionals develop throughout their careers, the portfolio is updated and new evidence is included.

Portfolios in the classroom have characteristics that differ from professional portfolios. Judith Arter and Vicki Spandel (1992) recommend that portfolios in an educational setting involve student participation in the selection of evidence (what is included in a portfolio) but that teachers provide specific, predetermined guidelines for the selection of materials and criteria for scoring. Defined in this way, portfolios in educational settings have the following essential characteristics. First, the educational portfolio has a *predefined, clear purpose*. Second, the portfolio includes *specific artifacts that students select based on the purpose* of the portfolio. Third, students are engaged in a *self-reflective process* that requires them to think about and articulate the learning achievements that each artifact displays. Fourth, based on clearly described *scoring criteria*, teachers examine and evaluate each student's learning achievements, weaknesses, and progress. Fifth, *teachers clearly communicate* these strengths and learning needs with parents and students.

Types of Portfolios

Portfolios have different structures depending on the purpose and context of the portfolio. And the purposes for a portfolio in the classroom context are connected to the learning purposes or objectives of a course of study. Because there are different learning purposes, the contents and the form of portfolios are equally diverse. Since portfolio use in the classrooms is fairly new, many different types of portfolio structures are being developed. The following categories represent the major portfolio structures that are now emerging (Burke, Fogerty, Belgard, 2004; McMillan, 2004; Stiggins, 2005).

Project or Product Portfolio A primary purpose of a project or product portfolio is to show the steps and/or the results of a completed project or task. Such a portfolio is useful because the final product does not always show the skills and knowledge that the student used in an effort to complete the project. By asking students to provide evidence of their work along the way, teachers can see both strengths and weaknesses in the thinking processes and skills the students used.

The specific type of project dictates what types of artifacts should be collected by the student for evaluation. For example, if students are to complete a science project, the artifacts that would be included in the **project portfolio** might consist of a hypothesis or prediction statement, the rationale, a design statement listing the steps or procedures that will be followed to answer the hypothesis, the tables of data that were collected, the conclusions concerning the patterns that these data tables show, and an interpretation of the overall results. At first glance, this list of artifacts sounds like a research paper. This is no surprise because a project such as this often lends itself to the development of a publication. However, when these separate pieces of evidence are compiled in a portfolio, they are displayed as single tasks that are performed along the way as the student does the project. In this way, both teacher and student can see the individual tasks clearly displayed in detail so that they can evaluate the strengths and weaknesses of each step of the project.

The **product portfolio** is similar to the project portfolio except that its focus is on the end product rather than on the process in which the product was developed. This type of portfolio contains the final product as well as detailed explanations of each part of the final product. These parts tend to be the key dimensions of learning that the product represents. For this reason, if the final product had to meet certain mathematical dimensions (such as a specific length, width, shape), these dimensions would be highlighted in the product description. If the product had to show efficiency or other design requirements, each of these would be described in the product portfolio. As you can see, the product portfolio contains the same information as the project portfolio except that in the product portfolio, there is little or no information about the process that was used to develop the product. The product portfolio therefore can be considered a subset of the project portfolio.

Growth Portfolio The purpose of a **growth portfolio** is to display changes and accomplishments related to academic performance over time. In a growth portfolio, students would be asked to collect artifacts of their accomplishments concerning a specific proficiency across a span of time. For example, at the end of each month, students could be asked to select their best narrative paragraphs written during that month. Students would then place those paragraphs in a growth portfolio and tell why the paragraphs they selected were worthy indicators of narrative writing. After several months, students could then look at their growth portfolio entries and describe improvements that they see in their work. In return, the teacher could do the same. This interactive assessment provides an excellent opportunity to communicate strengths and needed improvements both to students and parents. Also, the portfolio contents clarify the accomplishments of students, which may be less obvious when only summary statements are available.

Standards-Based Portfolio In contrast to collecting artifacts that relate to a specific project or a specific competency or skill, the purpose of **standards-based portfolios** is to collect evidence that links student achievement to particular learning standards. This type of portfolio focuses on specific standards that are predetermined by the teacher and clearly described to students at the beginning of an academic year. Students would then collect evidence of accomplishment for each of the standards and present these artifacts of accomplishment in clusters that relate to these standards.

For example, as students move through a continuous-progress mathematics program, they would display their ability to solve problems for different mathematical competencies linked to a standard. These problems could be in the form of multiple-choice questions that students answered in a testing situation or they could be homework or assignments completed during class time. The key to this type of portfolio is that students know what competencies they are expected to master, and they must show proficiency in the form of artifacts that display mastery of each competency.

Another version of a standards-based portfolio is sometimes required of students who are pursuing a degree in a field of study. The students would be asked to collect artifacts that address the field's stated standards. As they make progress in their courses of study, they collect products that were assigned along the way, place these products in their portfolio, and write a description of the standards that are being met by the products they have included. This approach focuses students on the key standards that represent their field of study and helps the students assess their success toward meeting the standards of their field.

Celebration Portfolio The purpose of a **celebration portfolio** is to collect examples of students' favorite works or accomplishments. This type of portfolio is based on students' personal criteria rather than the criteria of others. It allows students to answer the question, What works are meaningful to me and why am I proud of them? This type of portfolio requires a great deal of self-reflection, and it also helps students determine underlying criteria that account for their selections. Celebration portfolios extend the thinking of teachers in that they may uncover criteria from students' selections that should be emphasized more clearly in their instruction. In this way, such portfolios offer insights both to students' and teachers' growth.

Journal Portfolio The purpose of this type of portfolio is simply to provide a structure for students to collect and reflect on their work continuously. The **journal portfolio** can be conceptualized as a type of diary in which students keep examples of their work in progress and reflect on products or assignments as they go along. Such portfolios are not meant to be a display of finished products; rather, they provide a structure for preserving reflections and ideas. The use of such portfolios is to provide information about what a student has struggled with and now understands or about an insight that was achieved thanks to a work in progress. Journal portfolios are not meant to provide evaluative insights. Rather they provide a record of thinking and self-reflection for students to use as they prepare other portfolios.

A parallel to this type of portfolio in the world of work is found in the working journals of writers who regularly jot down ideas for characters and plots, or in the working papers of scientists who record possible hypotheses, experimental approaches, or notes from a lecture. Also in the working world, detectives may write down possible clues, evidence, and suspects. For this reason, the use of journals in the classroom provides an opportunity for ongoing self-reflection as well as preparation for the working world.

Student Reflection and Portfolio Development

We cannot overstate the importance of student reflection in portfolio development. Students are typically evaluated by others, yet the assessment process should also include *self-assessment*. For this reason, portfolios provide a practical and relatively easy opportunity to involve students in the assessment process without intimidation or fear of failure. For example, through the development of portfolios, teachers can provide students with a method for accumulating evidence and also with a vocabulary to use in communicating achievement. Teachers can help students achieve a clear sense of themselves as learners when they regularly ask students to write or talk about their evidence of achievement.

Most important, students who learn to reflect on their achievements and evaluate themselves become better achievers. The process itself enables them to understand both weaknesses and strengths so that they can make personal decisions about what they still need to know. They begin to see themselves (rather than the teacher) as being in the center of the assessment process. Assessment no longer is simply viewed as a matter of grading or summing. Rather, students begin to see assessment as a part of the self-regulated, continual process of learning. And they begin to see the inherent value of reflection, self-monitoring, self-assessment, and self-correction within the world of learning.

Ask Yourself

Recall a time when you, as a student, were asked to critique your work. What did the teacher do to make you feel comfortable in this effort? Once you completed the critique, were you provided with an opportunity to implement some of your ideas? Based on your experiences, how might you implement meaningful self-assessment in the classroom?

Designing and Using Portfolio Assessments in the Classroom

Now that you have an awareness of the many types of portfolios and their different uses, let's clarify the steps for designing and using portfolios as an assessment tool. In this section we describe a general procedure that you might use to design and implement a portfolio assessment in your classroom. We also present the strengths of portfolio assessment as well as the limitations. An awareness of these strengths and limitations will help you determine when (and if) to use portfolios as part of your assessment plan.

Resource for Your Assessment Toolkit
Self-Reflection Questions

The following questions and prompts can help trigger a variety of insights by students if they are used consistently in the classroom environment. The questions are straightforward, and their power resides not in their wording but in their regular use by teachers and students. The opportunity to help students gain metacognitive skills such as reflection and self-assessment provides a clear reason for employing one or more of these questions as part of every school day.

- Describe the steps that you used to complete today's assignment. Which steps really helped you complete the assignment and which ones were less useful? What would you change next time?
- What personal strengths did you notice in completing today's work? What difficulties did you have and how did you overcome them? What kind of help did you need that you could not get? Where might you find that help in the future?
- What aspect of today's work was meaningful to you? What effect did the work have on your attitudes, perspectives, or interests?

- What weaknesses did you find in your efforts to complete your work? How might you overcome one of these weaknesses? What resources could you use? What resources would you like to use that are not available to you?
- What makes your best work more effective than your other work? What does your best work tell you about your accomplishments? What could you still improve in your best work?
- Ask someone to look at your work and describe what they see. Carefully listen to the feedback and jot down what is said. Then make a list of the comments with which you agree and describe why you do not agree with others.

As you can see, these questions are organized in clusters so that your self-reflection is viewed from a variety of perspectives. Add some others to this list as you continue in your career, and you will find that, not only do students strengthen their self-reflection skills, but you will as well.

Source: Adapted from Camp, 1992 and McMillan, 2004.

Steps for Developing Portfolio Assessments

Developing a solid portfolio assessment requires some advance planning. The following steps provide a general set of directions that are applicable most of the time when developing an assessment for a portfolio. As with any general set of directions, however, you will find that the steps are sometimes completed in a different order or that some of the steps are not necessary.

Clarify the Overall Purpose of the Portfolio The design and use of a portfolio begins with a clear description of your purpose. We have shown that different structures or types of portfolios emerge based on different purposes. This first step requires that you clearly determine why you want students to create a portfolio. Do you want them to show you some growth toward a standard, do you want them to complete a project, or do you want them to show their thinking as they develop a solution to a problem? You may need to complete the next step before you make a firm decision about the purpose statement.

Relate the Portfolio Purpose to Your Learning Objectives and the Relevant Standards Using portfolios in the classroom necessitates that the portfolio matches your learning objectives and goals. It is critical to determine how the use of a portfolio will further your learning plans. Since portfolios are excellent tools to help students display their thinking and understandings, you will need to determine what thinking strategies you wish students to employ. This analysis will influence your decision concerning the purpose statement for the portfolio. It will help your focus if you write a purpose statement for the portfolio and then link that purpose statement to the learning goals.

Determine What Needs to Be Included in the Portfolio and Relate These Artifacts to Valued Learning Once you have clearly described the purpose of the portfolio, you must determine what artifacts (work samples, assessment results, and so on) should be included in the portfolio. Naturally, these artifacts are derived from your learning activities. The range of artifacts is determined by the extent of the subject matter and the unit of instruction, as shown in Figure 9.1.

Again, what goes into the portfolio should relate to the portfolio's specific purposes. If you want students to develop an understanding about some concept, there should be evidence that this concept has been mastered. You need to provide opportunities to complete artifacts that show this understanding. If you want students to show a specific skill, you need to include an artifact that requires the use of that skill. Ultimately, any artifact that you include in the portfolio should be considered an indicator of some important knowledge, skill, or disposition. Considering what each artifact tells you about student learning will help you determine if you have too many artifacts focused on the same learning target or too few that show mastery of another learning target.

Identify the Physical Structure of the Portfolio Now that you have a sense of the types of artifacts that you wish students to include in their portfolios, you must consider the physical structure of the portfolio. Where will students place their items? What type of container is appropriate? Do they need file folders, do they need plastic bins, do they need accordion files? How will the materials be organized—categorically, numerically, alphabetically, by subject area, or in some other way? Where can students store their portfolios so that they are easily accessible? Answers to these practical questions affect the successful use of portfolios in your classroom. If students cannot manage and access their materials effectively, they will become

Figure 9.1 *Examples of Artifacts for Portfolios, Organized by Subject Area*

Language Arts	Mathematics	Science	Social Studies
Favorite poems, songs, letters	Solution to an open-ended question	Prediction based on prior experience	Presentation of a view of society
Finished samples of different writing genres: persuasive, letters, poetry, information, stories	Graphs, histograms	Data tables	Written descriptions of different cultures, institutions, professions
Finished writings drawn from other subject areas	Geometric shapes	Concept maps	Discussion of equity, justice, democracy, freedom, rights, and other large social concepts
Literature extensions: scripts for drama, visual arts, webs, charts, timelines, murals	Examples of perimeter, area, cubic space	Drawings to scale	Drawings of artifacts
Audiotape of readings	Problem made up by student to display a concept	Graphs, inferences, conclusions based on data	Timelines
Notes from individual reading and research	Models, photo showing use of manipulatives	Diagrams, charts, interpretation of trends	Examples of constitutions and civic responsibilities
Writing responses that illustrate critical and creative thinking	Written discussion of mathematical concepts	Written discussion of science concepts	Position paper on a social issue
Writing responses to literacy components: plot, setting, point of view, character development, links to life, theme, criticism	Statistical manipulation of data	Inquiry designs	Investigation of a social issue
Items with evidence of style, organization, voice, clarity	Description of mathematical concepts found in the physical world	Science-technology-society connections	Family shield and explanation of symbols
Evidence of effort—first drafts, second drafts, finished drafts	Papers showing correction to mathematical errors	Example of a science misconception that is corrected	Proposal to respond to a social problem

discouraged. You may need to modify your original intentions based on your answers to practical considerations.

Because of the disadvantages of physical portfolios—their bulk, the difficulty in accessing a specific item in the portfolio, and the cost of maintaining multiple copies—the use of **e-portfolios** (electronic collections) has increased. Imagine preparing for the start of a new school year by logging in to your school's computer network, opening your new class list, and following a hyperlink to a developmental portfolio of each student's work from all previous grades. Each year's materials would include an assessment by the respective teachers to guide your understanding of each student's achievements, strengths, and weaknesses. How much more effective could this be in getting to know your incoming students than the paper file from the office or the discussions in the teachers' lounge?

While many schools have not reached the level of technology implementation just depicted, more basic approaches to e-portfolios are in widespread use. The most common is a CD of student work, organized generally by grade level and by subject at the secondary level. At the end of each school year as well as at various times during the year, learners add appropriate materials to the CD to create their evolving record. CD-based e-portfolios are within the technology skills range of most teachers and schools, and the cost for blank CDs is minimal.

Determine Sources and Learning Content That You Must Provide to Enable Students to Gather Evidence for Their Portfolio Once you have determined the purpose, content, and physical structure of the portfolio, it is important to examine your instructional plan. Carefully sequence what it is you will teach students to do and when and where you will provide time for the students to develop artifacts that show they have mastered the skill or content you have taught.

It is not enough to require students to complete an artifact; you must also provide the proper instruction. When using portfolios as assessments, this is especially tricky. You do not want to provide so much instruction that the students are no longer creating artifacts by using their own understandings and skills. If you tell students exactly what to do to create a product, the only thing that the product indicates is students' ability to follow directions. So, instruction needs to be more in the spirit of coaching rather than telling. However, this is easier said than done, and it can be difficult to determine that fine line. Ultimately, the key question to ask yourself is, Did I teach students the proper content and skill to create an artifact independently?

Determine Student Self-Reflection Opportunities Before implementing your portfolio assessment plan, establish guidelines to help students self-reflect along the way. The self-reflective questions in the Resource for Your Assessment Toolkit on page 244 give you a sample of different types of questions that may be helpful. The key at this point in the portfolio design process is to determine where and when to use which questions. And how will students answer these questions? Will they write their answers, discuss them with others, or simply think about them?

Identify Scoring Criteria for the Portfolio If you have carefully completed all the above steps, the task of developing scoring criteria will be a relatively easy one. Since scoring criteria relate to the specific artifacts you have already determined, you will find that developing the criteria for each artifact flows easily.

Share the Scoring Criteria with Students By discussing the scoring criteria prior to the development of each artifact, students can ask questions, suggest changes and additions, and ultimately develop a greater ownership of the process. Keep in mind that you as the teacher have the final responsibility and say-so about these evaluation procedures. You must be prepared to control the process to ensure integrity, quality, and fairness.

Clarify a Communication Method to Examine the Results of Portfolio Evaluation The final step for implementing portfolios is conducting a conference with each student to review its contents, the student's reflections, and your evaluations of the individual artifacts. Give your students guidelines for these conferences so that they can prepare some questions ahead of time. During the conference, allow students to do most of the talking. Make certain at the end of the conference that you and the student have a specific plan of action based on the strengths and limitations of the portfolio.

Strengths and Limitations of Portfolio Assessment

Portfolios have some compelling features that make their use attractive. They complement and encompass other assessment procedures, and they allow students to own the process and make it more meaningful. However, just like any other assessment procedure portfolios have both strengths and limitations. Review these so that you can better determine when and if you should take the time to design a portfolio assessment.

Benefits of Portfolio Assessment Portfolio assessments help students develop self-assessment skills. They provide opportunities for students to reflect on and see improvements in their work, and they provide motivation for students to continue to learn. Portfolio assessments provide excellent opportunities for students to practice thinking skills, to practice **self-assessment** by analyzing their work, to compare their work over time, to make decisions about what they need to do next, and to evaluate their own growth.

Portfolio assessments provide students with a level of control and responsibility for their learning. They afford students the opportunity to maintain and track their academic growth. Portfolio assessments involve a level of collaborative assessment; students are invited to add or modify evaluative criteria, and consequently the assessment process is partially theirs. Portfolio assessments are linked directly to instruction. The artifacts are developed as the instruction is provided, and this integrates portfolio assessment within the instructional process. For this reason, portfolios add a dimension of continuous improvement to assessment while reducing the stress that often accompanies the judgment dimension.

Limitations of Portfolio Assessment Like performance assessments, portfolio assessment is time-consuming. Many hours are needed to design a solid portfolio assessment plan, to integrate instruction properly, to review artifacts, to conduct student conferences, and to communicate results to parents and others. Portfolio assessments require extensive organization and management. Portfolios are filled with all sorts of artifacts that require room, organization, and resources. Portfolio assessment is not only time-consuming, but it may also be financially costly to provide videotapes, audiotapes, posters, boxes, files, paper, markers, and computer time.

Portfolio assessments, like performance assessments, tend to have limited generalizability. Because the scoring criteria is closely linked to specific artifacts and instruction is closely linked to the development of those specific artifacts, you must be careful not to overgeneralize the indicators. For example, if you evaluate a written artifact that is expository in nature, there is no guarantee that the student who receives a high score on that artifact will necessarily be able to write an expository piece in another discipline or another context. Your evaluation of the student's expository writing is limited to the context of the portfolio assignment.

?Ask Yourself

Consider a time when you were involved in selecting the criteria for an evaluation. What type of discussion did the teacher provide for student input? Did you find the experience meaningful? What would have made the experience more meaningful?

Rubric Development and Its Relationship to Assessment

The word *rubric* is used in many different ways in the field of education. These different uses have spawned different products all called rubrics that have very different structures. If you were to complete a web search based on the word *rubric,* you would find that the descriptions and examples vary greatly.

Digging Deeper
The Origins of Rubric

The word *rubric* is derived from the Latin word for "red clay." During the Roman empire, important laws were written in red clay, then baked and displayed on walls. Laws impressed in red clay were considered important, stable, and worthy of permanence.

In medieval times a rubric was considered a set of instructions or commentary attached to a law or liturgical service. These instructions were typically written in red, and, hence, rubric came to mean something that authoritatively instructs people.

Source: Popham, 1997.

Rubrics are sometimes used to describe a picture of what a scientist, mathematician, engineer, writer, or teacher is able to do at different points in their career. For example, a rubric of this sort would describe the characteristics of a beginning professional (sometimes called a novice), then describe an established professional, and then describe an expert. These labels (novice, established, expert) are termed *performance levels*. When a rubric is written for such a complex and abstract concept, the wording of the rubric is understandably abstract and general. A different use of the term *rubric* applies to a precise scoring guide used to evaluate a research paper, a project, or a performance. In this case, the wording for the rubric is far more specific and precise.

The Challenging Task of Defining Rubrics

Recall from Chapter 6 that a *rubric* is a set of rules specifying the criteria used to find out what students know and are able to do. In its simplest form, a rubric is nothing more than an answer key for a multiple-choice test. In this case, the only rule within the rubric is to count the number of correct answers and perhaps cluster the answers into different subtest scores. You normally do not write out this type of rubric because it is so simple. Nevertheless, whenever you score a paper-and-pencil test, you are creating a scoring rubric when you decide what criteria to use and how you will compile the scores (for example, whether to add all correct answers together or whether to weight certain answers to form a total score). While rubrics for multiple-choice tests are usually quite simple, much more thought and consideration is required when developing rubrics for a performance task or a portfolio.

One of the greatest challenges in assessing learning through performance tasks and portfolios is to identify the important knowledge and skill features of the task. As we suggested earlier, the process of figuring out those features can be likened to using an x-ray. An x-ray enables a physician to view the underlying structures that support the human body. In a sense, this is the view a teacher needs when determining how to assess a performance or a portfolio. Each performance task contains important underlying features, and each portfolio contains a number of artifacts that are *indicators* of the critical dimensions of learning and inquiry. In science, these dimensions include, for example, concept understanding, process skills, habits of mind, and science-technology-society (S-T-S) connections. In social studies these dimensions include concept understanding, critical thinking, and recognition of the rights of others. Teachers must step back from any educational performance or portfolio development task and, like a doctor with an x-ray, look beneath the surface of the performance to find the important dimensions that indicate knowledge or skill acquisition. Identifying these indicators is at the heart of conceptualizing rubrics.

There are many resources, especially online, that offer predeveloped rubrics. In general, these resources should be used with some caution. The key to developing a useful rubric is assuring that the set of rules specifically matches the task that you are trying to assess. Predeveloped rubrics most likely will not fully match the task that your students are being asked to complete. We recommend that you look at such predesigned rubrics simply to provide possible indicators or ideas for your context. On the other hand, websites that allow you to input relevant details—such as the behavior you are looking at, the dimensions of learning, the criteria of interest, and so on—may be useful in creating rubrics for your classroom. The key is that your set of rules validly matches what you intend to measure; only careful reflection can accomplish this task.

Types of Rubrics

Even though we have presented an overarching definition for rubrics as a set of rules that specifies what and how scoring criteria should be applied, the task of writing these rules is by no means simple. To add to the complexity, the form or structure of the rubric changes dramatically when applied to different targets. When a rubric is developed to answer a large and complex question such as, What is an expert scientist?, a generalized rubric is most appropriate. When writing a rubric to describe what criteria should be applied to a specific task, an analytic rubric is appropriate. It is important to understand these different types so that you will know which one to use and how to apply it to different types of targets.

Generalized Rubrics **Generalized rubrics** focus on large questions or concepts such as, What is the description of a good teacher? A competent scientist? A skilled mathematician? Or they focus on large tasks such as, What is the description of an excellent piece of writing? An outstanding science experiment? Brilliant detective work? A generalized scoring rubric focuses on the critical attributes of a task or professional as a single entity. Because the rubric must encompass a wide variety of contexts, the wording must remain abstract and general. Generalized rubrics are useful in that the description permits a

Figure 9.2 *Generalized Oral Presentation Rubric*

Expert	The presenter clearly describes the question and provides strong reasons for its importance. Specific information is provided to support the conclusions that are drawn. The delivery is engaging, and sentence structure is consistently correct. Eye contact is made and sustained throughout the presentation. There is strong evidence of preparation, organization, and enthusiasm for the topic. The visual aid is used to make the presentation more effective. Questions from the audience are clearly answered with specific and appropriate information.
Developed	The presenter describes the question and provides reasons for its importance. Adequate information is provided to support the conclusions that are drawn. The delivery is clear, and sentence structure is correct. There is evidence of preparation, organization, and enthusiasm for the topic. The visual aid is mentioned and used. Questions from the audience are clearly answered.
Developing	The presenter describes the question, conclusions are stated, but supporting information is limited. The delivery and sentence structure are understandable, but there are some errors. The visual aid is mentioned. Questions from the audience are answered.
Novice	The presenter states the question but fails to fully describe it. The delivery is difficult to follow, and the sentence structure may be weak. Few if any adequate conclusions are provided. There is limited evidence of preparation, organization, and enthusiasm for the topic. The visual aid is not used, or if so, ineffectively. Questions from the audience receive inadequate responses.

Source: Wiggins, 1998.

unity of focus. However, generalized rubrics do not yield precise assessment results. The best use of generalized rubrics is to aid communication by providing a common vocabulary across multiple settings.

Figure 9.2 identifies the criteria contained in a generalized rubric for an oral presentation task. Categories are listed on a continuum, describing the criteria from a novice presenter to an expert. The teacher uses the rubric by selecting the category along the continuum that best represents the student's performance during the oral presentation.

As you review the different descriptions of an expert, developed, developing, or novice oral presentation, you may find that there are dimensions that do not match a specific oral presentation that you assign to your students. For example, the rubric states that there is a question as the focus of the presentation. You may not have a question as the focus for your students, so this part of the rubric would need to be modified. You may have a more specific requirement for the use of a visual aid, so you would need to adapt this requirement. The key to using generalized rubrics is that they need to be carefully modified to match your actual assignments.

Developing Generalized Rubrics You might wonder how such generalized rubrics are developed. Often, experts come together to discuss the precise meaning of some general task or description of a professional in their field. As experts in the field, they share their different ideas about valued knowledge, skills, dispositions, or about the structure of some significant task. Generally, all the ideas are presented and saved in a master list.

Once all participating experts have had the chance to share their points of view, the different characteristics are categorized into key dimensions that make up an expert description or expert implementation of a task. Discussion continues until consensus is achieved.

Once a description of an expert professional or expert performance is written, the expert panel considers what a novice or beginner description or performance might include. The same listing and discussion occurs until agreement is reached. This process is repeated until the continuum of categories from novice to expert is finished. Finally, the rubric is released to other experts in the field for their review and comment. Modifications are made, and the generalized rubric is released for general use.

Unfortunately, this procedure is not always followed with care. Sometimes rubrics are developed by an individual or a company without such a precise process. It is wise to check how a generalized rubric was developed before you begin using it.

Figure 9.3 shows a generalized rubric for observing problem-solving skills. Note that the names of the various levels differ, and the indicators are described in simple, parallel, sentences.

Analytic Rubrics Another approach to developing rubrics requires teachers to identify the specific knowledge and skills features that are critical to and inherent in a task. By specifying these knowledge and skill features in advance, teachers can assess concept understanding, process skills, and habits of mind as separate components. **Analytic rubrics** yield more precise assessment results than do generalized rubrics. The limitation of analytic rubrics is that they focus on specific tasks and cannot be generalized across different contexts.

Developing Analytic Rubrics For a multifaceted assessment task (whether it is a performance assessment or a portfolio assessment), the teacher identifies

Figure 9.3 *Generalized Rubric for Observing Students Applying Problem-Solving Skills*

Level	Descriptors
Exemplary	Applies problem-solving skills *consistently*. Applies problem-solving skills *independently*. Explains rationale for *each step* of the process. Transfers skills to solve *more challenging* problems.
Accomplished	Applies problem-solving skills *most* of the time. Applies problem-solving skills with *some* assistance. Explains rationale for *most* steps of the process. Transfers skills to solve *most* similar problems.
Developing	Applies problem-solving skills *some* of the time. Applies problem-solving skills with *significant* assistance. Explains rationale for *some* steps of the process. Transfers skills to solve *some* similar problems.
Beginning	Cannot apply problem-solving skills even with assistance. Cannot explain the process to demonstrate understanding. Cannot solve similar problems even with assistance.

which of the many features of the task or portfolio artifacts will be assessed. Using learning dimensions of concept understanding, concept application, thinking strategies and process skills, habits of mind, and other valued areas of achievement as a guide, the teacher lists those student behaviors or indicators of learning that relate to the important learning dimensions that they have taught and expect students to be able to master. The teacher then assigns a rating of "complete" (there is sufficient evidence), or "almost" (evidence present but incomplete), or "not yet" (little to no evidence). "Complete" means that the student exhibited the indicator; "almost" means that there is some evidence that the student exhibited the indicator, but something is incorrect or missing; and "not yet" means that the student did not show evidence of learning for that indicator.

The analytic rubric provides separate scores for multiple dimensions implicit in each student's work. In this way, analytic scoring allows for more specific observation and detailed feedback than generalized rubrics. Scoring criteria include a description of the dimensions for evaluating a student performance, standards for judging performance, and a scale of values for rating the dimensions. Well-articulated evaluation criteria are needed to help teachers define excellence; to communicate goals and results to students and parents; to help the teacher be accurate, unbiased, and consistent in scoring, and to document the observation used to make judgments about the students.

Carefully crafted analytic rubrics not only point to the key learning dimensions that should be assessed, but, like all good assessments, they also illuminate instruction. Since analytic rubrics specify the key indicators of learning within a task, teachers can quickly note if one of those task indicators is consistently not evident in students' work. Immediately, the teacher has a specific target for further instruction.

Examples of Projects and Their Analytic Rubrics Let's examine some specific assessment tasks or projects that require the development of an analytic rubric. Figure 9.4 presents such an illustrative science task.

This analytic rubric relates to three tasks that students are asked to perform as part of a science study and assessment of fossil development. In Activity 1 students are given a fossil-rich "site." They are asked to make a scale drawing one-half the size of the site and label the coordinates on a grid. Using simple tools, students excavate four fossils from the site. They describe the fossils and use coordinate symbols to indicate the location of the specimens on the scale drawing.

Figure 9.4 *Analytic Rubric for a Study of Fossils Project*

Indicators of Learning Found in Performance Activities	Complete	Almost	Not Yet	Dimensions of Learning Related to Indicators
Activity 1 Indicators				**Dimensions of Learning**
The student				
Wrote a detailed description of the site.				Observation
Measured the size of the site in centimeters.				Measurement
Drew a model to scale—½.				Scale
Labeled the coordinates correctly.				Graphing
Gave coordinates of locations of four fossils.				Graphing
Placed fossils or letters correctly on the map.				Graphing
Gave logical answer regarding use of map.				Reasoning

(continued)

Figure 9.4 *Analytic Rubric for a Study of Fossils Project (continued)*

Indicators of Learning Found in Performance Activities	Complete	Almost	Not Yet	Dimensions of Learning Related to Indicators
Activity 2 Indicators				**Dimensions of Learning**
The student				
Drew or traced four specimens with detail.				Representation
Measured and recorded length of each fossil.				Measurement (length)
Measured and recorded width of each fossil.				Measurement (width)
Measured and recorded mass of each fossil.				Measurement (mass)
Made inferences about fossil relationships to exisng organisms.				Inference
Activity 3 Indicators				**Dimensions of Learning**
The student				
Listed one way two fossils are alike.				Comparison
Found and recorded names of four fossils.				Information gathering
Identified two organisms similar to fossils.				Properties of organisms
Listed characteristics of fossils that are similar to the two present-day organisms.				Properties of organisms

Source: Adapted from Hammerman and Musial, 2008.

In Activity 2 students are asked to make a drawing of each of the four fossils. This is an important skill that researchers need in order to record the intricate features of their finds. Students will measure the length, width, and mass of each fossil. Then they will study each fossil's characteristics to determine if any of them resembles organisms that are alive today.

In Activity 3 students are asked to compare their fossils to one another. Do they have any characteristics in common? Are any two alike? Students are challenged to find at least one way that any two of the fossils are alike. They are provided access to field guides and reference books for fossils to find the type and name of each specimen. From these resources and others, students can find names or pictures of similar present-day organisms. Students research and learn as much as they can about their four fossils and the organisms they resemble. The analytic rubric identifies the key learning indicators that relate to the three activities.

Figure 9.5 is an analytic rubric used to assess a student-designed TV commercial. Students study propaganda techniques and work in pairs to create a 1-minute commercial selling the product Cherry Crunch. Students are allowed to select a Cherry Crunch product (cereal, ice cream, makeup, and so on) and actually package the product for their commercial. The

Figure 9.5 *Rubric for Observing Student Presentation of TV Commercial*

Cherry Crunch Commercial

Stars *[Students' names]*

_____

_____

Criteria	Two Thumbs Up	One Thumb Up, One Thumb Down	Two Thumbs Down
Propaganda Technique	Clearly illustrated	Difficult to determine	Can't tell at all
Equal Parts	Fairly shared	One person has some-what larger part	One person dominates
Time: 55–60 sec.	55–60 sec.	61–65 sec. or 50–54 sec.	More than 65 or less than 50 sec.
Enunciation	Clear and distinct	Sometimes slurred	Very fast and slurred
Organization	Planned and pre-pared	Somewhat disorganized	Not ready, very disorganized
Originality	Brand-new idea	Looks a little familiar	Obviously copied
Neat Product Packaging	All elements are neat, clean, straight; spelling is correct	Missing one element	Missing more than one element

descriptors are those used by movie critics and are selected by the students. The teacher assigns the point values to the categories and creates an equivalent percentage scale.

An example of an analytic rubric for observing student behavior is shown in Figure 9.6. This is a rubric used to score individual students as

Figure 9.6 *Analytic Rubric for Evaluating Individual Group Members*

	4	3	2	1
Contributions	Routinely provides useful ideas when participating in the group and in classroom discussion. A definite leader who contributes a lot of effort.	Usually provides useful ideas when participating in the group and in classroom discussion. A strong group member who tries hard!	Sometimes provides useful ideas when participating in the group and in classroom discussion. A satisfactory group member who does what is required.	Rarely provides useful ideas when participating in the group and in classroom discussion. May refuse to participate.
Problem Solving	Actively looks for and suggests solutions to problems.	Refines solutions suggested by others.	Does not suggest or refine solutions, but is willing to try out solutions suggested by others.	Does not try to solve problems or help others solve problems. Lets others do the work.
Attitude	Never is publicly critical of the project or the work of others. Always has a positive attitude about the task(s).	Rarely is publicly critical of the project or the work of others. Often has a positive attitude about the task(s).	Occasionally is publicly critical of the project or the work of other members of the group. Usually has a positive attitude about the task(s).	Often is publicly critical of the project or the work of other members of the group. Often has a negative attitude about the task(s).
Working with Others	Almost always listens to, shares with, and supports the efforts of others. Tries to keep people working well together.	Usually listens to, shares with, and supports the efforts of others. Does not cause waves in the group.	Often listens to, shares with, and supports the efforts of others, but sometimes is not a good team member.	Rarely listens to, shares with, and supports the efforts of others. Often is not a good team player.

Source: Generated on RubiStar, *rubistar.4teachers.org.*

they work in a cooperative group, created on an Internet rubric generator site (http://www.rubistar.4teachers.org/), which is noted at the end of this chapter under Relevant Website Resources.

Holistic Rubrics Now that we have clarified the distinction between generalized and analytic rubrics, let's consider one other type of rubric that incorporates elements of both the analytic and generalized. **Holistic rubrics** are scoring guides that relate to an assessment task, test, or project in much the same way that analytic rubrics do. However, instead of identifying the specific criteria and detailing these criteria prior to assessment, some educators claim that it is better to examine the task as a whole (hence the *holistic*) rather than to look at the individual indicators separately.

Developing Holistic Rubrics In developing a holistic scoring guide, the teacher uses an overall judgment to determine the quality of an assessment task. One way of developing a holistic rubric in the context of a portfolio assessment is to first review all of the portfolio artifacts and then place them in piles based on their overall quality. The teacher might also try to rank all of the artifacts from best to worst. Once this is completed, the teacher would return to each artifact and identify both the strengths and weaknesses of the artifact, trying to determine what differentiates the best from the next-best, and so on down through the samples.

A more formal approach to developing a holistic rubric would be as follows. The teacher identifies a worthy task that students are capable of completing at a specific grade level. Then, instead of writing the rubric immediately, the students are told to perform the task while the teacher views the students' performances in their entirety. Having viewed the performances, the teacher separates the performances into two groups: those that were adequate and those that were not. Once the performances have been separated, the teacher reviews the adequate performances and selects a subgroup that performed more than adequately and labels that group "exceptional."

Then the teacher reviews the performances that were inadequate and once again separates the inadequate performances into two subgroups: those performances that were merely inadequate and those that were seriously inadequate. Finally, the teacher returns to each of the four groups from "seriously inadequate" to "exceptional" and writes a holistic description of the characteristics of each category. The descriptions are then analyzed and revised until they effectively distinguish each description from the others. These written descriptions make up the final generalized or holistic rubric that is now available for use to score other student work on the same performance. Figure 9.7 is a holistic rubric that divides the possible skill indicators for writing a story (the analytic rubriclike component) into four categories (the generalized rubriclike aspect).

Figure 9.7 *Holistic Rubric for Writing a Story*

Undeveloped Story/Serious Inadequacies	Paper is a listing of related events. More than one event is described but with few details about setting, characters, or the events.
Basic Story/Inadequate	Paper describes a series of events, giving details (in at least two or three sentences) about some aspect of the story (events, characters' goals, problems to be solved). However, the story is confusing or incomplete: At the end of the story the characters' goals are ignored or the problems inadequately resolved; the beginning does not match the rest of the story; the internal logic or plausibility of characters' actions is not maintained; the story lacks cohesion.
Developed Story/Adequate	Paper describes a sequence of episodes in which almost all story elements (setting episodes, characters' goals, or problems to be solved) are clearly developed with simple resolution of these goals or problems at the end. May have one or two problems or may include too much detail.
Elaborate Story/Excellent	Paper describes a sequence of episodes in which almost all story elements (setting episodes, characters' goals, or problems to be solved) are well developed. The resolutions of the goals or problems at the end are fleshed out. The events are presented and elaborated in a cohesive way.

Source: Adapted from "Writing Framework and Specifications for the 1998 National Assessment of Educational Progress." (1997).

Figure 9.8 is a rubric also focused on writing. In this case the task is part of the Illinois Standards Achievement Test (ISAT), developed by the Illinois State Department of Education. This figure shows a self-assessment version of a rubric for writing an extended response to a reading prompt. This rubric again is holistic, offering an overall judgment of the student's skills. Instead of category names (expert, novice, and so on), numbers are used in this student-friendly version.

Getting Rubrics Right

What flaws can make a rubric unusable? Several have been articulated by W. James Popham (1997):

- *Flaw 1: Task-specific rubrics that are too narrow.* When the criteria for an assessment task are linked only to the specific elements in that task, you cannot assume that the skills and concepts required in completing that specific task will generalize to other, similar, tasks.

Figure 9.8 *Student-Friendly Holistic Rubric for Illinois State Board of Education Extended-Response Reading Test, Grades 3 and 4*

4	I explain the main ideas and important information from the text. I connect my own ideas or experiences to the author's ideas. I use examples and important details to support my answer. I balance the author's ideas with my own ideas.
3	I explain some of the main ideas and important information from the text. I connect some of my own ideas and experiences to the author's ideas. I use some examples and important details to support my answer. I balance only some of the author's ideas with my own ideas.
2	I explain only a few ideas from the text. I summarize the text without including any of my own ideas or experiences. OR I explain my own ideas without explaining the text. I use general statements instead of specific details and examples.
1	I explain little or nothing from the text. I use incorrect or unimportant information from the text. I write too little to show I understand the text. I write nothing.
0	I do not respond to the task.

Source: Reformatted from "Extended-Response Reading Rubric, Grades 3 and 4 Student-Friendly Rubric."

- *Flaw 2: Rubrics that contain excessively general criteria.* On the other hand, when criteria are stated in a general manner without specifics, there is no certainty that the indicator has actually been achieved.

- *Flaw 3: Rubrics that have inappropriate detail.* Another shortcoming in some rubrics is detail that is not focused on the learning outcome. Rubrics should focus on the appropriate indicators and criteria and omit extraneous material. Lengthy, overly detailed, rubrics are apt to be used improperly because the excessive length confuses rather than clarifies.

- *Flaw 4: Equating the test of the skill with the skill itself.* Sometimes a rubric that matches the specific behaviors of the task gives the impression that the behavior itself is the criterion. In fact, the behavior in a

Resource for Your Assessment Toolkit
Guidelines for Selecting Rubrics

The following recommendations concerning the selection of a rubric were developed by teachers working in the Chicago public schools.

Considerations When Selecting a Rubric

- Does the rubric relate to the outcome(s) being measured? Does it address anything extraneous?
- Does the rubric cover important dimensions of student performance?
- Do the criteria reflect current conceptions of "excellence" in the field?
- Are the dimensions or scales well defined?
- Is there a clear basis for assigning scores at each scale point?

- Can the rubric be applied consistently by different scorers?
- Can the rubric be understood by students and parents?
- Is the rubric developmentally appropriate?
- Can the rubric be applied to a variety of tasks?
- Is the rubric fair and free from bias?
- Is the rubric useful, feasible, manageable, and practical?

Source: Chicago Public Schools: Instructional Intranet.

---

task, such as developing an operation definition, is not the focus of the rubric. Rather it is only one indicator for a process skill in science. More behaviors in different contexts are necessary to determine if the skill itself has been mastered.

The more quickly we abandon excessively detailed task-specific rubrics as well as excessively general and fuzzy rubrics the more likely we will come up with rubrics that actually enhance instruction. The best advice we can provide is to focus on learning targets and then make certain that the rubrics that are used match these targets. It is a challenging task, but over time and with practice the task of developing good rubrics can be achieved.

Ask Yourself

Review some of the rubrics that were used to evaluate your work in your courses. How might you describe the characteristics of rubrics that you believe really captured what you knew and could do? What types of rubrics seemed to be the most meaningful to you? Compare these rubrics to rubrics that you believe did not accurately capture what you knew and were able to do. How might you describe the characteristics of these rubrics?

Summary

- Portfolios are purposeful, organized collections of evidence (artifacts) that demonstrate a person's knowledge, skill, or ability.

- Portfolios require teachers to provide specific, predetermined guidelines but also allow student participation in the selection of evidence.

- Portfolios offer opportunities to observe students in a broader context: taking risks, developing creative solutions, and learning to make judgments about their performances.

- Portfolios allow students to assume ownership in ways that few other instructional approaches or assessments allow because they must collect and reflect on examples of their work to create the portfolio. Portfolios help students develop self-assessment skills.

- Different types of portfolios provide different assessment evidence. Project portfolios show the steps of a completed project or task. Product portfolios show the results of a completed project or task. Growth portfolios display changes and accomplishments related to academic performance over time. Standards-based portfolios collect evidence that link student achievement to particular learning standards. Celebration portfolios display examples of students' favorite works or accomplishments. Journal portfolios, or learning logs, provide a structure for students to continuously collect and reflect on their work.

- Portfolio assessment has a number of limitations. It is time-consuming, requires extensive organization and management, and has limited generalizability.

- Generalized rubrics focus on large questions or concepts such as, What is the description of a good teacher? Or on large tasks such as, What is the description of an excellent piece of writing?

- Analytic rubrics require teachers to identify the specific knowledge and skills features that are critical to and inherent in a task.

- Holistic rubrics allow teachers to use an overall judgment to determine the quality of an assessment task.

- Several common flaws should be avoided when writing rubrics: They can be too specific or too general, they can include excessive detail, and they can equate the test of a skill with the skill itself.

Key Terms

analytic rubric (253)

artifact (239)

celebration portfolio (242)

e-portfolio (247)

folio (239)

generalized rubric (251)

growth portfolio (241)

holistic rubric (259)

journal portfolio (242)

portfolio (239)

product portfolio (241)

project portfolio (240)

self-assessment (248)

self-reflection (239)

standards-based portfolio (241)

For Further Discussion

1. How might instruction differ when a teacher wants to assess a pupil's progress through a portfolio assessment rather than through selected-response assessments?

2. Why would a teacher choose to use portfolio assessments when there is currently so much emphasis in schools on standardized selected-response assessments?

3. What type of rubric do you believe best fits your teaching style? Discuss your reasons for your selection.

Comprehension Quiz

Part One

Indicate which type of portfolio best fits these purposes:

Celebration (C)

Growth (G)

Standards-based (S)

1. To show examples of all of a student's work that matches learning outcomes

2. To demonstrate students' best works throughout the year

3. To indicate progress on an important skill

Part Two

Indicate which of the following is an advantage (A) or disadvantage (D) of using portfolio assessments.

1. Collaboration between student and teacher

2. Student selection of contents

3. Continuous monitoring of student progress

4. Generalizability

5. Student self-reflection

6. Time needed to develop

Part Three

Indicate which type of rubric best fits these situations:

Generalized (G)

Analytic (A)

Holistic (H)

1. To assess what specific knowledge and skills have been mastered

2. To develop a common rubric for a science experiment throughout the district

3. To determine what learning objectives need to be retaught

4. To determine which students wrote excellent creative writing pieces

Relevant Website Resources

Electronic Portfolios: Students, Teachers, and Life-Long Learners

http://eduscapes.com/tap/topic82.htm

This website provides a mini-directory of website links concerning electronic portfolios. Here you can find articles and samples of electronic portfolios for teachers and students.

Office of Educational Research and Improvement (OERI) of the U.S. Department of Education: Consumer Guides

http://www.ed.gov/pubs/OR/ConsumerGuides/classuse.html

The U.S. Department of Education explains what a student portfolio is and how it could be beneficial in the classroom. For those who are interested in getting more information on student portfolios and their uses, different contact information is available on the website.

Rubistar

http://rubistar.4teachers.org/index.php

The website allows you to select the type of skill, behavior, or product; the dimensions of each criteria, and the number of levels of performance. You need to register in order to save your rubric, but the website is free.

References

Arter, J., & Spandel, V. (1992). Using portfolios of student work in instruction and assessment. *Educational Measurement Issues and Practice, 11,* 36–44.

Burke, K., Fogarty, R., & Belgrad, S. (2002). *The portfolio connection: Student work linked to standards.* 2nd ed. Thousand Oaks, CA: Corwin Press.

Camp, R. (1992). "Portfolio reflections in middle and secondary school classrooms." In K. B. Yancy (Ed.), *Portfolios in the writing classroom.* Urbana IL: National Council of Teachers of English.

McMillan, James H. (2004). *Classroom assessment: Principles and practice for effective instruction.* Boston, MA: Pearson Allyn and Bacon.

Popham, J. W. (1997). What's wrong and what's right with rubrics. *Educational Leadership*, October, 72–75. From http://www.newadvent.org/cathen/13216a.htm. Accessed December 12, 2007.

Stiggins, Richard J. (2005). *Student-involved assessment for learning.* Boston, MA: Pearson Prentice Hall.

CHAPTER 10

Developing Grading Procedures

Chapter Objectives

After reading and thinking about this chapter, you will be able to:

- **Explain the difference between assessment and grading.**
- **Explain the purposes of evaluating and reporting student work.**
- **Understand the importance of grading academic achievement.**

- **Recognize the problems of including behavior, attendance, and attitude in grades.**
- **Discuss the advantages and disadvantages of typical grading systems.**
- **Describe some alternatives to traditional grading systems.**

Two teachers—teaching the same course using the same syllabus and with identical course assignments—differ in one respect. Teacher A has a grading scale defined by percentage: 90 percent for an A, 80 percent for a B and so on. Teacher B announces on the first day of class that all students in the class will earn A's for the course if they actively engage in the class and submit assignments that reflect student effort. How do you think this would affect student motivation in both classes? Grades carry significant weight with students; honor societies, college admissions, athletic eligibility, and scholarships often depend on students' grades. But what does a grade communicate to others, and is a grade a meaningful indicator of student learning?

We have seen so far that designing and implementing valid assessment tools that help students learn is a complex and challenging task. Perhaps even more challenging is the task of assigning a grade to represent student progress. Grades can mean different things to students, teachers, parents, administrators, researchers, school boards, colleges and universities, potential employers, and the policymakers who write education law. For more than 100 years, the great majority of schools in the United States have used some form of letter grades (A, B, C, D, F), words (excellent, good, acceptable, needs work, poor), or percentages (90%, 80%, 70%) to describe student progress. The importance of these grades is so engrained in the minds of most of today's students that it may seem that learning itself is not as important as the grade that is received.

In this chapter we ask you to consider the role of grades and grading in interpreting and communicating student learning. We look at the way that educators translate the complex issues of learning and assessment into reporting systems that provide feedback to students, parents, and other interested parties. We examine common grading practices and the problems associated with them. We also take a look at what some schools are doing in search of grading systems that give better descriptions of student progress, that help students learn, and that provide valid information that is clearly understood by all interested parties.

Foundational Questions for Your Consideration

- In what ways does traditional letter grading help or hinder student learning?
- Does the fact that most colleges and universities use grades and grade point averages to help determine who gains access to these institutions justify the use of letter grades in elementary, middle, and high school?
- Should grades be permanent once they are assigned or should students have the opportunity to revisit course material and prove mastery at a later date?
- Who should be involved in determining grading policies: state boards of education, local school boards, administrators, individual teachers, parents, students?

What Is a Grade?

In Chapter 1 we defined *assessment* as the art of placing learners in a context that brings out what it is a learner knows and can do, as well as what a learner may not know or be able to do. We used the image of a teacher sitting beside a student to better understand what the student knows and can do. Grading is often confused with assessment, but the two are not the same.

Grading is the process of holistically evaluating student performance and assigning evaluative symbols to represent what a learner knows and can do, or may not know or be able to do, as evidenced by various assessments. Notice that *assessment* revolves around what the *student* does, whereas *grading* is a summative judgment made by the *teacher*. Teachers develop grading practices for their classrooms and "assign" or "give" grades, and students "receive" or "get" them.

A Grade's Essential Dimensions

A grade has two critical elements: It is based on an analysis of assessment data, and it involves an interpretation that is communicated to others. The two elements are sometimes in conflict in traditional grading practice.

Analysis of Assessment Data Data analysis is the element over which you as a teacher will have important control. You will be basing your grades on the assessment information you gather on each of your students. This again underlines the importance of creating meaningful and valid assessments, using the methods discussed throughout this book. If you develop ways to find out as precisely as possible what it is that your students know and can do, you will have a meaningful basis for making evaluative statements about them. If your assessments are poorly conceived and hastily made, you will be basing your grades on poor data, on information that does not truly reflect your students' achievement and performance.

Most people agree that the purpose of grades is to communicate students' academic achievement. The grades become blurred or distorted, however, when they include a variety of nonacademic factors such as attendance, tardies, effort, attitude, late work, class participation, group work, class discussions, or behavior.

Students who achieve high scores on end-of-course tests, state standardized tests, and national standardized tests may, in fact, receive low grades from their teachers because they lost points for nonacademic factors, such as behavior or effort. Students and parents are understandably concerned by the disconnect between students' grades and their academic achievement as measured by instruments outside of your classroom.

The opposite also occurs when teachers include extra credit points or add in bonus points based on students' perfect attendance, punctuality, cooperation, positive attitude, and good behavior. Some of these students may receive high grades enhanced by the bonus points for their class work but fail standardized assessments. We agree with Ken O'Connor, who says that "For grades to have real meaning, they must be relatively pure measures of each student's achievement of the learning goals for each course" (2002, p. 87). Grades that reflect valid data based on students' academic achievement related to standards provide an accurate picture for students, parents, and others.

Interpretation and Communication of Grades Having gathered and compiled data from your students' assessments, you will then make a judgment about the meaning of these data. This judgment requires that you interpret the assessment data you have analyzed. Your interpretation is based on a set of criteria that either you or your school district establish. Thomas Guskey and Jane Bailey (2001) describe the types of *learning criteria* used in grading and reporting as falling into three broad categories: product, process, and progress.

- **Product criteria** are favored by advocates of standards-based and performance-based approaches to teaching and learning. These educators believe the primary purpose of grading and reporting is to communicate a summative evaluation of student achievement and performance (Cangelosi, 1990). In other words, they focus on *what* students know and are able to do at a particular point in time. Teachers who use product criteria often base their grades or reports exclusively on final examination scores, final products (reports or projects), overall assessments, and other culminating demonstrations of learning.

- **Process criteria** are emphasized by educators who believe product criteria do not provide a complete picture of student learning. From their perspective, grading and reporting should reflect not just the final results but also *how* students got there. Teachers who consider effort or work habits when reporting on student learning are using process criteria. So too are teachers who count regular classroom quizzes, homework, class participation, or attendance.

- **Progress criteria** are used by educators who believe it is most important to consider how much students have gained from their learning experiences. Other names for progress criteria include educational growth, learning gain, improvement scoring, and value-added learning.

Even though some educators recommend basing all grades on the final product to communicate a summative evaluation of student achievement and performance, many teachers consider it fair to reward low-ability students who try hard and make progress and to penalize high-ability students who do not exert any effort to improve. Some report cards include sections for attributes such as progress, process, effort, and growth so it becomes evident that these criteria are being reported separately from academic achievement and proficiency in meeting standards. Regardless of the reporting system, teachers must communicate clearly to students and parents the criteria they use to interpret students' assessment data.

Sometimes the process for determining grades is not developed by the teacher alone. Many schools and districts have developed guidelines that must be followed by all teachers as a way to ensure consistency and fairness. But no matter who specifies the criteria, it is you who makes the judgment. You will assign a symbol to holistically describe the students' achievements in order to communicate simply and crisply to others. As an expert—and as a good teacher you will be an expert on the students in

Figure 10.1 *Two Critical Elements of a Grade*

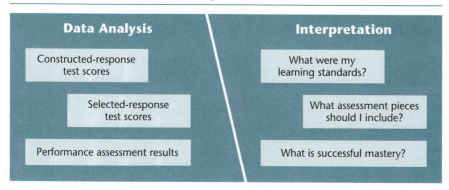

your classroom—you will be making a professional decision regarding the significance of the data you have compiled for your students. You will decide that *this* level of accomplishment is "an A" or "satisfactory" or "pass," or 93 percent, while *this* level of accomplishment is "poor" or "needs improvement" or "objective is not met." Figure 10.1 describes the two critical aspects of grading.

Given how difficult it can be to compile and analyze students' assessment data and how arbitrary it can be to interpret these data and assign grades to certain levels of achievement, why do we do it? Where did this kind of grading come from?

How Grades Came to Be: A Brief History of Grading Practices

Some writers have traced the beginning of letter grading in the United States to the late eighteenth century at Yale. Like other institutions, Yale had been using written descriptions of student work that were prepared by professors as final statements about students' proficiency in each class. During the 1780s they made the change to the use of a 4-point scale, which they saw as a way to add efficiency to their evaluative system (Durm, 1993). This "more efficient" practice spread to other American universities over the next century, replacing descriptive written statements first with percentages and later with letter grades to characterize student progress.

As universities looked for a way to ensure that only those who were truly prepared were accepted into their institutions of higher learning, they pressed high schools to be accountable for what students were learning. One important result was the establishment of Carnegie units (equal to 120 contact hours or 1 year of course credit) for subject area courses. Ultimately, the requirement of a minimum number of credits or Carnegie units in order to graduate from high school led educational institutions to implement and apply various grading systems in high schools. The grading trend eventually spread to elementary schools, and today even first-graders in many school districts receive report cards with letter grades.

Why Do We Grade Students?

Evaluating student performance and reporting the evaluation to others—the student, the parents, the school, colleges, or employers—serves a number of important purposes. The Joint Committee on Standards for Educational Evaluation (Gullickson, 2003) compiled the views of 16 North American associations ranging from the American Association of School Administrators to the National School Boards Association. They established Proprietary Standards to ensure that student evaluations will be conducted legally, ethically, and with due regard for the well-being of the students. Proprietary Standard P1 is "Service to Students" and it states, "Evaluations of students should promote sound educational principles, fulfillment of institutional missions, and effective student work, so that educational needs of students are served" (Gullickson, 2003, p. 27). The explanation of Standard P1 is as follows:

> A major purpose of student evaluation is to guide students, their parents/guardians, and educators in the students' acquisition of the knowledge, skills, attitudes, and behaviors that they will need as adults to participate in a democratic society. Student evaluations should help students and other stakeholders understand the goals and objectives of instruction and each student's status and progress in relation to these desired outcomes. In addition, student evaluations should help students, parents/guardians, and teachers plan future instruction and where needed, appropriate follow-up remedial action. (p. 29)

Feedback Students need feedback on their performance from their teachers. The most useful way to get that feedback is immediately from the teacher during learning activities. Students like and need to have a sense of how well they are meeting the expectations of their teachers. While they have received various types of feedback on quizzes, reports, and performances, they may find it difficult to mentally integrate these individual pieces of data to determine how they are doing. Grades can do this.

Communication Parents use grades to understand how their children are doing in school. Like students, parents may have difficulty assimilating the many different sources of assessment data available for their children, and the grade provides them with a quick and easy summary of their children's progress. Most parents are familiar with traditional letter grading from their educational past and expect something similar for their children. Some parents reward their children for getting good grades, or punish them for getting bad grades, sometimes going as far as paying them for each A or taking them on a vacation for making the honor roll.

Grades offer quick and concise data points for guidance counselors who are helping students plan their high school courses or apply to college. They also help employers determine the academic qualifications of students applying for jobs.

Accountability Elementary, middle, and high schools use grades as part of the formula to determine which students pass to the next level of study and which students are required to stay behind because they have not demonstrated sufficient knowledge to continue. This is another important reason for teachers to be sure that the grades they assign are valid and actually reflect what a student knows and can do.

Schools often use grades as a motivator: In many schools, students cannot participate in extracurricular activities unless they have a minimum grade point average. High schools sometimes attach privileges to students' GPAs by allowing off-campus lunch or parking permits to students performing above a certain level in a given semester.

Sorting True to their origins, GPAs and transcripts of grades are still used as part of the formula for determining entrance to most colleges and universities. Many universities require that students have a minimum GPA and/or be in the top 10 percent, 15 percent, or 25 percent of their graduating class in order to gain entrance. Grading in this context is not focused on how far a student has progressed on a learning continuum but instead is merely describing where the student sits in relation to others of the same age. For this purpose, grades are an easy and manageable way to separate out the "best" students from the rest.

Digging Deeper
Do Grades Motivate Students?

One of most common beliefs about grades is that, without them, students would not study or do their schoolwork. Grades are held out as the prize that you get when you apply yourself and learn and the punishment you receive when you do not work hard.

Although we would like to think that students have an innate love of learning and they are intrin-sically motivated to learn, grades are important factors in determining how much effort students put forth. Students are also motivated by the recognition they receive when they make the honor roll, win acceptance into national honor societies, get nominated for Star Student, win scholarships, and get recognized at awards ceremonies. Good grades have some perks—not to mention the

(continued)

Digging Deeper
Do Grades Motivate Students? (continued)

money for A's on report cards often awarded by proud parents and grandparents.

According to Guskey and Bailey (2001), no studies support the use of low grades or marks as punishments. Some students simply withdraw from learning and pretend that the low grades do not matter to them. They may become discipline problems as a result of trying to mask their embarrassment and protect their self-image among their peers. Teachers, in turn, may use grades to punish students who misbehave or demonstrate poor attitude toward the teacher or the work. If the students do not comply with the teacher's wishes, they will suffer the consequences of a failing grade—the most powerful punishment a teacher can give.

> Such practices have no educational value and, in the long run, adversely affect students, teachers, and the relationship they share. Rather than attempting to punish students with a low grade or mark in the hope it will prompt greater effort in the future, teachers can better motivate students by considering their work as incomplete and then requiring additional effort. (Guskey & Bailey, 2001, p. 35)

Just as some students are motivated by the recognition they receive for making good grades, students with low or failing grades also suffer from more than losing their self-esteem. Some districts enforce the "no pass/no play" rule where students who fall below a C average or who receive a D or an F in any subject are banned from participating in sports or extracurricular activities. Sometimes these students are not motivated by academic success but will make an extra effort because of their desire to play football, try out for cheerleading, or play in the band. When their reason for coming to school is eliminated by one or two low grades, their motivation to learn may also suffer. The most traumatic punishments for failing grades include

the students' embarrassment about flunking a course, getting assigned to summer school, being retained, or not graduating with their class. Retention in any grade is a strong predictor of dropping out of school later, and it can destroy the self-esteem of the students.

In fact, rather than grades being a motivator, research has demonstrated that students have a tendency to show less interest in learning when they are graded (Butler & Nisan, 1986; Grolnick & Ryan, 1987). The importance of grades is stressed to students from an early age and leads many to focus on simply doing what is necessary to get the good grade, instead of focusing on learning. It also leads some students to cheat in order to gain rewards or avoid punishment. Teachers say it is not uncommon for parents to help their children cheat in order to get a good grade. In this case, parents and students certainly may be motivated to get high grades, but learning may be incidental to the activities that produce the high grades.

With so much attention on the grade, students lose sight of actual learning as the goal of education. Research shows that the emphasis on grades tends to keep students from taking on challenging courses and assignments (Kohn, 1994). When grades become the goal of education, students of all ages realize that the easier the task, the higher the likelihood of getting a good grade. What motivation does a student have to choose difficult coursework or assignments if the consequence may be getting a lower grade?

The use of a traditional grading system may motivate students to do what is necessary to get good grades, but if we want to encourage deep learning, research shows that grades may be a direct hindrance to achieving that goal (Butler & Nisan, 1986; Grolnick & Ryan, 1987). In addition, for students who do poorly in school, grades are a strong deterrent to enjoying learning.

? Ask Yourself

How many times have you heard the following:

> I got a C on the test.
>
> She's grounded because she got bad grades on her last report card.
>
> His parents gave him $50 for each A he got.

What do statements like these reflect about how we think about grading? Did you ever receive some kind of incentive for getting good grades? Were you ever punished in some way for getting bad grades? How did this affect your attitude toward school and learning? How did the low grade affect your attitude toward the teacher who gave you the bad grade?

Types of Grading Systems

Even though difficulties surround the grading process, teachers are almost always required to grade students. It is important to understand different approaches to grading as well as the strengths and limitations of each approach. By developing an understanding of these different approaches, you will be better able to determine when to use a specific approach and also why you have chosen to use it. First, we will consider two fundamentally different types of grading systems: criterion-referenced and norm-referenced.

Criterion-Referenced Versus Norm-Referenced Grading

Criterion-referenced practices describe student progress in relation to predefined standards set by the teacher, the school district, or by state or national groups. In contrast, norm-referenced grading methods describe student progress in relation to other students.

Criterion-referenced grading allows room for all students to achieve at the highest level. For example, if all 20 students in a class score between 81 and 99 on a 100-point test, each student receives the grade that corresponds to his or her points or percentage according to the teacher-established scale. If 91–100 equals an A, and 81–90 equals a B, everyone in the class will have received an A or a B on the test.

Norm-referenced grading systems are designed to compare students to one another. Teachers who use norm-referenced grading often justify it as needed to keep students on their toes by requiring them to compete against others. Some teachers also justify norm-referenced grading as demonstrating their toughness or high teaching standards because their grading

Figure 10.2 *The Normal Curve*

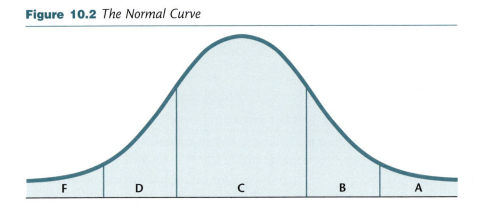

| F | D | C | B | A |

system allows them to consistently fail a certain percentage of their students, as shown on the curve in Figure 10.2.

This curve is the normal curve familiar to you through standardized testing; you will learn more about this curve in Chapter 11. The statistical properties of the normal curve include a large middle section and equal areas at each end of the curve. These properties are used to create a grading plan in which there are small but essentially equal percentages of A's and F's, slightly larger and essentially equal percentages of B's and D's, and a large number of C's. Students may expect this kind of grading system, due primarily to the effect of college admissions requirements and their trickle-down effect; and, as we said earlier, teachers sometimes see these grading methods as increasing motivation and demonstrating rigor.

The most important disadvantage of such systems is the lack of meaning of a given grade. In norm-referenced grading, regardless of the range of scores achieved by students on some assessment, the scores must be placed on a continuum that assigns an A to those in the top 5 percent and an F to those in the bottom 5 percent. For example, for the same 20 students who scored between 81 and 99 on a 100-point test, a teacher would curve their scores so that those at the highest end receive an A and those at the lowest receive an F. Therefore, a student scoring an 81 would receive an F by virtue of being the worst score in the class. Most people would assume that a grade of D or F means failure to master content, but in a norm-referenced grading system, it simply means that the student is at the bottom of the class.

If you have succeeded in helping all of your students learn and master content and skills, your grading on the curve will not reflect that. Instead, it will appear that a predetermined percentage of students are failing. Alternatively, we would normally assume that an A represents high achievement, but if all the students have done poorly on a particular assessment, the students who receive an A may have missed half or more of the items.

While certain grading methods are specifically criterion-referenced or norm-referenced, some, including those with which you are most familiar, can be either. We will begin our discussion by describing those systems.

Grading Systems That May Be Either Criterion- or Norm-Referenced

The two grading systems commonly used in the United States are letter grades and points or percentage grades. Both of these systems can be classified as either criterion-referenced or norm-referenced depending on the way in which they are used. When a teacher assigns a letter or percentage grade based on the performance of other students, the grading system is norm-referenced. When a teacher assigns a letter grade based on whether a student attained a predefined performance level (a standard) or a predefined percentage or number of points, the grading system is criterion-referenced.

Letter Grades We are all familiar with letter grading, and almost all of us have experienced years of this particular system in which a grade of A, B, C, D, or F denotes the level of achievement. The advantages of letter grades are their conciseness, familiarity, and correlation to college success. A single letter concisely expresses everything about a student's achievement in a given time period. Furthermore, most people believe that they know exactly what an A means or what a C means. And years of research on student achievement as measured by GPA have found correlations between grades in high school and success in higher education.

The disadvantages of letter grades are noteworthy, however. Because letter and percentage grading have been a part of education in the United States for more than 100 years, many people see these grades as not only inevitable but as correct. Letter grades are considered to be accurate indicators of student performance that can be easily interpreted by all and translated from one situation to another. Despite this widespread belief that an A is an A, however, letter grades vary widely in meaning from one context to another. In any given teacher's classroom, a grade may reflect mastery of content as shown by tests, quizzes, and projects. It may or may not include other factors such as effort, class participation, homework completion, attitude, attendance, or improvement over time.

Further, letter grades are ultimately arbitrary, and their meaning varies from teacher to teacher. Even within the same school and subject matter, different teachers may use different methods of computing a student's grade: meaning that even if the course content is the same, if you take the course with Ms. Horn, you might get a B, but if you take the same course with Mr. Bender, you might get an A. Some teachers use norm-referenced letter grades, with the grade indicating the student's status within the class. Others use letter grades in a criterion-referenced manner in which the grade indicates the level of mastery of classroom objectives. Concerns about grade inflation illustrate the fact that letter grades mean different things at different times and places.

Perhaps the most important disadvantage of letter grades, however, is the fact that they actually contain much less information than it appears. Imagine a food critic who reviews a restaurant and gives the restaurant a C without any further details. You probably understand that the meal was okay—not great, but not terrible. However, you do not know if it was the quality, temperature, or presentation of the food that could be improved. Were the raw ingredients of poor quality or was the preparation lacking? Was there a problem with the ambience of the room, the speed of the service, the friendliness of the staff, or the cleanliness of the dining room, kitchen, or restroom? The C gives the consumer a rough idea of something, but it provides no specifics to help the consumer make an informed decision and offers no useful feedback to the restaurant regarding how to improve.

In the same way, reducing student progress to one letter grade or descriptive word—however convenient and manageable it may be in terms of data storage or communication with parents—slights the different facets of student learning and does not give enough information to be helpful to students or any interested party. Although an A+ may tell us something about what a student knows and can do, a C or D or F tells us almost nothing. A D on a transcript does not tell us if the student has not mastered the information, did not show up for class, did not turn in homework, or misbehaved in class. It tells us that the student did not meet some requirements of the class, but we do not know which ones. Or, if the teacher assigns grades using a norm-referenced system, the student may have mastered the class content but perhaps was one of the lower performers in a group of high achievers. Near the bottom of the curve, he gets a D.

Points and Percentage Systems Some teachers use a point system in which they and students track grades by adding the points received during the term. This method is easily understood by students, parents, and teachers alike and has a history as old as letter grades. Students keep track of their grades, which helps students develop ownership over how they are doing in class as grade computation is no longer a mysterious secret formula.

Figure 10.3 displays an example of a total points grading system. This example shows the points that Kelly earned in senior English, along with the total points possible. The overall scheme for awarding a grade of A, B, C, D, or F is communicated to students ahead of time so that they can determine the progress they are making as they complete various assessments throughout the grading period. Since the range for an A is 90 percent or higher, the range for a B is 80–89 percent, the range for a C is 70–79

Figure 10.3 *Kelly's Senior English Grade in a Total Points Grading System*

Assignment	Points Earned	Points Possible
Quiz	10	12
Essay	22	30
Project	43	50
Presentation	13	20
Test	88	100
TOTAL	**176**	**212**

Overall Grade Awarded = B

A = 190–212   B = 170–189   C = 148–169   D = 127–147   F = 126 or less

percent, students can calculate how many points they need to earn a specific grade for each assignment. Because the grade is determined by a total point system, students can do poorly on some assignments and still earn an A or a B.

In this type of grading system, teachers determine the number of total points needed to earn each letter grade and students add up all of the points they receive on assignments and assessments throughout the term. This method shares the same major drawback as letter grading in that the scale used to determine the points and ultimately the letter grade the student receives is arbitrary and almost always beyond the control of the students. These grades still communicate little in terms of content standards or about what a student actually knows and can do.

The system shown in Figure 10.3 can be either criterion-referenced or norm-referenced. If it is criterion-referenced, the points for each assignment would be based on how closely the student's work met the criteria set by the teacher. If norm-referenced, the points would be assigned based on how well the student's work compared to the work of the other students in the class.

In addition, the points/percentage system can be *both* criterion- and norm-referenced at the same time. In this case, the points would be assigned on the basis of how well the student's work met the teacher's criteria (criterion-referenced), but the grade would be assigned on the basis of a comparison to the number of points that were achieved by the rest of the class (norm-referenced).

Grading Systems That Are Specifically Criterion-Referenced

Some grading methods are explicitly designed to evaluate student performance against a standard. Whether the student's performance is better or worse than that of other students is not relevant to the grading system. Included here are methods measuring students against instructional objectives, pass/fail systems, and grades based on contracts.

Instructional Standards Grading System One way to show a student's performance within the context of school district expectations is to use a list of standards that are checked off or rated on a scale using such points as "fully met," "partly met," and "not yet begun." The strength of this method is its tracking of students' progress through the list of standards over the course of the school year and also across years, giving a well-rounded picture of growth and improvement. By breaking down the grade into specifics, both students and parents receive information related to specific content and skills and target goals.

The difficult part of this system is that it requires the school district to prepare a sufficiently detailed list of standards to meaningfully express what is taught; at the same time, it cannot be so lengthy that it overwhelms the teachers who use it and the students and parents to whom it is intended to communicate.

Figure 10.4 provides an example of this kind of system. As shown in the figure, instead of assigning the student a C in Language Arts on the report card, teachers mark each area of his or her strengths and weaknesses.

Pass/Fail Grading **Pass/fail grading** is seen in universities, where this system serves to encourage students to try out classes that are especially challenging or outside their declared majors. One positive characteristic of a pass/fail grading system is that it requires teachers to carefully consider what exactly the standard is for passing an entire course of study. If this description of the standard for passing is published, the students, parents, and other educators gain some insight into the types of things students know or can do when they receive a passing grade for that course. This type of grading system is limited, however, because there is nothing you can say about a student who fails.

Some elementary schools also use this type of system, in which students are graded on a scale similar to that of the instructional objectives method: "excellent," "satisfactory," and "unsatisfactory." The rationale for such a system is the avoidance of emphasis on letter grades for younger students. At the same time, little information is given about student achievement, and this method often looks like a junior version of letter grades, using only A, C, and F.

Contract Grading Occasionally, teachers work with students to set learning goals. They help students figure out how to reach these goals, and they spell out the criteria that will be used to assess student progress. In **contract grading,** students and teachers develop a plan together, including how the student's grade will be determined, and they both sign it as a contract.

Figure 10.4 *Report Card Showing Progress Toward Instructional Standards*

Language Arts	Novice	In Progress	Proficient	Advanced
Writing Skills				
• Uses complete sentences			X	
• Varies sentence types	X			
• Punctuates correctly		X		
Reading Skills				
• Recognizes main ideas				X
• Uses context clues to discover meaning			X	
• Uses graphic representations to interpret meaning	X			
Speaking Skills				
• Speaks loudly			X	
• Uses inflections appropriately		X		
• Speaks clearly			X	
Listening Skills				
• Asks good questions		X		
• Understands key ideas		X		
• Demonstrates appropriate nonverbal expressions		X		

Under this kind of grading, students know exactly what is expected of them, and students are allowed to have differing goals, thus better meeting their individual learning needs.

Ask Yourself

Can a letter grade or a one-word description on a transcript ever truly represent student learning? If a student enters a class with a high degree of knowledge about the subject, can he or she receive a good grade without having actually learned anything? Is it possible that a student who has learned a lot can receive a bad grade? How might that happen? Did you ever decide not to take a difficult class because you were afraid that it would ruin your GPA?

Resource for Your Assessment Toolkit
Developing Your Personal Grading Philosophy

Thoughtfully answering these questions can help you develop a personal philosophy of grading.

1. What do you think a grade symbol should represent? Do you want grades in your classroom to represent how much students know, how they compare to others in their class or grade level, how much they have learned since the beginning of the term, whether or not they have completed assignments and/or homework, how well they behave in class, or how much effort they put into their work? Keep in mind that one symbol cannot tell all, so what vital information do you want to ensure that it communicates?

2. Do you believe that all students should be able to achieve an A, or do you believe that grades should be distributed in some way with relation to the class as a whole, limiting the number of A's, B's, C's, D's, and F's?

3. Do you believe in failing students or in giving a zero or no credit for any assignments or assessments? What does an F mean? That a student has not demonstrated that she has learned anything? That he knows nothing? That she has a bad attitude? That he does not meet minimum standards? That she is the worst in the class? That he has not turned in any work?

4. What components should go into a final grade? Do you think that all assessments—whether quizzes, tests, projects, writing assignments, or performance assessments—should form part of the final grade, or should the final grade be based on end-of-term assessments that show what students know and can do by the end of the grading period?

5. Do you think that all components of a grade should have equal value or should they be weighted according to what you or the school, the students, or the parents think is most important in learning?

6. What method of calculating grades makes most sense to you: total points, percentages, rubrics?

7. Do you believe that there are absolutes in grading, or can you as the teacher decide to change a student's grade because you think it is the right thing to do? If a student has a C+ according to your scale, but is "really close to a B−," is it okay to bump the grade up because you think the student has worked hard, or because you know the student had family problems that were distracting during the term? What about the other way around?

8. How will you address any inconsistencies between your personal beliefs and what your school requires of you?

Source: Adapted from Frisbie & Waltman, 1992.

How Can I Make Grading Meaningful and Fair?

Grades are communicated to students and parents in a variety of ways that are established by each school or school district. Teachers may or may not have input into or control over how these systems work. More often than not, the system teachers must use is the one produced by the software purchased by the school district. At the same time, you as a teacher will have to face the question of how to compile the grades, regardless of the reporting system used. Your students have spoken, written, and performed—all ways of showing what they know and can do in the classroom. How do you assemble and make sense of all of the information you have gathered in order to report on the students' achievement?

We have shown how a grade has two distinct elements: analyzing assessment data and then interpreting that analysis to provide an evaluative symbol that holistically communicates to others. Because these two elements are so intertwined, it is helpful to present an example of carefully combining assessment data and then interpreting them holistically.

Combining Assessment Data Holistically to Create a Grade

A primary step to combining information from multiple assessment opportunities is to make certain that each piece of information properly relates to the same achievement target or standard. Think of these different assessment pieces that you collect throughout the grading period as separate pieces of a puzzle. The intended representation for that puzzle is a picture of students' academic achievement in your classroom. There are two important decisions you now need to make. First, which assessment pieces should be included in the overall picture? And second, how big should each puzzle piece be?

For example, if you need to develop an overall grade for science knowledge, it is important that each assessment piece focus on science concepts. You might think this sounds easy, but often other dimensions of science (like process or reasoning skills) are included in an assessment record. You will need to carefully determine if the assessment records you have collected throughout the grading period are assessments of science knowledge or assessments of certain science skills or dispositions. Then, you must decide which assessment pieces should be included in the picture of science knowledge and which assessment pieces (like those that measure science skills) should be left behind. You may have collected assessment data from several selected-response and student constructed-response assessments that had a total of 60 questions focused on different science concepts and 40 questions focused on science skills (such as hypothesizing, inferring, graphing, and so on). If you wanted to provide a picture of science knowledge separate from science skills, you would only use the 60 questions for science knowledge for the knowledge grade and leave out the 40 questions for science skills.

On the other hand, you may want to provide a grade that represents a mixture of science knowledge and science skills. In this case you would include all the 100 questions to determine the science grade. Although this might make the grade a bit confusing because it is measuring two things simultaneously, teachers sometimes must do so because the report cards that they are using only allow for one grade per subject area. The key here is that you should always keep a clear record of the thinking that informs the assessment pieces of a grade.

Once you have determined which assessment records should be included in your science knowledge grade, it is equally important to ascertain what science concepts were measured by which assessment piece. You may find that you have assessed one science concept (like electrical force) multiple times and another concept (like magnetic force) only once. You must determine whether you will combine all the assessment records for the first concept (electrical force) and summarize them with a single score before combining that score with the score for the second concept (magnetic force). Or you may wish to have your overall grade for science knowledge represent the average score for all the assessment pieces. If you choose to do this, then the overall grade for science knowledge is automatically an assessment that primarily represents students' knowledge of electrical force and only secondarily of magnetic force.

Ultimately you will find that you often need to weight the different assessment pieces that you have collected throughout the grading period so that each piece accurately represents the specific learning objectives that were the focus of your teaching. Assigning some sort of percentage or number of points is useful in this task.

The key to making the correct decision about what assessment records to include or to weight is always the specific learning objectives or standards that you have decided to emphasize during your teaching. When it comes time to develop an overall grade, you must carefully consider which pieces of assessment information provide the clearest and most accurate picture of the objectives that were the focus of your instruction. Once you have determined which pieces are to be included and perhaps weighted, put your decisions in writing. This written rationale becomes an invaluable tool to share with students, parents, and administrators.

Some Practical Suggestions

Even when you do your best to develop a grading system that matches your learning objectives and state standards and that communicates clearly to students, parents, and other educators, there are always a few snags. Some of them can be anticipated. In this section, we share some practical suggestions that may assist you in grading.

Dealing with Cheating Whether it involves getting the test answers from a student in an earlier class period, looking at another student's paper, text messaging another student, or pulling out the old-fashioned cheat sheet,

Resource for Your Assessment Toolkit

Pulling Assessment Data Together to Create the Grade

The following steps provide a template for clearly analyzing the assessment pieces to ultimately interpret the data and assign a grade symbol.

Part I: Analyzing Assessment Data

1. Establish a deadline for students to complete all incomplete work.
2. Bring together all the assessment data you have collected for one particular standard.
3. Review the assessments to assure that they all truly target the same learning standard.
4. Decide which assessments are important enough to include in the grade.
5. Organize the assessments by levels of performance correlated to subject-area criteria or benchmarks.
6. Decide which assessments are recent enough to include and give priority to the final assessments because they reflect progress or growth over time.
7. Review the remaining assessments to determine how well they have covered the target standard.

8. Consider weighting the scores in areas that focused on the most important part of the standard.

Part II: Interpreting the Data and Assigning a Symbol

1. Once you have clarified what learning standards you have taught and assessed, consider what it means to have achieved each of the standards completely. This provides you with the image of an A.
2. Now examine each of the assessment pieces for your learning standards and consider how important each assessment piece is in comparison to the other pieces. Give priority to evidence related to the most important standard. Weight each assessment piece accordingly.
3. Either through a percentage or point system, create a range for a grade of A that matches your image of a student who has achieved each of the learning standards completely. Then consider a range for a B, C, D, and F.

at times students cheat. Perhaps the newest trend in cheating involves plagiarized papers purchased on the Internet or from another student. Sometimes students plagiarize large portions of others' work or get substantial assistance from a peer or parent.

There are a number of motivations for cheating, and these need to be investigated and understood by both parents and teachers. Sometimes cheating is the result of fear and undue pressure to succeed. Sometimes cheating is an act of defiance of authority. Sometimes cheating can be a cry for attention. No matter the reason, when it comes to assessing academic achievement, cheating needs to be separated from grading. The reason is that assessment is about academic achievement. If you choose to assign a zero or a failing grade for an assessment because a student cheats, that assessment is no longer a measure of that student's achievement. Rather, it is a measure of an unethical action. One of the most important characteristics of good grading is that it measures what it says it measures.

So, as tempted as you may be to punish a student by assigning a poor grade for a test on which that student has cheated, try to refrain from this practice. You must create a grade that represents what that student has learned, not the cheating. The actual act of cheating must be handled through another means such as a sanction that limits privileges or places students on probation or requires students to redo the work with integrity and honesty.

Some schools establish honor codes that set the standards for honest and ethical behavior and require each teacher to enforce those policies. Schools that have effective policies targeting academic dishonesty with appropriate consequences help their teachers handle cheating situations fairly and consistently.

Everyone makes mistakes, but in this case the punishment must fit the crime. If the student misses an algebra question on a test, his score suffers. If he cheats on the test, he must face the consequences of his dishonesty and retake the test.

Borderline Cases Another common occurrence when trying to summarize multiple assessment pieces into a single grade is having a student's assessment total fall on the borderline between two grades. Sometimes teachers will allow extraneous factors to influence them, such as the student's level of effort or the fact that the student generally does work that is on one side or another of the borderline. Although it is tempting to make the decision on the basis of prior patterns of behavior, to do so only complicates an already complex process. Once again, a grade should represent specifically the academic achievement that has been shown by the student, and all data should relate to that academic achievement.

A much sounder approach requires some advance planning. It is wise to, as a matter of course, collect one or two additional pieces of relevant assessment data that overlap the assessment results you have already collected. In general, these extra pieces of assessment would not be used in the grading procedure unless a borderline case occurs, when the results of these parallel assessments would be used to determine which grade to assign. This approach keeps extraneous factors from complicating both the grading procedure and the communication process.

Norman Gronlund (1998) sounds a note of caution about borderline cases that applies to all grading situations. He points out that assessment scores may contain clerical errors. Or one low test score that contributes to the lower composite score might have been due to illness or some other extraneous factor. "In any event," he says, "it is wise to review the data for borderline cases and make any needed adjustments. When in doubt, fair grading would favor giving the student the higher grade" (p. 175).

Even though the emphasis in grading is on academic achievement, another approach could be to allow data related to process and progress to influence the grade if a borderline problem emerges. Jane Pollock (2007) discusses how one teacher had two separate sections in her grade book: one related to Academic Achievement Standards and the other related to an Approach to Learning scale. On a given assignment, the teacher could write one score for the achievement standard and then turn the page over and write another score based on such issues as participation, homework, effort, or other dispositions. If you have collected this information systematically, these factors could be allowed to be the tipping point for determining the grade of a student on the borderline.

The Issue of Zero The zero has become a controversial issue in grading. Teachers will say they do not "give" zeroes to students who do not turn in their assignments; students "earn" the zeroes by not caring enough to exert any effort to comply with the instructions. The use of zeroes by a teacher can cause students to give up early in a grading period when they do the math and discover the three zeroes they earned at the beginning of a course have ruined any chance of passing. Often students say they quit trying midway through the course because they calculated they would need to score 100 percent on every upcoming assignment and test in order to have a chance to pass.

The first problem relates to the mathematical impact of a zero. Dingles Reeves (2004) says even teachers who subscribe to the "punishment theory" of grading might want to consider the difference between assigning a zero on a 5-point grading scale versus using a zero on a 100-point grading scale. It can make sense to use a zero within a 5-point scale (4, 3, 2, 1, 0) that correspond to grades of A, B, C, D, and F, because the increment between each letter grade is proportionate to the increment between each numerical grade, that is, 1 point. He points out, however, that most teachers use the zero based on a 100-point scale. Reeves argues,

> This defies logic and mathematical accuracy. On a 100-point scale, the interval between numerical and letter grades is typically 10 points, with the break points at 90, 80, 70, and so on. But when the grade of zero is applied to a 100-point scale, the interval between the D and F is not 10 points but 60 points. Most state standards in mathematics require that fifth-grade students understand the principles of ratios—for example, A is to B as 4 is to 3; D is to F as 1 is to zero. Yet the persistence of the zero on a 100-point scale indicates that many people with advanced degrees, including those with more background in mathematics than the typical teacher, have not applied the ratio standard to their own professional practices. To

insist on the use of a zero on a 100-point scale is to assert that work that is not turned in deserves a penalty that is many times more severe than that assessed for work that is done wretchedly and is worth a D. (pp. 324–325)

Here is an example. Jason could have taken three tests in his American History class and received grades of 95, 85, and 100. On the day of the fourth and final test, Jason had an unexcused absence because he did not have a note from his doctor. His average of 93 percent (A) for the three test scores drops dramatically to an average of 70 percent (D−) when a zero is included in the final average for the four grades.

Others recommend that a more equitable solution to the problem of missed work is to have the student make up the work after school or during a lunch period or study hall (Stiggins, Arter, Chappuis, & Chappuis, 2004). Give Jason an "incomplete" until there is enough information to make a judgment on his level of achievement on the course learning targets. The unexcused absence should be dealt with by administrators with a detention or disciplinary action or recorded separately on a conduct or behavior record, but it should not provide misleading information about his academic achievement.

Extra Credit Often teachers provide opportunities for students to earn extra credit toward a grade. If extra credit is conceptualized as another opportunity for students to show what they know or can do, such a practice can be a motivation for students to strengthen their assessment profile. And such extra credit assessments also provide additional information when a borderline case occurs.

The only caution concerning extra credit is that such a practice should not send a message that students will receive a higher grade simply for redoing their work over and over. You need to clarify for students that completing extra credit work is more than repeating something that has been shown already. Extra credit should provide a different opportunity for students to show what they have learned and can now apply in a more challenging assignment.

One example of acceptable extra credit work is as follows. Imagine that you have already assessed students' ability to reason to a logical conclusion using an essay question. An appropriate extra credit assignment might permit students to solve a different problem by completing some independent research and then writing a short report that describes how they solved the problem. This extra credit permits students to show their ability to draw a logical conclusion based on their own data collection. It is not simply a repeat of an essay question.

Just be careful not to allow students to do so much extra credit that the bonus points inflate their grades. If the extra credit is closely linked to the academic goal, it can be judged appropriately as another opportunity to meet the academic target. If the extra credit involves more generic or fluffy skills—like creating a poster about World War II or designing a costume for a favorite character in a book—the extra point could inflate the academic grade beyond what the student has achieved academically. The student who received the grade inflated by the bonus points may still flunk the final exam or do poorly on the state standardized tests.

Cooperative Learning and Grading Another frequent challenge in determining a grade relates to assessment in cooperative learning contexts, in which students work together to solve problems, answer questions, or create products. There is no question that such collaborative contexts are useful learning environments and that collecting assessment data in such environments is appropriate. When grading cooperative projects, the teacher must carefully assess each student in light of her or his specific contribution to the answer or product. This is difficult but possible. One technique requires students to individually display their specific contribution to an answer by placing it in a color that uniquely identifies each student.

Another method that enables the teacher to assess the work of the individual student in a group setting is to have students complete different aspects of the project and then assess each aspect separately. Then the teacher can carefully match each part of the project to a specific aspect of achievement that the project part represents. According to Spencer Kagan (1995), group grades can penalize students who work hard but have cooperative learning partners who do not; as well, these grades can inappropriately reward students who do not work hard but have hard-working partners.

Using the Most Recent Assessment Information When summarizing assessment data, it is important to recognize that the most recent assessment data is the most valuable. By the time a grade is to be determined, the assessment data from the first part of a grading period may be outdated. For example, a second-grade student may have been assessed on adding two-digit numbers with no regrouping at the beginning of a grading period. Perhaps at this early point the student was not yet fully focused and scored poorly on several assessments. Over the grading period, however, the student's progress accelerated and revealed subsequent mastery for not only adding two-digit numbers but other related mathematics competencies. If students demonstrate consistent achievement at a later time that overrides earlier assessment results, the earlier assessment results should be discarded in favor of the current data. The key is that a grade should represent the current academic achievement of a student.

Some school districts have a policy against grading formative assessments, such as rough drafts of papers. Instead, teachers might use these rough drafts in progress reports to parents. Only the summative product (the final research paper) is assigned a grade. Once again, you will need to follow the policies of your school or district to be in compliance with specific grading procedures.

How Can We Shift Attention from Grades to Academic Achievement?

Reducing the focus on grades can be a challenge for teachers, students, and parents. After all, we have all been conditioned to think about grades as part of education. It is easier with younger students who have had less exposure to grading, but for high school students who have already had ten years to focus on grades, the change is radical. Students need to be helped through it and encouraged to focus on learning and how they can apply the learning to their lives. Here are a few suggestions for reducing the focus on grades in the classroom:

- *Don't grade everything that students do in your class.* This helps students concentrate on learning and on what they are doing in class, instead of thinking about what grade they are getting. Provide specific feedback such as written narrative commentary, conferences with students about assessments, and peer feedback from other students regarding presentations, group projects, and so on. Specific feedback goes beyond "good job" or "needs work" to provide adequate information for students to understand exactly what they are already doing well and how they can improve.

- *Don't grade students while they are learning new concepts.* Practice, rough drafts, homework, and ongoing assessments to see how students are progressing should not be part of a grade. Pop quizzes to "motivate" students to study do not work—they often seem threatening and unfair to the students. The best motivating technique is to provide instruction that students find interesting and challenging.

- *Send the message that all students can learn and succeed in your classroom.* Eliminate norm-referenced grading practices that force students to compete against one another. Create a trusting learning environment in which students feel comfortable exploring, risking, and even failing. Emphasize to students and parents that grades simply represent demonstrated learning; they are not a statement about the quality of the student.

- *Remove "grade talk" from your classroom vocabulary and conversations with parents.* Refrain from reminding a student that he needs to turn in a project to "get an A" or that she will "fail" if she does not make up a test. Talk to students constantly about learning; explain to and remind them why they are doing what they are doing in terms of their learning goals. Instead of calling a parent to express your concern that Tim's "grade has suffered" in recent weeks, phrase your concern in terms of the behaviors that you see (Tim seems preoccupied and has not turned in his homework for the past two weeks).

- *Provide an appropriate engaging curriculum framework, and allow students to participate in determining what to study, how to study it, and how to assess their learning and determine their grade.* This does not mean giving students free rein in the classroom, it means including students in the discussion about what they do for 6 hours every day. Provide options and choices so that each student can pursue what is most interesting to him or her within the framework. Students who are excited about and challenged by what they are exploring worry less about their grade simply because they are more engaged in and committed to their own learning.

- *Invite parents to get involved in your classroom and in their child's education.* Explain to them what grades mean in your classroom and how and why emphasizing grades over learning for their children is unhealthy.

Improving Grading Practices to Help Students Learn

Are there ways of summarizing student progress that provide better feedback for students, parents, schools, colleges and universities, and potential employers while remaining manageable for teachers? Many schools are committing significant time and energy toward developing alternative reporting systems. It is important to remember that there is not one right answer to this complex issue but that the search for better models of grading and reporting is continuing.

We review here several methods for communicating student progress to parents and others. Each represents a way of providing meaningful and often detailed information about student progress, and each can include letter grades as an adjunct. Many schools are finding that letter grades, while lacking information when used alone, can be combined with one of the reporting methods discussed to provide meaningful feedback.

Standards-Based Report Cards Standards-based grading systems differ from traditional grading systems in a several significant ways. Instead of providing letter grades focused on a subject area, standards-based grading systems provide information about students' progress for specific learning goals and performance standards. Standards-based grading is criterion-referenced and measures achievement or progress about learning, instead of an uncertain mix of attitude, effort, and behavior. Standards-based grading emphasizes the most recent evidence of learning and carefully describes that evidence rather than simply including every score for every assignment and recording the average. In general, a **standards-based report card** provides much more detailed and clearer feedback to students and parents than do traditional grading systems.

Student-Led Conferences Many schools are experimenting with **student-led conferences** that provide students, parents, and teachers with the opportunity to talk together about student work and progress. Although these conferences may take a variety of forms depending on the school, in general they include similar characteristics. Students keep an ongoing portfolio of all of their work in each class, and, in preparation for their conferences, they work with their teachers to select their best pieces of work from each class to present to their parents at the conference.

Conferences last 20 to 30 minutes, during which the student leads the conversation by showing and discussing his or her work sample from each class, and the teacher or teachers discuss the student's report card with the student and parent. Teachers highlight student progress and provide suggestions for improvement and support services for students who need extra assistance. Parents have the opportunity to ask questions. These conferences help students take responsibility for their learning and help students and parents talk to one another about school and what students are learning.

Narrative Evaluations Some schools have opted to drop letter grades in favor of written **narrative evaluations** of student strengths and weaknesses. Just like the reviewer who writes a narrative evaluation of a restaurant instead of merely assigning a letter grade, a well-written narrative evaluation of a student's progress provides more useful information to all interested parties than a letter grade.

Several institutes of higher learning are using this system, including Alverno College in Milwaukee, Evergreen State College in Olympia, Washington, and New College of Florida in Sarasota. For example, New College states on its website: "Students' progress should be based on demonstrated competence and real mastery rather than on the accumulation of credits and grades. Non-graded, narrative evaluations encourage exploration and mastery instead of competition."

The Illinois and Mathematics and Science Academy, a public high school, does not provide grade point averages. The school is committed to assessment that is displayed in the form of key performances matched to Standards of Significant Learning the school has adopted.

Portfolios of Student Work Chapter 9 addresses the use of portfolios as assessment tools, showing ways to collect, interpret, and display student work over time. In this chapter, we are referring to a portfolio as a final product showing a student's best work and used as a substitute for a letter grade. Just as a prospective employee might bring a portfolio to a job interview, a student presents a portfolio to showcase his or her learning. In comparison with letter grades, portfolios provide a more complete picture of what students know and can do. They also demonstrate students' progress over time and their reflections on their learning.

Thornton Friends School in Silver Spring, Maryland, is one of a number schools that use portfolio assessment in lieu of letter grades. As they describe the benefits,

> Portfolios can be much more valid than one-time tests or quizzes, because they measure a student's progress over a longer period of time and on different types of assignments. They can give us a more multifaceted view of the student and allow her to demonstrate a wider variety of skills and intelligences. For example, a passing or failing report card grade from the year before does not give a teacher as much information as a portfolio full of that student's actual work would. (www.thortonfriends.org)

Making Sense of Grading Practices This chapter has shown that grading remains a difficult and complex process. Grades have had a long history in the United States, and they continue to provide information to parents and students that is often unclear, confusing, and misinterpreted. We have shown how grades are determined by many types of evidence and that there is no clear agreement across teachers and school districts about the quality or legitimacy of these evidence types. So, what is a teacher to do in the midst of such complexity? Always analyze and question the specific characteristics of any grading system that you use. By carefully clarifying the characteristics of your grading system, you will be able to determine, with some precision, how your grading system matches the grading systems of others. By discussing the specific differences between grading systems, you will determine, over time, what aspects of a grading system you value, and you will be able to explain to others why you value these aspects. Ultimately, grading is an area that calls for changes, and you can help make changes by clarifying what you want to see in a grade and by developing grades based on evidence that is appropriate and clear.

Summary

- Grading is the process of holistically evaluating student performance and assigning evaluative symbols to represent what a learner knows and can do, or may not know or be able to do, as evidenced by various assessments. Good assessment revolves around what the student does, while grading is a summative judgment made by the teacher.

- A grade has two critical elements: It is based on an analysis of assessment data, and it involves an interpretation that is communicated to others.

- Letter and percentage grading have been used for more than 100 years in the United States.

- Grading serves several important purposes in education: feedback to students, communication with parents and others, accountability for the school district and state, and sorting of students from "best" on down.

- Norm-referenced grading methods describe student progress in relation to other students. Norm-referenced grading views student scores in a classroom as if they were distributed along the normal or bell curve. This is the familiar practice called grading on a curve.

- Criterion-referenced practices describe student progress in relation to predefined standards set by the teacher, the school district, or state or national groups. Criterion-referenced grading allows room for all students to achieve at the highest level. Included here are methods measuring students by instructional objectives, pass/fail systems, capstone grading, and contracts-based grading.

- Letter grades and grades based on percentages or points can be either norm- or criterion-referenced systems.

- To create grades for your students, you will need to combine assessment data you have collected over some period and then assign meaning to this summary.

- The overemphasis on letter grades has some negative consequences for students and schools alike. There are a number of things you can do as a teacher to minimize these negatives, given that some kind of grading is required in most school districts.

- Some schools and colleges have developed "nongraded" grading systems that may be useful models for you and your school.

Key Terms

contract grading (280)

criterion-referenced grading (275)

grading (268)

narrative evaluation (292)

norm-referenced grading (275)

pass/fail grading (280)

process criteria (270)

product criteria (270)

progress criteria (270)

standards-based report card (292)

student-led conference (292)

For Further Discussion

1. Consider one subject area that you intend to teach. What type of grading system would you employ in your classroom and why?

2. Take a look at the way you are assessed in this course of study. Is it norm-referenced or criterion-referenced? How would you interpret the meaning of an A based not simply on scores but in terms of learning?

3. In what ways have grades motivated or failed to motivate you? What lessons does your experience provide to help you develop a good grading system?

4. What can you do to discourage cheating in your classroom?

5. How are rubrics integrated into traditional letter grades and percentage grades?

Comprehension Quiz

Case Study 1

You have spent the past grading period teaching students the following learning objectives in mathematics:

- Students will understand the relationship of length and width as these concepts relate to area.
- Students will apply the concept of area to their daily life.

Throughout the grading period, you have collected the following assessment pieces:

- Three quizzes that ask students to calculate the area of different shapes:
  - Quiz 1 at the beginning of the semester
  - Quiz 2 at the middle of the semester
  - Quiz 3 at the end of the semester
- Final multiple-choice examination containing 20 questions:
  - 5 questions require students to calculate the area of different shapes
  - 5 questions are word problems that ask students to consider which shape provides the most space for a backyard
  - 5 questions require students to calculate the perimeter of different shapes
  - 5 questions are multiplication questions involving decimals
- Performance assessment in which students are asked to select the best shape for a 140-foot perimeter backyard that provides the most space for their pet to run
- Six weeks of homework assignments that focused on the calculation of different-shaped areas

Consider the four assessment pieces that are available to you. Determine which assessment pieces should be included in the final grade for mathematics and which should not. Identify your reasons for including or excluding any of the assessment pieces.

Case Study 2

You are reviewing the summary grades of three students at the end of the marking period in a writing unit:

Grading Standards

$$90–100 = A$$
$$80–89 = B$$
$$70–79 = C$$
$$60–69 = D$$
$$59 = F$$

Consider the grades and the circumstances of the missing writing assignments. Determine each student's final grade, and explain your rationale for what you could do to address these issues.

Writing Unit	Narrative Paper	Informative Paper	Persuasive Paper	Original Short Story	Research Paper	Average Score	Grade
Jody	50	75	80	F for cheating	85		
Kevin	95	85	0, not turned in	70	65		
Juan	50	55	65	70	75		

Relevant Website Resources

EASL: Equity and Achievement for Standards-Based Learning

www.ease-equity.org

This site explains an outcome-based nongraded system for ongoing student evaluation designed to help students persist and take responsibility for their learning.

Grading: Selected Resources for the Middle School Teacher

http://www.middleweb.com/Grading.html

This site features a review of grading software, teacher discussions about giving failing grades for late assignments, not grading everything the students do, and grading correlated to standards. It also has articles about grade inflation, performance-based assessment, matching assessment with curriculum, competitive grading, and report card grading and adaptations.

ACT Information or Policymakers: High School Readiness

http://www.act.org/path/policy/education/k12.html

Two research articles on differential grading standards among public high schools and high school grade inflation from 1991 to 2003 are available to review. The sources were included in ACT Policy Reports from 2004. The research studies noted that a student's grades depend not only on the student's achievements but also on the achievement of the student's schoolmates, and different schools can have student populations with different average levels of achievement.

Grading Students' Classroom Writing

http://www.kidsource.com/education/grading.classroom.writing.html

This article discusses grading in the writing process. It shows how to use grading to promote students' learning, provide feedback to help students revise their writing, and effectively grade students' writing products.

Hawaii's General Learning Outcomes for Essential Overarching Goals

http://doe.k12.hi.us/standards/GLO_rubric.htm

Teachers in Hawaii gather classroom-based evidence on General Learner Outcomes. The outcomes include: self-directed learner, community contributor, complex thinker, quality producer, effective communicator, and effective and ethical user of technology. This site includes indicators for these outcomes and rubrics to help teachers assess their students and help students self-assess their progress.

Ontario's Provincial Report Card Grades 9–12

http://www.edu.gov.on.ca/eng/document/forms/report/sec/not1e.pdf

This report card is an example of how teachers can communicate behaviors they think are important but separate them from academic achievement. This allows everyone to know as accurately as possible what a grade really means. The report card has a section for course grades that includes comments about strengths, areas for improvement, and next steps; attendance that targets classes missed and times late; and learning skills that include working independently, teamwork, organization, work habits/homework, and initiative.

References

Butler, R., & Nisan, M. (1986). Effects of no feedback, task-related comments, and grades on intrinsic motivation and performance. *Journal of Educational Psychology, 78,* 210–216.

Cangelosi, J. S. (1990). Grading and reporting student achievement. In *Designing tests for evaluating student achievement* (pp. 196–213). New York: Longman.

Du rm, M. (1993). An A is not an A is not an A: A history of grading. *Education Forum, 57,* 294–297.

Farrington, C. A., & Small, M. H. (2006). *Removing structural barriers to academic achievement in high schools.* http://www.ease-equity.org/files/uplink/Removing_Structural_Barriers_to_Academic_Achievement.pdf. Accessed September 26, 2006.

Frisbie, D. A. & Waltman, K. K. (1992). Developing a personal grading plan. *Educational Measurement: Issues and Practice.* From http://depts.washington.edu/grading/plan/frisbie.html.

Grolnick, W. S., & Ryan, R. M. (1987). Autonomy in children's learning: An experimental and individual difference investigation. *Journal of Personality and Social Psychology, 52,* 890–898.

Gronlund, N. E. (1998). *Assessment of student achievement,* 6th ed. Needham Heights, MA: Longwood Division, Allyn and Bacon.

Gullickson, A. R. (2003). The student evaluation standards: How to improve evaluations of students. Chair of the Joint Committee on Standards for Educational Evaluation. Thousand Oaks, CA: Corwin Press and ETS Educational Policy Leadership Institute.

Guskey, T. R., & Bailey, J. M. (2001). *Developing grading and reporting systems for student learning.* Experts in Assessment™. Series eds. T. R. Guskey & R. J. Marzano. Thousand Oaks, CA: Corwin Press.

Kagan, S. (1995). Group grades miss the mark. *Educational Leadrship, 52* (8), 68–71.

Kohn, A. (1994). Grading: The issue is not how but why. *Educational Leadership.* http://www. alfickohn.org/teaching/grading.htm. Accessed October 4, 2007.

O'Connor, K. (2002). *How to grade for learning,* 2nd ed. Thousand Oaks, CA: Corwin Press.

Pollock, J. E. (2007). *Improving student learning: One teacher at a time.* Alexandria, VA: Association for Supervision and Curriculum Development.

Reeves, D. B. (2004, December). The case against the zero. *Phi Delta Kappan, 86*(4), 324–325.

Reeves, D. B. (2006). *The learning leader: How to focus school improvement on better results.* Alexandria, VA: Association for Supervision and Curriculum Development.

Stiggins, R. J., Arter, J. A., Chappuis, J., & Chappuis, S. (2004). *Classroom assessment for student learning: Doing it right—using it well.* Portland, OR: Assessment Training Institute.

CHAPTER 11

Statistical Applications to Assessment

Chapter Objectives

After reading and thinking about this chapter, you will be able to:

- **Describe and calculate statistical concepts commonly used by classroom teachers, such as central tendencies and measures of variability.**

- **Explain the special characteristics of the normal distribution.**

- **Describe typical item analysis procedures and how they can be used to inform assessment-based decisions.**

If you score a 95 on a math test, would you be pleased? Your first response might be, "Of course!" But what if there were 200 possible points? Or, if it were a 100-point test, would you be pleased to know that a 95 was the lowest score in the class? The score on an assessment tells only part of the story. To be meaningful, the score must be interpreted with respect to other variables, such as the scores of other students, the student's prior performance on similar assessments, the content of items answered correctly and incorrectly, and so on. In this chapter, we will introduce you to statistical concepts that will help you interpret scores in a meaningful way; but, in doing so, we urge you to think about how your interpretation might differ from the interpretation of another teacher, the student, or the student's parents.

This chapter introduces you to basic statistical concepts that can help you describe student performance on assessments and help you evaluate the effectiveness of your instruction. Students are often most interested in their own performance, but their teachers need to know more. Teachers can gain insight about the effectiveness of their instructional approaches based on the way the entire class performs on an assessment. This chapter will give you an understanding of several common statistical procedures that can be used to look for patterns across the whole class of students. It will provide the tools to compare one student's performance to the performance of the whole class, to determine if your learning targets have been met, and to evaluate the assessment itself.

Statistics provide pictures or insights about groups and provide information about individuals. Examining patterns across many students is very helpful for determining the effectiveness of an instructional method. If an instructional approach helps a large number of students, it is worth continuing. Of course, those students who do not benefit from the approach need to be provided other options. Foundational concerns about using statistics stem from the delicate balance between the importance of the individual versus the importance of the group. As teachers we must always be wary of making decisions that only benefit the larger group at the sacrifice of the individual student.

Foundational Questions for Your Consideration

- When is it appropriate for a teacher to compare a student's performance on an assessment to the performance of other students?
- When is it useful to know how a class performed overall? Would that knowledge provide insight into how well students learned and how effective instruction was?
- How do you know if an assessment item achieved its purpose?

Looking Beyond the Test Score

As we begin our discussion of statistical applications to classroom assessment, let's take a look at a typical classroom. The community the students come from is diverse. About half of the students are male and half female, with varying socioeconomic backgrounds. The school racial/ethnic makeup is 25.5 percent White, 35.2 percent Black, 38.4 percent Latino, 0.8 percent Asian, and 0.1 percent Native American. Fifty-three percent are low income, and 18.9 percent are English language learners. There are 26 students in the classroom.

The class has just completed an American history unit on the Great Depression, culminating in a summative assessment, a 50-item multiple-choice unit test. Each item is worth 1 point, so the highest possible score is 50 points. The teacher, Ms. Dailey, scores each student's test and enters the score in the grade book as shown in Figure 11.1.

Figure 11.1 *Student Scores on the Great Depression Unit Test*

Name	Score	Name	Score
Anderson, Jennifer	42	Johnson, Takesha	38
Bennett, Wilma	27	Kendall, Randall	47
Billings, Sam	43	Kent, Lucy	34
Cheng, Joshua	33	Lenning, Lemont	46
Cuerritto, Rosita	45	Leopold, Pegi	42
Esposito, Maria	47	Maudlin, Elroy	47
Etner, Robert	23	McFadden, Tracey	50
Fuentes, Jose	44	Puentino, Andreas	37
Fuentes, Lucinda	40	Stephano, Maria	48
Gomez, Roberto	43	Trapo, Joseph	22
Guttman, Steve	44	Venito, John	44
Henry, William	44	Williams, Belinda	41
Jennings, Sophia	44	Wyndot, Rolin	43

Ms. Dailey is aware that some students did not perform as well as she expected or hoped. She notices this when hand-scoring the test and when entering the scores into the grade book. She also notes a few students did exceptionally well. She is not sure what to make of the assessment information. Did all students meet the learning objectives? Is there a pattern to the assessment data? That is hard to tell based on the list of scores in the grade book. Should she reteach part of the unit or move on to the next unit? Should she provide additional instruction for some students, but not all? Ms. Dailey is having a hard time deciding what to do. This is a common situation for many teachers.

An additional factor is weighing on Ms. Dailey's mind. While scoring the test, she noticed that some of the items were answered correctly by all or almost all the students, a good thing from her perspective. She is also aware that a number of students performed poorly on specific items. She is concerned that perhaps the class did not learn certain aspects of the unit. Again, Ms. Dailey is not sure what to make of her observations and the data.

There are often subtle patterns of correct and incorrect answers on an assessment. It is difficult to detect such patterns when scoring and grading assessments, especially with a large class. If Ms. Dailey were able to detect these patterns, she might be able to place individual and whole-class performance in a better context. That level of detail and analysis could be useful in making good instructional decisions.

Fortunately, there are tools available to the teacher to help determine what typical student performance is for the class based on their distribution of test scores, how spread out these scores are, and how an individual fits into that spread. There are also tools to analyze the quality of test items that can tell the teacher how easy or difficult an item is and how well an item measures a concept or construct.

Statistical Concepts

Let's think about Ms. Dailey, the assessment data she has, and how she could use the data. She could use the data to

- See if students met learning objectives.
- Gauge the effectiveness of her instruction.
- Plan future instruction.

For example, it would be useful to know what the typical student performance was on the assessment. Overall, did students perform well or poorly? How spread out are the scores? What is the lowest score? What is the highest?

Distribution of Scores

A good place to begin detecting patterns in scores is to consider what the data really look like. We need to see the data in some organized way to extract meaning from it. It would benefit Ms. Dailey if she were able to detect *patterns* in the distribution of scores.

Frequency Table Many teachers begin looking at test scores and other numerical assessment data by arranging them in a **frequency table.** This lets us get a sense of the data, to look for trends. The easiest and quickest way to do this is to arrange the data in a list from lowest score to highest score. We could then tally the number of times a particular score occurred. Figure 11.2 is Ms. Dailey's unit test data arranged from lowest score to highest score. The tally marks indicate the frequency of each score. Note

Figure 11.2 *Frequency Table of Student Scores on Great Depression Unit Test*

Score	Tallies
22	I
23	I
24	
25	
26	
27	I
28	
29	
30	
31	
32	
33	I
34	I
35	
36	
37	I
38	I
39	
40	I
41	I
42	II
43	III
44	IIII
45	I
46	I
47	III
48	I
49	
50	I

the use of tally marks instead of Arabic numerals (IIII I instead of 6). This helps us see the shape of the data. What shape do you see?

Ms. Dailey could begin interpreting her test scores using this frequency table. For example, she could see where a particular student performed compared to other students. She could more easily see what the highest scores are, what the lowest scores are, and what the middle scores tend to be. She could also see that a few students performed poorly on the assessment, while the majority of the students did very well.

Figure 11.3 *Histogram of Student Scores on Great Depression Unit Test*

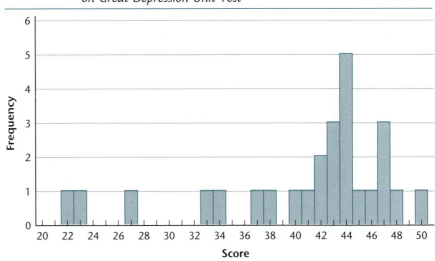

Histogram Another useful way to display a frequency distribution is to create a **histogram,** a pictorial representation of data in the form of a bar graph. Each score can be listed on the horizontal axis (the X-axis), and the tally or frequency of each score can be displayed on the vertical axis (the Y-axis). Figure 11.3 shows the histogram of the assessment scores earned by the students on the unit test. The histogram shows roughly the same shape as the tally marks in the frequency table in Figure 11.2. (Note how rotating the frequency table of tally marks in Figure 11.2 counterclockwise gives you the same view as the histogram.)

There is a lot more meaningful information conveyed in a histogram than in an unorganized set of assessment scores. We can already see several patterns from this pictorial representation. Again, it is easy to note how a few students performed poorly on the assessment in contrast to the majority of the students who earned scores of 42 or more. Do you see the really low scores of 22, 23, and 27? Also, it looks as if most students did fairly well, given the cluster of students scoring 42 or better on the 50-item test.

Besides looking at individual scores, Ms. Dailey could group scores together into intervals that might represent specific grades earned by students. Ms. Dailey uses the grading scale shown in Figure 11.4 to assign letter grades to unit test scores. With the grading scale shown in the figure, a student earning a score of 48 would earn an A, a student earning a 42 would earn a B, and so on.

We could display the frequency of each grade in a histogram by counting how many students received a particular grade on the unit test. Figure 11.5 shows what the unit test grades would look like.

Figure 11.4 *Great Depression Unit Test Scores Grouped for Grading*

Score Interval	Grade
45–50	A
40–44	B
35–39	C
30–34	D
29 and below	F

Figure 11.5 *Histogram of Student Grades on Great Depression Unit Test*

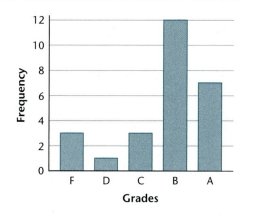

Histograms provide a way of visually detecting patterns in assessment data. A quick glance at the histogram of the grades suggests a number of students in Ms. Dailey's class performed quite well. More than half the students earned either an A or B. Of course, this is the same pattern we saw in the histogram of individual scores in Figure 11.3.

Frequency Polygon Another useful representation of assessment data is the **frequency polygon,** a line graph similar to the histogram. Test scores are again written along the X-axis, while the frequency of each score is on the Y-axis. A dot is placed at the intercept of the midpoint of the interval for a particular score (above the X-axis) and the frequency of that particular score (along the Y-axis). A line is drawn between adjacent dots. A frequency

Figure 11.6 *Frequency Polygon for Student Scores on Great Depression Unit Test*

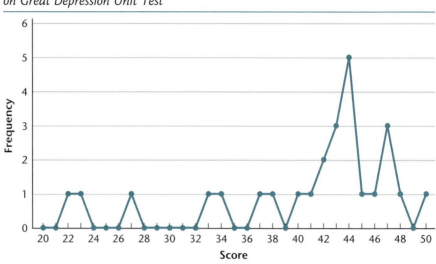

polygon created from the Great Depression unit test scores in Ms. Dailey's class is shown in Figure 11.6.

The shape of the frequency polygon in Figure 11.6 is similar to the shape of the histogram in Figure 11.3. Frequency polygons and histograms essentially convey the same information. Ms. Dailey could use either to gain a better understanding of her assessment data.

Now that she has the frequency table, the histogram, and the frequency polygon, Ms. Dailey is in a position to begin to answer the question, "What is the typical student performance?" And, "How well did I do in helping students meet the learning outcomes?" How would you answer these questions? While it is possible to get a rough idea by observing the pictorial representations of the set of scores, the answer would lack precision. And that leads to another question, namely, "What exactly is typical performance?"

Measures of Central Tendency

There are several ways to measure typical performance numerically. The statistical term for typical performance is **central tendency,** which is a numeric summary of a set of scores. Think of central tendency as a measure of where data tend to cluster together. There are three common measures of central tendency: mean, median, and mode. Each of these is a different way to summarize the scores into a single number.

Mean The **mean** $(\overline{X})$ is already familiar to you. It is simply the arithmetic average of a set of scores. As you recall, the average is calculated by taking all the individual scores, adding them together, and dividing by the total number of scores. The formula is written as

$$\overline{X} = \frac{\Sigma X}{N}$$

which you read as, "The mean equals the sum of all scores divided by the number of scores."

Σ is the capital Greek letter sigma and stands for *the sum of* a group of numbers. X represents each *individual score* and N is the *total number* of scores. So, what is the average (mean) score of Ms. Dailey's class on the unit test? Here is how the mean is calculated:

$$\overline{X} = \frac{\Sigma X}{N}$$

$$\Sigma X = 42 + 27 + 43 + \ldots + 44 + 41 + 43 = 1058$$

$$N = 26$$

$$\overline{X} = \frac{\Sigma X}{N} = \frac{1058}{26} = 40.7$$

The mean score is 40.7, or approximately 41. Ms. Dailey could use this measure of central tendency to characterize the typical performance of her class. Overall, the typical student answered about 81 percent of the items correctly (40.7 items correct divided by the total of 50 is 0.81 or 81%). She could also get an idea of how individual students performed compared to the typical student. For example, it looks like Maria Stephano did very well compared to the average student in class. Maria's score of 48 is clearly above average. Robert Etner, with a score of 23, appears to have performed well below the average. Lucinda Fuentes and Belinda Williams appear to be typical, with scores of 40 and 41 respectively, right at the mean.

Note that the mean uses all scores in the set of data. Every assessment score is used to calculate the mean, including those who did *extremely* well and those who did *extremely* poorly. Take a look at the frequency table again in Figure 11.2. How did Robert Etner's score of 23 and Joseph Trapo's score of 22 impact the mean? And Wilma Bennett's score of 27 was also lower than the rest of the class. A look at the frequency table will show that most scores seem to be in the range of 37 to 50, while those below 33 certainly seem to be unusual. Scores that are quite different from the majority (either higher or lower) are called **outliers**. Could these outliers be distorting the mean by pulling it lower than what might be the typical or average performance on this test?

If these three students (Robert, Joseph, and Wilma) had not taken the test, their low scores would not have been calculated into the class mean. The average score, if we recalculated it, would be 43 instead of 40.7. This difference may seem small, but it points out that the mean is influenced by

Figure 11.7 *Comparison of Two Distributions—With and Without Outliers*

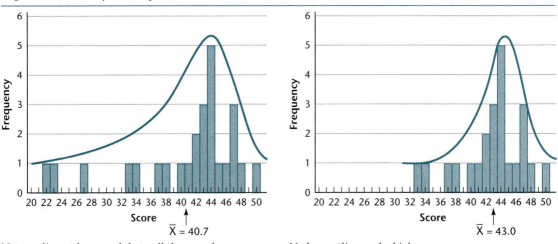

Note outliers at lower end that pull the mean lower.

No low outliers and a higher mean.

all assessment scores, including outliers. Since all data points are included in the mean, we must be careful of our interpretation of the mean. It may or may not represent what is considered to be typical student performance. Always look at the set of scores once they are arranged in a frequency table or a histogram. Figure 11.7 illustrates this.

Only by examining the data in an organized way would we have a sense of how the scores below 33 are skewing or pulling the mean lower than we might expect. A **skewed distribution** that is pulled lower by outliers is a **negatively skewed distribution.** A distribution that is pulled higher by outliers is a **positively skewed distribution.** Did you get the clues? Positive distributions pull toward the more positive end, while negatively skewed distributions pull toward the more negative end. (In this usage, positive does not necessarily mean good, it simply means a higher number.)

Figure 11.8 shows three distributions; a positively skewed distribution, a normal distribution, and a negatively skewed distribution. Note how the tails pull the distribution in a particular direction. Knowing the shape of the distribution can have important classroom implications. For example, at the beginning of a unit of instruction, student performance on a pretest might take the shape of a positive distribution (most students perform poorly and have not mastered the instructional material). That is to be expected. At the end of instruction, it would be desirable that most students perform quite well on the end-of-unit assessment. In other words, the shape of the distribution becomes negatively skewed. This would indicate that most students learned the material and met desired expectations.

Seeing a change in the shape of a distribution from a positive skew to a negative skew would be a good thing in the classroom. A shift in skew suggests there has been a growth in student learning. Figure 11.9

Figure 11.8 *Changing Shapes of Distributions—Positively Skewed, Normal, and Negatively Skewed*

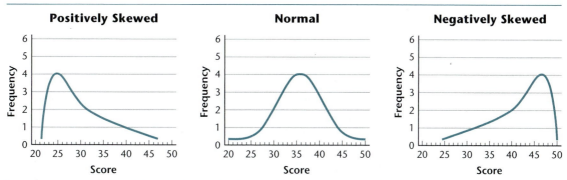

Note the direction of the tail. It pulls the distribution in either a positive, neutral, or negative direction.

Figure 11.9 *Expected Shift in Skewness When Teaching Is Effective and Students Have Met Desired Outcomes*

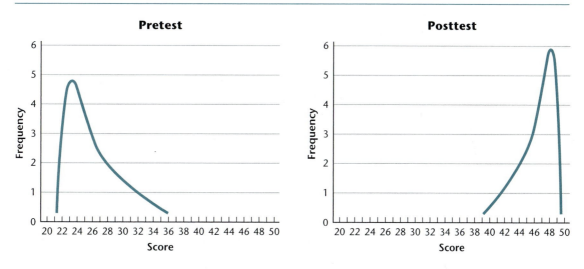

represents a shift in student performance between a pretest at the beginning of a unit of instruction and a posttest at the end of instruction if teaching was effective and students met desired learning outcomes.

Median A second measure of central tendency is the **median,** the middle score in a set of scores. Half of the scores are above the median, and half are below the median. The median represents the score of the individual who would be right in the middle of the set of scores. To find the median, you would first arrange the scores from lowest to highest. Then determine which score is in the middle, with half of the scores below it and half above. That score is the median. For an example, look at the following score set, which has been arranged from lowest score to highest score.

23   26   27   29   30   34   36

↑
median

The middle score is 29. Three scores are below 29, and three scores are above it. Note that there are an odd number of scores in this set. It is easy to determine the median when there are an odd number of scores. Here is another example, with an even number of scores. The median will be between the two middle scores.

23   26   27   29   30   34   36   48

↑
median

In this case, the median is 29.5, halfway between 29 and 30. That is, the median is a number that is *not actually a score in that set*. When the score set contains an odd number of scores, the median will be the middle score. When there is an even number of scores, the median will be the average of the two scores that straddle the middle of the score set.

Note one other thing about this second example. Although the one additional score (48) is quite a bit higher than the rest of the scores, the change in the median is very small. The median is not affected by outliers the way that the mean is. In fact, substitute a score of 98 instead of 48 and the median is still unchanged. *The median is best used when you are concerned that outliers might be affecting the mean by making it less representative of a group of scores.*

Now let's examine Ms. Dailey's classroom results. What is the median for Ms. Dailey's class on the unit test? We obtain the median by arranging the scores from lowest to highest, which we have already done in Figure 11.2. The total number of scores is 26, an even number, so we will need to identify score number 13 and score number 14, which would represent the two middle scores in this set. You can do this easily by starting at one end of the frequency table and counting the tally marks until you get to scores 13 and 14. In this case, both number 13 and number 14 are among the tally marks for score 43. The average of 43 + 43 is 43. Therefore, the median of this set of test scores is 43. Using the median as a measure of central tendency, we would say that the typical student performance is 43 correct out of 50, or 86 percent correct.

Note how the median score is higher than the mean we calculated earlier. The median is 43, while the mean is 40.7. Is this what we would have predicted given the skewed data? The answer is yes. In Ms. Dailey's class, several students had unusually low scores that pulled the mean lower. The mean used all the scores, while the median did not. When the data may be skewed, consider the median as more representative of typical student performance than the mean.

Reexamine Ms. Dailey's frequency table in Figure 11.2 to see if the mean or the median appears to be more representative. The median, at 43, appears to be more typical than the mean of 40.7. A look at Figure 11.7 will confirm this. This highlights the importance of first visually examining assessment scores with a frequency table.

Mode The third measure of central tendency is the **mode,** the most frequent score in a set. If you had the frequency distribution shown in Figure 11.10, the mode would be 18, the most frequent score.

Note the similarity between the words *mode* and *most*. This may be a helpful way to recall that the *mode* is the *mo*st frequent score. Be aware that it is possible for a set of scores to have a tie among scores for the most frequent. The example in Figure 11.11 illustrates this.

In Figure 11.11, the most frequent scores are 16 and 20, with three tallies each. In this case, there are two modes. We call this a **bimodal** distribution (*bi* for "two"). We could have three, four, or more modes. We would call these **multimodal** distributions. This would change our picture of the typical student performance. Figure 11.12 provides histograms of a unimodal distribution and of a bimodal distribution. What do you think is the typical student performance in the bimodal distribution? Which measure of central tendency is most accurate? Or should you use several?

Figure 11.10 *Example Frequency Distribution 1*

Score	Frequency
15	I
16	
17	II
18	ШI
19	III
20	I

Figure 11.11 *Example Frequency Distribution 2*

Score	Frequency
15	I
16	III
17	II
18	I
19	
20	III

Figure 11.12 *Histograms of Unimodal Distribution and Bimodal Distribution*

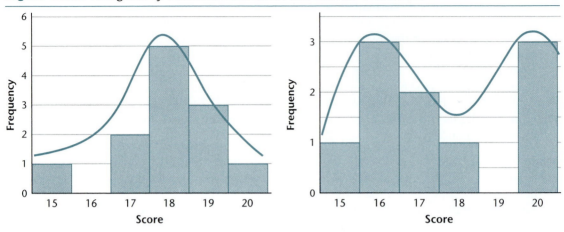

Let's look at Ms. Dailey's assessment results. What was the mode of the unit test scores? Look at the frequency table again in Figure 11.2 and identify the most frequent score. In this case, the mode is 44. Like the median, the mode does not take into account all scores. It has the advantage of not being influenced by outliers to the same extent as the mean. But, be careful, the mode can occur anywhere in a set of scores and may not actually represent the most typical performance. It may also occur at several scores (such as bimodal or even multimodal). Again, a visual examination of a frequency table is in order to make sure you are not making incorrect inferences that could lead to poor decision making. Nonetheless, knowing what the most common scores are can help a teacher make an informed decision about a class as a whole and about individual students. It is possible to detect trends and patterns by looking at the mode.

Measures of Variability

So far, we have examined patterns in assessment data that can give us an idea of what typical student performances might be. These are the measures of central tendency. We might also ask, "How consistent or spread out are the student scores?" The answer could give us an idea of the variability of student learning and the overall effectiveness of our teaching. Measures of **variability** help inform teachers about student learning because they examine the consistency of student performances and whether scores are spread out or bunched together. We will look at two common measures: range and standard deviation.

Range When we think about how consistent or diverse a set of assessment scores might be, we often look at the lowest score and the highest score.

Resource for Your Assessment Toolkit
A Quick Overview of Central Tendency Statistics

Since norm-referenced standardized testing uses central tendency statistics to make inferences and draw conclusions, it is helpful to have a quick review of some of the benefits and limitations of central tendency statistics. Sometimes it's efficient to describe a whole group of scores by giving a single number. An *average* summarizes a group of numbers by calculating a central tendency. There are three main types of averages: mean, median, and mode. Each of these can be used to quickly describe a set of test scores or other numbers in a group.

However, even though all three numbers provide a measure of central tendency, they must be carefully interpreted because they represent different ways of thinking about the center of a group. The following examples will help you quickly recall the issues that surround the use of means, medians, and modes.

Mean

The mean is the average you are already familiar with. It's also called the arithmetic average because it's the average you use simple arithmetic to calculate. To find the mean of a group of test scores, for example, you add up all of the scores and divide by the number of scores you have.

Let's try an example. Suppose you have the following group of ten student scores after giving a 100-point test in your class:

85 88 92 90 90 85 85 90 95 80

First, we add up the scores, giving us a total of 880. Next, we divide 880 by the number of student scores, which is 10. This gives us a mean of 88. So you can quickly describe this group of test scores by saying, "Ten students took this test and their average or mean score was 88 points."

Advantage of the Mean: The advantage of the mean compared to the other measures of central tendency is that it takes all of the scores into account. None of the scores is left out or given any special weight in the calculation.

Disadvantage of the Mean: The mean's advantage can become a disadvantage. Because the mean takes all of the scores into account, it can be skewed or distorted by a small number of scores that are quite different from the rest, or even by just one very different score. When this happens, the number you use to describe your set of test scores may also be distorted.

Let's go back to our example and add a couple of *outliers,* that is, scores that are quite different from the rest. Suppose two of the scores were 0 instead of 90:

85 88 92 0 0 85 85 90 95 80

Again, we add up the scores and this time we get 700. Dividing by ten gives us a mean of 70 instead of 88. Now if we say, "Ten students took this test and their average or mean score was 70 points," how accurately are we describing the group of test scores? Seventy points is lower than almost all of the scores and is not very accurate description of the group as a whole.

Median

The median is the number in the middle of your set of test scores after you have arranged them in order from lowest to highest. Let's go back to our first set of scores:

85 88 92 90 90 85 85 90 95 80

If we arrange them in order, this is what we have:

80 85 85 85 88 90 90 90 92 95

(continued)

Then we count to the middle number—except there is no number in the middle since we have an even number of test scores. So we look at the two middle scores, which are 88 and 90, and the median will be the point halfway between them, or 89. This number is almost identical to the mean of this group of scores, which is 88.

You can use a little arithmetic to calculate the median when you have an even number of scores. Add the two middle scores (88 + 90 = 178), then divide by two to get the mean of these two numbers (178 / 2 = 89). So when you have an even number of scores, you may find yourself calculating a mean while you are on your way to finding the median!

Now let's find the median of the second example, the set of scores with two zeroes. If we put those scores in order from lowest to highest, we get:

0   0   80   85   85   85   88   90   92   95

The median again is halfway between the two center numbers, both of which are 85. But since they're the same, the median is simply 85. This median is not very close to the mean we calculated for this set (70), although it is close to the median of the previous set of scores (88). Looking at this second set of test scores, which average seems more accurate for the group as a whole, the mean of 70, which is lower than most of the scores, or the median of 85, which is close to most of the scores?

Advantage of the Median: In contrast to the mean, the median is affected very little by outliers. As a result, it tends to be a more "natural" description of the overall group performance than the mean is when outliers are present.

Disadvantage of the Median: Sometimes the median is a number that is not actually in the set of scores (like 89). Also, when there is a large number of scores, it can take a lot of time sorting the scores from smallest to largest and then counting to the middle. Of course, with the help of a computer-sort program, this problem is resolved.

Mode

The mode provides another way of looking at the central tendency of a group of scores. This type of average is the score that occurs most often in the group. To determine the mode, you simply look at all the scores and determine which score occurs most often. Returning to our example, you can see that the score of 85 and the score of 90 each occur three times. All other scores occur fewer times, so the mode is both 85 and 90. There are two modes or two central tendencies. Sometimes this is called a bi-modal distribution of scores.

80   85   85   85   88   90   90   90   92

Now let's find the mode for the set of scores with two zeroes. In this example the number 85 occurs the most often, hence the mode is simply 85. The spread or range of scores does not affect the mode. The only thing the mode represents is the score that occurs most frequently.

0   0   80   85   85   85   88   90   92   95

Advantage of the Mode: The mode is simple to determine and accurately represents the most frequent score or scores in a group.

Disadvantage of the Mode: The mode only focuses on the most frequent number or numbers in a group. The mode completely leaves out all other scores even if other scores occur quite frequently.

These two scores indicate how wide the set of scores is. We call the difference between the highest score and lowest score the **range**. For example, suppose the highest student performance was 29 correct out 30 possible. The lowest score was 16 out of 30 possible. The range is simply 29 minus 16, or 13.

What is the range on Ms. Dailey's unit test? Again, look back at the frequency table in Figure 11.2, and you will see the highest score was 50, while the lowest score is 22. The range is 50 minus 22, which is 28. What does this tell us about the student performance in Ms. Dailey's class? It tells us that the scores, with a high of 50 to a low of 22, were quite spread out. Of course, this is only a limited picture of how the students performed. We only have two data points. What if the high score or the low score is an outlier—unusually high or unusually low? How might this affect our interpretation and use of the range as an indicator of how variable the scores are?

In the case of Ms. Dailey's class, we already determined that the low scores are outliers—out of the ordinary and not typical. Recall the negative skew to the data. Maybe the use of the range would lead us to conclude the scores are more spread out than they really are. A different measure of variability is in order—one that uses more of the data. In fact, what if we could use all of the assessment scores to gauge how spread out the scores are? The standard deviation is just such a measure.

Standard Deviation The **standard deviation** (SD) is a measure of the average distance each individual score is from the mean. It is an indicator of how spread out the scores are around the mean. If the standard deviation is relatively small compared to the mean, then the scores are bunched together. We say that they are more *homogeneous* (that is, on average, the individual scores do not deviate much from the mean). On the other hand, if the standard deviation is relatively large, the scores are more *heterogeneous* and spread out (that is, on average, the individual scores do deviate quite a bit from the mean). It might be helpful to think of the word *standard* as "average" and the word *deviation* as "distance." You can think of standard deviation as the *average distance* that individual scores are from the mean.

Figure 11.13 shows two sets of test scores. In each case the average (mean) score earned by students is 50, but the scores are not distributed in the same way. The first has a smaller standard deviation (SD = $+/-3.0$), the second a larger standard deviation (SD = $+/-5.3$). Note how the scores in the smaller standard deviation example are homogeneous—in other words, grouped together. On average, most students are clustered around the mean by plus or minus 3.0 points. Scores are more spread out and heterogeneous in the larger standard deviation example. Most students in this example are spread out from the mean by plus or minus 5.3 points. The standard deviation is one way to tell how spread out or clustered a set of scores are from the mean. This helps you as the teacher see how variable student performance is on a classroom assessment.

Figure 11.13 *Two Distributions with the Same Mean but Different Standard Deviations*

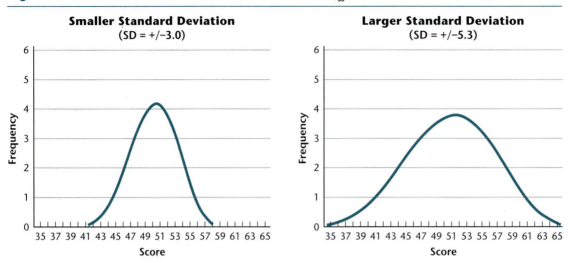

The formula for calculating the standard deviation appears complicated, but conceptually it is really quite simple. The formula is

$$SD = \sqrt{\frac{\Sigma(X-\overline{X})^2}{N}}$$

where $(X-\overline{X})^2$ represents each individual score minus the mean, squared; and N is the number of scores that you have.

An explanation for the squaring and square root are in order. Let's assume we have the following individual scores from an assessment.

15   15   20   20   25   25

We are interested in determining the average distance of each score from the mean. Our first step is to calculate the mean. Note in Figure 11.14 that we calculate the mean in the first column by summing all the individual scores (ΣX) and then dividing by the number of scores (N). In the second column, we write the mean $(\overline{X})$. In the third column, we subtract each individual score from the mean.

Recall that our goal is to calculate the average distance each score is from the mean. It would seem reasonable to just calculate the average by summing all the differences (the deviations) and dividing by N. If we did that, however, we would get zero when we summed all the differences! Well, we know that the average distance is not zero, so how could that be? This happens because half of the differences between each score and the mean will be negative, and the other half will be positive. When we sum

Figure 11.14 *Calculating a Standard Deviation*

Individual Score (X)	Average Score ($\overline{X}$)	Deviation ($X - \overline{X}$)	Squared Deviation ($X - \overline{X}$)²
15	20	−5	25
15	20	−5	25
20	20	0	0
20	20	0	0
25	20	5	25
25	20	5	25
$\Sigma X = 15 + 15 + 20$ $+ 20 + 25 + 25$ $= 120$			$\Sigma(X - \overline{X})^2 = 25 + 25$ $+ 25 + 25 = 100$
N = 6			N = 6
$\overline{X} = \dfrac{\Sigma X}{N} = \dfrac{120}{6} = 20$			$\dfrac{\Sigma(X - \overline{X})^2}{N} = \dfrac{100}{6} = 16.7$

them, they will add up to zero. Double-check this by adding together the differences found in the third column of Figure 11.14. You should have found that $(-5) + (-5) + 0 + 0 + 5 + 5 = 0$.

A partial solution to this dilemma is to square the differences. Remember, squaring a negative number gives you a positive number. In the fourth column, you will see what happens when we square the differences and add them together. We arrive at what is called the *sum of the squared deviations* (SS). The average sum of the squared deviations is the *variance*. This is simply the SS divided by N (the number of scores). We eliminated the zero, but now we have inflated deviations because of the squaring. To bring the inflated deviations back in line with the original set of scores, we take the square root of the average squared deviations.

The standard deviation (SD) for our set of scores is

$$SD = \sqrt{\frac{\Sigma(X - \overline{X})^2}{N}} = \sqrt{\frac{100}{6}} = \sqrt{16.7} = 4.1$$

You can translate this as, "The average distance of each score from the mean of 20 is 4.1." This lets us know that, on average, the scores in this example are approximately 4 points above or below the mean. We can use the standard deviation as an indicator of how spread out the scores are around the mean of 20. Remember, the larger the SD, the more spread out the scores.

On the surface the formula seems complicated, but if you work through a few examples, it will become clear why we square the difference between each individual score and the mean and why we take the square root of the average squared deviations. Try practicing the steps outlined above on Ms. Dailey's unit test scores. You should find

$$\Sigma X = 1058$$

$$N = 26$$

$$\overline{X} = 40.7$$

$$\Sigma(X - \overline{X})^2 = 1355.5$$

$$\frac{\Sigma(X - \overline{X})^2}{N} = \frac{1355.5}{26} = 52.1$$

$$SD = \sqrt{\frac{\Sigma(X - \overline{X})^2}{N}} = \sqrt{\frac{1355.5}{26}} = \sqrt{52.1} = 7.2$$

Compared to the range, the standard deviation has the advantage of using all the scores in a set, so it is more likely to be representative of the spread of scores. Rather than reporting only that the scores had a range of 28, Ms. Dailey now has a reference point (the mean) and a number that tells her the average distance of the scores from that reference point. In fact, the standard deviation is often used as a *unit for measuring*. Ms. Dailey could use the standard deviation to answer such questions as which students scored one standard deviation (1 SD) higher than the mean or how many scores on the test were more than one standard deviation (>1 SD) below the mean.

The standard deviation does take more effort to calculate, though. The range is easier and quicker to estimate but has the disadvantage of being greatly influenced by unusually high or low scores (outliers).

So far, we have looked at several ways to visualize assessment data and at statistical concepts that can help a teacher make more informed decisions in the classroom. As a teacher, you can display your test scores in meaningful ways, using a frequency table, a histogram, or a frequency polygon. You can extract the meaning from a hodgepodge of scores by looking at measures of central tendency—the mean, the median, and the mode. And, you can gauge the variability among scores by calculating the range and the standard deviation. These statistical measures are tools that help shape and guide instructional decision making in the classroom. The measures of central tendency and variability can be used to judge whether students met learning objectives and how effective instruction was.

?Ask Yourself

We have demonstrated several ways in which you can interpret the performance of students individually and in groups (such as classes or grade levels). Think for a moment about the kinds of questions that parents might ask you: How is my child doing in class? How have her test scores been? Have you seen a change or growth in my child's scores? What is her average score on the assessments? Now, with an understanding of central tendency and variability of scores, what additional information might you share with parents? How could you make such information meaningful to parents who seem interested, for example, only in their child's test scores? Can you show a change in learning over time?

The Normal Curve

In our discussion of statistical concepts, we have highlighted the fact that it is good practice for teachers to graphically and pictorially represent a set of assessment scores. This is done to get an initial sense of the shape of the distribution. We noted that measures of central tendency are often different and that a set of scores may very well be skewed positively or negatively. The **normal curve,** or the **normal distribution,** is a special case. It is a theoretical, mathematically derived frequency distribution.

Look at the normal distribution in Figure 11.15. Note how the shape is symmetrical around the mean. If you draw a vertical line through the middle of the distribution, you will see that the left side of the distribution is a mirror image of the right side. Notice that the tails of each half do not actually touch the horizontal base line, that is, there never is a frequency of zero. Instead, the tails extend infinitely because the normal curve is a theoretical concept that could apply to an infinite number of observations.

Figure 11.15 *The Normal Curve*

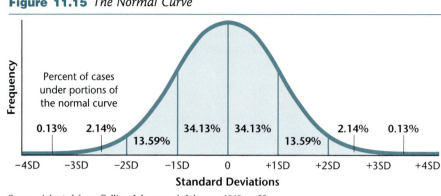

Source: Adapted from Collins, Johansen, & Johnson, 1969, p. 23.

In a normal distribution, all of our measures of central tendency are the same. Mean = median = mode. The average score ($\overline{X}$) is right in the middle. The median, by definition is also the middle score. Half of the scores are above it, and half are below it. And the mode (the most frequent score) happens to be the same score as the mean and the median. This is indeed a special situation.

The variability of scores as measured by the standard deviation also takes on special significance here. It turns out that in a normal distribution, a specific proportion of scores will be within a given distance from the mean. In this case, about two-thirds (68.26%) of the scores will be within one standard deviation below and one standard deviation above the mean (that is, $+/-$ 1 SD). Furthermore, 95.44 percent are within *plus or minus two* standard deviations of the mean, and 99.72 percent are within *plus or minus three* standard deviations of the mean.

Because of these unique mathematical characteristics, the normal curve can be used to estimate the overall performance of a group of individuals and also to place an individual score in context with a group of scores. The normal curve is critical to the proper construction, scoring, and interpretation of norm-referenced, high-stakes assessments, which we will be discussing in Chapter 12. Measurement specialists assert that many human behaviors approximate a normal distribution. When a large enough sample of data is obtained, it is often the case that the distribution will take on characteristics of the normal curve. For example, the normal curve provides the foundation for creating, scoring, and interpreting intelligence (IQ), aptitude, and achievement assessments, such as the Stanford-Binet Intelligence Scale, the Weschler Intelligence Scale, the American College Testing Program tests (ACT), and the Scholastic Assessment Test (SAT).

Digging Deeper
What Is "Normal" Behavior?

A number of social scientists and measurement specialists contend that, if our sample is large enough, natural phenomena will arrange themselves along a normal curve. Think about it for a moment: Whether we are measuring IQ, height, shoe size, or time to complete the Chicago marathon, all have extreme scores or values, but the majority of values will cluster around the middle of the curve (that is, the mean, median, and mode will all be nearly the same value). But there is an important differ- ence between one's height and one's intelligence. Height is an absolute value that really cannot be argued. But intelligence, achievement, aptitude, and other such constructs are not absolute and are subject to error in measurement and interpretation.

So, when we are asked to describe "normal" behavior or performance on an intelligence test, for example, perhaps we should acknowledge that our measures are always imprecise and open to interpretation.

Ask Yourself

Would you expect classroom assessments to have a normal distribution? Do you think the size of most classrooms (number of students) will provide the variability needed to achieve a normal distribution? Would you be satisfied if your instructionally oriented assessments demonstrated a normal distribution? What would that say about your ability to effectively guide students to meet learning objectives or demonstrate mastery of knowledge, skills, and attitudes if only a few achieved the highest levels of performance? As you think about your classroom assessments, which measure of central tendency would be most useful?

Item Analysis

We now shift our discussion to item analysis. **Item analysis** is one of several ways to judge the quality of both teacher-made and published tests that use selected responses, the forms of assessment we discussed in Chapter 5. Far too often, teachers give an assessment, score it, and record the results without examining the quality of the items. Item analysis is a set of procedures designed to evaluate the quality of items that make up assessments.

Individual items on an assessment can have specific, unique characteristics. Two prominent and useful characteristics are *item difficulty* (how hard an item is) and *item discrimination* (how well an item distinguishes those who know the material well from those who do not). We will look at each from the vantage point of teacher-made classroom assessments.

Item Difficulty

An initial estimate of the quality of an item can be easily found by calculating the item difficulty. **Item difficulty** is simply the ratio or percentage of individuals who answered an item correctly. The item difficulty index is calculated using this formula:

item difficulty index = number of correct answers / total number of students who answered the item

The ratio of students answering an item correctly can range from 0.00 to 1.00 (or from 0 to 100% of the students answering the item correctly). The easier the item, the larger the item difficulty index. For example, if item 1 is answered correctly by 15 out of 20 students, then the item difficulty index is 15/20, which is 0.75 or 75 percent. If item 2 is answered correctly by 18 out of 20 students, then the item difficulty index is 18/20, which is 0.90 or 90 percent. Item 2 has a larger item difficulty index and is therefore an easier item.

It is fairly easy to obtain the item difficulty index for test items. After an assessment has been given, responses to each item are recorded and counted, including those that are correct and those that are incorrect. You can record the frequency of responses in the margin of the assessment next to each item and set of answers. Then calculate the difficulty index for each item based on the number of students getting that item right, divided by the number who answered that item. Remember, you may be dividing by different numbers if some students failed to answer some of the items.

Let's look at Ms. Dailey's unit test results for an example. Data from item 1 is given in Figure 11.16. Note the numbers written in the left margin. They are *the number of students who selected each response.*

It apears that for item 1, there were 22 students (out of the total of 26 who answered the item) who selected b, the correct answer. Therefore, the item difficulty index is 22 divided by 26, which is 0.85. Since 85 percent of the students answered item 1 correctly, the item difficulty index equals 0.85 or 85 percent.

Item difficulty is often used as a measure of how hard an item is. On a classroom assessment, you can gauge an item as being easy, medium, or difficult. If a number of students get an item correct, it can be inferred that the item is relatively easy. If a number of students get an item wrong, then it can be inferred that the item is difficult. A good assessment is one that

Figure 11.16 *Number of Student Responses to Item 1 on Great Depression Unit Test*

Item 1. The Dust Bowl covered the central part of the United States during the 1930s. What was one of the consequences of the Dust Bowl?		
4	a.	Farmers shifted to growing more corn and less wheat.
18	b*	Many families became homeless.
2	c.	Herbert Hoover was elected president.
2	d.	The draft was instituted for all young men between the ages of 18 and 25.
Note: * is the correct response.		

balances the difficulty of items to provide information about a range of student abilities and performances. All students should have an opportunity to demonstrate what they know and can do. This necessitates a range of item difficulties on an assessment. Students who are doing well overall will need the opportunity to show that with difficult items. By successfully answering difficult items, they are able to show the full extent of what they know and can do. Low-performing students will likewise need a chance to show what they know and can do. This can be achieved by including easier items on an assessment. Since the item we looked at above was the first test question, Ms. Dailey probably wanted to start off the test at a fairly easy level, to draw students in and reduce test anxiety.

When you look at item difficulty, it is also a good practice to compare the calculated item difficulty to the probability a student would guess the correct answer by chance alone. For items with only two response choices (such as true-false), the chance probability of guessing the correct answer is 1 out of 2, or 0.50 (50%). For a multiple-choice item with four options, the chance probability of guessing the correct answer is 1 out of 4, or 0.25 (25%). Clearly, *the calculated item difficulty index should be greater than the probability of correctly guessing the answer.*

The item difficulty index gives an estimate of how hard an item is for all students—those who performed well overall and those who performed poorly. But it would also be interesting to know how an item functions with high-performing students compared to low-performing students. If an item is working effectively, it should be answered more frequently by those students who know the content than by those who do not. This leads to the second indicator of item quality—item discrimination.

Item Discrimination

Item discrimination is defined as the degree to which an item differentiates those who have higher levels of achievement from those who have lower levels of achievement. Item discrimination values range from -1.00 to $+1.00$. The discrimination power of an item is a measure of the ability of an item to distinguish between those students who performed well overall on a test and those who did not.

A *positive discriminator* is an item that is answered correctly at a higher rate by those who did well on the test compared to those who performed poorly. That is, the item is positively differentiating those who know from those who do not. Values above 0.00 indicate positive discrimination. The more positive the discriminator, the better the item is functioning in differentiating among varying levels of achievement. Such an item is thought to have more precision and thus is a more useful and effective test item.

A *negative discriminator* is an item that has a higher proportion of poorly performing students answering it correctly compared to those who did well overall. Such an item is, in essence, operating in the opposite direction one would expect (values below 0.00). This is undesirable. An item that is a *nondiscriminator* is one that does not differentiate between the high-performing and the low-performing students. This, too, is undesirable.

On published norm-referenced tests that have large numbers of students providing assessment data, the discrimination index is often estimated by calculating a correlation coefficient for the relationship between individual items and a student's overall performance on a test. But what can teachers do in the classroom? There is an alternative way to estimate the discrimination index that, while less sophisticated, is an effective approach for classroom tests. The procedure is similar to the one used earlier in calculating item difficulty. The goal is to compare the response rate of the high-performing students to the low-performing students on individual items. This is essentially the same thing as comparing the item difficulty for the high group to the item difficulty for the low group.

The first step is to identify the three groups of students in the classroom: the high-performing group, the middle-performing group, and the low-performing group. Rank order all of the tests from highest score to lowest score. If you have a typical classroom with between 20 and 30 students, you can split the class in three groups, as long as each group has roughly the same number of students.

The second step is to calculate the item difficulty index on each item for the high group and the low group. Since we are interested in seeing how well an item differentiates the high group from the low group, we do not use the middle group. (Their scores would needlessly complicate our calculations.) Now, for the high group, take the number of high-performing students who answered the item correctly and divide by the number of students in that group. The result will be the item difficulty for the high group. Do the same for the low group, and you will have the item difficulty for the low group.

The third step is simply to take the item difficulty for the high group and subtract the item difficulty for the low group. The difference is the item discrimination. Restated then, item discrimination in a classroom context is

item discrimination index = item difficulty index of high group
— item difficulty index of low group

Figure 11.17 shows an example from Ms. Dailey's classroom assessment. There are 26 students, with 9 in the high group, 8 in the middle group, and 9 in the low group. The response rates for each group to the correct answer and alternatives to item 6 are written in the left margin of the scoring key of the test.

Figure 11.17 *Number of Students Answering Each Response Option to Item 6*

Item 6. Which of the following was one of the results of the Great Depression?

H	M	L		
1	2	3	a.	Congress passed the law authorizing an income tax.
0	1	2	b.	Congress passed the law authorizing Medicare.
8	5	3	c.*	Congress passed laws that have been called the New Deal.
0	0	1	d.	Congress passed laws that gave Native American nations greater control over their own affairs.

Note: * is the correct response.

The item difficulty for the high group is

number of correct answers / total number of students in high group who answered the item

$$8 / 9 = 0.72$$

The item difficulty for the low group is

number of correct answers / total number of students in low group who answered the item

$$3 / 9 = 0.33$$

The item discrimination index is

item difficulty index of high group – item difficulty index of low group

$$0.72 - 0.33 = 0.39$$

It appars that item 6 is a positive discriminator since the discrimination index is a positive number, 0.39.

Resource for Your Assessment Toolkit

What Teachers Should Know and Be Able to Do: National Board for Professional Teaching Standards

The National Board for Professional Teaching Standards (NBPTS, 2002) has a set of five core propositions regarding what every teacher should know and be able to do. The third and fourth core propositions are directly relevant to the concepts covered in this chapter. Note in the following the role of assessing individual students as well as placing individual student performance in the context of the class as a whole. All five core propositions can be viewed online at http://www.nbpts.org/the_standards/the_five_core_propositio.

Core Proposition 3. Teachers Are Responsible for Managing and Monitoring Student Learning

Accomplished teachers create, enrich, maintain and alter instructional settings to capture and sustain the interest of their students and to make the most effective use of time. They also are adept at engaging students and adults to assist their teaching and at enlisting their colleagues' knowledge and expertise to complement their own. Accomplished teachers command a range of generic instructional techniques, know when each is appropriate and can implement them as needed. They are as aware of ineffectual or damaging practice as they are devoted to elegant practice. They know how to engage groups of students to ensure a disciplined learning environment, and how to organize instruction to allow the schools' goals for students to be met. They are adept at setting norms for social interaction among students and between students and teachers. They understand how to motivate students to learn and how to maintain their interest even in the face of temporary failure.

Accomplished teachers can assess the progress of individual students as well as that of the class as a whole. They employ multiple methods for measuring student growth and understanding and can clearly explain student performance to parents. (pp. 3–4) [emphasis added]

Core Proposition 4. Teachers Think Systematically about Their Practice and Learn from Experience

Accomplished teachers are models of educated persons, exemplifying the virtues they seek to inspire in students—curiosity, tolerance, honesty, fairness, respect for diversity and appreciation of cultural differences—and the capacities that are prerequisites for intellectual growth: the ability to reason and take multiple perspectives, to be creative and take risks, and to adopt an experimental and problem-solving orientation. Accomplished teachers draw on their knowledge of human development, subject matter and instruction, and their understanding of their students to make principled judgments about sound practice. Their decisions are not only grounded in the literature, but also in their experience. They engage in lifelong learning which they seek to encourage in their students. *Striving to strengthen their teaching, accomplished teachers critically examine their practice, seek to expand their repertoire, deepen their knowledge, sharpen their judgment and adapt their teaching to new findings, ideas and theories.* (p. 4) [emphasis added]

Source: National Board for Professional Teaching Standards, 2002.

Calculating the item difficulty and item discrimination indexes requires time and effort, but it can deepen your understanding of both your students and your assessment. The results of such an analysis can provide an opportunity to increase the effectiveness of class discussion of assessment results, improve the quality of remediation (if needed), and improve the effectiveness of instruction. Knowing the quality and effectiveness of items to measure specific content and constructs will give the teacher insight into what students know and can do. During class discussion, the teacher can use the knowledge of item effectiveness to address student misunderstandings and misconceptions. There is an opportunity to seek and receive feedback on improving the quality of poorly performing items. Students will benefit from an honest attempt on the teacher's part to be fair and purposeful. The teacher has an opportunity to hone skills at test construction by receiving the feedback of item analysis and modifying items to improve their effectiveness.

?*Ask Yourself*

Item analysis tells us how effective a particular test item is. Over time, as you refine your classroom assessments, you will find that some items are more effective and discriminating than others. How might you work with your colleagues (say, teachers of the same grade or subject) to develop a test item bank for items that have proven effective? How could you communicate the importance of such analysis to effective assessment?

Summary

- Examining sets of scores is often the first step in understanding group test scores. Frequency tables are probably the simplest arrangement and allow you to understand assessment data by identifying frequencies of scores.

- Histograms are a pictorial representation of data in the form of a bar graph in which each score is listed on the horizontal axis (the X-axis), and the tally or frequency of each score is displayed on the vertical axis (the Y-axis).

- There are three common ways to measure typical performance numerically. They are called measures of central tendency, and they summarize a set of scores.

- The mean is the arithmetic average of a set of scores and is calculated by taking all the individual scores, adding them together, and dividing by the total number of scores.

- The median is the middle score in a set of scores. To obtain the median, arrange the scores from lowest to highest and determine which score is in the middle, such that half of the scores are below it and half are above. When the score set contains an odd number of scores, the median will be the middle score. When there is an even number of scores, the median will be the average of the two scores that straddle the middle of the score set.

- The mode is the most frequent score in a set of scores.
- Measures of variability help inform teachers about the consistency of student performances and whether scores are spread out or bunched together. The two most common measures are range and standard deviation.
- Range represents the difference between the highest score and the lowest score.
- The standard deviation is a measure of the average distance each individual score is from the mean and indicates how spread out the scores are around the mean.

- Item analysis is one of several ways to judge the quality of teacher-made and published assessments. Item analysis is an empirical process and set of procedures designed to evaluate the quality of items that make up assessments.
- Two prominent and useful item analysis statistics are item difficulty (how hard or difficult an item is) and item discrimination (how well an item sorts those who know the material well overall from those who do not). Item difficulty is the ratio or percentage of individuals who answered an item correctly. Item discrimination is the degree to which an item differentiates those who did well on the test from those who did poorly on the test.

Key Terms

For Further Discussion

1. Statistics are useful in explaining scores to others, but in what ways can they inform your teaching?

2. Students often are concerned with how well they did on a test—what grade they received. Consider the statistics that you have encountered in this chapter. In what ways do they lead you to ask how well your students performed on a test and, perhaps, how well you did in developing your test?

3. At what point would you say an individual student performed considerably below average or considerably above average compared to classmates? Would the individual score be 1 standard deviation above or below the mean? 2 standard deviations above or below mean? 3 standard deviations above or below the mean? At what point would you say an individual score is not typical (average)?

Comprehension Quiz

1. You have just scored a 50-point midterm examination in your freshman math class and calculate a mean score of 40. What does the mean score reveal about your students' performance?

2. You look across two of your classes and find that both groups have a mean score of 40. But you notice that one group has a standard deviation of 5 and the other an SD of 10. What would you know about the performance of both groups?

3. On this same test, if you found that all of your students answered question 15 correctly, this would be an indicator of what form of item analysis? What are some things that this analysis might reveal to you?

4. Which of the three measures of central tendency is (are) influenced by extremely high or extremely low scores? Which is (are) not?

Relevant Website Resources

Practical Research, Evaluation & Assessment

http://pareonline.net/Home.htm

This online journal is supported by volunteers and presents refereed journal articles on all areas of educational assessment. There are many articles that address the use of statistical analysis in the classroom.

Testing and Evaluation Services

http://testing.wisc.edu/WhatDoThoseNumbersMean.htm

What do those numbers mean? This is a summary of test statistics and item analysis. The site offers a quick, one-page guide to interpreting the statistics you might encounter as part of the results of a classroom assessment and accompanying item analysis.

References

Collins, H. W., Johansen, J. H., & Johnson, J. A. (1969). *Educational measurement and evaluation: A worktext*. Glenview, IL: Scott, Foresman.

National Board for Professional Teaching Standards (NBPTS). (2002). *What teachers should know and be able to do*. Arlington, VA: Author.

CHAPTER 12

Using Standardized Achievement Tests as Assessments

Chapter Objectives

After reading and thinking about this chapter, you will be able to:

- **Understand the role of standardized tests and testing in an educational setting.**
- **Articulate the differences between norm-referenced tests and criterion-referenced tests.**

- **Articulate the differences between achievement tests and aptitude tests.**
- **Interpret and summarize students' performance on standardized tests.**

In this chapter we guide teachers in the administration, use, and interpretation of standardized assessments. We ask you to consider how you can meaningfully apply standardized tests to classroom practice and how other assessments can provide complementary and supporting evidence of student growth.

Standardized testing, which we define below, is the topic of much discussion in today's educational climate. College entrance, high school graduation, teacher and school evaluations, and assessments of student skills in a variety of areas rely on students' performance on similar or common measures. Standardized tests inform many important educational questions, but have we come to rely too heavily on them? Think about this: In some districts and schools, admission to specialized or gifted programs is weighted heavily (and in some instances solely) by a test score. So a student who has a fight with her parents or stays up too late the night before or is just recovering from a lengthy illness finds herself excluded from a program because of the difference in 2 or 3 points on a standardized test. And there can be consequences for schools or teachers whose students perform poorly.

Standardized Tests in the Current Educational Climate

A major purpose of this textbook is to help you understand that assessment takes many forms. Student learning in all its complexity can never be fully understood or characterized by one single measure—a test score, an observation, an oral examination, or a performance. And, as you have seen, when properly developed and administered, any assessment can give some important information about how and what your students have learned. In this chapter we will examine standardized tests and consider their intended purposes. We use a foundational perspective to help you become a more critical consumer and interpreter of standardized tests as they become increasingly visible in the public educational landscape.

What Is a Standardized Test?

A standardized test is one that (1) is administered and scored following a common protocol; (2) provides **normative scores,** that is, scores that allow you to interpret students' performance relative to others who have taken the test; and (3) is developed and evaluated by experts to ensure that the test consistently measures what it says it is measuring (that is, it has content validity).

Think for a moment about the tests that you may have taken in your educational history—teacher-made tests, physical fitness tests, intelligence tests, and so on. Each of these tests tells us something important about you at various points in your schooling—how well you understand algebra, how many sit-ups you can perform in 2 minutes, or how your verbal abilities compare to your spatial abilities. Now consider the tests that you took as you began the process of college admission and selection. Some of you took the ACT, others the SAT, and, once you were admitted to college, you may have taken college placement exams or CLEP tests. These are all examples of standardized tests—developed and refined by experts, usually administered in large-group settings and interpreted in such a way that you (and the college admissions team) know how well you performed relative to other students taking the identical tests under identical conditions.

Why Are Standardized Tests Important?

The SAT (which used to stand for "Scholastic Aptitude Test" but now, according to its publisher, is no longer an acronym for anything) is a widely administered standardized test used in the college admissions process. Based on your score, college admissions personnel can predict how likely it is that you will succeed at their institution. Of course, the SAT is but one assessment that an admissions office might use, but it can be an important one.

Consider now what might happen if, in place of SAT scores, colleges ask students to report their test scores from teacher-made classroom tests that they have taken in the last two years of high school. How would the admissions personnel know if the tests were of equal quality and equal difficulty? How could they easily and meaningfully interpret the classroom test scores of thousands of applicants from hundreds of different high schools? With standardized tests, these questions are irrelevant. The admissions personnel use scores from a test administered in the very same way to all students, knowing that all students were given the very same test items— and that the test has been shown to correlate with college performance.

What Else Do Standardized Tests Offer?

As research has found, standardized tests can help us predict future student performance. In addition, the tests allow us to look at how student performance changes over time, how schools perform relative to state or national norms, or how groups of students compare to one another. Standardized tests can also contribute to decision making about school programs and curricula, and they can become part of an ongoing school or district program evaluation process. While we are primarily concerned in this chapter with standardized tests as they relate to teaching and learning, you may be interested to know that standardized tests are used in many contexts for a variety of purposes. For example, they are used to measure intelligence, to describe personality, and to identify occupational interests and preferences.

Digging Deeper
Early Use of the SAT

The first administration of the SAT occurred in 1926, and, for several years, the results of the SAT were used to conduct research on the relationship between students' scores and their performance in college. The plan was to develop normative data that would determine whether the test could accurately predict students' college grades. In the 1930s, Harvard President James Bryant Conant decided to use the SAT to identify academically capable students from the midwest-ern section of the United States. Historically, Harvard had attracted its students from the Northeast, and Conant used the SAT as a way to offer Harvard scholarships to nontraditional applicants. In the first 2 years in which Harvard employed the SAT to this end, one of the students accepted was James Tobin, who went on to win a Nobel Prize in economics.

Source: Lemann, 1999.

Most important, though, in this chapter we urge you to think about how standardized testing might influence classroom practice, both in terms of content and instructional methods. The debate surrounding the proper role of standardized testing in education is not new; but, in an era of heightened accountability for teachers, schools, and states, testing has become a source of contention among parents, educators, legislators, and other stakeholders.

The No Child Left Behind Act

As we have described in earlier chapters, standardized testing was thrust into prominence when the federal No Child Left Behind (NCLB) Act placed accountability on individual states to raise academic proficiency for all learners to 100 percent by 2014. NCLB was designed to address concerns about academic performance of students nationally. In Chapter 3 we discussed how the results of standardized tests such as the National Assessment of Educational Progress (NAEP) showed that subgroups compared on the basis of gender, race/ethnicity, or socioeconomic status (SES) achieved differently. NCLB was designed to hold schools and districts accountable to bring all student achievement to a standard, regardless of SES, race, or gender. The law requires that progress be measured through annual testing in grades 3–8.

In this explanation written for parents, the language of NCLB clearly articulates the crucial role of testing.

> *No Child Left Behind* requires states to test your child in reading and math every year in grades 3–8. Your child will also be tested at least once in high school. The tests will help you, your child, and your

child's teachers know how well your child is learning and when he or she needs extra help.

Although states have been given some latitude in determining how they will improve low-achieving schools and groups, the measure of student learning must be standardized tests that are given statewide. As a teacher, how will you respond to state or national testing? How can you use the results of such tests to enhance your teaching? We know that students who have deep understanding of concepts perform better on standardized tests than students who have a superficial content knowledge. How do you teach toward such understanding when students and parents value high scores and when the testing culture itself encourages performance over mastery?

Meaningful Learning in an Age of High-Stakes Assessment

Throughout this chapter, we will refer to the concept of *high-stakes assessment*, which we discussed in Chapter 3. This refers to any test for which there are significant consequences for the student, for the teacher, or for the school. For students, a college placement exam or the Law School Admissions Test, for example, carries important consequences. The performance of subgroups of students can carry significant weight in the assessment of a school under NCLB.

Remember that whatever measure you employ to assess students' understanding always provides an incomplete picture. If your teaching is characterized by helping your students fully master important concepts rather than simply perform well on a standardized test, your students will demonstrate deeper and more authentic learning through all of their assessments. And, as they prepare for high-stakes testing situations, they will display greater confidence and persistence and achieve consistent performance results.

Ask Yourself

Think about two testing situations. First, recall a time when you were expected to participate in a large-group testing situation in your school, perhaps a state-mandated achievement test. Now, consider the weeks leading up to your college admissions testing—the ACT, SAT, or a placement exam. Did you approach these two testing situations differently? Were they equally important to you? As a teacher, how might your answers to these questions help you interpret the results of your students' performance?

Types of Tests

You and your students will encounter several types of standardized tests that differ in important ways. Perhaps the most critical difference is that between norm-referenced and criterion-referenced tests.

Norm-Referenced Versus Criterion-Referenced Tests

Think of a teacher-made test with 100 multiple-choice items. If a student correctly answers 83 items, this may translate to a letter grade of B in your class. But how does this student compare to the rest of the class or to the rest of the students in the same grade? Standardized tests allow us to answer these questions.

We can characterize student performance even further if we know whether we are interpreting a norm-referenced or a criterion-referenced test. In assessment, **norms** refer to the statistics that describe the performance of the entire group of test takers. As introduced in Chapter 1, *norm-referenced tests*, then, are tests in which a single student's performance can be compared to the performance of a larger group. It is expected that students' scores will be distributed from low to high, and, when we examine a student's score on a norm-referenced test, we will be able to see how the student scored with respect to all other test takers.

On a norm-referenced test, we are able to compare a person's score with a group of people who have taken the same test. This comparative group, which usually includes thousands of test takers, is referred to as a *norming group.* You will often see a school's aggregate scores on an achievement test reported as a percentile, say the 70th percentile. It is likely that this test was a norm-referenced test, and a large number of students provided the norm from which we are able to derive the percentile rank of a student or school.

You may already recognize some of these commonly administered, norm-referenced tests. These are tests that assess various skills and compare students' performance to the performance of a norming group: the California Achievement Test (CAT), the Iowa Test of Basic Skills (ITBS), and the Stanford Achievement Test.

Criterion-referenced tests, on the other hand, indicate how well developed a person's skills or understanding are as compared to an established standard or criterion. In a high school health class, for example, many students will be expected to pass a test of their knowledge of cardiopulmonary resuscitation (CPR). In a test on this topic, is it useful to know how many questions a student answered correctly relative to other students? Probably not. In this instance, we are most interested in how much of the process students understand and can perform. In assessing a skill such a CPR, we include on the test all the skills that make up CPR because we want to know how many of these skills a student has successfully mastered.

How does this distinction come into play in the schools? Consider a state-level assessment of mathematics achievement among eighth graders. A criterion-referenced test would allow you to see whether your eighth-graders achieved at a certain standard that the state had set in mathematics. The standard would probably be expressed in terms of a *cut score* or *cut-off score.*

Suppose the cut score was 150 points out of a possible 200 on this eighth-grade math test. We would say that students who scored at or above 150 on this test "met the standard." Those who scored below 150 "failed to meet the standard." There may also be a category called "exceeds the standard." If so, students who scored at, perhaps, 180 or above would be labeled "exceeds the standard."

A norm-referenced test, such as the SAT, would be interpreted and applied differently. For example, we know that the mean (average) score on the verbal component of the SAT is 500, and the standard deviation is 100. As you learned in Chapter 11, roughly two-thirds of all test takers will score between plus or minus one standard deviation (SD) from the mean, that is, between 400 and 600 on the SAT verbal test. The higher the score, the fewer people there will be who have earned that score.

Now think about how colleges and universities interpret such scores. Colleges can be fairly certain that if they receive an application from a student with an SAT verbal score of 780, which is almost 3 SDs above the mean, that student scored at a level that few students will reach. Therefore, they might make a decision (hopefully using other criteria as well) that this student is worth admitting because of his performance on the SAT relative to all other test takers.

Achievement Tests Versus Aptitude Tests

Achievement versus aptitude. The distinction between the two terms may not be familiar to you, and to be sure, the difference between achievement tests and aptitude tests is lost on many educators. The truth is that in practice, while there is a definitional difference between the two types of test, it is sometimes difficult to distinguish one from the other. What is the difference and why is the difference important in understanding learning? What does each type of test contribute to student success?

As we discussed in Chapter 5, *achievement tests* are assessments intended to measure students' accumulated knowledge in a particular area. Published, standardized achievement tests are invariably norm-referenced tests. Standardized achievement tests are intended to measure student learning in a particular academic area. They may measure achievement in

Resource for Your Assessment Toolkit
Building a Standardized Norm-Referenced Achievement Test

Although you may never take part in developing a standardized norm-referenced achievement test, it is helpful to understand how such tests are created. Such an understanding will help you answer parents' questions about standardized testing. It will also enable you to participate in a standardized test selection committee for your school district.

The steps taken by a testing company to create a new standardized achievement test begin at the same place that a teacher does when preparing to write a classroom test. The major difference is that the testing company moves beyond the classroom test level to make its test standardized, culture-fair, and norm-referenced. Here are the steps needed to build such a test.

1. *Clearly identify the test's purpose.* What should the test tell us about students' knowledge and skill?
2. *Determine the test's format.* While most standardized tests use selected-response items, some also include essay items.
3. *Create the test items.* This process involves curriculum experts and item writers, who go through several rounds of writing items, critiquing them, and rewriting them. As a part of this step, items

are also reviewed for bias. Typically, many more items are written than will be needed for the test.

4. *Pretest the items.* Items are administered to groups of students. Their responses are analyzed statistically using item analysis methods. Items that perform poorly (that is, items that students apparently misunderstand or that are too easy or too hard) are dropped and replaced. This process of item analysis and replacement continues until there is a large enough group of items assembled that perform well.

5. *Establish test norms.* At this point, the test is considered to be complete. Creating norms for a test involves administering the test to a large and varied sample of students. The test scores for the thousand of students in the sample will be the basis for the norms that all future testing will use when interpreting student scores. Consequently, testing companies work hard to collect a group of schools that are representative of the nation as a whole. Information about the size and composition of the norm sample (racial, ethnic, SES, size of community and school) will be printed in the test manual.

a specific area, or they may comprise several subtests, each of which measures a separate area or skill. The purpose of the test is to cover the entire academic area with a small number of test items, given that many areas must be covered during the testing.

Consequently, the test typically is composed of items of varying levels of difficulty—from relatively easy to very difficult—because the test is designed to assess a wide range of student knowledge. Nearly all students at a particular grade level will correctly answer the simpler items, while few students at a particular grade level will be able to answer the more difficult items. Generally only one item—or at the most two—will deal with a particular topic within each area. Figure 12.1 illustrates the kind of items that

Figure 12.1 *Example Test Items from an Elementary Norm-Referenced Standardized Achievement Test Battery: Social Studies Subtest*

1. What did the American colonists want to gain by fighting the English?
   a. freedom from England
   b. a better economy
   c. George Washington for president
   d. to build new colonies

2. What is *one* way that colonial life is different from life today?
   a. Most children lived in a house with their parents.
   b. Children went to school to learn reading and writing.
   c. People worked to earn a living.
   d. Food was cooked in the fireplace.

3. What was the purpose of the Underground Railroad?
   a. It connected the East and West Coasts.
   b. It helped pioneers cross the Great Plains.
   c. It helped southern slaves escape to freedom in the North.
   d. It carried miners to Alaska.

4. What was the name of the new country formed by the southeastern states that favored slavery?
   a. the Constitution
   b. the Confederacy
   c. the Conflagration
   d. the Civil War

5. Immigrants have come to the United States for many reasons. Which statement is NOT a reason for immigrating?
   a. to have more freedom
   b. to find a job
   c. to own land
   d. to take a long vacation

6. Who was president of the United States during the Civil War?
   a. George Washington
   b. Frederick Douglass
   c. Abraham Lincoln
   d. Patrick Henry

7. How often is the president of the United States elected?
   a. every 2 years
   b. every 4 years
   c. every 5 years
   d. every 6 years

might be found on the social studies subtest of a standardized achievement battery.

As you can see from reading the test items in Figure 12.1, there is often limited coverage of any one topic on a test. This illustration has 3 items on the Civil War era, for example. This differs greatly from the kind of test you might typically create for your students after studying a unit on the Civil War. Rather than 3 items, you might have 30 items on a multiple-choice quiz—and such a quiz could also be called an achievement test. Your classroom achievement test would not be a standardized test, and it would be criterion-referenced rather than norm-referenced. In addition to the test, you might have your students prepare a report or presentation or other product to show their mastery of your classroom learning outcomes related to the Civil War. In short, you would give many opportunities for them to show what they know and can do in this area, if you were assessing students in your classroom. You would not limit yourself to 3 test items.

This example shows one of the limitations of standardized achievement test batteries—the narrow coverage of any one topic. Another limitation is that these tests are timed, which can impact student performance and cognitive demands put on students as they read one item on topic 1, then one or two on topic 2, and so on. The need to quickly change gears mentally from one test item to another and to finish a section within a specified time period when taking this kind of test can add a layer of strain and anxiety to the testing experience that may influence some students' scores.

When would such a test be appropriately used? The answer lies in the test's intended purpose: Standardized, norm-referenced achievement tests are specifically designed to broadly assess students in a way that can compare one group's achievement with that of others. Although coverage is narrow in any single area, the test items have been written by experts to match the topics that are most likely to be covered in schools nationally. It can be useful to see how a school or school district compares to the country as a whole in each academic area. School administrators and school boards often like to review this kind of data in order to compare their district's performance with others. Only a standardized, norm-referenced achievement test will provide this comparison.

Aptitude tests are designed to measure not accumulated knowledge but rather a student's *capacity* to achieve or perform at certain levels. In other words, while an achievement test measures what a student has done, an aptitude test intends to predict what a student is capable of doing.

Historically, the SAT and the ACT exams have been used to predict with some level of precision how well a student will perform in college. (As we have noted, SAT was originally an acronym for Scholastic Aptitude Test.) Currently, such tests have come under scrutiny for several reasons.

First, as has been their purpose for many decades, aptitude tests are intended to predict success in a subsequent context. We are most familiar with this in the form of the SAT or the Graduate Record Examination (GRE), which serve to predict a student's success in higher education or graduate school, respectively. But, if aptitude implies potential, then performance on an aptitude test should not be influenced by extensive preparation or studying. Nevertheless, students and their parents spend significant amounts of time and money in preparation for such tests.

Second, research has suggested that an achievement test (such as the SAT II) is a better predictor of college success than an aptitude test like the general SAT. (Geiser & Studley, 2001).

?Ask Yourself

Think about your last experience in a standardized testing situation.
How did your performance on that test influence the way in which you approached your subsequent learning strategies? As a teacher, how can you meaningfully communicate your students' performance to them? To their parents?

Interpreting Results of Standardized Tests

According to the **Family Educational Rights and Privacy Act (FERPA)** of 1974, parents have a legal right to examine their child's academic records, including scores from any tests they have taken. As a classroom teacher or as an administrator, then, it becomes especially important for two reasons for you to be able to understand and communicate the results of a standardized test. First, you will have another insight into your students' learning in key areas; and, second, you will be able to demystify the process for parents and other stakeholders in the community. Here we will introduce several key statistics related to norm-referenced tests that will allow you to understand student performance and meaningfully communicate that performance to others.

In our discussion of the SAT verbal scores, we referred to the characteristics of the normal curve. In particular, the normal curve and the standard deviation, which we covered in detail in Chapter 11, are critical to the interpretation of standardized test scores. Standardized test score norms are derived from testing a large number of students and, as a result, the scores when plotted on a graph will be very close to a normal curve. Test manuals that list the norms for the test will provide you with means for test scores and subtest scores, standard deviations, and the distribution of scores based on the norming group's test scores. The following sections provide you with a vocabulary for understanding and communicating test scores.

Types of Scores

We will start with two types of scores that are quite familiar—raw scores and percent correct. These two kinds of test scores are the most frequently used in classrooms today, and they communicate an important level of understanding about our students.

Raw Scores Quite simply, a student's **raw score** on an assessment is the number of items he or she answered correctly. For example, on a 50-item multiple-choice test of mathematical concepts, a student who correctly answers 37 items out of 50 would have a raw score of 37.

Percent Correct To calculate the **percent correct**, then, we simply divide the raw score by the number of items on the test. In this case,

$$\text{Percent correct} = 37/50 = 74\%$$

The percent correct is a more useful measure of performance than a raw score because it allows us to begin to compare performance among different assessments. If, for example, you looked at a student's performance on two different assessments—a midterm and a final—and the student had a raw score of 35 on the midterm and a raw score of 70 on the final, you might assume that she had performed significantly better on the final. But if the midterm contained 50 items and the final had 100 items, then the percent correct on the two assessments—70 percent on the midterm and 70 percent on the final—tells you that the student's performance was the same on both tests.

Neither the raw score nor the percent correct, however, reveals anything about how one student performs relative to another student, group of students, or all students who took the same test. For a fuller understanding of one student's performance relative to a larger group, we look to several statistics that are commonly used in reports of standardized tests.

Percentile Rank A **percentile rank** is the most typical norm-referenced test score. It refers not to the percentage of items answered correctly but rather to a student's performance relative to all other test takers. When a test report indicates that a student performed at the 60th percentile, it means that he or she performed better than 60 percent of the students in the norm sample. Percentile ranks are in widespread use because they are so easy to understand and interpret.

Take a look at Figure 12.2, which displays the scores of a group of 485 tenth-grade students at one high school who took the verbal portion of the SAT (formerly called the SAT-V, now called the critical reading section of the SAT). Among this group of tenth-graders, the lowest score was 420 and the highest score was 790, which is slightly lower than the highest possible score of 800. And the mean (average) score for these students was 570, slightly higher than the mean of 500 that we noted earlier.

But how might you understand and communicate an individual student's score more meaningfully? A student comes to you and asks what a score of 630 on the SAT-V means. If you have a table of percentile ranks like that in Figure 12.2, you can see that a score of 630 corresponds to a percentile of 75, which means that your student has a higher SAT-V score than 75 percent of the 485 test takers at this high school.

Figure 12.2 *SAT Verbal Scores of Tenth-Grade Students with Percentile Rank*

SAT Verbal Score	Percentile Rank	SAT Verbal Score	Percentile Rank
790	99	570	50
710	95	560	45
670	90	550	40
660	85	530	35
640	80	520	30
630	**75**	510	25
620	70	500	20
610	65	480	15
600	60	470	10
580	55	420	5

Percentile ranks have the advantage of being easy to understand and interpret. They give a quick and clear picture of a student's standing within the total group who took the test.

Stanines Scores that are reported as **stanines** (short for "standard nine") indicate where student performance falls on a scale of 1 to 9. Because it is a simple system with only a few numbers, stanines can be especially easy to explain to parents and students.

Stanines are a form of standard score. Each stanine does not represent 11 percent of test takers but rather one-half of a standard deviation, with stanine 5 straddling the midpoint of the standard curve. Stanine 1 represents the lowest scores, 9 represents the highest scores. On a standardized test, most test takers would fall in the average range, in stanines 4 to 6. Therefore, stanine 7 or above could be considered above average, and stanine 3 or below would be considered below average. Stanines are closely related to percentile ranks, in that each stanine covers a certain range of percentiles. Figure 12.3 shows the relationship between percentile ranks and stanines.

Let's look again at our tenth-grade SAT-V example, as shown in Figure 12.4. Stanines communicate relative standing without the precision of a

Figure 12.3 *The Meaning of Stanines and Their Relationship to Percentile Ranks*

Percentile Ranks	Stanine	Descriptive Label
96–99	9	Well above average
89–95	8	
77–88	7	Above average
60–76	6	
40–59	5	Average
23–39	4	
11–22	3	
4–10	2	Below average
Less than 4	1	Well below average

Figure 12.4 *SAT Verbal Scores of Tenth-Grade Students with Percentile Rank and Stanine*

SAT Verbal Score	Percentile Rank	Stanine	SAT Verbal Score	Percentile Rank	Stanine
790	99	9	570	50	5
710	95	8	560	45	5
670	90	8	550	40	5
660	85	7	530	35	4
640	80	7	520	30	4
630	**75**	**6**	510	25	4
620	70	6	500	20	3
610	65	6	480	15	3
600	60	6	470	10	2
580	55	5	420	5	1

percentile rank. Using once again our student with an SAT-V score of 630, we know that the student scored better than 75 percent of this group of 485 students. The corresponding stanine score is a 6, which indicates that the student's SAT-V is at the high end of the average stanine scores of 4, 5, and 6.

Why would we want to use a stanine for interpreting test results when it is not as precise as a percentile? There are two reasons. The first is its status as a standard score, which makes it possible to combine stanines from different tests to create a total or overall score. We can also directly compare a student's stanine on one test with her stanine on another. As stanines are usually interpreted, a 2-stanine difference between two scores is considered a significant difference. For example, if a student had a stanine of 4 in reading and 6 in math, we would conclude that his math achievement was higher than his reading achievement. However, if his reading stanine was 5 and math stanine 6, we would not conclude that the difference in the scores was a significant one.

This issue of significance is also related to the second advantage that stanines provide: They are a reminder not to overinterpret any particular test score. With high-stakes testing, we can become too invested in the scores produced by these tests. Going back to the student who scored 630 on the SAT verbal test, we noted that this score is equivalent to a stanine of 6. How low a score would another student have to have in order to be considered "significantly lower" than 630? The answer is 530 or lower. That is the highest SAT score that corresponds to a stanine of 4, which is 2 stanines lower than a stanine of 6. That is a 100-point difference on the SAT scale, or about one standard deviation. Using stanines reminds us that often, a few points difference in standard scores have little meaning.

In any case, any one score is simply one piece of data about what a student knows or can do. A stanine is a rather general score, in which a number of raw scores and a number of percentiles all have the same stanine score. Small and unimportant differences between students and small differences among a particular student's subtest scores disappear when expressed as stanines. Consequently, we are less likely to impart too great a meaning to a single test score.

Grade Equivalents **Grade equivalent (GE) scores** are easy to understand and easy to misinterpret. Think about your grade school years. In September of your fourth-grade year, you had achieved a certain proficiency in mathematics, but how did your performance compare to students who were also in the first month of their fourth-grade year? Do you believe most parents would be interested in knowing how their children were performing in mathematics or reading compared to test takers at the same place in their schooling?

Quite simply, a grade equivalent score communicates a level of performance relative to test takers in the same grade. The GE score is represented as two numbers separated by a decimal. The first number represents a grade in school, and the second a tenth of a school year, or about a month. For example, a GE score of 5.2 represents the expected performance of a student in the second month of fifth grade.

So what would you make of a fourth-grade student who receives a grade equivalent score in math of 7.4? It is tempting to think that this student is ready for junior high school math because her score indicates that she is performing at the level of a seventh-grade student in the fourth month of school. The grade equivalent score, however, can be misleading for a number of reasons, and most assessment experts argue that stanines or percentile ranks are more informative and precise. Using the above example of a fourth-grader with a math grade equivalent score of 7.4, it is important to understand that the student is likely ahead of her same grade peers in math, but she should not necessarily be placed in seventh-grade math. Instead, this GE score suggests what the score of a seventh-grader would likely be on the math test normed for fourth-grade students.

In other words, if you have evidence that the student is above grade level, you would want to assess the student using a test that has been normed for seventh-graders to get a more accurate picture of the student's math abilities. Although you should never use grade equivalent scores alone as the justification for acceleration and promotion, it can be helpful in recognizing students who may be ahead of their grade peers in specific areas.

Reading and Interpreting a Standardized Test Score Report

Now that we have introduced some important ideas in standardized testing, let's take look at how such ideas can be applied using a common achievement test, the Terra Nova California Achievement Test (CAT). The Terra Nova measures concepts, processes, and objectives found in the major academic content areas in American schools, such as reading, language arts, mathematics, science, and social studies. Students' scores are compared to national normative data, and reports on each student's performance are generated.

The Terra Nova characterizes student performance relative to a nationally representative, random sample of test takers from different geographic regions and school sizes, varying socioeconomic status, and representative ethnic groups. For our purposes, the Terra Nova is a useful instrument in that the student report uses percentiles, stanines, and grade equivalents to show student achievement.

Take a look at the report in Figure 12.5, which is a sample report for the Terra Nova. Spend a few moments reading the sample report and try to interpret this student's performance. How did Ken score relative to the

Figure 12.5 *Sample Home Report for the Terra Nova CAT*

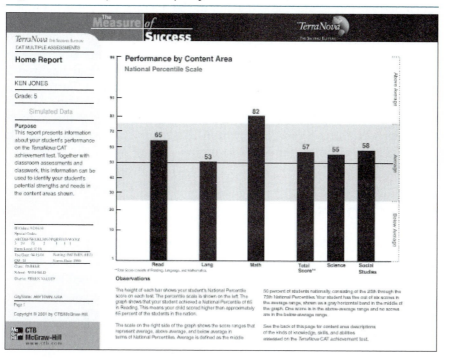

other students who took this test? Which areas appear to be his strong areas? How would you explain his performance to his parents?

You may first notice that the report conveys quite a bit of information on a single page. What does the black, horizontal line in the middle of the graph tell you? Notice that the line connects the number *50* on the left (Y-axis) of the graph to the word *average* on the right. The 50 represents the 50th percentile, indicating that half of all test takers scored below that line and half scored above. Where did our student fall? He scored almost exactly average in reading (53rd percentile) and science (55th percentile) and somewhat higher in all other areas.

Now notice the slightly shaded background. Notice that it covers the middle third of the graph. Recall that in a normal curve there will be few extremely high or low scores, so the area covered in the shaded area represents the area where the largest number of scores will fall. In terms of stanine scores, this area represents scores of 4, 5, and 6. What more can you now say about your student? His overall score and his scores in reading, language, science, and social studies could fairly be characterized as average. Notice that stanines and percentiles convey information differently, and while percentiles are more precise and descriptive, both lead us to conclude that this student is achieving in the average range for his grade level in most areas.

Our student is, however, performing above average in one area: mathematics. He has a percentile score of 82 and this rank is above the shaded background. So, imagine again that your principal has asked you to communicate with parents about your student's Terra Nova report. Where would you begin? What would you emphasize? What other evidence, besides the Terra Nova, might you bring to the conversation to corroborate your observation that your student is average in some skills and somewhat better in math?

Ask Yourself

Think back to your senior year in high school, when you were making important choices about college. You probably took the ACT, SAT, various AP tests, or some form of college placement exam. Who helped you interpret and fully understand what those tests conveyed about your level of achievement or aptitude? How about the other high-stakes tests you took along the way? How might you, in your own classroom—whether you teach fifth-graders, ninth-graders, or twelfth-graders—effectively advise your students about what those tests mean about their learning? Even if this task is officially handled by your school's counselors, you can add another important perspective from your content area.

Preparing Students for Testing Situations

Think about your high school experience and recall those activities in which you participated outside of class: sports, theater, music, or math team. What might have been the consequences if you had skipped a couple weeks of practice prior to a big game or the last two weeks of rehearsals before the spring musical? It certainly would have been evident in your performance. You might look back on that time and conclude that your game or performance really did not reflect your true talent.

Now apply those circumstances to tests. Most students would agree on the importance of studying for a test, but do they prepare properly? Just as you need a basketball coach or a stage director in extracurricular activities, as a teacher you will help your students prepare properly and effectively for the standardized testing situations they encounter in school.

Student Motivation and Standardized Tests

We can be fairly confident that students will prepare and perform better on assessments that carry some personal meaning or value for them. Classroom tests that influence their semester grade, competitive tests that will earn them personal or team recognition, and standardized tests that will determine college admission carry significant value for students. So, in an era of high-stakes testing, the true high stakes for students are not the same as those for their schools, districts, or states. That is not to say, of course, that students generally dismiss such tests, or that, overall, we cannot get a reasonable picture of our students' learning. But if we use our understanding of motivation, we can enhance the likelihood that students will approach standardized testing situations with purpose.

As we have indicated, each of the authors of this book has experience in working with students with exceptionalities, particularly giftedness and learning disabilities. Within both of these specialized groups, students are regularly administered standardized tests for a variety of purposes. For example, within our gifted population of approximately 600 students, we regularly administer a variety of standardized tests that help us to better understand and serve them as learners. Our instruments include the Ravens Progressive Matrices Test, the Cornell Critical Thinking Test, the Watson-Glaser Critical Thinking Inventory, the Learning Context Questionnaire, the SAT, the PSAT, and many others. In fact, over 3 years of school, these students take over ten standardized instruments.

While the students do not always enjoy taking the tests, they are quite interested in finding out the results. They want to know, "What does this test tell me about myself?" We build on the students' curiosity about their test results in two ways. First, we spend some time clarifying the purposes of the tests to the students. Next, when we receive the actual results, staff members meet with each student to report her or his test performance and to discuss what specific insights about the student's abilities and needs the results offer. Staff members are careful to make the individual conference experiences diagnostic and supportive.

We use this example to suggest ways in which you can effectively engage students in the process of standardized testing. First and foremost, you want to be sure that students are not anxious about the testing event but also that they are invested in the testing process. The above example suggests that you can achieve this twofold goal by carefully explaining how the purpose of the standardized test relates to students' lives. Then, because you have shown students that the tests have useful information to offer them, you can emphasize the need to take these tests seriously so that the test results accurately show what students know and can do. Also, you can help students by carefully refraining from expressing your own worry or anxiety about how the test results will be used.

Finally, and most important, effective assessment relies on your timely and meaningful feedback. As a practice, providing student feedback on all assessments helps develop students' *efficacy* (confidence to do well in a particular setting) and resilience and helps them in assessing their short- and long-term goals. Your regular classroom feedback lays the groundwork for using standardized tests as another source of information that can reinforce the students' active monitoring of their own learning.

To this point, you should discourage students from using their performance on the test as a source of comparison with other students. Making unreasonable comparisons on performance (for example, when a low-achieving student compares his or her score to the top scorer in the class) can negatively affect student efficacy. Such comparisons become much more common as students move into early adolescence.

Students often view poor performance on a standardized test as evidence of low ability or intelligence. You might think about providing a safety net for students who perform poorly. For example, if the test includes subscores indicating achievement in different areas, and you have a student who does poorly on the mathematics section, you might consider creating alternate assessments that allow your student to demonstrate that he, in fact, can perform well in that area. By doing so, you can address issues of math efficacy and develop confidence for future tests.

Test Anxiety and Your Students

Test anxiety is a real educational phenomenon, and when words such as *high stakes* are used to describe standardized tests, that anxiety may undermine the test performance of a number of students. You may know of classmates who say that they are not good test takers and that they believe their poor performance on the ACT was a function of test anxiety. But high-achieving students with a strong understanding of concepts and content, according to research, generally tend to perform well in testing situations. In fact, as we have discussed elsewhere, higher levels of efficacy are related to lower levels of test anxiety.

There may be several other factors at play in student anxiety or low performance on standardized tests. First, student performance can sometimes be related to familiarity with the format of the test itself. Testing guides, such as those that are published to prepare students for tests such as the ACT or teacher certification exams, are often helpful in acquainting students with the scope of the test's content, the types of test items, and the time limits allowed to complete different sections of the test. Students who enter a testing situation without any idea of the format, scope, or type of items they will encounter are not likely to perform as well as students who have some familiarity with the test's expectations. Second, students may have inaccurately assessed their readiness to perform well on the test, and a poor performance may reflect true achievement rather than true test anxiety.

Robert L. Ebel and David A. Frisbie (1986) suggest some considerations that teachers might take into account as they assess students' readiness for a standardized test. First, test anxiety appears to be negatively correlated with level of ability. In other words, the students who demonstrate the greatest levels of test anxiety tend to be the least ready for the testing situation, and those students who show the lowest levels of anxiety tend to be the most prepared and competent. Second, the importance of the test to the test taker is related to level of anxiety. That is, the more important it is to do well on a test, the more likely a student is to show some anxiety. Third, a mild level of anxiety can actually enhance student performance on a test.

Taking into account what may be true test anxiety and what might be a lack of readiness for a testing situation, what can you do as a teacher to prepare your students for standardized testing situations—even high-stakes testing?

Teach for Conceptual Understanding Rather than Test Content "Teaching to the test" is a practice that is derided as an outcome of high-stakes testing. The argument is that as teachers begin to worry about the consequences of low test performance, they begin to tailor their lessons to the specific content of an upcoming test. This practice, however, points to two important considerations for test preparation. First, students who cram in late-night sessions as a study habit for a test typically demonstrate only superficial understanding on a test that is intended to be an authentic measure of knowledge and achievement. Second, and certainly more important, abundant research suggests that students who have deep conceptual understanding of content are consistently higher performing on tests. They are more persistent in their problem solving, and they are able to draw on more complex understanding in testing situations than students who have simply memorized.

Help Students Become Properly Oriented to Standardized Testing
Think about the construction of your own tests leading up to the standardized testing session. When possible, create and administer some test items that are similar to those on an upcoming standardized test to allow your students a chance to practice. Consider this scenario: Throughout your course, you administer to your students five paper-and-pencil tests, all of which comprise only multiple-choice, true-false, and short-answer items. On your final exam you ask students' to respond to three essay questions. You have not prepared them in advance by describing the test format. How might this affect the students' performance? If instead, you had allowed your students to articulate their understanding through essays or constructed-response items throughout the semester, they would be prepared both for the content and possible item types on the final assessment.

Familiarizing your students with the format of the test items and with the general content is not the same as "teaching to the test." Introducing students to the format of the items, with an overview of the content they can expect, is an appropriate practice that does not undermine the intent of the test.

Having to encounter time limits for the first time on a standardized test can be especially intimidating. So if your students are relatively new to standardized testing, give them some practice with timed activities.

Further, let your students know that achievement tests are intended to include items that are beyond their level of knowledge. Students may spend too much time on such problems, which leads to frustration with the test and may discourage them in future testing settings. Students should be advised not to spend too much time on any one question and to return to the most difficult questions after they have completed the remainder.

Provide Occasional Practice Exercises Although some rare practice opportunity is helpful, we recommend that this classroom practice not be too widely utilized because it can have the effect of directing students' test preparation efforts toward the test itself. Nevertheless, it can be effective at preparing students through sample questions and formats. It is important, though, that the practice exercises be clearly linked to learning outcomes that you have identified for your course. In other words, use materials and questions on topics that you would be addressing regardless of the upcoming standardized tests.

?*Ask Yourself*

In testing situations, boys prefer and tend to perform better than girls do on timed tests that involve objective-type items This is a persistent criticism of tests that are intended to predict performance. When the element of time is removed and when the test contains more constructed-response items, male/female differences tend to disappear. Knowing that your students will likely be taking tests that are timed and that will include many multiple-choice items, what might be an effective classroom strategy that would address this testing issue?

Making Standardized Tests Meaningful

In our presentation of the psychological foundations of assessment, we have pointed to the importance of understanding student motivation in developing assessments that accurately reflect and indicate student learn-

Resource for Your Assessment Toolkit
More Information on Standardized Tests

In this chapter we have characterized the types of standardized tests that your student might encounter. As examples, we have also identified a few specific and widely administered tests to illustrate the uses and limitations of such tests. There are, however, standardized tests that assess many different learner characteristics, and there are several online resources that will give you brief overviews and, in some cases, reviews and evaluations of published tests. The Educational Testing Service (ETS) offers such a resource at its website (www.ets.org/testcoll/). If you would like more information about a particular test (to communicate with parents, for example), or if you are looking for a test that will help you understand your students better (such as a critical thinking instrument), the ETS website contains a large number of useful entries.

ing. It is important to think about motivation as a process. It is tempting to think of motivation as something that we do *to* our students—we certainly want to motivate them to learn. But motivation begins with engagement, and, while some students will be intrinsically motivated to learn, we must find meaningful ways to engage other students and lead them to become active monitors of their own learning.

For these reasons, making standardized tests meaningful carries with it two important implications. First, we should actively seek ways to make all tests meaningful to students. Second, the results of any test should carry some meaning for our own instruction and planning.

As classrooms become more diverse in terms of ethnicity, socioeconomic status, and other learner characteristics, the challenge of teaching diverse groups becomes increasingly complex. And legislation such as NCLB clearly charges educators with meeting those diverse needs and measuring learning through standardized tests. So how can teachers interpret and communicate student performance on standardized tests in such a way that they meaningfully communicate learning?

As we have already suggested, student performance on any assessment is influenced by a variety of factors in addition to the student's knowledge and skill—student motivation, testing conditions, the match between the assessment and the content that has been covered, as well as unknowable personal factors that have an effect on a particular student. But, the most significant point to remember when interpreting or communicating test scores, regardless of the stakes involved, is that *no single test can fully communicate any student's learning or understanding.*

Whether you spend your career as a classroom teacher or whether you take on a different role in the field of education, you will be in a position to interpret and explain test scores for students, parents, and others. In the previous chapter, we considered more specifically the types of data and statistics that are typically included on standardized test reports, but here we focus on three important considerations in communicating test results in a meaningful way.

1. *Familiarize yourself with both the purposes and the report format of the test results.* Parents and students have a right to know why they are being tested. The more you are able to demystify the test and testing situation, the more likely students are to engage in the task and the more confident you can be in explaining student performance to parents.

2. *Connect student performance on a standardized test to other assessments that your students have taken.* As a teacher, you know that one test cannot tell the full story of a student's learning, but this understanding is not shared by all. Unfortunately, today's educational climate leads some parents or other stakeholder groups to look at performance on tests as the single strongest indicator of achievement, when other school- or classroom-level assessments could tell a clearer or more complete story. So, while you rarely would dismiss a student's test score, be prepared to share with parents other ways in which student understanding has been assessed that show how your students have performed.

3. *Be aware that there may be other factors that influence test performance and be prepared to note these to parents.* Illness on the day of the test, low motivation, circumstances in your student's home, or some other factor may lead to low test performance. In some instances, such as with the ACT or perhaps an aptitude test required for admission to a gifted program, students may have the opportunity to take the test again. So, if parents ask why their child's performance appears below ability, you may be able to indicate to parents what you observed about the student on the day of testing.

We conclude with a thought on the temptation and perhaps the tendency to overinterpret student performance on standardized tests. Because two students have similar scores on a standardized test does not necessarily mean that they are equally prepared academically. In a classic collection of essays on learning and understanding, Lev Vygotsky discusses the situation of two girls of the same age and grade, who have identical scores on a standardized achievement test. From the test scores, both girls seem equally and adequately prepared for next year's school work. One of the girls, however, had been ill and had missed much of the school year and had not been present for daily lessons, group work, and assessments. Although she was able to answer the same number of test items as the other girl, she may have a more superficial understanding of the topics covered in the test, having missed so much of the school year. Consequently, she may not be as well prepared to move ahead and may need extra help in mastering the next year's curriculum. The difference in these two girls, then, is not in any outward, standardized measure of achievement, but rather in the level of support they would need to continue their learning—and this is something that a standardized test does not capture.

Ask Yourself

Our colleague related a story of the influence that high-stakes standardized testing can have on teaching and learning and even on a school system. Her son arrived home from school one afternoon distraught over an upcoming test that was to be administered in his school. After some discussion, her son disclosed that his teacher had warned the class that, if they performed poorly on the test, she would lose her job! Whether or not the teacher was exaggerating the consequences in order to boost class performance, the message was clear: Student performance carries significant consequences. How urgent is it to communicate the importance of schoolwide testing to students? Would NCLB influence the way you communicate this? How might you communicate the importance of such testing to your students?

Summary

- Standardized tests are those tests that:
  - Comprise items that are developed and evaluated by experts to ensure that the test consistently measures what it purports to measure.
  - Are administered and scored following a common protocol.
  - Provide normative data that allow you to interpret student performance relative to others who have taken the same test.
- Norm-referenced tests are tests in which a single student's performance can be compared to the performance of a larger group and that typically comprise items of varying levels of difficulty,

from relatively easy to very difficult and challenging. Norms are created by the performance of large groups of test takers on the same measure.

- Criterion-referenced tests are tests that indicate how well developed a person's skills and/or understanding are within a particular area.
- Achievement tests are assessments intended to measure students' accumulated knowledge in a particular area.
- Aptitude tests measure a student's capacity to achieve or perform to certain levels. While an achievement test measures what a student has done, an aptitude test intends to measure what a student is capable of doing.

- Test results are often reported and may be communicated meaningfully to parents using several statistical concepts.
    - Raw scores and percent correct are the simplest and most common. Raw score indicates the number answered correctly, but the percent correct is a more useful measure of performance because it allows us to begin to compare performance among different assessments.
    - A percentile refers to a student's performance relative to all other test takers. A test report indicating performance at the 85th percentile means that the test taker performed better than 85 percent of all students who took the same test.

- Stanines (short for "standard nine") indicate where student performance falls on a scale of 1 to 9, in which a stanine score of 1 represents the lowest scores, and 9 represents the highest scores. On a standardized test, most test takers would fall in the average range, in stanines 4 to 6.
- Grade equivalent (GE) communicates a level of performance relative to test takers in the same grade. The grade equivalent score is represented as two numbers separated by a decimal. The first number represents a grade in school and the second a tenth of a school year. A GE score of 9.1 represents the expected performance of a student in the first month of ninth grade.

Key Terms

Family Educational Rights and Privacy Act
     (FERPA) (341)
grade equivalent (GE) score (345)
normative scores (332)
norms (336)

percent correct (342)
percentile rank (342)
raw score (341)
stanines (343)

For Further Discussion

1. Do you think that student performance on a standardized test is an appropriate way to assess the effectiveness of a teacher or a school?

2. Think about the age group or grade that you intend to teach. How might you communicate the importance of standardized tests?

3. Do you believe that a test developed at the classroom or school level is a better indicator of student learning than standardized tests? How might you use both to understand and communicate your students' performance?

Comprehension Quiz

1. Consider the following tests. Determine whether each is more likely a norm-referenced test or a criterion-referenced test.

a. Law School Admission Test (LSAT)
b. a pre-service teachers' basic skills test
c. a state medical licensing examination
d. a real estate broker's license test

2. In your own words, how would you define the following types of score:

Stanine

Percentile rank

Grade equivalent

Raw score

Percentage

3. What are the strengths and weaknesses of each of the scores listed above in interpreting and communicating student performance?

4. List three things teachers can do to prepare their students for a standardized testing situation.

5. Imagine that in a parent–teacher conference you are expected to communicate the results of a standardized test to your parents. How would you communicate the following in a meaningful way to parents?

a. a student who has a percentile rank of 74 on a science test

b. a 7th grade student who has a math grade equivalent score of 8.7

c. a student with a stanine score of 4 on a reading comprehension test

References

Ebel, R. L., & Frisbie, D. A. (1986). Essentials of educational measurement. Englewood Cliffs, NJ, Prentice Hall.

Geiser, S. & Studley, R. (2001). UC and the SAT: Predictive validity and differential impact of the SAT I and SAT II at the University of California. http://www.ucop.edu/sas/research/researchandplanning/pdf/sat_study.pdf. Accessed June 1, 2007.

Lemann, H. (1999). *The Big Test. The Secret History of American Meritocracy.* New York: Farrar, Straus, & Giroux.

Relevant Website Resources

National Assessment of Educational Progress: The Nation's Report Card

nces.ed.gov/nationsreportcard

This site provides results from the only nationally representative assessment of America's students in reading, math, science, writing, U.S. history, civics, geography, and the arts.

FairTest: The National Center for Fair and Open Testing

http://www.fairtest.org

FairTest offers a critical evaluation of tests, testing practices, and legislation related to testing. The website is dedicated to informing parents and educators about equitability and fairness in the administration of tests in the United States.

ETS TestLink

www.ets.org/testcoll

Operated by the Educational Testing Service (ETS), TestLink contains a catalogue of more than 25,000 tests and other measurements. The test collection at ETS is the largest library of test references and resources in the world.

CHAPTER 13

Assessment and the Law

Chapter Objectives

After reading and thinking about this chapter, you will be able to:

- **Identify legal issues related to the use of high-stakes tests to determine eligibility for high school graduation.**

- **Understand how the fourteenth Amendment and Title VI of the Civil Rights Act provide students with important rights against discriminatory high-stakes assessments.**

- **Discuss the impact of statutes such as the No Child Left Behind Act and the**

- **Individuals with Disabilities Education Act on student assessment.**

- **Comprehend the legal issues surrounding test bias and teacher certification tests and the use of standardized test results in determining teacher tenure, promotion, and merit pay.**

- **Recognize how the First Amendment affects the creation and utilization of classroom assessments.**

Most of us proceeded through school without much consideration of the legal dimensions of educational assessment. We may have grumbled about the difficulty of a final exam or haggled with the teacher over the possibility of dropping that low test score. As teachers, we will be faced with such issues as test bias, state-mandated testing, accessibility of test scores, and the various ways that a test score might be interpreted and applied. We must balance the rights of the individual student with the purposes of the assessments that student will encounter from kindergarten through college. The foundational questions for you to ponder throughout this chapter are ones that you should consider regularly as you prepare to enter the profession of teaching.

Foundational Questions for Your Consideration

- What are the consequences of testing, and do those consequences conflict with my understanding of the rights of my students?
- How can students' rights and schools' responsibilities be reconciled in high-stakes testing situations?
- What legal claims are available to students faced with an unfair standardized test?
- How can a teacher ensure that classroom assessments do not trample students' legal rights?

High-Stakes Assessment

Students in American public schools are constantly assessed: Homework is evaluated, essays and projects are graded, class exams are corrected, and comprehensive standardized tests are administered. Courts of law have consistently ruled that assessing students is a legal, even necessary, function of public schools. At the same time, the law protects students against unfair or invalid assessments. School districts must be particularly careful to ensure that assessments are fair, unbiased, and educationally valid when the stakes for failing the assessment are especially high. Consider what is at stake for the students in each of the following scenarios:

Scenario 1   A teacher gives students in his fifth-grade language arts class a spelling test. Although the test is supposed to cover words that the fifth-graders have already been exposed to, 3 of the 20 words on the test have never been introduced to the students. Consequently, most students receive lower-than-average grades on the test.

Scenario 2   During the fall semester of their senior year, students at the local high school are informed that the district has adopted a new policy requiring students to pass a graduation exam in order to be eligible for a high school diploma. The graduation test, based on a curriculum that is being phased in beginning with this year's ninth-graders, contains large sections of material that this year's seniors have never been taught. Consequently, nearly half of the senior class taking the exam (including a number of honor roll students) fail the assessment.

The assessments given in both scenarios are unfair because students are being tested on material they have never had the opportunity to learn. Also, students in both scenarios will face academic consequences as a result of an unfair assessment. However, the academic consequences of the two scenarios are very different in scope. In the first scenario, it is possible that a number of students in the class will receive a language arts grade lower than they truly deserve. While this is a problem, it pales in comparison to the consequences suffered by students in the second scenario, who face the real possibility that their high school diploma will either be denied or delayed.

While *all* assessments should be fair and valid, this is especially important when the stakes for failing an assessment are particularly high. As you read in Chapter 1, valid assessment evidence clearly relates to and measures what it is that we are trying to assess. Consider a legal analogy to the situation in the two scenarios above. A radar gun (the assessment) is faulty and does not accurately reflect a targeted car's speed. As a result, a number of people who are driving their cars at or below the speed limit may undeservedly receive speeding tickets. In contrast, consider a faulty DNA test used to analyze evidence in a murder investigation that leads to an innocent person's wrongful conviction. There is a tremendous difference in consequences for individuals wrongly convicted of speeding as opposed to those wrongly convicted of murder! These examples indicate the importance of assessment validity *especially* when stakes are high.

High-stakes standardized testing in the form of graduation exams has become commonplace in the United States. While graduation exams were once only rarely used, now 25 states require a high school exit exam. Figure 13.1 lists the states that have graduation exam policies currently in place. One additional state has similar policies that are "under development."

The consequences for failing a high school exit exam vary. In many states, students who ultimately do not pass the required exit exam are not eligible to receive a high school diploma. Failure to receive a high school diploma has been linked to serious consequences, both for the individual student and the community at large. Students without a diploma are more likely to be incarcerated, more likely to have no health insurance, more likely to have a child out of wedlock, less likely to receive prenatal care, and more likely to be dependent on public aid. And, of course, failure to receive a diploma limits an individual's opportunities for postsecondary educational and job opportunities (Rowe, 2004). Given these high stakes, it is not surprising that students from a number of states have filed lawsuits that have challenged the legality of high school graduation exams.

Debra P. v. Turlington

The earliest and perhaps most significant case challenging a high-stakes graduation test is *Debra P. v. Turlington*. In the late 1970s, the Florida legislature passed (and later amended) its Educational Accountability Act, which

Figure 13.1 *States That Currently Have Graduation Examination Policies*

State	Test(s)
Alabama	Alabama High School Graduation Exam
Alaska	Alaska High School Graduation Qualifying Exam
California	California High School Exit Exam
Florida	Florida Comprehensive Assessment Test
Georgia	Georgia High School Graduation Test
Idaho	Idaho State Achievement Test
Indiana	Indiana State Testing for Educational Progress, Plus
Louisiana	Graduation Exit Exam
Maryland	High School Assessment
Massachusetts	Massachusetts Comprehensive Assessment System
Mississippi	Functional Literacy Examination
Nevada	High Proficiency Examination
New Jersey	High School Proficiency Assessment
New Mexico	NM High School Competency Exam

required that high school students pass a test in order to receive a high school diploma. The act included a provision ensuring that graduating seniors who failed the test would not leave empty-handed. Students who met all of the standard graduation requirements but failed the test could receive a certificate of completion but would be ineligible to receive a diploma until the test was successfully passed. However, a certificate of completion was not academically equivalent to a high school diploma because "only those who received a diploma were eligible for certain state jobs and admission to the state university system" (Moran, 2000, p. 120). As a result, seniors who failed Florida's graduation exam could face serious academic and/or vocational consequences.

The student plaintiffs in *Debra P.* challenged Florida's graduation test on a number of different grounds, including claims that the test was racially

New York	Regents Comprehensive Examinations
North Carolina	North Carolina Competency Test
North Dakota	Terra Nova (CTB/5) and Test of Cognitive Skills
Ohio	Ohio Graduation Tests
Oklahoma	(under development)
Pennsylvania	Pennsylvania System of School Assessment or Local Assessment
South Carolina	High School Assessment Program
Tennessee	Gateway Examinations
Texas	Texas Assessment of Knowledge and Skills
Utah	Utah Basic Skills Competency Test
Virginia	Virginia Assessment Program
Washington	Washington Assessment of Student Learning (WASL)

Source: Adapted from Council of Chief State School Officers (CCSSO), Key State Education Policies on PK–12 Education: 2006, Table 13, p. 20, "High School Exit Exam Requirements—2004." Found at http://www.ccsso.org/publications/details.cfm?PublicationID=348. Accessed January 8, 2008.

biased and violated students' due process rights. The courts ultimately decided that while there was nothing unconstitutional about the state of Florida instituting a graduation test, the way in which the test had been proposed and used violated students' rights. The state of Florida was instructed to refrain from using the graduation test until it could be fairly and properly implemented.

Ask Yourself

Many states require high school students to pass a graduation exam before they may receive a high school diploma. While this is a common requirement, it is not universal. Each state individually decides if a graduation test will be used and what the consequences of failure to pass the test will be. Consider how this variation in state policy might affect a student faced with the following scenario.

At the beginning of her senior year, LaShonda moves from a state that does not require a graduation test to one that does. The curricula of the two states, while similar, are not identical. LaShonda is concerned that she will be tested on material to which she has not been exposed. Additionally, while her classmates in her new school have been preparing for a graduation exam for many years, this requirement is new to LaShonda. While she is a good student who would have easily graduated from high school in her original state, she is worried that she may not pass the required test in her new state and might be denied a high school diploma.

- How are LaShonda's concerns similar to those addressed by students in the *Debra P.* case?
- Assume her new state permits her to apply for a graduation exam waiver. What arguments might she include in her waiver application?

Assessment and the Fourteenth Amendment

The U.S. Constitution can be interpreted as a type of contract, or written agreement, between the government and its citizens. Any time federal or state employees (such as public school teachers or administrators) carry out their professional duties, they are required to abide by the Constitution and its amendments. If a student believes that a public school or its employees have not followed the requirements of the Constitution, they may file a lawsuit outlining their complaints and indicating which section(s) they believe the school has not properly followed.

Lawsuits brought by students challenging high-stakes tests often assert that students' due process or equal protection rights as guaranteed by the Fourteenth Amendment have been violated. The text of this amendment states,

> No State shall make or enforce any law which shall abridge the privileges or immunities of citizens of the United States; nor shall any State deprive any person of life, liberty, or property, without due process of law; nor deny to any person within its jurisdiction the equal protection of the laws.

At first glance, it may seem that this amendment would have little applicability to public school employees. For example, how could any state "deprive any person of life, liberty, or property" in a public school situation? Courts have interpreted the term *state* to include not just the state itself, but

Digging Deeper
Brown v. Board of Education

Brown v. Board of Education, decided in 1954, is one of the most significant decisions ever issued by the U.S. Supreme Court. Were it not for this decision, many school districts would have continued to require Black and White students to attend separate and unequal schools. While most people would acknowledge *Brown's* importance in the realm of school desegregation, the significance of this case goes far beyond issues of student integration.

Today, education is perhaps the most important function of state and local governments.

Compulsory school attendance laws and the great expenditures for education both demonstrate our recognition of the importance of education to our democratic society.
Brown v. Board of Education, 1954

Considering the great emphasis placed on education by the nation's highest Court, it is essential that the process of educating students—including the administration of both classroom and high-stakes assessments—be carried out in a legal, constitutionally sound manner.

anyone acting on behalf of the state. Teachers employed in a public school are state employees and, in carrying out their contracted duties, each is considered to be a **state actor**—that is, someone acting on behalf of the state. In their professional lives, teachers—just like state governors or legislators—are required to refrain from depriving anyone of their "life, liberty, or property" without due process of law.

Due Process Claims

Just as courts have broadly interpreted the term *state,* they have interpreted the phrase *life, liberty, or property* very broadly. After all, a public school teacher will not be involved in executions (the taking of life), locking up students (the taking of liberty), or seizing, for example, high school students' cars (the taking of property). But courts have interpreted *schooling* as a property right. In the U.S. Supreme Court case *Goss v. Lopez,* the Court ruled that a student's "legitimate entitlement to a public education [is] a property interest which is protected by the Due Process Clause" (p. 574). Courts have also indicated that a high school diploma (provided students have met all standard requirements) can also be considered as a form of property.

For this reason, before a student's property can be taken (by suspending or expelling the student, for example), the Fourteenth Amendment requires that the student be given due process rights. Two types of due process rights are important to consider here.

Procedural Due Process First we will discuss the right to **procedural due process,** which is an issue that comes up most often in school disciplinary situations. Teachers and administrators provide a student facing suspension with his or her procedural due process rights by giving the student *notice* of what the student has done ("Sonya, I saw you trip Juan in the hallway") and the opportunity to respond to the claims, or a *hearing.* The hearing can be as simple as asking the student, "Sonya, what do you have to say about that?" or it can be a formal event in which the student is presented with the charges against her and is given the opportunity to respond.

In addition to disciplinary situations, courts have held that students have procedural due process rights in high-stakes testing situations. In the case we discussed in the previous section, *Debra P. v. Turlington,* the plaintiffs successfully claimed that Florida's graduation test violated both students' property and liberty interests. We already pointed out that courts have interpreted schooling and the high school diploma to be property under the Fourteenth Amendment. In addition, the court in *Debra P.* agreed with the plaintiffs that a graduation test would have an effect on students' liberty rights. Just as courts have interpreted property to be more than physical objects, *liberty* has been interpreted as more than physical freedom. The court found that the use of an unfair high-stakes test would influence "a student's right to be free of the stigma of being labeled 'functionally illiterate' by state officials" (Moran, 2000, p. 122).

Just as students are entitled to due process before their property is taken away, they are entitled to due process of the law before a liberty interest (in this case, the receipt of a high school diploma) may be threatened. A high-stakes standardized test that has the real effect of denying a student a diploma is, in essence, a form of taking both a student's property and liberty away. For this reason, students facing a newly enacted graduation test must be given adequate notice of the high-stakes test in order to ensure their due process rights.

Substantive Due Process Protecting a student's **substantive due process** rights requires that the actions of a teacher or administrator be *inherently fair.* In addition to adequate notice, substantive due process rights entitle students to a "fair opportunity to learn" what they will be tested on (Moran, 2000, p. 122). Telling students in first grade that they will have to pass a high school graduation exam would certainly give them the notice required by procedural due process rights. But if the exam contained material that was not in the curriculum and was never taught to students, it would violate their substantive due process rights.

Equal Protection Claims

Like the Due Process Clause, the Equal Protection Clause of the Fourteenth Amendment gives students protections in high-stakes testing situations. The Equal Protection Clause requires state actors such as public school teachers and administrators to treat groups of students equally. At the same time it is important to note that this clause does *not* require students to be treated *identically.* Instead, it requires that "equally situated students" be treated equally.

Resource for Your Assessment Toolkit
Checking Your State's Testing Policies

When it comes to standardized tests, as a classroom teacher or administrator you will be asked to administer, rather than to design, the assessments. It is important to be familiar with the testing policies of your state. This information is easily accessible via each state's Department of Education website. Listed here are links to each of these departments.

Alabama: http://www.alsde.edu

Alaska: http://www.educ.state.ak.us/

Arizona: http://www.ade.az.gov/

Arkansas: http://arkansased.org/

California: http://www.cde.ca.gov/

Colorado: http://www.cde.state.co.us/

Connecticut: http://www.state.ct.us/sde/

Delaware: http://www.doe.k12.de.us/

District of Columbia: http://www.k12.dc.us

Florida: http://www.fldoe.org

Georgia: http://public.doe.k12.ga.us/

Hawaii: http://doe.k12.hi.us/

Idaho: http://www.sde.state.id.us/Dept/

Illinois: http://www.isbe.state.il.us/

Indiana: http://www.doe.state.in.us/

Iowa: http://www.state.ia.us/educate/

Kansas: http://www.ksbe.state.ks.us/

Kentucky: http://www.education.ky.gov

Louisiana: http://www.doe.state.la.us/lde

Maine: http://www.state.me.us/education/

Maryland: www.msde.state.md.us

Massachusetts: http://www.doe.mass.edu/

Michigan: http://www.michigan.gov/mde

Minnesota: http://education.state.mn.us

Mississippi: http://www.mde.k12.ms.us/

Missouri: http://www.dese.mo.gov/

Montana: http://www.opi.state.mt.us/

Nebraska: http://www.nde.state.ne.us/

Nevada: http://www.doe.nv.gov/

New Hampshire: http://www.ed.state.nh.us/education/

New Jersey: http://www.state.nj.us/education/

New Mexico: http://sde.state.nm.us/

New York: http://www.nysed.gov/

North Carolina: http://www.dpi.state.nc.us/

North Dakota: http://www.dpi.state.nd.us/

Ohio: http://www.ode.state.oh.us

Oklahoma: http://www.sde.state.ok.us

Oregon: http://www.ode.state.or.us/

Pennsylvania: http://www.pde.state.pa.us//

Rhode Island: http://www.ridoe.net/

South Carolina: http://ed.sc.gov/

South Dakota: http://doe.sd.gov/

Tennessee: http://www.state.tn.us/education/

Texas: http://www.tea.state.tx.us/

Utah: http://www.usoe.k12.ut.us/

Vermont: http://education.vermont.gov/

Virginia: http://www.pen.k12.va.us/

Washington: http://www.k12.wa.us/

West Virginia: http://wvde.state.wv.us/

Wisconsin: http://www.dpi.state.wi.us

Wyoming: http://www.k12.wy.us/

There are many instances in which students are rightfully treated differently. For example, while high school seniors in a district may enjoy open-campus privileges that allow them to leave school during their lunch period, the same privileges would not be extended to the district's kindergartners. The Equal Protection Clause would not be violated by such a policy. Why? Because high school seniors, many of whom may already be legal adults (having reached the age of 18), and kindergartners (all minors, for whom open-campus privileges could present a real danger) are *not* "similarly situated" groups.

Courts frequently use two types of analysis (often referred to as *tests*) to determine whether students have been denied their equal protection rights: the rational basis test and the strict scrutiny test. The **rational basis test** is used when students are treated differently based on relatively inconsequential differences such as grade level. For example, a court addressing a challenge to the open-campus lunch policy would most definitely apply the rational basis test. In order for the differential classifications (that is, treating seniors and kindergartners differently) to pass constitutional muster, the school district will only need to show that there is a rational reason for the classification—for example, that seniors have driver's licenses, kindergartners do not.

But when groups of students are treated differently or policies have a differential effect on groups because of classifications such as race or national origin, the Court uses the **strict scrutiny test.** School districts have a much more difficult time convincing courts that the differential treatment of students by race does not violate the Equal Protection Clause. For example, a district policy that treats students differently by race would need to demonstrate that the practice (1) serves a compelling interest, (2) is narrowly tailored, and (3) is the least restrictive means for achieving the desired outcome. The same is true in the case of other groups that have been historically discriminated against.

The *Debra P.* court decided that the Florida graduation exam violated the Equal Protection Clause because the test had a "disproportionately negative effect on black students" who had been disadvantaged by attending racially segregated schools (O'Neill, 2003, p. 644). At the same time, the court found that the state *could* require the graduation exam for students who had *not* been subjected to the unequal educational opportunities created by racially segregated schools, agreeing that a graduation test can serve a legitimate purpose in improving student achievement.

Ask Yourself

You are a teacher employed in a state that requires that students pass a high school graduation exam before they are eligible to receive a diploma. The state relies on a private testing company to develop and distribute the test to all state high schools, which then administer the tests.

When this year's test results were announced, a number of districts in one large metropolitan city were unhappily surprised by the results: Nearly one-third of test takers in these districts failed the exam. For the past 5 years, the failure rate had never been greater than 20 percent. Teachers, administrators, parents, and students alike questioned the validity of the test.

After some investigation into their concerns, the testing company found that students in the low-scoring districts had accidentally been given a future version of the test (a test designed for the following year). After comparing the test questions to the state standards, it was determined that the test covered material aligned with some soon-to-be-adopted curriculum changes—material to which this year's students had not yet been exposed.

- Could students who took the future version of the test claim that their Fourteenth Amendment rights were violated? How so?
- Would it be appropriate for the school to deny high school diplomas to students failing this version of the test?

Standardized Testing and Title VI of the Civil Rights Act of 1964

While the majority of high school students in the United States live in states in which graduation exams are required, there is some indication that the required exams are not evenly distributed across the student population. States with large numbers of minority students are more likely to have graduation exam requirements than are states with smaller numbers of minority students (Littleton, 2004). Also, minority students often perform more poorly than their majority counterparts on standardized tests.

One of the most important aspects of standardized testing is to ensure that the tests do not have a discriminatory effect. Title VI of the Civil Rights Act of 1964 states that

No person in the United States shall, on the ground of race, color, or national origin, be excluded from participation in, be denied the benefits of, or be subjected to discrimination under any program or activity receiving Federal financial assistance.

Racially discriminatory standardized tests would fall in the domain of Title VI protections.

GI Forum v. Texas Education Agency

In *GI Forum v. Texas Education Agency,* plaintiffs claimed that the graduation test then used by the state of Texas was racially biased and therefore was in violation of Title VI. At the time of the case, Texas students were given the Texas Assessment of Academic Skills (TAAS) beginning in third grade. The final administration of the TAAS was given to tenth-graders and served as a high school exit exam. Students who failed any section of the test (reading, writing, or math) received remediation in the subject(s) failed and had the opportunity to retake the TAAS as many as seven or eight times (Anthes, 2000). In this case, the plaintiffs stated that their due process rights had been violated and that the TAAS had an "adverse impact" on minority students in violation of Title VI (*GI Forum,* p. 668). They presented data showing that while more than two-thirds of White students passed the TAAS (69%), fewer than half of Hispanic students (41%) and just one-third of Black students (33%) passed the test (*GI Forum,* 2000). White students were more than twice as likely to pass the TAAS than were Black students.

Statistically it is not unusual for there to be different pass rates for student groups. For example, students born in January may have a 51 percent test passage rate while students born in May may have a 49 percent passage rate. This does not mean that a test is biased against students born in May. Rather, minor statistical differences between groups are to be expected. But when test passing rates are significantly different (such as 69% of White students passing the TAAS as compared to 33% of Black students), random statistical variations alone cannot explain the difference. Tests that result in one racial group performing in a significantly different way than another are said to have a *disparate impact* on test takers.

Courts have interpreted tests that have a disparate impact on minority examinees as being a problem under Title VI. As the statistics above demonstrate, the TAAS clearly had a disparate impact on minority test takers. However, disparate impact alone is not enough to prohibit the use of a high-stakes test under Title VI. Although the court agreed that the passing rate statistics showed that there was a disparate impact on the TAAS between minority and majority students, the court concluded that the use of the test was an educational necessity required to "hold students, teachers, and schools accountable for learning and teaching" (*GI Forum,* 2000, p. 681). The plaintiffs in *GI Forum* were unable to convince the court that there were any alternatives to the TAAS that would achieve the same goals but not have a disparate impact on minority test takers. The court decided that Texas could continue using the TAAS and concluded its opinion by stating that "the system is not perfect, but the court cannot say that it is unconstitutional" (*GI Forum,* p. 684).

?Ask Yourself

You live and work in a state where more than 90 percent of Hispanic students attend inner-city schools. Severe budget cuts at the state level in recent years have led to major cuts in all state schools. However, the inner-city schools have been the hardest hit. To compensate for the loss of funding, most inner-city schools now offer a curriculum that does not include art, music, or foreign language classes.

Each year, eighth-grade students throughout the state are required to pass a standardized exam as a prerequisite to high school admission. The test is quite comprehensive in nature. While it focuses mainly on math and reading, there are a number of questions that presuppose that test takers have had exposure to classes in art and music.

When the test scores are released, not surprisingly, inner-city school students perform poorly in comparison to other students around the state. A group of Hispanic students and parents bring a lawsuit claiming that the test is biased.

- Given the facts of the case, do you think that Title VI applies? Why or why not?

Assessment Mandated by State and Federal Entities

As we have discussed throughout this book, the No Child Left Behind Act (NCLB) is perhaps the most significant piece of federal education legislation enacted in recent history. While NCLB originally enjoyed widespread support, it has recently come under fire from many groups, some of which initially supported the legislation. This change is due in large part to the controversial testing requirements required by this law.

NCLB places a heavy emphasis on standardized testing. As of the 2005–06 school year, NCLB required districts to test students in reading and math yearly in grades 3 through 8, and at least once in grades 10 through 12. In the 2007–08 school year, additional testing requirements went into effect: Students must be assessed in the area of science at least once in grades 3 through 5, grades 6 through 9, and grades 10 through 12. The decision about what test(s) to administer is left to each individual state.

After assessing students, NCLB requires that student results be made publicly available. As one of the major goals of NCLB is to close the achievement gap among groups of students, achievement data is reported separately for major racial and ethnic groups, students with disabilities, students with limited English proficiency (English language learner, or ELL, students), low-income students, migrant students, and both genders. Figure 13.2 outlines the current reporting requirements.

The most critical issue for each state is to define what will constitute annual yearly progress (AYP) under NCLB. *Annual yearly progress* is the measure used to tell the federal government whether each school within the state is improving, and it is tied to student performance on a standardized test. Each state then sets the benchmark (the percent of students who must pass each section of the test) in order for the school to claim that they are making annual yearly progress.

Because schools must also report progress of the subgroups listed in Figure 13.2, each state must also decide on the minimum number of students on which they will report the subgroup data. Why would this decision be necessary or important? Why not set a federal standard? Primarily because schools across the nation differ so widely in size. In some schools, it will not make sense to report certain kinds of subgroup data. For example, a school in a particular neighborhood might have only two students classified as a racial minority—meaning different racially from the majority of the population of students. It would not make good statistical sense to report data on this tiny subgroup of students. Also, reporting group data with such a small sample size could affect student privacy. In this example, suppose that the school reported that 0 percent of minority students met AYP standards. Anyone looking at the data, which is available to the public, would know that both of the students in the subgroup did not meet AYP. Therefore, in addition to offering more statistical validity, larger subgroup sizes provide an extra measure of privacy protection for students.

A school will fail to achieve AYP if *either* the student population as a whole *or* one of the following subgroups fails to meet AYP: major racial and ethnic groups, students with disabilities, students with limited English proficiency, and low-income students. As mentioned above, each state determines their individual AYP goals. Annual state benchmarks increase incrementally because all states are expected to have 100% of students meeting or exceeding state proficiency standards by the 2013–14 school year. For example, a state may mandate that 72% of a school's student population as a whole and each of its subgroups demonstrate proficiency in mathematics on the state-designated standardized test in order for that school to make AYP in 2008–09. The following year, however, the percentage of students required to demonstrate proficiency in order to achieve AYP may rise to 78%; two years later the required percentage may be 86%, and so forth until 2013–14, at which point 100% of students are expected to demonstrate proficiency.

Figure 13.2 Federal Data Requirements for Report Cards for Title I, Part A Recipients, under No Child Left Behind

	Level of Reporting			Subgroups								
	State Level	Local Level (i.e. district)	School Level	All Students	Major Racial & Ethnic Groups	Students with Disabilities	Limited English Proficient	Economically Disadvantaged	Migrant[1]	Gender[1]	High Poverty Schools[2]	Low Poverty Schools[2]
Reading and Mathematics Assessment Data[3]												
Percentage of students tested	✓	✓	✓	✓	✓	✓	✓	✓	✓	✓		
Percentage of students achieving at each proficiency level	✓	✓	✓	✓	✓	✓	✓	✓	✓	✓		
Most recent 2-year trend data in student achievement for each subject and grade assessed	✓		✓	✓								
Local (i.e. district) achievement compared to state achievement		✓		✓	✓	✓	✓	✓	✓	✓		
School achievement compared to local and state achievement			✓	✓	✓	✓	✓	✓	✓	✓		

Accountability Data

Comparison between actual achievement and state's annual measurable objectives	✓	✓	✓	✓	✓	✓	✓	✓
Student achievement on other academic indicators used for AYP (e.g., high school graduation rate)	✓	✓	✓	✓	✓	✓	✓	✓
Number and names of local education agencies (i.e. districts, etc.) and schools identified for improvement, corrective action, and restructuring	✓	✓	✓					
Percentage of schools identified for school improvement, corrective action, or restructuring		✓						

[1]Subgroups of migrant and gender are required subgroups for reporting purposes, but are not among the required subgroups for AYP determinations.

[2]High poverty refers to top quartile, and low poverty refers to bottom quartile.

[3]Beginning in 2007–08, science assessment data will be included in this requirement.

Source: Adapted from *Report Cards: Title I, Part A Non-Regulatory Guidance*, U.S. Department of Education, September 12, 2003, http://www.ed.gov/programs/titleiparta/reportcardsguidance.doc

Schools failing to consecutively make AYP (either within the student population in general or in any of the four specified subgroups) face penalties, as outlined in Figure 13.3. Note that penalties are more severe for Title I, or high-poverty, schools.

Failing to make AYP can lead to serious consequences. Because student scores are directly tied to making AYP, classroom teachers often feel a great

Figure 13.3 *NCLB/Title I School Improvement Continuum*

Year	Status	Interventions for Title I Schools
Year 1	**Early Warning**—Did not make AYP for one year.	None.
Year 2	First year of *school in need of improvement* status. Did not make AYP for two consecutive years in the same content area.	Parent notification, public school choice (or supplemental educational services), school improvement plan, technical assistance from district.
Year 3	Second year of *school in need of improvement* status. Did not make AYP for three consecutive years in the same content area.	Parent notification, public school choice, supplemental educational services, school improvement plan, technical assistance from district.
Year 4	Third year of school in need of improvement status—*corrective action.* Did not make AYP for four consecutive years in the same content area.	Parent notification, public school choice, supplemental educational services, school improvement plan, technical assistance from district and state, corrective action, participation in CAPA [Collaborative Assessment for Planning and Achievement]
Year 5	Fourth year of school in need of improvement status—*school restructuring plan.* Did not make AYP for five consecutive years in the same content area.	Parent notification, public school choice, supplemental educational services, school improvement plan, technical assistance from district and state, development of restructuring plan (governance).
Year 6	Fifth year of school in need of improvement status—*implementation of restructuring plan.* Did not make AYP for six consecutive years in the same content area.	Parent notification, public school choice, supplemental educational services, school improvement plan, technical assistance from district and state, implementation of restructuring plan.

Source: Available from the New Jersey Department of Education website, 2005 NCLB Report, http://education.state.nj.us/rc/nclb05/ayp.html.

deal of pressure to ensure that their students are prepared for the standardized test. Some parents have claimed that this increased pressure forces educators to "teach to the test" and focus almost exclusively on subjects covered in the high-stakes exam. Art, music, and physical education teachers often express concern that, given the great emphasis on the standardized testing requirements of NCLB, their subjects take a backseat to the core curriculum areas.

?Ask Yourself

One of the stated goals of the No Child Left Behind Act is to hold educators accountable for the academic performance of students in their care. While this is a laudable goal, there is significant disagreement as to whether the determination that a school has made (or not made) AYP tells the whole story when it comes to teacher and student success.

Assume that you are a new teacher at South Middle School, a Title I school. While student test scores at your school have actually *increased* in recent years, they are still well below the state benchmark for making AYP. Because your school has failed to make AYP for several years, you are facing many of the consequences outlined in this section. In contrast, one of your friends has taken a job at North Middle School, a Title I school in a neighboring district. Test scores at your friend's school have remained relatively stable, even *decreasing* slightly in a few recent years. Despite this, the school has managed to just scrape by and make AYP each year.

When South Middle School's test results are published in the local newspaper, many teachers in your school—including yourself—feel frustrated. The newspaper headline reads "Incompetent Teachers? School Fails to Make AYP Again." In contrast, a newspaper article discussing AYP at North Middle School appears under the headline, "Teachers lead students to successful completion of exam: School makes AYP for fourth consecutive year!" Consider the following questions:

- How do you think community members from each district will interpret the results?

- Considering the trend in test scores for each district (and assuming a direct link between teaching and student performance), how might you argue that teachers at South Middle School are actually outperforming their counterparts at North Middle School?
- Assume that you are new to the area and have a job offer from each of these schools. Would their respective AYP results influence your decision? Why or why not?

Assessment of Exceptional Students and the Law

In the past it was routine for students with special physical, emotional, or learning needs to be denied an adequate education. Sometimes this took the form of a school denying admission to a student based on his or her special needs. Other times students were admitted to public schools but did not receive the services and accommodations necessary for them to benefit educationally. Today, special education students are protected by powerful federal legislation that ensures that they will have access to a free, appropriate public education.

The Rehabilitation Act of 1973

The first significant federal law protecting children with special needs, the Rehabilitation Act, was passed in 1973. **Section 504** of this act provided disabled individuals with significant protections against discrimination. The act mandated that

> No otherwise qualified individual with a disability in the United States, as defined in section 7(20), shall, solely by reason of her or his disability, be excluded from the participation in, be denied the benefits of, or be subjected to discrimination under any program or activity receiving Federal financial assistance.

Public schools receive Federal financial assistance, so eligible students (and teachers) in public schools are affected by this legislation.

Public Law 94-142, the Education for All Handicapped Children Act

Two years later, in 1975, Congress passed a law that became the precursor to our current special education law. **Public Law 94-142, the Education** for All Handicapped Children Act, included a number of important pro-visions aimed at addressing the educational needs of special education students. P.L. 94-142 provided much-needed federal funding for special education programs. Additionally, the act highlighted the unique skills necessary for teachers to work with special education students by requiring specialized certification for special education teachers (Rowe, 2004). The act also outlined disabled students' rights to a free, appropriate public education in the least restrictive environment.

Disabled students are entitled to educational services through the age of 21. Students' individual needs are assessed, and an **individualized education plan** (IEP, discussed further in Chapter 14) is drawn up by a team that includes both school personnel (teachers, a school psychologist, and so on), the students' parents or guardians, and often the student him- or herself. Instruction and assessment guidelines are governed by the student's IEP. For example, a blind student may receive textbooks, classroom materials, and tests in Braille. Or, a student with a learning disability may be allotted extra time to complete an assessment. Student needs, modifications, and accommodations are specifically outlined in a student's IEP.

In 1990, P.L. 94-142 was renamed the **Individuals with Disabilities Education Act (IDEA)** and has been subsequently reauthorized and amended, most recently in 2004. The requirement of a free, appropriate public education offered in the least restrictive environment is maintained and underscored in IDEA.

Special Education High-Stakes Testing Litigation

Litigation involving special education students and high-stakes tests began soon after P.L. 94-142 went into effect. In *Board of Education v. Ambach,* parents of two disabled New York high school students in the class of 1979 sued their school district when they were denied diplomas after failing a graduation exam. Students in the class of 1979 first learned of the graduation test when the Board of Regents passed the requirement in 1976. However, there was considerable disagreement as to whether students with disabilities would be required to meet the new graduation requirement. Clarification came in April 1979, just a few months before the two students involved in the lawsuit were set to graduate, when the district definitively stated that *all* students would be required to pass the test in order to receive a high school diploma. The two students in question subsequently took and failed the exam. When the Board of Education attempted to invalidate the students' diplomas, their parents decided to sue the district (Gerber, 2002). The court determined that the students had both a property interest and a liberty interest (as was the case in *Debra P.,* discussed above) in their diplomas. As such, students were entitled to adequate notice (more than a few months) before being required to pass the graduation exam.

An Illinois court agreed with the *Ambach* decision 2 years later in *Brookhart v. Illinois State Board of Education.* Like *Ambach,* plaintiffs in *Brookhart* challenged a newly enacted policy requiring students to pass a graduation exam in order to be eligible to receive a high school diploma. The court stated that graduation tests may be required of special education students. However, they noted that the plaintiffs in this case had not been given adequate notice to prepare for the exam. In a recent case involving a similar challenge, *Rene v. Reed,* the court decided that an Indiana graduation exam did not violate the constitutional rights of disabled students when students were provided with adequate notice of the requirement—3 years, in this case (Gerber, 2002).

Are Standardized Tests Fair to Exceptional Students?

There is widespread concern that standardized test scores for special education students may do little more than display students' disabilities rather than measure their academic skills. A student with certain learning disabilities can be disadvantaged by the format of standardized tests. For example, a student with a reading disability would likely not perform as well as a student without such a disability on a math assessment even if the mathematical skill and knowledge level of both students are identical. Would the poor score of the former student be reflective of her math skills? Probably not. It is far more likely that her score on the math section of the assessment would be more reflective of her reading disability than it would demonstrate her ability or skill in solving mathematics problems. IDEA mandates that special education students be given only assessments that have been validated for the purpose in which the assessment is being used. So, a mathematics assessment that tests reading comprehension as much as it does math skills would unfairly disadvantage students with reading comprehension disabilities.

To ensure that standardized assessments are fair and free from bias, assessments are routinely field tested before widespread use, but the population used for these field tests rarely includes students with disabilities. As a result, test makers have little information about the validity of using the test on special education students (Rowe, 2004). So, it is not surprising that there are wide test score gaps between regular and special education students. One researcher reports that "in no state does the passage rate for disabled students equal that of all students" (Rowe, 2004, p. 119).

Figure 13.4 *Comparison of Regular Education and Special Education Test Scores on Graduation Tests, Selected States*

State	Reading/Language Arts Pass Rates (all students/special education students)	Math Pass Rates (all students/special education students)	Writing Pass Rates (all students/special education students)
Alabama	88% / 58%	83% / 51%	—
Alaska	66% / 21%	44% / 16%	47% / 4%
California	64% / 18%	44 % / 9%	—
Georgia	94% / 68%	91% / 57%	92% / 62%
Indiana	66% / 19%	65% / 24%	—
Massachusetts	82% / 46%	75% / 39%	—
Minnesota	80% / 40%	75% / 33%	91% / 63%
New Mexico	92% / 66%	82% / 43%	—
South Carolina	85% / 49%	81% / 51%	86% / 57%
Virginia	82% / 43%	—	84% / 43%

Source: All data compiled from Rowe, 2004.

Figure 13.4 illustrates the difference between regular and special education student test scores on standardized graduation tests given by selected states in 2001–02.

Special education students are, as a group, less likely to receive a high school diploma in states requiring a graduation exam. As discussed previously, students who do not have a high school diploma may face serious personal, educational, and vocational consequences. Given these high stakes, especially in light of the already existing test gap, it is essential that education professionals ensure that the needs of special education students are met when taking standardized assessments. IDEA requires that students with documented disabilities receive reasonable accommodations. Reasonable accommodations, as defined by the U.S. Department of Education (2003), are "changes in testing materials or procedures that ensure that an assessment measures the student's knowledge and skills rather than the student's disabilities."

Accommodations vary by student need and could include any or all of the following: reading the test questions aloud, allowing the use of reference materials, administering the test individually in a quiet room, or providing extended time to complete the assessment (Norlin & Gorn, 2005). Additionally, provisions are made for students with the most severe disabilities to complete alternate assessments in certain cases. States individually determine which accommodations are acceptable and which are not for each standardized test utilized. An accommodation allowed by one state may very well be prohibited by another.

We will discuss this important issue further in the next chapter. And we will provide guidelines for making appropriate accommodations for all exceptional students.

Ask Yourself

Imagine that you are a special education teacher at a large suburban high school. Recently, your local newspaper has been publishing a series of articles entitled "Failing Our Special Needs Students." In one of the articles the authors note that while 91 percent of regular education students at your school either meet or exceed expectations, only 57 percent of special education students meet or exceed expectations. A parent interviewed in one of the articles has called for the school board to look into what he calls "a special education department which is clearly not doing its job." You are familiar with the special education staff at your school and know that every teacher is dedicated to the students and gives 110 percent. Still, the article's statistics are correct. What could you say in a letter to the editor of the newspaper? Consider these issues:

- Are standardized test scores an authentic measure of achievement for all special education students? Why or why not?
- Assume that your state-mandated exam does not allow for any accommodations for special education students. Describe how this might impact standardized test scores.

Assessment of English Language Learners

Changing demographics in many states have created new challenges for standardized testing policies and procedures. For example, in the 2004–05 school year, one-quarter of all California public school students were classified as English language learners, or ELLs. This trend will likely continue in coming years since at present more than one-third of all California kindergartners through third-graders are classified as ELLs (Archerd, 2006). Not surprisingly, students still in the process of learning English do not fare as well on English-language standardized tests as do those who are native or experienced English speakers.

A recently filed case, *Coachella Valley v. California,* addresses these concerns. California, like every other state, is required to test students in order to comply with NCLB. However, unlike 14 other states that (as of 2005) provide accommodations for ELL students, California has an "English-only testing policy" (Archerd, 2006, p. 163). Plaintiffs in *Coachella* argue that such a policy violates the provision of NCLB, which states that students are to be given "to the extent practicable, assessments in the language and form most likely to yield accurate data on what such students know and can do in academic content areas, until such students have achieved English language proficiency" (*Coachella,* p. 1).

A Pennsylvania court addressed a similar situation in which some districts were offering Spanish-language standardized tests while others were requiring ELL students to take exams in English. In *Reading School District v. Pennsylvania Department of Education,* the court stated that while native-language (in this case, Spanish) testing was not mandatory, that it should be provided "to the extent practicable" (p. 172).

? Ask Yourself

Imagine that you are an A student attending high school in Michigan. Your mother receives word that her company is transferring her from the U.S. office to the Japan office. Having only a few months' notice before the move, you have not had time to learn Japanese, and you enter your new Tokyo school speaking only a handful of Japanese words. After a few short months, imagine you are given a high-stakes test—perhaps one that would be tied to your successful high school graduation. The test is entirely in Japanese, and there are few accommodations for nonnative speakers. Although you were an A student in Michigan and have an excellent understanding of the content matter being tested, it is highly unlikely that you will perform well on this standardized test.

- Would a failing grade on a standardized math test, for example, indicate that you were not proficient in the math skills being tested?
- How would you be able to tell whether a low score was reflective of content knowledge or language comprehension?
- Would your Japanese test scores adequately reflect your academic abilities?

Teachers and Assessment

Preservice teachers in all 50 states and in the District of Columbia are assessed in one form or another in order to qualify for their professional careers: For example, in 2004, all 50 states and the District of Columbia reported requiring preservice teachers to take at least one written test (CCSSO, 2005, p. 25). Forty-three states require a field-specific subject-matter test, 35 require an "assessment of professional knowledge of teaching," and a third require some type of performance assessment (CCSSO, 2005, p. 25). For teachers working in the vast majority of states, state requirements do not end once certification or licensure is obtained. In 2004, teachers in 48 states and the District of Columbia were required to successfully complete a prescribed number of professional development hours in order to be eligible for teacher license renewal (CCSSO, 2005, p. 26).

While testing preservice teachers is common, the practice is not without controversy. The validity and fairness of teacher certification tests has come into question in a number of different states in which there are significant gaps in pass rates for White and minority test takers. For example, Black preservice teachers in Florida are more than three times more likely and Hispanics are almost twice as likely as White preservice teachers to fail at least one section of the state teacher certification test (Davis & Doig, 2004). The scores of California preservice teachers taking the CBEST (California Basic Education Skills Test) also vary widely by race. While 80 percent of Whites successfully pass the test, only 47 percent of Hispanics and 37 percent of Blacks fare similarly (Rebell, 1997). When the reading section of the Praxis test (an assessment used by a number of states in the teacher certification process) was analyzed to compare 2 years of passing scores by test takers from 29 states, the researchers found that 86 percent of White examinees received passing scores, compared to 65 percent of Hispanics, 59 percent of Asian Americans, and 50 percent of Blacks (National Research Council, 2001).

There is some disagreement as to the reason for the precertification test score gap for White and minority applicants. Some argue that the disparity in minority/majority test scores is a result of inadequate educational opportunities for minority youth who subsequently prepare to enter the teaching profession. On the other hand, there has been widespread concern that some standardized teacher certification tests have inherent racial biases that lead to a disproportionate number of minority test takers receiving failing marks. These issues have led to litigation in several states.

Alabama's teacher certification test, the Alabama Initial Teacher Certification Testing Program (AITCTP), was challenged by a group of Black teachers who claimed that the test "impermissibly discriminate[d] against black persons seeking state certification" (*Allen v. Alabama State Board of Education*, 1985, p. 1048). A settlement was agreed on which awarded plaintiffs $500,000 in damages and permanent Alabama teaching certificates, and Alabama agreed to modify its teacher certification process (Ludlow, 2001).

In *Association of Mexican-American Educators [AMAE] v. California*, minority teacher candidates in California challenged the state's use of the CBEST by claiming, in part, that the standardized test violated Title VII of the Civil Rights Act of 1964. Title VII prohibits employers from discriminating against employees because of their race, color, religion, gender, or national origin. Employment tests that disadvantage minority candidates are impermissible "unless the tests have a manifest relationship to the job in question and no less discriminatory alternatives are available" (Blotevogel, 2003, p. 563). Expert witnesses demonstrated that passing rates for White and minority first-time test takers varied widely. While nearly three-quarters of White test takers pass the CBEST on their first attempt (73.4%), fewer than half of Hispanics (49.4%) and just over one-third of Blacks (37.7%) pass the CBEST (*AMAE*, 1996). The Ninth Circuit Court of Appeals ruled that states may be liable for high-stakes testing that disadvantages minority applicants under Title VII.

NCLB and Teacher Assessment

While testing of teachers is not expressly required under NCLB, the act does include provisions addressing teacher quality assessment. NCLB requires that teachers, at a minimum, have full state certification and a bachelor's degree and demonstrate subject-matter competency for the subjects they teach. Teachers of core academic areas (defined as English, reading, language arts, mathematics, science, foreign languages, civics and government, social studies, economics, arts, history, and geography) are required to be "highly qualified" no later than the 2005–06 school year.

Just as NCLB allows individual states great latitude in determining which standardized tests to use to meet the act's requirements, it similarly allows such flexibility in determining how teachers will be deemed to be "highly qualified." To make such a determination, states may use a "high, objective, uniform state standard of evaluation" (HOUSSE). State HOUSSE plans often take into account factors such as the years of successful teaching and the number of professional development experiences. Figure 13.5 is a table compiled by the Education Commission of the States to show the type of assessment(s) used by states' HOUSSE programs.

Figure 13.5 *Type of HOUSSE Used by Each State to Determine Highly Qualified Teachers*

States are using one or more of the options below in their proposed or final HOUSSEs.

HOUSSE Type	Middle Grades	Secondary
Point System*	**17 states** AL,AZ,CA,GL,KS, KY,MD,MA,NJ,NY,NC, ND,OH,OK,TN,TX,UT	**17 states** AL,AZ,CA,GA,KS, KY,MD,MA,NJ,NY,NC, ND,OH,OK,TN,TX,UT
Professional Development	**9 states** AR,IL,LA,MI,MS, NV,NH,OH,TN	**8 states** AR,IL,LA,MI, NV,NH,OH,TN
Performance Evaluation	**9 states** FL,GA,MI,NH,NM, NC,VA,WA,WV	**9 states** FL,GA,MI,NH,NM, NC,VA,WA,WV
Classroom Experience (Please note that no states, except SD, are solely using this option.)	**9 states** IL,LA,MI,NV, NM,NC,OR,SD,TX	**8 states** IL,LA,MI,NV, NM,NC,SD,TX
Portfolio	**3 states** LA,NH,NM	**3 states** LA,NH,NM
Student Achievement Data	**3 states** CO,TN,VA	**3 states** CO,TN,VA
No HOUSSE (Does not include HOUSSEs under development)	**2 states** ID,WI	**3 states** ID,OR,WI

*In cases where a point system included the other options (professional development, student data, classroom experience, etc.), those activities were not counted as separate types offered.

Source: Azordegan, 2004.

The majority of states use some type of point system to evaluate teachers for the purpose of NCLB. An equal number of states (nine each) use, in part or combination, a review of teachers' professional development activities, a teaching performance evaluation, and an audit of classroom experience. Three states use portfolio review for evaluation purposes, and three apply the controversial method of using student achievement data to determine whether a teacher is highly qualified. The two states that report no HOUSSE (Idaho and Wisconsin) assert that their rigorous state licensure requirements result in all certified teachers in their state being highly qualified. Just as states are required to collect and publish student data, states must also report teacher qualification data. NCLB requires that states break down teachers into "highly qualified" and "not highly qualified" categories and further indicate the percentage of each class of teacher working in high- and low-poverty schools.

Linking Teacher Evaluations to Student Test Scores

While teachers' test scores on preservice examinations determine whether an individual will receive a teaching job, in some districts student standardized test scores may influence whether the teacher receives continued employment. This practice was challenged in *Scheelhaase v. Woodbury Central Community School District* in the 1970s. In *Scheelhaase,* an untenured Iowa teacher's contract was terminated, in part as a result of her students' performance on two standardized tests: the Iowa Tests of Basic Skills (ITBS) and Iowa Tests of Educational Development (ITED). The teacher, Ms. Scheelhaase, felt that her firing because of low student test scores was unfair and filed a lawsuit against the district.

In her suit, Scheelhaase claimed that the district's decision to fire her "on the ground of allegedly low test scores" violated her due process rights under the Fourteenth Amendment (p. 239). At the trial court level, Scheelhaase won. The court ordered that she be reemployed and awarded her monetary damages. But the appellate court disagreed, holding that her constitutional rights had not been violated and dismissing her case. That is, the higher court found that the district could consider student test scores when deciding whether to continue employing an untenured teacher.

Even when student test scores do not factor into tenure decisions, they may be used to determine teacher pay. Minnesota has used a pay-for-performance plan for faculty teaching Advanced Placement (AP) courses. Students scoring at least a 3 on an AP test earned their classroom teacher a $25 bonus (Allen, 1999). While this per-student amount is small, a teacher instructing multiple sections of an AP class could receive a net bonus of over $1,000. Since the 2006–07 school year, raises and bonuses for Florida teachers are directly linked to their students' performance on standardized tests. Lawmakers in Alaska, Massachusetts, and Mississippi are considering similar initiatives (Peterson, 2006). Some individual districts in states without policies explicitly linking teacher pay to student test scores have enacted pay-for-performance plans. For example, districts in both Denver and Houston employ such a plan.

Ask Yourself

Inner-city schools often face greater challenges than do schools in the suburbs. For example, students attending inner-city schools may be more likely to live in poverty, more likely to live in a one-parent family, less likely to receive adequate nutrition and/or medical services, and so on. As you learned in Chapter 3, inner-city students often score lower on standardized tests than do their suburban counterparts. Additionally, many inner-city districts have difficulty hiring enough teachers to serve their students. Consider the impact of using student test scores as a part of teacher evaluations in districts like the ones in this scenario.

- Do you think a policy of linking student performance on standardized tests to teacher evaluations would impact the number of applicants to inner-city schools? To suburban schools?
- As a prospective employee, would this type of policy influence where you chose to apply?

Assessment and the Family Educational Rights and Privacy Act (FERPA)

As mentioned in Chapter 12, the Family Educational Rights and Privacy Act (FERPA) was signed into law in August 1974. The statute addresses, among other things, the privacy of educational records at institutions receiving federal funding. The privacy of educational records is guaranteed protection, and the statute defines these records as "files, documents, and other materials which . . . contain information directly related to a student . . . and are maintained by an educational agency or institution by a person acting for such agency or institution." FERPA notes that certain types of "directory information" about a student can be released without violating the act. A student's name, address, and telephone number are all considered directory information. This means that protection of student information under FERPA is based on determining whether such information is an "educational record" or if it is "directory information."

A recent U.S. Supreme Court decision, *Owasso Independent School Dist. No. I-011 v. Falvo,* addressed the question of whether student grades were educational records protected by FERPA. Ms. Falvo, a parent suing on behalf of her middle school–aged son, alleged that his teacher's practice of having students correct each other's papers and subsequently call out the grade violated FERPA by making an educational record public without prior consent. She claimed that her son, a special education student, was publicly embarrassed when his lower-than-average quiz grades were announced to the class. While Falvo won at the Tenth Circuit Court of Appeals, this decision was quickly overturned by a unanimous U.S. Supreme Court on appeal.

The Supreme Court stated that peer grading and oral reporting of student marks did not violate FERPA. They said that holding otherwise would "impose substantial burdens on teachers across the country. It would force all instructors to take time, which otherwise could be spent teaching and in preparation, to correct an assortment of daily student assignments" (p. 435). The Court neglected to decide whether FERPA would apply to a student's grade *after* it had been entered in the teacher's gradebook. However, they noted that one student calling out the grade of another student before a grade was recorded by the teacher could not violate FERPA, in part, because students are not acting on behalf of the school (as are teachers and administrators).

Teachers may legally continue to use peer grading as a classroom practice. However, because the Court did not address whether recorded classroom grades are student records, teachers and administrators should take care to keep this information private. As with all rulings, just because a court has determined that a practice is legal it does not mean that the practice should be used. Educators should make determinations at the individual classroom level about the pros and cons of using peer grading by taking into account student characteristics and the classroom climate. If the calling out of grades will result in students being teased, the time saved by the practice would not outweigh the negative effects on the classroom climate and the psychological or social effects on the children.

Ask Yourself

Consider how teachers' classroom practices would have been altered if *Owasso v. Falvo* had been decided differently. How would in-class assessment practices be altered if the Court had decided that every assignment completed by a student is an educational record protected by FERPA? How would the following practices be affected by such a decision, if at all?

- A teacher has students grade each other's work but does not have students call out the grades to the class.
- A teacher has a "student of the week" bulletin board where samples of a student's best work is displayed.
- Students collaborate on group projects.

First Amendment Guidelines for Classroom Assessments

In much of this chapter we have directly addressed the law and high-stakes assessments like graduation exams. While high-stakes assessments are often the subject of legal challenges, students are only subjected to a handful of such assessments throughout their K–12 years. On the other hand, classroom assessments are an almost daily occurrence for the vast majority of students, so it is important for classroom teachers to make sure that the assessments they give in the classroom meet constitutional guidelines.

The First Amendment of the Constitution provides citizens, including public school students, with important protections. As we said earlier, public school teachers and administrators are considered by the courts to be state actors. As such, in their professional duties they are legally bound to respect their students' constitutional rights. The text of the First Amendment states that

> Congress shall make no law respecting an establishment of religion, or prohibiting the free exercise thereof; or abridging the freedom of speech, or of the press; or the right of the people peaceably to assemble, and to petition the Government for a redress of grievances.

The first sentence of the amendment specifically addresses the issue of religion and the state in two clauses. The first clause is often referred to as the Establishment Clause; the second, the Free Exercise Clause.

Even though the amendment states that "Congress shall make no law respecting an establishment of religion," courts have interpreted this **Establishment Clause** to mean that no state actor (including public school teachers) can "establish" a religion. Actions that would establish a religion widely vary. For example, a biology teacher sharing his opinion that evolution cannot be true because it says nothing about it in the Bible would be establishing a religion. A physical education teacher sharing her slides from a recent trip to Mecca while explaining that Islam is the only true religion would be establishing a religion.

At first glance it may seem that any mention of religion in the public schools would violate the Establishment Clause. This is not the case. There are many instances in which the subject of religion will naturally intersect with a public school curriculum. For example, it would be difficult, if not impossible, to study world history or Renaissance art without mention of religion. The subject of religion is not constitutionally off limits provided that it is discussed for legitimate pedagogical reasons in a neutral manner. Proselytizing, or trying to convert someone to one's own religious beliefs, obviously would be unconstitutional. Consider the following test questions

Resource for Your Assessment Toolkit
First Amendment Checklist

When designing classroom assessments, the following test will help you in determining whether an assessment you are considering would violate the First Amendment. If you answer yes to any of the following statements, consider altering your assessment.

- Is the purpose of the assessment to promote religious belief in general?
- Is the purpose of the assessment to promote one religious faith over another?
- Is the purpose of the assessment to discourage or belittle religious belief?
- Does the assessment require students to support or oppose personal religious belief over nonbelief?

- Does the assessment require students to support or oppose the truth of one religion over another?
- Does the assessment require students to personally engage in religious practices or services?
- Would completion of the assignment require students to compromise their religious beliefs or nonbelief?
- Could a different assessment achieve the same pedagogical goals and *not* address religious belief or nonbelief?

given to students enrolled in a music class studying music history at a high school:

- Citing at least three examples, demonstrate how classical music from the Renaissance and Baroque periods illustrates the composers' religious beliefs.
- Citing at least three examples, demonstrate how classical music from the Renaissance and Baroque periods illustrates the truth of Christianity.

Although both questions ask students to discuss aspects of religion, the first question would be permissible while the second would not. The first question asks students to apply knowledge of history. It is an undisputable fact that religious belief, namely Christianity, greatly influenced Renaissance and Baroque composers. Note that there is no editorializing—that is, there is no suggestion in the text of the question that religious belief in general, or Christianity in particular, is right or wrong. This is not the case with the second question. While this question also asks students to apply historical knowledge, the phrase "illustrates the truth of Christianity" is constitutionally problematic. The very question itself could be interpreted as an endorsement of one religious faith over another and of belief over nonbelief.

The Supreme Court has used a three-pronged test known as the *Lemon test* to determine whether something is in violation of the Establishment

Clause. While this was originally designed to be used by judges and justices, it can be used as a good rule of thumb for teachers trying to determine whether an assessment might cross the line. According to the *Lemon* test, something violates the Establishment Clause of the Constitution if any of the following are violated. (The prongs have been reworded to present the test in the context of a classroom assessment.)

1. The assessment must have a secular (nonreligious) purpose.
2. The primary effect of the assessment must neither advance nor inhibit religion over nonreligion, or one religion over any other.
3. The assessment should avoid excessive government entanglement with religion. (adapted from *Lemon v. Kurtzman,* 1971)

The second religion clause contained in the First Amendment is the **Free Exercise Clause.** This can be thought of as a bookend to the Establishment Clause. Whereas the Establishment Clause mandates that educators do not force their belief or nonbelief on students in their charge, the Free Exercise Clause requires that they do not unnecessarily inhibit students' expression of their religious beliefs.

Courts have recognized that there are time, place, and manner restrictions to this protection for students. For example, a student taking a geometry quiz does not have the choice to omit some of the questions and instead write about his personal belief in Hinduism. However, students asked to complete a creative writing assignment entitled "What inspires me" could address (and, arguably, would have to address in order to fulfill the requirements of the assignment) their religious beliefs or nonbelief. Additionally, students are free to engage in religious activities (prayer and study) during their free time, such as at lunch, in after-school clubs, and so forth. *Preventing* students from discussing religion during appropriate times is as unconstitutional as *requiring* them to do so.

Ask Yourself

Assume you are a history teacher working on a final exam question for students enrolled in your world history course. You would like to construct a question asking students to address how the Roman Catholic Church influenced life for the average European during the Middle Ages. One of your colleagues has told you that such a religious question could be unconstitutional. Using the *Lemon* test, consider the following:

- What would be an example of a question that might violate the First Amendment?
- What would be an example of a question that would not violate the First Amendment?

Summary

- While graduation tests are not federally mandated, they are used by a majority of the states and the District of Columbia.

- Students required to pass a graduation exam have both property and liberty rights under the Fourteenth Amendment of the Constitution.

- Tests that have a disparate impact on different groups of test takers are discriminatory and violate Title VI of the Civil Rights Act of 1964.

- Annual standardized testing is mandated by the federal government through the No Child Left Behind Act.

- Students with disabilities can be required to take high-stakes assessments, often with appropriate accommodations as outlined in a student's IEP.

- English language learners are required by the NCLB to complete standardized tests along with the rest of the students in their schools.

- All 50 states and the District of Columbia subject preservice teachers to one or more assessments in order to be qualified to be a teacher.

- The NCLB requires that teachers be highly qualified in the core subjects in which they teach. The definition of highly qualified is left up to each state to determine.

- The courts have interpreted the First Amendment to the Constitution to mean that educational assessments must be free from both religious and antireligious bias.

Key Terms

Establishment Clause (389)

Free Exercise Clause (391)

individualized education plan (IEP) (378)

Individuals with Disabilities Education Act (IDEA) (378)

Lemon test (390)

procedural due process (365)

Public Law 94–142, the Education for All Handicapped Children Act (377)

rational basis test (368)

Section 504 of the Rehabilitation Act of 1973 (377)

state actor (365)

strict scrutiny test (368)

substantive due process (366)

For Further Discussion

1. Knowing that you have studied the legal aspects of student assessment, your principal asks you to provide a brief presentation outlining some key points new teachers should keep in mind when creating classroom assessments. What do you include in your overview?

2. Your school district is considering adopting a mandatory graduation test for high school seniors, beginning later this year. What legal issues are important for the district to consider before its adoption?

Comprehension Quiz

Indicate whether each of the statements below is true or false.

1. Courts have determined that special education students are *not* required to take standardized tests.

2. A world history test may include factual questions about religion.

3. NCLB requires states to give graduating seniors a high school exit exam.

4. A school directory that publishes students' names and phone numbers violates FERPA.

5. It is illegal for school districts to take into account student performance on standardized tests when evaluating teachers.

6. Preservice teachers are given a qualifying assessment, in one form or another, in all 50 states and the District of Columbia.

7. The U.S. Department of Education sets annual AYP benchmark scores that schools and districts are required to meet.

8. Courts have determined that students facing high-stakes tests that may result in the denial of a high school diploma have due process rights under the Fourteenth Amendment of the Constitution.

9. NCLB requires that standardized test results be made publicly available.

10. Continuous failure to make AYP will result in increasingly severe penalties.

Relevant Website Resources

Contact Information for All State/Territory/District Departments of Education

http://wdcrobcolp01.ed.gov/Programs/EROD/org_list.cfm?category_ID=SEA

Published by the U.S. Department of Education, this website provides contact information (address, telephone, fax, e-mail, and website address) for all available U.S. states and territories.

Education Commission of the States—Assessment Data

http://www.ecs.org/html/issue.asp?issueid=12

This website provides information and links to publications dealing with the issue of student assessment published by the Education Commission of the States. The site features "issue breakout" sections covering these assessment subtopics: accommodations, college entrance exams, design/technical quality, high stakes/competency, national tests, and technology/computer-based assessments.

Education Commission of the States—Online Teaching Quality Database

http://www.ecs.org/ecsmain.asp?page/html/educationissues/teachingquality/nclb-hqtp/db_intro.asp

This website features a link to the ECS's online teaching quality database. Additionally, the site includes a clickable map allowing users to access all 50 states' definitions of "highly qualified" teachers and state HOUSSE standards.

ERIC Clearinghouse on Assessment and Evaluation

http://www.ericae.net/

Users are able to search abstracts of more than 1 million research articles and education resources. This site also features a test locator database, allowing users to find information on various assessments including test descriptions, addresses of test publishers, and location of test reviews.

U.S. Department of Education—FERPA

http://www.ed.gov/policy/gen/guid/fpco/index.html

This U.S. Department of Education website addresses the Family Educational Rights and Privacy Act (FERPA). Site explains the act in easy-to-understand language and provides contact information for the Family Policy Compliance Office for users seeking additional guidance.

U.S. Department of Education—IDEA 2004

http://www.idea.eg.gov

This site provides information on the most recent authorization of the Individuals with Disabilities Education (Improvement) Act, or IDEA 2004.

Users can click on links from this page and access the text of the act, read the regulations, and download forms that can be utilized by faculty and administrators working with special education students.

U.S. Department of Education—NCLB

http://www.ed.gov/nclb/landing.jhtml

This website contains a wealth of information on the No Child Left Behind (NCLB) Act. Features include information on NCLB reauthorization, an NCLB roadmap, a teacher's toolkit, and 50-state information on the implementation of the act.

References

Allen, M. (1999). *Student results and teacher accountability.* Denver: Education Commission of the States.

Anthes, K. (2000). *Competency testing for high school graduation: Notes on the Texas lawsuit.* Denver: Education Commission of the States.

Archerd, E. (2006). Spanish-language test accommodations: Recommended or required by NCLB? *Harvard Latino Law Review, 9,* 163–178.

Association of Mexican-American Educators v. California, 937 F.Supp. 1397 (1996).

Azordegan, J. (2004). *Initial findings and major questions about HOUSSE.* Denver: Education Commission of the States.

Blotevogel, M. T. (2003). Testing title VII's patience? The need for better remedies when state "teacher testing" requirements have a disparate impact on employment opportunities for minority populations. *Washington University Law Quarterly, 81,* 561–589.

Council of Chief State School Officers (CCSSO). (2005). *State education policies on PK–12 education: 2004.* Washington, DC. http://www.ccsso.org/content/pdfs/FINAL%20KSP%202004.pdf. Accessed June 24, 2006.

Davis, C., & Doig, M. (2004, December 14). Minority teachers struggle on exams. *Sarasota Herald-Tribune,* p. A1.

Gerber, B. A. (2002). High stakes testing: A potentially discriminatory practice with diminishing legal relief for students at risk. *Temple Law Review, 75,* 863–890.

Littleton, M. (2004). High stakes testing. *West's Education Law Reporter, 187,* 389–396.

Ludlow, L. H. (2001). Teacher test accountability: From Alabama to Massachusetts. *Education Policy Analysis Archives, 9, 6.* http://epaa.asu.edu/epaa/v9n6.html. Accessed July 17, 2006.

Moran, R. F. (2000). Sorting and reforming: High-stakes testing in the public schools. *Akron Law Review, 34,* 107–135.

National Research Council. (2001). *Testing teacher candidates: The role of licensure tests in improving teacher quality.* Committee on Assessment and Teacher Quality. K. T. Mitchell, D. Z. Robinson, B. S. Plake, & K. T. Knowles, eds. Board on Testing and Assessment, Center for Education, Division of Behavioral and Social Sciences and Education, Washington, DC: National Academy Press.

Norlin, J. W., & Gorn, S. (2005). *The answer book on special education law.* Horsham, PA: LRP Publications.

O'Neill, P. T. (2003). High stakes testing law and litigation. *Brigham Young University Education and Law Journal,* 623–662.

Peterson, K. (2006). Teacher pay reform challenges states. *Stateline.org.* http://www.stateline.org/live/ViewPage.action?siteNodeId=136&languageId=1&contentId=93346.

Rebell, M. (1997). *The present and the future; Linking standards and assessment.* National Evaluation Systems, Inc.

Publication. http://www.nesinc.com/PDFs/1997_12Rebell.pdf. Accessed July 17, 2006.

Rowe, J. R. (2004). High school exit exams meet IDEA: An examination of the history, legal ramifications, and implications for local school administrators and teachers. *Brigham Young University Education and Law Journal*, 75–137.

U.S. Department of Education. (2003). *Standards and assessments: Non-regulatory guidance*. Washington, DC: Author.

Chapter Objectives

After reading and thinking about this chapter, you will be able to:

- **Define IDEA and explain what that means within our educational system.**

- **Explain accommodations in assessment and how they fit into classroom assessment.**

- **Describe the role of the classroom teacher in the education of students with disabilities.**

- **Explain alternative assessment methods for students with disabilities.**

- **Describe alternative assessment methods for students with gifts and talents.**

- **Explain instructional elements that can be utilized when teaching English language learner (ELL) students.**

We have already discussed what assessment is, what it can tell us, and what kinds of assessments are used in classrooms. In this chapter we focus on how we can modify assessments when necessary to fit the individual needs of students without compromising the integrity of the assessment.

There are many reasons that assessment accommodations may be needed. For example, students may have disabilities or physical impairments; they may live in difficult or problematic situations; they may have little experience in testing; they may be learning English; or they may be from backgrounds that differ culturally from the larger society. Students who are exceptionally gifted may also need accommodations.

We will spend a good part of this chapter on accommodating students who have been identified as in need of special education. These students' needs have been addressed in our legal system, and you as a classroom teacher will need to be aware of the important role you play in this area. But it is essential to remember that disabilities are only one segment in the larger idea of exceptionality. As we said in Chapter 2, we are all unique and exceptional in some ways. In this chapter we describe various methods, strategies, and accommodations to help keep a classroom inclusive for all students, while remaining fair in the testing process.

Foundational Questions for Your Consideration

- Should all students be assessed using the identical test administered in the identical manner?
- Have Section 504 and IDEA improved education for all students?
- Should teachers be expected to accommodate all individual needs? What would be reasonable limits?

Assessment and Exceptionality: A Short History of Legislation

Before 1975, hundreds of thousands of students with disabilities were denied access to an education and other necessary services. Some who were attending public schools were not learning successfully because their disabilities were undetected, while those with known disabilities were generally excluded from the public school system. Often this forced families to seek alternative educational opportunities for their children, perhaps traveling a great distance from home to get educational services. In general, the burden was on the family of the student with disabilities to figure out how and where to get an education for their child and how to pay for it.

The Individuals with Disabilities Education Act (IDEA)

As we discussed in Chapter 13, several important pieces of federal legislation were passed in the 1970s that, along with subsequent court cases, changed opportunities for students with disabilities. The Individuals with Disabilities Education Act (IDEA; originally Public Law 94-142, the Education for all Handicapped Children Act of 1975), requires that public schools provide to all children with disabilities, as defined in the eligibility requirements, a free and appropriate public education in the least restrictive environment that accommodates the individual's needs. This law requires that students with disabilities be provided reasonable accommodations and auxiliary aids and services to make it possible for them to get the education they need either in the regular classroom or else in a setting that is as close to it as possible. It includes protection of the rights of children with disabilities and of their parents or guardians.

This legislation has dramatically changed the lives of these children and their families. They now have opportunities to learn and are able to achieve goals that were previously thought to be unattainable. Students with special needs are graduating from high school and from college and are becoming productive members of the workforce. And, along the way, IDEA has changed the climate of the classroom and the responsibilities of the teacher.

Section 504 of the Rehabilitation Act of 1973

The Rehabilitation Act of 1973 was passed almost simultaneously with P.L. 94-142. Qualified individuals are protected from discrimination under Section 504 of this act, the name by which this law is commonly known in the field of education. Section 504 specifies that individuals with disabilities have the right to participate in and have access to the same programs, benefits, and services as nondisabled persons. Therefore, any employer or organization that receives federal tax dollars is required to provide equal opportunities to individuals with disabilities. Public schools receive federal money, so education falls under this law, reinforcing the accountability of schools to be inclusive with students who have disabilities.

Under Section 504, the definition of a disabled individual is any person who has a physical or mental impairment that substantially limits one or more major life activities. Major life activities include such things as independently caring for one's self, seeing, hearing, walking, breathing, working, speaking, performing manual tasks, and learning. Examples of impairments that may impede major life activities run the gamut from blindness or visual impairments, deafness or hearing impairments, to AIDS, alcoholism, cancer, diabetes, drug addiction, heart disease, and mental illness. To be clear, any student who may have one or more impairment is allowed to be an active participant in school, with all of the rights and responsibilities of his or her peers.

In summary, the purpose of both IDEA and Section 504 is to provide a free, appropriate public education to all students with disabilities. Also, they both have nondiscrimination protection for these students and their families. However, Section 504 has broader eligibility criteria than does IDEA, and therefore it covers students with a wider range of disabilities.

Digging Deeper
The Future of IDEA?

The public education system has greatly expanded the opportunities for students with disabilities over the past 25 years. Will IDEA continue to successfully meet the needs of these students and their educators?

In the United States, education of students with disabilities was viewed as a privilege, rather than a right, until the early 1970s. We have come a long way since then with laws and amendments to help accommodate those students and their families and to protect their rights. On November 29, 2000, the 25th anniversary of the IDEA, the Secretary of Education Richard Riley stated,

IDEA opened doors to our schoolhouses for our students with disabilities. Today, millions of students with disabilities attend our public schools. We have made steady progress toward educating students with disabilities. . . . We must continue to build on the experience and research developed during the past 25 years in order to give all students with disabilities the opportunity to attain economic self-sufficiency, independence and integration into society. We also must continue to develop and disseminate information to support and implement effective practices to meet the higher expectations that IDEA has created. (Katsiyannis, Yell, & Bradley, 2001)

Ask Yourself

Given that legislation has ensured that students with disabilities have a right to and access to an education, where do we go from here? How can we make the education of our students with disabilities more meaningful for them? What new and better opportunities can we provide for these students? In what ways is there room for improvement in the quality of their education? What implications arise for preparing the teachers of these students? Where do you see legislation going over the next 25 years?

What Is the Role of the Regular Classroom Teacher?

In compliance with IDEA, students with disabilities are to be included in the regular education classroom to the greatest extent possible. And regular classroom teachers are required to be involved with the decisions regarding the implementation and evaluation of these students. These teachers play a critical role in the student's educational process. Often the regular classroom teacher has spent a great deal of time interacting with the child and has been the sole link between school and home. All of this experience is pertinent to providing appropriate educational opportunities for the student. The regular classroom teacher has the knowledge as well as the responsibility to play an active role in educating the child with a disability.

As a classroom teacher, you will be an integral part of the education of a student with disabilities. You will be involved in some way in all parts of the process of identifying and monitoring the special educational services for the student. The steps in this process are

1. Identification: referring a student for screening.

2. Specialized comprehensive assessment of the student.

3. Development of the individualized education plan (IEP).

4. Preparation and administration of appropriate instruction.

5. Review of the student's IEP.

Identification of a Student with Special Needs

A student is usually referred for consideration for special education because the teacher has serious concerns about the student's performance or behavior. While there are cases where the student may be referred by parents, a family physician, or other school personnel, there is an increased likelihood that you, the classroom teacher, will be the person making the recommendation because you have worked closely with that student.

Each school has a Child Study Team (or similarly named committee) that has the task of accepting referrals from teachers and others and then gathering preliminary or screening information. The Child Study Team will expect you to provide certain kinds of information when you make your referral and will use that information to decide if the student should be assessed further. You will collect information that supports your concerns about the student, such as

- Student's grades and other achievement information
- Documented classroom observations
- Special efforts you have made to help the student, with the results
- Standardized test scores
- Information you have collected from your contacts with the parents

The team will consider your information and may also gather additional screening data. This would consist of observations, interviews, checklists, or tests that can be administered quickly to give a snapshot of the student's performance. When this preliminary information is collected, the committee meets to discuss it in light of the student's educational needs. If the team decides that a more comprehensive study is needed to determine the extent of the student's problems, the team will then begin a specialized and more thorough assessment.

Specialized Assessment of the Student

As the next step in this process, specialists (such as the school psychologist, speech clinician, physical and occupational therapists, and the social worker) conduct a detailed individual assessment of that student. The purpose of this comprehensive assessment is to gather enough information to determine if the student has a disability as defined in state and national rules as well as to pinpoint clearly and thoroughly the student's strengths and weakness. The following areas are assessed:

- Mental, physical, or emotional challenges.
- Educational challenges.
- Individual competencies that could be strengthened and maintained with additional services.

Although this evaluative process is primarily conducted by trained professionals who routinely assess children with disabilities, as the teacher, you will substantiate their results with data from your classroom. All the documentation and data you have been collecting will be of utmost importance during this process.

Development of the Individualized Education Plan (IEP)

When the specialized assessment is completed, a meeting, often called an IEP staffing, is scheduled to discuss the findings. Those present at the staffing would include an administrator, the student's classroom teacher, a special education teacher, the parents, and the specialists who tested the student. The purpose of the staffing is to evaluate the assessment data collected and to decide whether the student qualifies for special educational services. If the student does qualify, those present will develop an individualized educational plan (IEP) for the student.

The IEP is written to establish the learning objectives for the student within the regular classroom setting, explain how these objectives will be measured to determine if they have been met, and specify how instruction can be administered. The IEP must be specific, clear, reasonable, measurable, and complete. The tasks for the student must be manageable and the goals attainable. This is why the regular classroom teacher *must* be involved in the IEP staffing and in the development of the IEP. You will be the one who monitors the student's progress and reports the outcomes to the IEP team on a regular basis. You are the vital link between the child and the IEP team, as well as between school and home.

The IEP for a student with disabilities has many elements. Let's look at a few of them:

- A list of the student's current competencies in such things as academic content areas, physical abilities, and social, emotional, and behavioral factors that may inhibit the student's progress within the regular classroom.

- A statement of short-term and long-term goals. In addition, a professional is designated who is responsible for working with the student to attain the goals. The short-term goals must lead to fulfillment of the long-term goals.

- A statement of the educational services that will be scheduled for the student within and outside of the regular classroom.

- A schedule of the services: when they will begin, how much time will be allowed for each service, as well as a description of how the services will aid the student and the settings in which the services will be provided.

- A schedule for evaluating each goal and the criteria for doing so.

- An indication of which accommodations will be provided during required statewide and districtwide assessments.

Preparation and Administration of Individualized Instruction

The next step in the process of educating a child with disabilities is to actually provide the individualized instruction on a daily basis in compliance with the student's IEP. The objectives in the IEP dictate how the specialized instruction will fit into the general curriculum within the regular classroom. Your responsibilities might include

- Creating learning activities that are appropriate to the child's learning style.

- Devising supplemental instructional materials.

- Creating a versatile classroom setting whereby many learning styles are accommodated.

- Documenting the student's progress efficiently and accurately.

- Developing a contingency plan for behavioral problems that may arise.

- Developing individualized objectives for instruction that follow the student's IEP, as well as monitoring the progress of the student toward meeting those objectives.

While these tasks may sound daunting to you at this point, be assured that the IEP team will assist you in all these responsibilities. The team as a whole has the ultimate responsibility for creating and implementing the IEP. You will be one of the team members who makes these decisions and plans how the decisions can be implemented. You will find collaboration with your colleagues helpful in carrying out the requirements of the IEP.

Review of the Student's IEP

At regular intervals the student's IEP will be reviewed by the IEP team to determine if the student is making progress toward the stated objectives. During a review, the IEP can be modified to more closely meet the changing needs of the student and to perhaps arrange for additional special services. However, if there are any major modifications needed in the IEP, the team will gather additional assessment data to illustrate how the current instructional objectives have been attempted but cannot be met and how the proposed changes will be more effective for the student.

In summary, the regular classroom teacher is required by federal law, not only to be involved in various aspects of the education of a student with disabilities, but to actively be the liaison for the student with the IEP team. That is an important responsibility because you are the voice for the student. You are the one who will determine if the services provided for the student are adequate and are offering the best possible educational services available. This multidisciplinary team will rely on you to provide data that support various recommendations and then to follow-up with the progress reports on the instructional outcomes of the objectives set forth in the IEP.

Response to Intervention (RtI)

The 2004 Reauthorization of the Individuals with Disabilities Education Act (IDEA) introduced an alternative way to identify students who may be in need of special education services. Called **Response to Intervention (RtI),** this approach again begins with the classroom teacher and a student who is experiencing academic or behavior problems in the regular classroom. However, instead of employing the typical formal testing process, the classroom teacher tries out a variety of instructional methods within the classroom setting in an effort to determine which of these methods can provide the support that the student needs. RtI requires that the student's learning be closely monitored and that decisions be based on assessment results.

RtI is conceptualized as a multi-step problem-solving approach that explicitly involves the classroom teacher in the use of alternative instructional methods that are research based. As the intervention is provided to the student, the teacher uses the results of classroom assessments to decide whether the student needs additional instruction or intervention in the regular classroom or if he or she needs additional assistance. The teacher may bring in a school team to provide more intensive interventions to the student who is not achieving academically or behaviorally. If appropriate, the problem-solving team may then refer the student for special education services if the interventions have not helped the student improve. With RtI, it is possible to identify students in need of special education without going through a formal testing process.

The emphasis in RtI is on research-based instructional interventions and carefully planned assessment. It is expected that the assessments will be administered often, perhaps daily, and that they provide quick and detailed feedback to the teacher. Clearly, developing assessments that match alternative instruction is an increasingly important skill for classroom teachers.

?*Ask Yourself*

Think of a time when you or a fellow student felt trapped in a classroom because your learning needs were not understood by your teacher. What could the teacher have done to uncover your learning needs? What did the teacher do that made you unable to ask for help? What could a regular education teacher learn from the identification process described above?

Accommodations

It is critical that students with disabilities participate in assessments, but equally critical is the provision of **accommodations** or appropriate modifications for students who need them. By providing the necessary assessment accommodations, we make sure that all students are participants in the assessment process. Let's consider some questions related to providing appropriate accommodations during assessment for students who qualify under IDEA. The National Center on Educational Outcomes (1997) has addressed these questions:

- What does assessment accommodation mean?
- Who makes the decisions about the individual accommodations?
- Are the accommodations to be provided all of the time during all assessments?
- What types of accommodations could be available, and what principles should guide accommodation decisions?
- What do these accommodations do to the results of the assessments? Do they unfairly skew the results?

Let's examine each question separately and discuss examples that illustrate the accommodations.

Defining Assessment Accommodations

First, to help us understand the concept of assessment accommodations, let's note what an accommodation is not. It is *not* an advantage given to a student who is able to participate in the assessment process without any modification. It *is* a modification in the way a test is administered to a student with disabilities who qualifies for special education services and has an IEP. Its purpose is to help the student effectively communicate knowledge, progress, or skills without being impeded by the particular disability. Reasonable accommodations, as defined by the U.S. Department of Education, are "changes in testing materials or procedures that ensure that an assessment measures the student's knowledge and skills rather than the student's disabilities" (U.S. Department of Education, 2003). For example,

> *John is a student who has severe visual impairments. He is working toward the same academic achievements as his classmates; however, in order to demonstrate his intellectual ability he needs his tests transcribed into Braille, access to a Braille writer during class and test-taking times, and extended time to complete tests because it takes longer to read and write Braille. In addition, his answers need to be transcribed back into written form for the teacher to grade.*

The transcribing and timing accommodations allow John to participate in the same assessment process as his classmates. The modifications are employed not because the teacher feels sorry for John or wants to make life easier for him, but, rather, because without them John would not have an equal opportunity to show the teacher what he knows and can do. Without the extra time during the test for John to read and write using Braille, for example, the teacher will not know if he failed to finish the test because he did not know the material or because the Braille slowed him down. The two possibilities lead to two very different implications in teaching John, and the teacher needs to know which direction to follow.

Most educators realize the importance of developing technically sound assessments and ensuring that test implementation is carried out in a fair and nondiscriminatory manner. But, as we pointed out in Chapter 13, the potential is high with any disabled student for inadvertently testing the student's disability rather than his or her knowledge and skills. That is why an accommodation is a *necessary* modification for a student to ensure equal participation in an assessment. Another example:

> *Sarah has dyslexia (a reading disability). She is taking a science test but is not processing the written test like her peers. When Sarah reads the directions to the test or reads the test questions, it is as if she is encountering those words for the first time. Hence, reading the test is a slow, laborious process. Her inability to quickly and easily decode written communication becomes an impediment to her test taking. Sarah's efforts are focused on*

deciphering the questions on the test rather than on answering the questions. An appropriate accommodation might be to have the test tape recorded and have Sarah listen to the questions on headphones and complete the test by speaking the answers into a tape recorder.

A written test causes Sarah to struggle with reading and comprehending the test, not with answering the test questions. Unfortunately, then, Sarah's limitations caused by the dyslexia are being assessed rather than her knowledge of the subject. When the test itself creates a barrier for the student, an accommodation is needed. The accommodation suggested above, then, would be necessary in an effort to allow Sarah to participate in written tests on an equal footing with classmates.

Of course, it is essential when accommodations are developed that the purpose of the test is not compromised. We have emphasized many times in this book that any assessment you plan must have a clear purpose and a specific blueprint for the skills or constructs you want to measure. So the first step in developing an appropriate accommodation is the same as in creating any assessment: You must have a clear sense of what you want to find out about the student's knowledge, skills, understanding, and so on. Once you know that, you are prepared to develop an assessment with the accommodations needed to get you that information.

Who Decides about Assessment Accommodations?

One important point must be kept in mind. As a classroom teacher, you will not be alone in figuring out when accommodations need to be made and how to make them. The IEP team, of which you would be a member, will work together to make these decisions and will collaborate in developing accommodations, both in teaching and in testing.

When Are Accommodations Appropriate?

Educators and the IEP team will consider the circumstances of both the learning and testing environments as they are making decisions about accommodations. For example, if there are accommodations made during the instructional phase, then it is also appropriate for those accommodations to be provided during the assessment phase of learning. The factors that the committee will consider when determining the appropriateness of accommodations are the specific individual needs of the student and the purpose of the assessment and what it is intended to measure. For example,

The IEP team looks at whether a student should memorize the chemistry formulas the class has been learning or whether the formulas could be provided to this particular student by the teacher. If the team decides the test is measuring the student's ability to apply the formulas to solve a chemistry problem, then the IEP team might agree that it is appropriate for the teacher

Resource for Your Assessment Toolkit

Considerations for Assessment Accommodations

As a teacher, you will work with the IEP team to consider whether your student needs assessment accommodations. By giving careful thought to the issues listed here, you can help to make sure that your IEP reflects serious consideration about how to best meet the needs of your student.

- The strengths of the student.
- Parental concerns for enhancing the student's education.
- The results of the initial or most recent evaluation of the student.
- As appropriate, the results of the student's performance on any general state or districtwide assessment programs.
- Whether the student requires assistive technology devices and services.
- Whether the student has any special needs related to communication.

- In the case of a student with limited English proficiency, the language-related needs of the student.
- In the case of a student who is deaf or hard of hearing, the student's language and communication needs, opportunities for direct communication with peers and professional personnel in the student's language and mode of communication, academic level, and full range of needs, including opportunities for direct instruction in the student's language and mode of communication.
- In the case of a student who is visually impaired, instruction in Braille and/or whether the use of Braille is necessary.
- In the case of a student whose behavior impedes her or his learning or the learning of others, the strategies and supports to address that behavior, including positive behavioral interventions.

to supply the formulas. But, if the test is measuring the student's ability to remember the formulas and correctly apply them to a problem, then supplying the formulas may be inappropriate.

This example reinforces the necessity of *understanding the purpose* of the assessment and its underlying constructs so that the modifications are not in any way providing an unfair advantage over students who are not allowed the modifications.

Consider another example:

If the purpose of a reading test is to measure a student's ability to decode letters and words, then having someone read the test to the student would compromise the assessment, and the accommodation would not be appropriate. Why? Because it will not tell the teacher if the student himself or herself can decode the letters and words. On the other hand, if the purpose of the reading test is to show understanding of written language and to draw conclusions and provide interpretations, then the use of a reader for the student could be appropriate.

Here again it is crucial to know *what* the test is measuring so that accommodations are appropriate and necessary, without providing an unfair advantage.

> *If a student is unable to communicate verbally because he is mute but can express himself in written form, then during an oral exam he could record his answers on paper, and someone else could immediately vocalize his written response for him.*

These examples illustrate how students with specific disabilities can still be included in the assessment process simultaneously with their peers. With appropriate accommodations, they can be tested in a way that uncovers what they do and do not know, while being held accountable to the same standards as their peers.

Basic Guidelines for Accommodations

States vary considerably in their policies concerning the modification of assessments for those students with disabilities. There are, however, some common guidelines among their accountability systems (NCEO, 1997). Some of the common guiding principles are listed here:

- *Decision makers must know the student well.* Ensure that the decision makers are people who are familiar with the student's needs and abilities. This is typically the IEP team, which includes the student's classroom teacher.

- *Accommodations must focus on student needs.* Be sure that decisions are based on the student's needs, as well as practical issues in implementing accommodations, to ensure that the student has an even playing field with peers who do not have disabilities.

- *Continuity is critical.* Ensure there is continuity during the entire teach-test-teach instructional cycle. The student should feel the flow between the instructional phase of education and the assessment phase in terms of appropriate, helpful modifications. There are instances, however, where the same assistance given during instruction would not be appropriate during testing. For example, giving guided prompts might be helpful when teaching a topic but not suitable during the testing of that topic.

- *Understand the purpose of the test.* Consider the type of test being administered. Norm-referenced tests and criterion-referenced tests have different purposes, for example, so be sure you know the purpose of the test and how accommodations can be used without impairing test results.

- *Consider all the important factors.* Use a form that lists the variables that should be considered when making accommodation decisions.

This helps the team of decision makers focus on the relevant variables (such as, how will the specific disability interfere with the student's performance) rather than irrelevant variables (for instance, what program is the student in). This form should be part of the student's IEP in order to provide essential information about accommodation expectations for various testing requirements.

Categories of Accommodations

The National Center on Educational Outcomes (NCEO) described six categories of accommodations (1997). Let's explore examples of those six categories and examine sample questions within each category that could be used in making recommendations for accommodation.

Setting Perhaps there are aspects of the setting that are an impediment to the student completing the assessment. For example,

- Can the student take the test in the same way as it is administered to the other students?
- Can the student focus on the task at hand with other students present?
- Are there other distractions that prevent the student from completing the assessment?

Presentation The way an assessment is presented to a student may affect the outcome of a test, rather than it being an accurate indicator of the student's abilities. You will be considering such variables as

- Can the student read?
- Can the student see and hear?
- Can the student understand English at grade level?

Timing In some cases students need modifications in the time allowed to complete tests. You will need to determine

- Is the student able to work continuously for the length of time that the test is typically administered?
- Do the accommodations or special devices the student is using require extra time in order for the student to complete the test?

Response Students may know the answers to test questions but have difficulty communicating them. For example,

- Can the student manipulate a writing instrument?
- Can the student follow from a test to a test response form?
- Can the student speak or write English as needed?

Resource for Your Assessment Toolkit
Examples of Students' Problems and Possible Accommodations

Students with disabilities may need various accommodations when they are completing a test. These accommodations will vary according to individual needs and disabilities. This resource for your assessment toolkit provides a table with potential problems that some students with disabilities may have and offers various accommodation ideas that fit the disability (Wood, 2002). This may be useful if you are contributing ideas to the IEP team about how to accommodate an individual student during assessments.

Besides the disabilities, we include here other problems faced by students when taking a test, such as limited English proficiency or test anxiety. *These problems are not disabilities, but they can present barriers to students in showing what they know and can do in a testing situation*, and they should be considered as possible reasons for accommodation.

Barrier	Accommodations
Below Average IQ for Grade Level	Give test directions in both oral and written form. Correct for content only, not for spelling or grammar. Remind student to check the test for unanswered questions. Allow the use of multiplication tables or calculators during math tests, if the test deals with problem-solving skills. Provide a written outline for essay questions.
Poor Auditory Perception	For oral spelling tests, go slowly, enunciating each syllable and sound distinctly. Avoid oral tests in other curriculum areas. Seat student in a quiet place for testing. Allow tests to be taken in an alternate test site, such as the resource classroom. Place a "TESTING" sign on the classroom door to discourage interruptions.
Poor Visual Perception	Give directions in both oral and written form. Check student discreetly to see if he or she is on track. Provide special lighting. Give exam orally or tape-record it. Allow student to take entire test orally in class or in the resource room. Seat student away from distractions (for example, windows, door). Use a carrel or put desk facing the wall.
Poor Work with Time Constraints	Allow enough time for completion of the test. Provide breaks during lengthy tests. Give half of the test on one day and the remainder on a second day. Allow student to take the test in a resource room. Use untimed tests. Give oral or tape-recorded tests. If the student has slow writing skills, have student answer orally to the teacher or on tape.

(continued)

Resource for Your Assessment Toolkit

Examples of Students' Problems
and Possible Accommodations (continued)

Limited Proficiency in English	Give test directions in both oral and written form. Avoid long talks before the test. Allow responses to test questions to be tape-recorded. Correct for content only, not for spelling or grammar. Read the test aloud. Provide a written outline for essay questions. Tape-record instructions and questions for a test.
Anxiety	Avoid adding pressure to the test setting by admonishing students to "hurry and get finished" or "do your best; this counts for half of your six-weeks' grade." Give a practice test. Give a retest. Do not threaten dire consequences for failure. Avoid calling attention to the student as you help him or her. Confer with the student privately to work out accommodations for testing. Use flexible scheduling. Change the order in which subtests are given.

Source: Wood, 2002.

Scheduling Another area where accommodations may need to be made is in the scheduling of the administration of a particular test. Some considerations you must evaluate are

- Does the student experience excessive anxiety during a certain content-area test? If so, should that test be administered when the assessment for all of the other content areas has been completed?

- If the student takes a medication that wears off over time, and testing is scheduled during that time, should testing occur at a more optimal time of the day?

Other The remaining accommodations did not fit into the other categories so they are considered here. For example,

- Is the student equipped with the necessary test-taking skills?

- Is this assessment the first time the student will be taking a formal district or state test? Is practice needed?

How Do Accommodations Affect Test Results?

The provisions for accommodation are appropriate and needed for the disabled student. But there remains an obvious question. How do these accommodations affect the outcome of the test results? How do the test results impact the data for the classroom, the grade level, or the school?

While there are not statistically clear-cut answers to those questions at present, federally funded research projects are currently being conducted to explore the validity and reliability of tests when accommodations are appropriately provided. These validity issues are more critical for norm-referenced tests, however, than for the typical tests given by classroom teachers. As we have emphasized in this chapter, accommodations must be in line with the test's purpose, so you will be using accommodations that do not affect the validity of your classroom test results.

As a teacher, you will see how effective and helpful it is for students with disabilities to have these accommodations in order to give them the opportunity to be treated equally and have accountability for their learning just as their peers have. Teachers who are accommodating these students are having a powerful impact on the future of these learners and consequently on society.

Ask Yourself

How can we be assured that all students are treated equally and fairly if there are no "standards" in accommodations? If accommodations are developed for a specific individual, is it possible to provide accommodations that are considered standard from state to state (or even from school to school)? Is it possible that one state will offer more opportunities than another?

Accommodations for English Language Learners

It is becoming increasingly common to find yourself teaching in a classroom where one or more of your students may not speak English proficiently, or even at all. They may have grown up in another country or in a home where the primary language is not English. These students may have very different backgrounds, skills, and experiences than the other students in your classroom. However, English language learner (ELL) students are *not* disabled. Instead, their limited proficiency in English is a barrier to their ability to perform well on assessments that are administered in English.

These students may come from highly educated families where their parents were once professionals in their home country. These students may be exceptionally literate and have an extensive knowledge base acquired through formal education, but their education was obtained in another language. For this reason, assessment of these students is difficult. To accurately depict their abilities and aptitudes in a testing situation, these students must understand the assessment, and that may only be possible in their native language.

As educators we should embrace the diversity that ELL students bring to the classroom. These students need an active learning environment that addresses the special language-related needs and the cultural differences of students who are learning English. Here are five key instructional elements to be aware of when teaching ELL students (Zehler, 1994):

1. *Make the classroom predictable and accepting of all of your students.* Make them feel safe in their surroundings. Have structured rules for your classroom, predictable patterns, clear expectations, and genuine concern for each student.

2. *Make sure the instructional activities provide opportunities for language use.* Each student should be able to verbally communicate ideas, formulate questions, and convey higher-order thinking.

3. *Students should be active participants in the instructional tasks.* Students will learn more effectively if they help structure their own learning to make it more meaningful.

4. *Student understanding is key in instructional interactions.* Be sure all students, especially ELL students, understand the instructions presented.

5. *Student diversity should be utilized during instructional content.* When we incorporate diversity into our classroom instruction, we help recognize and validate different cultural perspectives. This provides all students with exposure to other languages and allows ELL students a way to connect their background with the content they are learning. This helps facilitate retention during assessment.

These instructional elements are ways to make ELL students feel connected to their learning and provide them with opportunities to practice English and understand content. Again, these students are not disabled in any way because of their language barrier. They are just restricted in their expression of knowledge and their understanding by not being proficient in the English-speaking classroom in which they are being educated. Our goal is to help them communicate more efficiently using the English language in order to more accurately reflect the extent of their knowledge during assessment.

?Ask Yourself

Consider a time when you attended class with a student who was still learning English. Imagine how it would feel if you tried to attend class in another country where you did not understand the primary language used for instruction.

Assessing Students with Exceptional Gifts and Talents

Making modifications in assessment for students with disabilities or for students with exceptional gifts and talents can be a real challenge for teachers. But the effort to meet the needs of these exceptional students is a matter of **fairness,** and it provides its own reward when you see that all students are learning in their unique ways. Now it is time to focus on assessment modifications for students who have been identified as having exceptional intellectual capabilities or other gifted characteristics.

The federal government does not include gifted students in P.L. 94-142 or subsequent legislation. Some states require that gifted and talented students be identified, while others do not. And, within the states that do not require identification, some school districts maintain their own gifted and talented programs. If your school district has a program for gifted students, you will need to operate within the requirements of that program. But whether or not they are officially identified through a program, the gifted students are present. They represent another form of exceptionality that you will want to accommodate in the best and fairest way you can.

The Multidimensional Qualities of Giftedness

Before we can begin to think about assessments for gifted students, let's examine the many different ways of thinking about **giftedness.** The Marland Report (1972) contains a definition of giftedness that has been the one most widely adopted by federal, state, and local education agencies. The report explains that gifted and talented students are capable of high performance but require **enrichment** in educational programs that extend beyond those provided in the regular school curriculum in order to realize these students' contribution to society and to themselves. The following are areas of giftedness included in the Marland definition:

- General intellectual ability
- Specific academic aptitude

- Creative or productive thinking
- Leadership ability
- Visual and performing arts
- Psychomotor ability

The Marland Report points out that a student with an IQ of 160 is as different from the student with an IQ of 130 as that student is from the student of average ability. The kinds of educational program developed for these differing ability levels should be markedly different from one another, although in most cases gifted programs are designed for the moderately gifted. An exceptionally gifted student may have difficulty finding challenges even in the gifted class because he or she moves at such an accelerated pace, processes information at greater depths, and has such an intensity toward learning that he or she can become bored and unchallenged very quickly.

As a teacher you may wonder why the gifted child in your classroom has grades that are average or even below average. A student's grades may not be high for several reasons. A student's circumstances are as different as each child. Is the student on free or reduced lunch? Has the student changed schools frequently? You learned in Chapter 3 that poverty and mobility are significant factors in achievement. Or perhaps the student is not yet proficient in the English language. There are many reasons why a gifted student may not achieve at the level expected.

Teachers' incorrect beliefs or biases about giftedness may create a climate for underachievement (National Association for Gifted Children, 2007):

- *The one-size-fits-all approach to curriculum.* "Special treatment just leads to elitism."

- *Hidden biases or prejudices against gifted students.* "I don't care if she was identified as gifted; Cathy is not gifted."

- *Acceptance of "happy, well-adjusted" as the main criterion for the appropriateness of gifted instruction.* "He's making straight As and enjoys doing what other students do."

- *Refusal to consider the option of acceleration.* "He may be smart, but I'm afraid acceleration may harm him socially or emotionally."

And the way that the classroom is structured can create barriers for gifted students' learning

- *Excessive use of gifted students as tutors.* "When do I get to learn something new?"

- *Unmonitored cooperative learning groups.* "The other kids dump all the work on me because they think it is easy for me." "No matter how hard I work, we all get the same group grade."

Challenges in Assessing the Gifted Learner

Let's now consider some assessment options for gifted students. Keep in mind that any assessment option first and foremost must take into account the multidimensional quality of the gifted student. For example, the gifted student might demonstrate talent in different ways, such as

- Ability to improvise with commonplace materials and objects
- Enjoyment of and ability in creative movement, dance, dramatics, music, rhythm, and so forth
- Use of expressive speech
- Richness of imagery in informal language
- Originality of ideas in problem solving
- Articulateness in role playing, sociodrama, and storytelling

Dynamic Assessment One approach to assessing gifted students is through the use of dynamic assessment. **Dynamic assessment** is a nontraditional approach to assessing cognitive ability. It involves instructing students on how to perform on certain tasks and then measuring their progress in learning to solve similar problems. Because it consists of a pretest-intervention-retest format, the focus is on improvement in student performance when a teacher provides mediated assistance on how to master the task. This approach helps identify and measure abilities (and deficiencies) prior to receiving the intervention and mediation.

The goal, then, of this assessment technique is to help students, through mediation, to develop skills commensurate with their true intellectual ability, not to increase IQ scores. This technique is especially helpful in recognizing gifts and talents in the underrepresented populations, such as the economically disadvantaged, English language learners, rurally isolated, or physically and mentally challenged. Since academic deficits can be due to environmental variables rather than to a lack of inherent ability, the use of dynamic assessment with these populations could provide greater access to gifted and talented programs.

You may recognize dynamic assessment as being related to Vygotsky's concept of the zone of proximal development, which we discussed in Chapter 2. According to Vygotsky, you can learn important information about a student if you sit beside the student, continuing to assess as you provide assistance and support. The information you gain can be difficult to get through other assessment methods.

Here is an example illustrating the use of dynamic assessment:

A student who is learning the English language is asked to tell a story about a picture book. The teacher evaluates the use of story ideas and the use of the English language (pretest). Based on that evaluation, the teacher targets areas in which the student had difficulty. For example, the student was unable to connect ideas in a logical order and was unable to grammatically formulate sentences. The teacher addresses these target areas with the student and provides instruction on how to work on these areas (intervention). They practice with more sample stories. Finally, the student is asked to re-tell the story (posttest), and then the teacher assesses the gains from the pretest to the posttest.

Dynamic assessment is unique in that it incorporates a learning component. It examines the learner's responsiveness to instruction and measures the amount of change produced during the process (Jitendra & Kameenui, 1993). This technique, however, is not meant to be a substitute for existing traditional, psychometric assessment approaches. Instead, it is meant as a supplementary approach for discerning students' abilities to maintain and transfer what was learned.

Authentic, Problem-Based Assessment and Gifted Students Students who are gifted often have an ability to see relationships among topics, concepts, and ideas without any formal instruction geared toward that specific topic. Mathematically gifted students, for example, may have an intuitive understanding of the functions and processes of mathematics and reasoning. They may even skip steps to derive an answer to a problem without being able to explain how they did it. For example,

Jack is a sixth-grade pre-algebra student who frequently seems uninterested in his math class. He draws pictures in his math notebook and goes through his folders while the teacher is explaining steps for solving the problem $8b + 22 = 4b + 46$. Jack solves these linear algebraic equations in one step, without acknowledging the teacher, taking notes, or writing his assignment down. He finds these step-by-step instructions to finding solutions boring and a waste of time.

Students who are gifted in mathematical thinking and problem solving need greater depth and breadth of topics and open-ended opportunities for solving more complex problems. These students are creative with divergent problem-solving strategies and have advanced ability to acquire content. They need opportunities to reach their mathematical potential, and the instructional and evaluative settings need to adequately reflect modifications for these students (Kongel & Fello, 2004).

For example, an assessment accommodation for a mathematically gifted student could be as simple as this:

The entire class must calculate the area of polygons and other geometric figures using basic formulas they have been taught. Gifted students, though, would instead have real-world application problems where they calculate the area of such things as rooms in a home or the size of various aspects of a building site.

This assessment adds a level of complexity and challenge. It gives gifted students the opportunity to see the connection between the mathematical concepts they have learned and the real world. The advanced complexity of contemporary real-world problems requires the use of higher-order thinking skills and allows more opportunities for open-ended responses.

Notice, however, what the assessment is *not*. The assessment for the gifted student is not merely completing 30 problems while the remainder of the class only has to complete 15 problems. Gifted learners would consider this increased repetition boring and unfair, and it could ultimately lead gifted students to conceal their abilities in order to avoid the painful repetition of material they would consider tedious.

Gifted students often want to gather and use information, as though they were professionals in that field, from the vantage point of inquiry rather than simply recalling the relevant facts. Instead, they want to use the facts and evidence that they have learned to support their ideas. Allowing gifted students to respond to more complex essay questions, to develop answers to ill-structured problems, and to defend answers with evidence they have identified are all legitimate options for modifying their assessments.

In summary, the dynamic and problem-based approaches provide assessment modifications that take into consideration the need for gifted students to be challenged. These students need opportunities to reach their potential and to be curious and creative and think deeply. The object is not for teachers to assign more-of-the-same work but to ascertain how they can promote higher-order thinking, encourage students to create and seek knowledge, and provide opportunities for students to be excited and motivated by learning. By fostering this type of learning and assessment within your environment, students are able to pursue their own interests at their own pace. By having choices, the students tend to be more motivated to explore areas of learning and develop new interests. You are in a unique position to help students advance their talents within a stimulating environment of original thinking and discovery.

Ask Yourself

Think of a time when you were bored in a class and felt like the teacher was just assigning busy work. How did you feel about learning? How did you feel when you were attending each session of that class? What things would you have liked to be doing to feel challenged?

Summary

- Special education has changed dramatically over the past few decades since the Individuals with Disabilities Education Act (IDEA) has been implemented.

IDEA requires all public schools to provide a free, appropriate education to all students with disabilities as defined in federal and state eligibility rules.

- Section 504 of the Rehabilitation Act of 1973 specifies that individuals with disabilities have the right to participate in and have access to the same programs, benefits, and services as nondisabled persons.
- The classroom teacher has an important role to play in assessing and educating students with disabilities. The classroom teacher knows the student best and acts as the voice for the student in each step of the special education process.
- The Individualized Education Plan (IEP) for a student with disabilities has a number of critical elements, including the student's current competencies and factors that may inhibit progress, short- and long-term goals, educational services that will be provided and their scheduling, plans for evaluating each goal, and accommodations to be provided during assessments. Assessment accommodations include setting, presentation, timing, response, and scheduling.
- Reasonable accommodations for special education students, as defined by the U.S. Department of Education, are "changes in testing materials or procedures that ensure that an assessment measures the student's knowledge and skills rather than the student's disabilities."
- English language learners are exceptional but not disabled; they have a language barrier in communicating their acquisition of knowledge and skills.

In classrooms, educators need to provide opportunities for meaningful dialogue in English where students feel safe to communicate their ideas, questions, and higher-order thinking. In addition, try to include other cultural backgrounds and languages in examples so all students have exposure to other languages.

- Gifted students require differential educational programs in order to fully develop their talents and to further develop their desire to be curious and creative and think deeply. The object is not for teachers to assign "more of the same," but to ascertain how they can promote higher-order thinking and encourage students to create and seek knowledge.
- Dynamic assessment consists of a pretest-intervention-retest format in which the focus is on improvement in student performance when a teacher provides mediated assistance on how to master the task. This technique is especially helpful in recognizing gifts and talents in the underrepresented populations.
- Authentic, problem-based assessment is especially appropriate for gifted students. The advanced complexity of contemporary real-world problems requires the use of higher-order thinking skills and allows more opportunities for open-ended responses.

Key Terms

accommodations (405)

dynamic assessment (417)

enrichment (415)

fairness (415)

giftedness (415)

Response to Intervention (RtI) (404)

For Further Discussion

1. Think about being a teacher in a classroom where you have 25 students, one of whom has physical disabilities that require the use of a wheelchair or crutches. What challenges will you face during instruction and assessment as you try to provide accommodations? Even though it is the law, is inclusion the best situation for everyone involved? Why or why not?

2. Should there be more resources allocated to gifted and talented programs and accommodations? If you have gifted students in your classroom, what kinds of enrichment activities would you provide to keep them challenged and stimulated? How would you accommodate them during assessments across various content domains (such as science, mathematics, reading, physical education)?

3. If you were having a conversation with someone outside the field of education, what would you tell that person when he or she stated that IDEA has negatively impacted our educational system?

Comprehension Quiz

1. Determine which of these problems or barriers to achievement are accommodated by each of the practices listed.

below average IQ

limited English proficiency

poor auditory perception

poor visual perception

time constraints

anxiety

  a. Keep sentences simple and short.

  b. Provide breaks during lengthy tests.

  c. Speak slowly, clearly and enunciate each syllable.

  d. Tape-record instructions and questions for a test.

  e. Provide a practice test.

  f. Use untimed tests.

  g. Highlight keywords in the test directions.

  h. Seat student in a quiet place for testing.

  i. Increase the size of the answer space or bubble.

  j. Correct for content only, not for spelling or grammar.

  k. Allow the use of multiplication tables or calculators.

2. Read the following scenario and indicate what was correct and what was lacking in the teacher's assessment accommodations.

Mr. Ortiz carefully read all the directions aloud, and he provided examples for the different question formats. He also provided one sample test question for each part of the test and orally stated the question and the answer. Mr. Ortiz prepared a separate set of directions for students with special needs. He underlined keywords in the short-answer questions. He also designed the test so that there were as many test questions as possible on the page. He told students that they had 18 minutes to complete the test. Mr. Ortiz did not permit any questions once students began the test, and he placed a sign on the door indicating that the test was taking place.

3. Read the following scenario and determine whether the teacher has properly followed the steps necessary to refer a student for identification.

Ms. Jackson observed that Renee might have a learning disability. Renee was easily distracted and often did not complete her assignments. She did not perform well on tests and showed little interest in class work. After checking Renee's previous test scores, Ms. Jackson decided to refer her for identification.

4. Read each assessment approach and determine if it is a dynamic assessment (DA) or a problem-based assessment (PBA).

  a. Students are asked to explain how they determined an answer.

  b. As students are learning a concept, the teacher asks probing questions.

  c. Students are asked to provide real-world applications to a concept.

d. Students are asked to identify the biases that may have influenced them.

e. Students are given a pretest and immediately provided feedback concerning questions that they answered incorrectly.

f. Students are permitted to determine when they want to take a posttest.

5. The National Center on Educational Outcomes describes six categories of accommodation for students with different needs: setting, presentation, timing, response, scheduling, and other. For each category, what kinds of questions might you ask about a student in order to appropriately recommend an accommodation?

Relevant Website Resources

Council for Exceptional Children

http://www.cec.sped.org

This website offers many links to various topics regarding IDEA and other aspects of our educational system. The tabs include discussion forums, law and resources, and professional development training events. From the law and resources tab, you have access to a teaching and learning center with many useful topics, such as instructional strategies, professional standards, subject areas, and support for teachers. This website also provides the latest news and updates on education.

Neag School of Education—University of Connecticut

http://www.gifted.uconn.edu

This website provides details on the Schoolwide Enrichment Model, graduate programs, and many resources. The site provides various links that could be helpful for teachers, parents, students, and researchers, and there is coverage on topics from educational policy on the gifted and talented, to identification of the gifted, to talent development. In addition, "Online Resources" offers information that can be utilized for researching gifted education within various content areas, as well as some of the latest research findings about gifted programs and gifted children.

National Association for Gifted Children (NAGC)

http://www.nagc.org

This site offers information regarding gifted students, their characteristics, and current research in the field. Educators will benefit from access to available resources such as research, journals, conventions, and a nice collection of publications in the bookstore area.

University of Northern Iowa—Inclusion

http://www.uni.edu/coe/inclusion

"Children who learn together, learn to live together." This website offers brief, informative critiques about inclusion and related issues. Alternative assessments for students who participated in inclusion are expected to be provided on this website.

The Institute for Community Inclusion

http://www.communityinclusion.org

The Institute for Community Inclusion site provides information on training, clinical and employment services, and research. ICI promotes assistance to organizations to include people with disabilities in school, work, and community activities. The University of Massachusetts, Boston, and Children's Hospital, Boston, are sponsors of ICI. This interactive website is a great learning tool for those who deal with inclusion.

Education World: Inclusion: Has It Gone Too Far?

http://www.education-world.com/a_curr/curr034.shtml

Writer Sharon Cromwell asks just how far schools should go when dealing with inclusion. Cromwell lists the disadvantages and the advantages of inclusion, and she gives advice on how to make inclusion successful for the class.

References

Jitendra, A. K., & Kameenui, E. J. (1993). Dynamic assessment as a compensatory assessment approach: A description and analysis. *Remedial and Special Education, 14*(5), 6–18.

Katsiyannis, A., Yell, M. L., & Bradley, R. (2001). Reflections on the 25th anniversary of the Individuals with Disabilities Act. *Remedial and Special Education, 22*(6), 324–334.

Kongel, J. V., & Fello, S. (2004, fall). Mathematically gifted students: How can we meet their needs? *Gifted Child Today 27*(4), 46–65.

Marland, S. P., Jr. (1972). *Education of the gifted and talented: Report to the Congress of the United States by the U.S. Commissioner of Education.* Washington, DC: U.S. Government Printing Office.

National Association for Gifted Children. (2007). www .nagc.org.access?data

National Center on Educational Outcomes Policy Directions. (1997, June). *Providing assessment accommodations.* Minneapolis: University of Minnesota, National Center on Educational Outcomes, ERIC Document Reproduction Service No. ED 416 628.

U.S. Department of Education. (2003). *Standards and assessments: Non-regulatory guidance.* Washington, DC: Author.

Wood, J. W. (2002). *Adapting instruction to accommodate students in inclusive settings.* Upper Saddle River, NJ: Merrill/ Prentice-Hall.

Zehler, A. (1994, summer). *NCBE Program Information Guide Series, 19.*

CHAPTER 15

Technology and Assessment

Chapter Objectives

After reading and thinking about this chapter, you will be able to:

- **Describe and explain multiple uses of technology for assessment.**
- **Select one basic technology application and explain why you would choose to use it as an assessment tool.**
- **Compare several approaches to assessment data analysis.**
- **Choose a technology for student performance demonstration and describe a concrete application of it in your teaching area, including your assessment plan.**

- **Describe benefits and barriers to using student response systems as assessment tools.**
- **Evaluate the potential for implementing an electronic portfolio in your teaching.**
- **Explain appropriate assessment uses of reflective journaling and WebQuests.**
- **Discuss benefits and barriers to use of a learning management system, an integrated learning system, and computer-assisted instruction for assessment.**

arly on in your study of this text, you learned that there are divergent purposes for assessment. You also learned that a common thread through all forms and purposes of assessment is gathering and interpreting evidence of student learning and teaching effectiveness.

In this chapter, you will learn ways in which technology supports and enhances assessment, whatever the purpose, benefiting both teachers and learners. Technology may serve to simplify assessment data gathering and analysis, automate parts of the processes, allow greater variety in assessment techniques, and support the varied needs of diverse learners. Whether you are assessing knowledge, skills, or even dispositions, technology can contribute to assessments that are fair, consistent, equitable, and just. You may use technology within an authentic context or to help create an authentic context for assessment.

The International Society for Technology in Education (ISTE) has developed and promoted the National Educational Technology Standards (NETS), with separate sets of standards for students (NETS•S), teachers (NETS•T), and school administrators (NETS•A). The NETS standards have been adopted, adapted, or aligned to by nearly every U.S. state (ISTE, 2006). Section IV of the NETS•T is Assessment and Evaluation, which reads in part: *"Teachers apply technology to facilitate a variety of effective assessment and evaluation strategies. Teachers . . . apply technology in assessing student learning of subject matter using a variety of assessment techniques. . . . use technology resources to collect and analyze data, interpret results, and communicate findings to improve instructional practice and maximize student learning"* (ISTE, 2003, p. 3).

According to J. D. Fletcher (2002, p. 36), "technology will change not only the way we do assessment but our objectives and expectations for assessment as well. . . . What we seek are better (more reliable, valid, and precise) inferences and decisions based on our assessment." Your study of assessment would be incomplete without consideration of some potential applications of technology in the process. We have divided the chapter into sections on basic technology applications for assessment, student performance and assessment, and integrated technology systems.

Foundational Questions for Your Consideration

- How does technology benefit you as a teacher in aspects of assessment?
- How will your students benefit from assessments you create or implement using technology?
- What challenges do you foresee to using technology in your school and, more specifically, your classroom assessment program?

Basic Technology Applications for Assessment

The most basic teacher applications of technology for assessment involve creating assessments, completing assessments and providing feedback, recording and analyzing assessment data, and qualitative assessment using observation and interviews.

Creating Assessments

Technology can assist any teacher in creating assessments. We will look at uses of word processing, online assessment creation, and test item banks as particularly common and useful tools.

Word Processing Teachers have been using personal computers to create assessments as long as they have had access to the technology. Anyone who has had the experience of using a typewriter in the past already appreciates the quantum leap in ease of writing that word processors provide. Creating on a computer what might once have been typed is a significant gain for teachers because it is easy to correct errors and to format each page to look just as you would like. This is particularly true when you use columns and tables effectively to achieve layouts other than single-column, full-width pages.

However, there are further benefits to creating assessments using a word processor that may be less obvious. You may want to have multiple versions of any test for various reasons, including a make-up exam for absent students, alternating versions among class members to reduce the potential for "borrowing answers," or pre- and posttesting on a given topic.

Developing your assessment items initially is the difficult part. Rearranging them into differing sequences requires little effort with a word processor and, in fact, makes multiple versions truly feasible. When you set up your test items as a numbered list, you can rearrange them at will without concern for renumbering them as you move them about.

If you have access to a computer lab, at least for assessment day, consider how constructed-response assessments benefit when students respond using **templates,** which are word processor documents that provide the structure for the desired responses. Students are less likely to neglect some expected part of a response if they have prompts to follow. Such templates can be helpful to students at any grade level who must write at least a short paragraph. Term papers can also benefit from structured templates that students receive, perhaps by e-mail from their teacher, for use at home, in the library media center, or other times and locations outside of class.

To create such a template, you set it up as a form in Microsoft Word (Figure 15.1), which enables you to lock your prompt text to prevent student editing, while allowing the user to fill in the designated areas, which expand automatically to accommodate as much as the learner writes. Alternately, use a color such as red for the prompt text, and instruct the students to remove it or leave it as part of the final document they prepare.

Figure 15.1 *A Word Document Form Partially Completed by a Student*

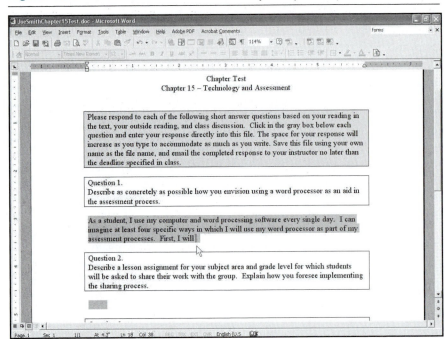

Online Assessment Creation Tools Teachers have long used a range of worksheets, puzzles, quizzes, and tests to support and measure student learning. Many websites enable teachers to create such materials quickly, easily, and at no cost. One top-quality site is Discoveryschool, a unit of Discovery Education, parent of the Discovery Channel. The Teaching Tools page (http://school.discovery.com/teachingtools/teachingtools.html) provides access to a variety of puzzle and worksheet generators, as well as the Quiz Center for creating quizzes online.

Test Item Banks Many textbook publishers offer test item banks for teachers to use, sometimes as standalone support materials and sometimes within the teacher's edition of the book. These resources can be a significant time-saver for busy teachers, as you will appreciate from discussions in previous chapters of assessment construction. However, the quality of test items varies widely, so do not assume you can just use what is there. In addition to selecting from among available items, you also need to examine each one carefully and modify items as needed to better suit the emphasis you have given to the content in your lesson.

Additional item resources are available on the Internet, of course. One particularly interesting site is part of the Schools of California Online

Resources for Education (SCORE). In addition to test banks that educators have evaluated as high quality, there are also links to a wide range of sample rubrics. You can check out these and many other resources at http://score.rims.k12.ca.us/sub_standards/alt_assessment_res_on_web.html. Also, the Pennsylvania Department of Education includes an item bank for reading and math as part of its assessment area, which you will find at http://www.pde.state.pa.us/a_and_t/.

Because of the wide variation in content and the frequent changes to websites, it is best to conduct your search for appropriate test banks using your favorite search engine. A search term as broad as "test banks K12" will provide a start, and then you can refine the search as needed.

On the commercial front, in 2005 the Educational Testing Service first offered the ETS Formative Assessment Item Bank. This resource contains tens of thousands of items for K–12 math and language arts, aligned with state standards. Users access the items through the ETS Instructional Data Management System, which schools must purchase. You can view sample items on the ETS website (http://www.ets.org) to get a sense of this resource.

Assessing Student Work and Providing Feedback

To achieve consistency and fairness in assessing student work, rubrics can be helpful for veteran teachers as well as newcomers to the field. You learned about developing and using rubrics in Chapter 9. As you realize, developing good rubrics can be difficult and time-consuming.

Technology can assist the rubric developer. Many educators turn to free online resources such as Rubistar (http://rubistar.4teachers.org) to help them develop sound rubrics (Figure 15.2). This website provides an explanation of rubrics and a tutorial on using the Rubistar system, which is available in Spanish as well as English to support bilingual class needs. Registration is free and allows you to save and edit your rubrics online for 1 year. Since Rubistar is online, you have access to your rubrics anywhere you have Internet access.

Rubistar offers many sample rubrics for you to explore to learn from the assessment approaches of other teachers. The rubrics can become interactive, if you subscribe to the service, meaning you can use them online rather than in print.

Kathy Schrock's Guide for Educators (http://school.discovery.com/schrockguide), a phenomenal resource for teachers, gives links to many other related resources. The direct link to her compilation of assessment and rubric materials is at http://school.discovery.com/schrockguide/assess.html. Also check out the many resources at http://www.4teachers.org, a service of the Advanced Learning Technologies project, Center for Research on Learning, at the University of Kansas (http://www.altec.org).

Figure 15.2 *Rubistar Website*

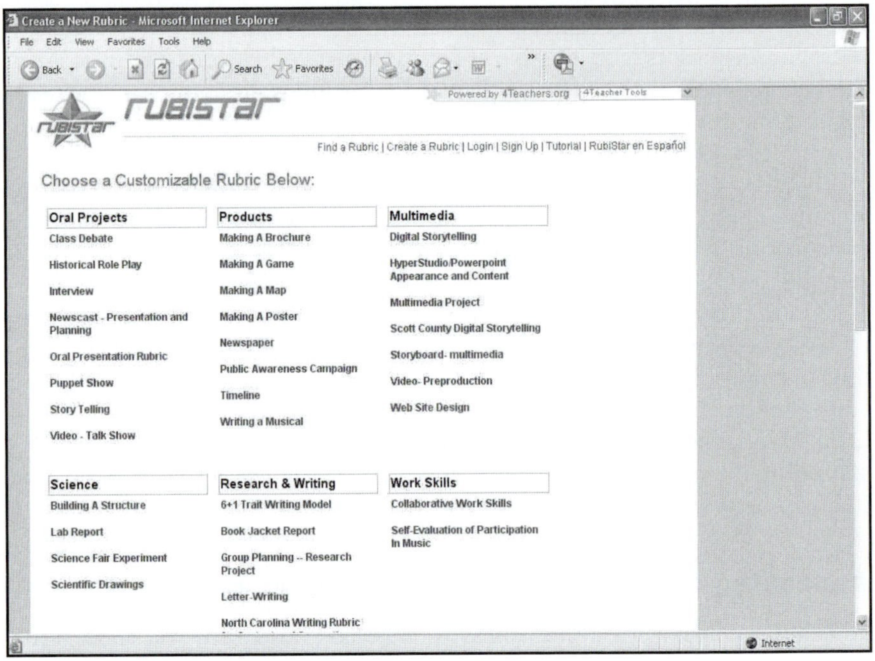

Online assessment systems such as Chalk & Wire (http://www .chalkandwire.com), TaskStream (https://www.taskstream.com/pub), and LiveText™ (http://www.livetext.com) offer yet another option for creating and using electronic rubrics. As an example, LiveText is a self-contained system in which teachers create assignments for students and rubrics for assessing the student work (Figure 15.3). Students submit their documents electronically for review by their teacher, who can provide comments for formative assessment and assess the work using the relevant rubric while adding comments for each criterion. The teacher returns all comments and the marked rubric to the student on completion of the assessment. Students need not wait until the next class session to receive their feedback. The original document is unchanged, and, if appropriate, the student may revise the assignment, which is then available for reassessment.

Many teachers save time by requiring electronic submission of written assignments, which they then review electronically and return to the author for further editing, in the case of formative assessments, or with grading comments inserted. Microsoft Word supports this step toward paperless written work through the 'Reviewing' feature. Your e-mail inbox replaces carrying stacks of paper from school to home and back again. If you permit students to resubmit work after improving it, they can easily accept, reject,

Figure 15.3 *Creating an Assessment in LiveText*

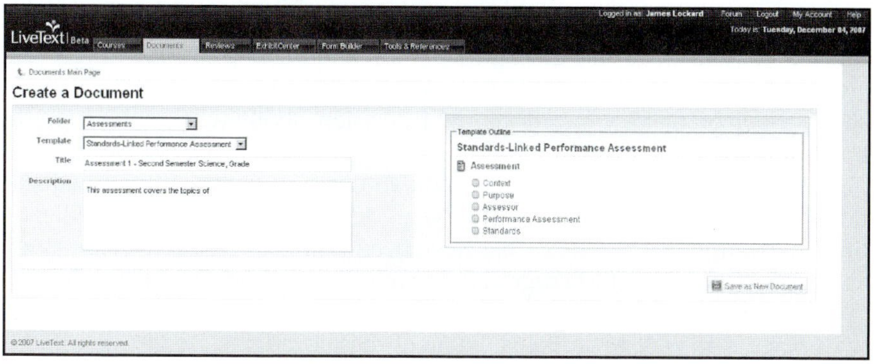

or remove your comments and edits within the document file. If you are unfamiliar with Reviewing and other functions of Word, many fine books are available to help you learn these techniques, such as *Microsoft Office for Teachers* (Fewell & Gibbs, 2006).

Tablet PCs are portable computers that enable the user to interact with computer documents by writing, drawing, and tapping directly on the screen, which swivels to fold down over the keyboard to create an electronic tablet. Depending on your point of view, tablet PCs offer a step forward or backward when it comes to reviewing and assessing written documents. Among the many features of a tablet PC is the ability to mark up any document directly on the screen using electronic colored pens and highlighters. Teachers can provide the same kinds of written feedback within an electronic document that they previously would have given with their red pen on paper. Some teachers find this easier and thus more acceptable than electronic reviewing in Word, and students are intrigued when they receive a "hand-marked" electronic copy of their work.

Recording and Analyzing Assessment Data

Once students have completed a task and you have assessed their work, you need to record your assessment data and, at some point, probably analyze it. There are a number of approaches to doing so using technology. Our consideration covers electronic grade books, data analysis tools, and computer-based testing.

Electronic Grade Books Many teachers have forsaken the traditional paper grade book for a technological alternative. Options range from creating your own basic system in a spreadsheet program, to specialized grade book software installed on an individual teacher's computer, to complete student information systems (SIS) that manage everything from attendance and lunch money to electronic grade submission and posting to student records. Teachers are usually required to use an SIS, if the school has one. Of course, each school or district makes its own decision about what, if any, grade book options are available.

For a lengthy listing of grade book software, visit http://www.educational-software-directory.net/teacher's/gradebook.html, where you will find links to commercial products that have been popular for many years (such as Grade Machine and Micrograde), as well as free products such as Think-Wave Educator Basic that offers online grade posting for communicating with parents as well as students. Some of these products are very rudimentary recordkeepers, while others include seating chart and lesson plan management, attendance records, and more. Some run on a personal digital assistant (PDA), such as the Palm devices, making them completely portable. Furthermore, learning management systems such as Blackboard and WebCT include online grade books to simplify managing and maintaining assessment data for the teacher and to give students flexible access to their course record.

Data Analysis Once you record student assessment data, you frequently need to analyze the data in some way. Analysis may be as simple as calculating the mean (average) score for each student to determine a grade or far more sophisticated, including analyzing the assessment items themselves to determine their relative ability to differentiate among learners. If you record your grades using spreadsheet software such as Microsoft Excel, you can easily perform basic to moderately complex statistical analyses within the spreadsheet. Many electronic grade books include analysis features to determine means, standard deviations, and so forth.

We mentioned Rubistar previously as an aid to creating rubrics, but the website also supports item analysis of data that you input after scoring with your rubric. Learning management and assessment systems such as Task-Stream can generate reports to show student attainment of standards to which the assessment is aligned. Finally, for the most sophisticated analyses, educators can turn to powerful tools such as SPSS, the Statistical Package for the Social Sciences.

Computer-Based Testing Some of the test generators we mentioned previously also support fully electronic assessment. Students complete the assessment at a computer and receive feedback by item and/or at the end. Scoring is automatic and instantaneous, ready for entry into a grade book or other record keeper. Students benefit from immediate feedback, and teachers save the time normally required for scoring.

Qualitative Assessments

So far, we have presented the technology tools that focus on common quantitative assessments, in other words, assessments that are scored by item. Other assessments may be more qualitative in nature, such as observation and interviewing.

Observation Skills performance assessment, such as in physical education and even art or music, typically depends on observation of each student attempting to perform the skill, which is then rated. As you learned in Chapter 7, checklists are commonly used and range from simple yes/no or present/not present marks to more finely differentiated levels of performance. Assessment of oral presentation skills, multimedia presentation skills, and student behavior or disposition may be similar. PDAs and tablet PCs offer electronic means to record observations using checklists or written notes, which you can then transfer to other software or summarize as appropriate.

Observing in group settings is challenging. One alternative is to videotape the group, then complete the assessment while viewing the tape. This approach permits reviewing segments as necessary. The teacher may view alone or with the individual or group at the same time, combining the assessment with immediate feedback to the student(s). At a higher level of sophistication, it is possible to capture the video from tape onto a computer, then analyze the performance using stop motion and video analysis software. This technique is most appropriate for critical learning situations, such as medical education.

Interviews Yet another form of assessment involves recording interviews with individuals, then reviewing the interviews using a rubric or checklist to identify specific points. Computer technology offers much greater control over audio playback than a tape player. You can record first to tape, then digitize the recording for analysis, or you can record directly using a digital recorder or onto a computer. Many notebook computers have built-in microphones, making the process of direct recording quite simple.

If you need a transcription of the recording, hardware and software combinations such as WavPedal provide easy control over playback as you type a verbatim transcript. Furthermore, continuing advances in voice recognition software are making automated transcription of voice to text possible, both during initial recording and from existing recordings.

Susan Williams (2002) describes another use for speech recognition to assess early reading skills. Watch Me! Read is a computerized coach that uses speech recognition to assess a child's reading and tailors feedback to the performance. The teacher receives a copy of the text that the child read, a recording of the reading session, and notation of whether the software accepted each word spoken as a match for the text. The goal of this software is to increase the child's opportunity for reading practice, while providing you, the teacher, with data to interpret as to the child's developing proficiency.

?*Ask Yourself*

If you have had the opportunity to examine a test item bank, perhaps one for a textbook in your teaching area, how do you feel about this approach to creating an assessment compared to developing one from scratch?

Describe any experiences you have had when you received feedback on an assessment by some technological means. How did this compare to more typical means of receiving feedback?

Given your experiences as both a K–12 student and now as a future teacher, what advantages and disadvantages do you see in using rubrics to guide assessments? How might technology fit into your use of rubrics in the classroom?

What experiences have you had with any kind of student information system or electronic grade book that provided access to your performance record? Compare your reaction to these experiences to more traditional assignment grading.

Have you ever received feedback on some assessment that included statistical analysis of the group's performance and your standing within the group? Other than your own score, did you find the information helpful? Why?

Think of a time when someone assessed your performance of some task or skill by observation. Examples might include giving a speech or presentation, taking your driver's license road test, or an activity unit in physical education. Did the assessor use technology as part of the process? If not, how might technology be used in such a situation, and how would it change the assessment process for both the assessor and the assessee?

Have you experienced a one-on-one oral interview/test with a teacher to demonstrate your understanding of a topic? If yes, how did you feel about this form of assessment? Were you more or less nervous than with a typical test? If you have not had this type of assessment experience, how do you think you would react to it?

Student Performance with Technology

In the previous section you learned about technological support for assessment in ways that parallel traditional assessment methods. Now let's turn to specific practical ways by which students can use technology to demonstrate their learning. Examples include sharing student work with the class, student response systems, electronic portfolios, reflection via journaling, and adaptive technology.

Sharing Student Work in Class

Before the arrival of newer technologies, students typically demonstrated their learning or shared their work with their classmates by writing on the board or passing papers around. Starting in the mid-1980s students whose classes met in computer labs found great benefit in technologies that allowed the teacher to view any student's screen from the teacher's computer. The student received help more quickly than when the teacher had to move around the room, especially in often-overcrowded labs. Furthermore, the teacher could project the student's screen for the entire class to see particularly good work or to learn from a common error.

What was once an expensive hardware-based technology is now even more flexible and far less expensive in any networked classroom thanks to software such as NetOp. With NetOp, in addition to the sharing functions, you can distribute documents to and receive documents from class members and even take control of the student's mouse to demonstrate procedures or correct errors, and create and give tests.

Wireless technology adds another dimension to sharing student work. Data projectors are becoming common in classrooms at all levels, whether permanently mounted or on mobile carts. Newer models may have wireless communication capabilities so that a computer need not be within the typical 6 feet of the projector as dictated by common video cable length. Rather, the computer screen can be transmitted to the projector from anywhere in the room using standard wireless communication. Using a notebook computer, you can potentially move around the room while projecting from your computer. For student performance, you would give your computer to a student who could, for example, demonstrate for the entire class how to search for resources on the Internet or how to use an online thesaurus.

Sharing student work takes another leap forward if you have a tablet PC rather than a standard notebook. Now your students can project actions previously possible only at the board, if at all, such as sketching a science diagram, writing and solving math problems, using electronic ink to highlight writing errors in a document, and more. The possibilities are limited only by the teacher's creativity.

Furthermore, you can save projected screens as images and use them to review the class session at the end of the period or any later time. A slideshow of these images could become make-up materials for students who were absent as well as cumulative review in preparation for unit testing. You must still assess the projected student work using the same approaches as for other forms of student work, and both formative and summative evaluations are possible.

An advantage of projected student work is that it potentially creates another authentic context in which students demonstrate their learning. Students may be more attentive to the quality and accuracy of their work if they know their classmates may see it projected in class.

Student Response Systems

Teachers routinely attempt to gauge student learning by posing questions in class. However, in most classes there are students who never volunteer to answer, while others have their hands in the air instantly for every question. In the end, one student responds, hopefully correctly, and the teacher assumes at least most of the others also understand. If no one attempts to respond, the teacher will recognize a problem and try to present the question, or even the previous material, in a different way to further probe student learning. Even with a teacher's best efforts, it is rarely possible to really know which class members understand and which do not, and the best intentions to reach all students may not be successful.

One technology that offers a different potential for assessing student learning is the **student response system (SRS),** or *clicker*. Example products include Qwizdom, eInstruction, Beyond Question, and TurningPoint, among many others. A clicker is a small, handheld device that somewhat resembles a TV remote control. Each student in a class has a clicker. Your teacher station computer has the system software installed and a receiver for the clicker signals. At the start of class, your students send a signal from their clicker, often just by turning it on, which logs them in and effectively takes attendance.

Prior to class or during instruction, you enter questions into the SRS system software and project them on the wall screen. Students respond using the appropriate button(s) on their clicker. Questions can be any format supported by the specific clicker, most commonly multiple-choice and yes/no type items. When a question appears, typically a timer starts, and students must respond before the time expires. When the allowed time ends, your computer immediately shows the distribution of responses, which you can display as a graph for the class to see. More advanced systems have small keyboards and screens, enabling students to enter constructed responses to questions and receive your feedback.

With an SRS, all students in the class respond, even those who may be shy about responding verbally. The pattern of responses provides formative data from which you can decide whether to move ahead or to revisit the topic to help those who did not understand. The National Research Council (2002) noted the potential of such systems, especially for formative evaluation. For many resources related to SRS use and benefits, visit the EDUCAUSE website (http://www.educause.edu) and enter "student response systems" into the search box. Included are several studies at universities that have implemented systems extensively. Arizona State University provides a detailed discussion of SRS at http://clte.asu.edu/wakonse/ENewsletter/

studentresponse_idea.htm. For information specifically about SRS use and K–12 teachers, see an article by William Penuel and colleagues (2007).

E-Portfolios

One common concern about traditional testing is that each test is just one snapshot in time. Such a snapshot may not accurately demonstrate a student's learning, such as if the student was ill at the time of testing. This is a particular concern with the high-stakes testing that has resulted from the No Child Left Behind legislation and other initiatives.

As discussed in Chapter 9, portfolios represent a more comprehensive and potentially more authentic approach to gathering evidence of student learning. Creative fields such as the fine arts, advertising, mass media, and graphic design have long relied on work samples, gathered in a physical portfolio, to assess the skills of individuals in the field. However, physical portfolios have many disadvantages including their bulk, the difficulty and/or cost of maintaining multiple copies, and the logistical challenges facing job applicants who need to get a copy to a potential employer immediately. These are among the reasons for the movement to electronic portfolios, starting in the lower elementary grades.

Many schools have implemented basic approaches to e-portfolios. The most common is a CD of student work, organized primarily by grade level and secondarily by subject. At the end of each school year, as well as at various times during the year, learners add appropriate materials to the CD to create their evolving record. CD-based e-portfolios are within the technology skills range of most teachers and schools, and the cost of CDs is minimal.

On a slightly higher level of sophistication, most schools have their own website. An e-portfolio adds little to existing school costs for web services. Creation of a web-based portfolio requires a greater level of technical skill, though many schools provide templates that are relatively easy to fill in and post onto the server.

Another approach to portfolio development is to subscribe to a service such as TaskStream or LiveText. Schools can develop their own templates for the structure of the portfolio, similar to the previous description of Word forms to guide a writing assignment.

Portfolio assessment need not differ from assessment of other types of student work. A rubric or other scoring guide is comparable for any means whereby students demonstrate their learning. Sophisticated systems incorporate assessment within the system, which we will discuss in the final section of this chapter.

Since 1991 Dr. Helen Barrett has devoted her career largely to electronic portfolios and is widely recognized as a leading authority in this area. Her website (http://electronicportfolios.org/) is a must-visit resource for anyone interested in this topic.

Reflection via Journaling

While assessments readily indicate what students know (and do not know), they seldom offer much insight into student thought processes, including reasons for errors and misconceptions. Many teachers require students to submit periodic reflections on their learning through a process called **journaling.** According to Jonnie Phipps (2005, p. 64), "Reflective writing can aid learners in synthesizing new information, and it is often used to improve reading comprehension, writing performance, and self-esteem via self-examination." At its simplest, journaling requires no more than paper and pencil with which to record one's thoughts, but naturally there are technological alternatives that can enhance the experience. Students can write their reflections using a word processor, of course. Teachers may prefer that students journal in e-mail messages or submit their reflective writing as e-mail attachments.

In comparison, Microsoft OneNote software offers some distinct advantages over more common technologies. OneNote is an all-purpose tool for organizing text and multimedia (audio and video) in one place with powerful search capabilities to later retrieve whatever you are looking for. OneNote uses the visual metaphor of a notepad with tabs across the top to organize the contents by chosen category and tabs down the right side to provide quick access to individual "notes" within a category. If students are required to reflect periodically on a class or their learning in it, the class might be the category at the top while each reflection entry would be a side tab within that category. This form of organization is significantly different from the way that individual files are normally stored on the computer, not interconnected in any way.

While a OneNote "page" looks much like a word processor document, it is more flexible and natural. You can place the cursor and type anywhere on the "page" just as you would jot notes anywhere on a pad of paper. This creates a more natural note-taking environment.

Still greater power lies in OneNote's ability to integrate images, audio, and even video clips with other content. Using a notebook computer with a built-in microphone, a student could record all or part of a class session live, review the audio recording later, then write or record a journal reflection about it to submit. With a small webcam, users can integrate video into their journals as well. All these capabilities are available to users who do not have a portable computer as well, but they are obviously limited to journaling where their computer is located.

Tablet PC users write directly on the OneNote notepad with their stylus, as on any paper writing surface, which allows them to make sketches, doodles, and diagrams along with other content (Figure 15.4). After you write with the tablet's electronic ink, OneNote can convert that handwriting into editable text on the page and save it in Word format for sharing with individuals who do not use OneNote. OneNote and a tablet PC offer a unique potential in reflective journaling.

Figure 15.4 *Microsoft OneNote for Taking Handwritten Notes*

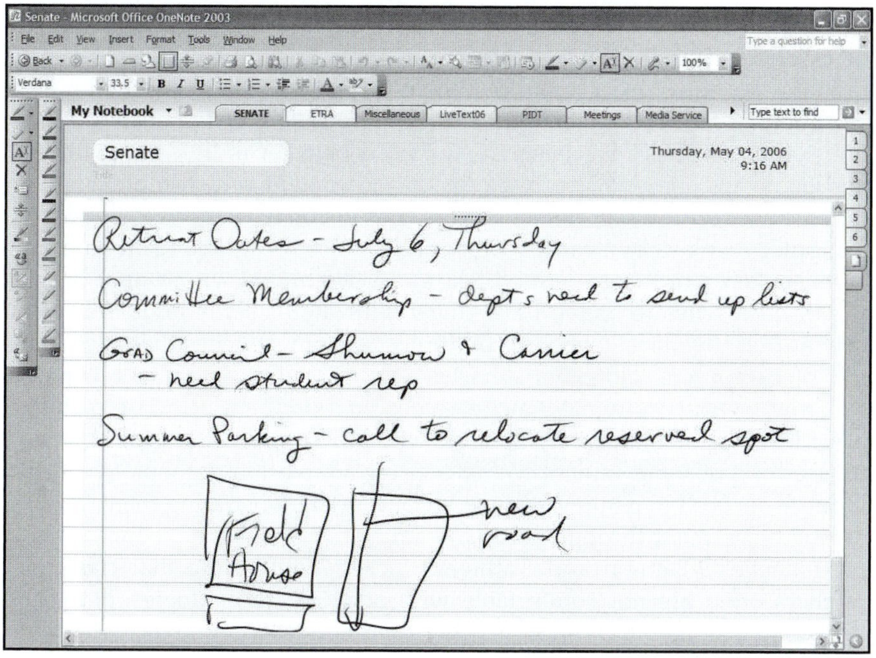

Another feature is a screen capture tool that allows the OneNote user to capture any part of the computer screen and incorporate it into a document. If both teacher and student use OneNote, its integrated collaboration features allow them to share a single notebook either online or offline. Changes made by either person will automatically update in the other's copy in real time or when that person next goes online. This means you can assess student work at your convenience and automatically return the work with comments as soon as you finish.

As a standalone application, OneNote did not attract the attention and use that it merits as a collaboration and assessment tool; but, as an integral part of Microsoft Office 2007 Home and Student Edition, usage seems certain to grow. For now, OneNote appears to be the ultimate tool for electronic journaling and general note taking with built-in assessment potential.

Adaptive Technologies

Since passage of the Americans with Disabilities Act in 1990, awareness of individuals with special needs has become much more prominent throughout society. The law requires reasonable accommodation of special needs, and a wide range of technologies enables many individuals to participate more fully in education than previously. Educators must become familiar with the technologies that exist and be alert to new ones as they appear, so that the individualized education plan (IEP) for each student includes the best possible learning and assessment options. **Adaptive** or **assistive technologies** are the subject of entire books, so treatment here will be limited.

Looking first at software that enables individuals to demonstrate learning, speech synthesis has been an enormous help for individuals with limited or no vision. JAWS software reads the content of a computer screen that the user cannot see, enabling users with vision limitations to learn from computer displays by hearing. Conversely, voice recognition software converts spoken words into written text to assist learners who cannot hear.

In the hardware arena, individuals with motor skills limitations may benefit from oversize keyboards and mice or from switches that allow control of computers and other devices by puffing into a straw, raising an eyebrow, or using minimal hand–eye coordination (Figure 15.5). On a more basic level, a calculator may be an essential accommodation for assessing the learning of some students. Whatever the adaptation, technology can aid individuals both in gaining knowledge and in demonstrating their learning during assessment through accommodations.

Blanche O'Bannon and Kathleen Puckett (2007) note that classroom teachers often are not comfortable with adaptive technologies. However, they are not alone. Classroom teachers serve as collaborative partners on IEP teams with special educators, who are the experts. An IEP will specify both instructional and assessment plans for the student, and federal law mandates consideration of adaptive technologies when writing an IEP (Marino, Marino, & Shaw, 2006). Beyond gaining general familiarity with adaptive software and hardware, the classroom teacher's critical roles are to "(observe) student performance when using technology [and to keep] the IEP team informed of successes and concerns" (p. 49). The Technology and Media Division of the Council for Exceptional Children (www.tamcec .org) offers many resources on adaptive technologies and their uses.

WebQuests

In the early days of educators' use of the World Wide Web, Professor Bernie Dodge, San Diego State University, drafted a short paper entitled "Some Thoughts about WebQuests" (Dodge, 1997). Dodge wrote, "A WebQuest is an inquiry-oriented activity in which some or all of the information that learners interact with comes from resources on the internet, optionally supplemented with videoconferencing." His concern in proposing the model for a **WebQuest** was that the concept of "surfing the Web" was all too often literally true—that is, teachers were turning students loose with little direction to find information on the Internet. Surfing might start with a clear purpose, but it often became aimless wandering rather quickly—

Figure 15.5 *Adaptive Keyboard for Learners with Limited Motor Control*

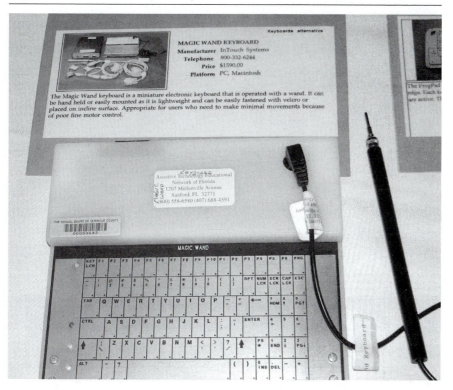

aimless in the sense that the original purpose was lost. Dodge and others recognized the vast potential of the information resources available at the fingertips of anyone with a computer and Internet access. The question was how to harness the potential productively.

In collaboration with his Australian colleague Tom March, Dodge developed the WebQuest concept, as well as the first examples. Teachers quickly accepted the challenge of guiding student learning using Internet resources following a basic template with six key elements (Dodge, 1997):

- An introduction to prepare the learner for the activity.
- A task that is both interesting and possible to do—a problem to solve.
- Information resources, generally provided as links within the WebQuest.
- A process presented as a set of clearly described steps.
- Guidance for structuring the information that is found.
- A conclusion to achieve closure.

Teachers assess student learning from WebQuests using rubrics or scoring guides, as appropriate to the style of the activity and its learning goals.

Initially, teachers created WebQuests for their students, but, as increasing numbers of teachers adopted constructivist learning principles, WebQuests became another means for students to construct and demonstrate their own learning. Student-created WebQuests often become valuable learning materials for other learners, demonstrating that the best way to learn something is to prepare to teach it to someone else. WebQuest enthusiasts comment on the extraordinary level of engagement they witness as students create new projects and the depth of learning the finished projects document. You can learn all about WebQuests and work through some of the countless examples by visiting the WebQuest Portal at http://webquest .org, one of the most popular educational sites on the Web (Figure 15.6).

Figure 15.6 *The WebQuest Homepage*

❓ *Ask Yourself*

Student response systems are widely used for instantaneous formative assessment. How would you use a class set of clickers to enhance the learning process for your students?

Describe your perceptions of e-portfolios as a means of assessment, both for shorter periods (such as within one course) and over longer periods (end of grade level or graduation requirement). What use of an e-portfolio do you believe would be more beneficial? Why?

If you have ever been asked to keep a reflective journal for a class, what challenges and benefits do you see in journaling now? How do you feel about journaling as an assessment technique for the students you will teach? Does your view depend on whether technology is used to support journaling?

How could WebQuests support a constructivist learning experience? How would you assess that experience?

Integrated Technologies

Some applications of technology combine elements of instruction, ranging from simple delivery of learning materials to full-blown independent learning systems, with basic to highly sophisticated assessment capabilities. Let's consider these technologies in the categories of learning management systems, integrated learning systems, and computer-assisted instruction.

Learning Management Systems

Learning management systems (LMS) are computer systems that assist teachers in managing all aspects of instruction. The most popular systems are also online systems, meaning users access them on the Internet. However, they do not necessarily involve distance education or delivery of instruction to learners who do not participate in classes physically. Hybrid or blended classes in which some portion of the instruction takes place in the classroom, are very common, and the LMS extends learning and assessment opportunities beyond class time. Learning opportunities may range from access to relevant course materials, such as syllabi and readings, to full-content presentations using tools such as PowerPoint or video clips and other multimedia, to interactive discussion boards that students visit at their convenience between class sessions or on specified dates.

For **synchronous** discussions, class members all log in to the system at the same time, and the discussion occurs live, in real time. **Asynchronous** discussions occur over some time frame, with participants reading what others have posted and adding contributions at their convenience.

Online discussions can serve a formative assessment function. Somewhat analogous to student response systems, electronic discussions actively engage participants who otherwise seldom contribute in class, perhaps due to shyness. All students have the opportunity, especially in an asynchronous discussion, to consider their response thoughtfully and refine it before sharing it with the group and to do so in the comfort of their own environment rather than the classroom. All students are expected to participate, and their contributions give the teacher insight into each student's understanding, not just those who contribute in class. The teacher has evidence of how well the students learned and can facilitate supplemental learning opportunities as needed.

Teachers may post a discussion question to which students respond and at the close of the discussion assess the responses in a variety of ways, ranging from holistically to using a detailed rubric to identify and give credit for specific contributions. Many teachers assign group projects, part of which could be to develop and post online discussion questions for other class members. Assessment of the group's work may focus on the questions developed as well as the group's ability to stimulate and manage the discussion. The teacher may assess the participants' comments as well, perhaps using a checklist. As for assessing level of participation, teachers can monitor student access to the system and record, for instance, which students have viewed assigned readings for how long and which have not.

Among the most widely used learning management systems are Blackboard and WebCT, once independent companies that merged in early 2006. According to company materials (Blackboard, 2006, p. 3), Blackboard, shown in Figure 15.7, is in use in more than 1,200 schools across the United States, including 41 of *Newsweek*'s top 100 high schools.

Both systems offer comprehensive capabilities to store all forms of electronic materials for students to access at will, organized as desired by the teacher. Both also provide complete discussion board capabilities. In addition, they can assist in course management by handling class lists, providing electronic means for students to submit assignments to their teachers, and managing grades with an integrated grade book. These systems support both formative and summative assessments using test items created by the teacher or the publisher of the class textbook. Students take these tests online, and then the system grades them, enters the results into the grade book, and offers analysis of the assessment data. Students can monitor their grades at any time; schools may choose to give parents access to student records as well. In fact, an LMS can serve as a communication tool between school and home to better inform parents of their child's assignments and progress using the assessment data. Parents need not wait for the next report card or parent–teacher conference to learn of their student's progress.

Blackboard and WebCT became commercially available in 1997 and served primarily as materials repositories and delivery systems. Over time both added features to become comprehensive learning management systems. Both are instructor-oriented, meaning the teacher creates the course, determines its content and structure, and makes it available to students. In contrast, LiveText's founders recognized in 1997 the growing movement toward standards-based assessment in education; they focused from the start on lesson planning and assessment as the core functions, both aligned with state and national standards.

To assist teachers with these tasks, LiveText defines all content as documents, which are actually web pages developed from templates that help guide the process. Creating a document from a template is similar to creating a Word document, and there is no need to learn web programming. Basic document types are lesson plans, assessments, projects, portfolios, and courses, each of which can be aligned with standards by selecting the relevant standards from hundreds of sets entered and maintained by LiveText. Students share their work with the teacher through the LiveText system. The teacher reviews and assesses the work electronically using an assessment document that contains the appropriate

Figure 15.7 *The Blackboard Learning Management System*

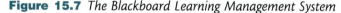
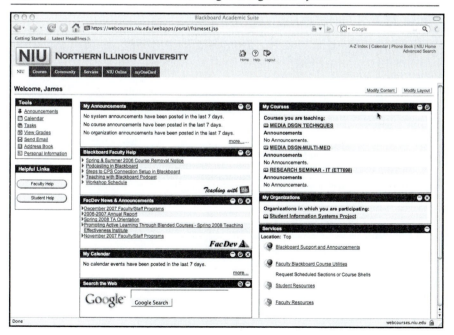

rubric, which the teacher also develops with the assistance of the system. Assessment data are stored in a grade book and can be aggregated into reports for local, state, or national reviewing bodies, such as licensure and accreditation agencies. Figure 15.8 shows one page in a course in LiveText.

Although teachers can do most of the same tasks within LiveText as within Blackboard, including delivery of materials and conducting online discussions, LiveText is more student-oriented. Students can set up their own work groups without teacher involvement and can share their work with one another for peer review and comment at any time. Student accounts have nearly all of the same functionalities that teachers have, and users are free to create documents of all types according to their needs. For example, preservice teachers can develop lesson plans in their methods courses, then deliver them in the classroom during clinical experiences, including student teaching. The cooperating teacher and clinical supervisor then assess the lesson and its delivery following institutional guidelines.

In addition to commercial, subscription systems such as Blackboard/ WebCT and LiveText, a growing number of educational institutions at all levels worldwide are using a free LMS called Moodle, which resembles the commercial products in features. Other free, open source LMS and assessment systems with a range of features include LON-CAPA,

Figure 15.8 *A Course in LiveText*

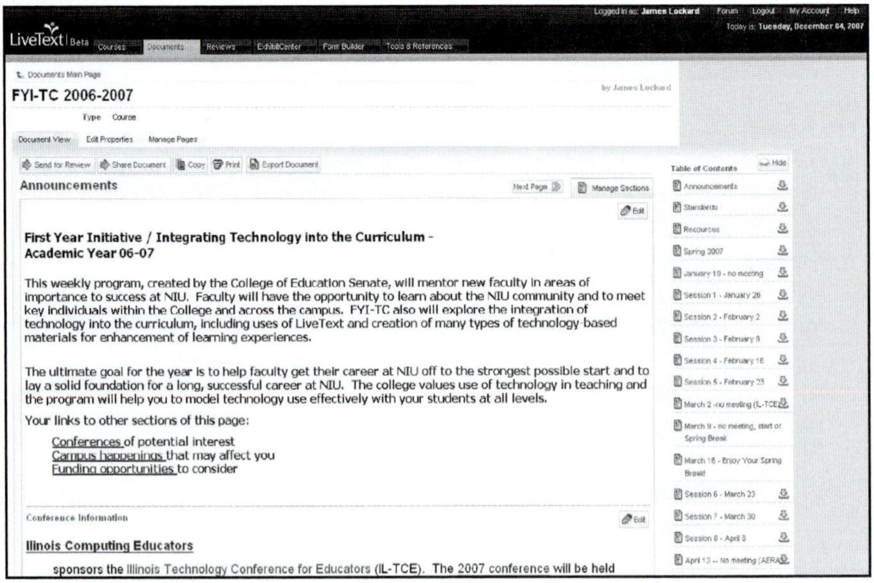

OpenMark, and Sakai. Look for more information about these systems in the end-of-chapter resources section as well as on the EduTools site (www .edutools.info), which compares many technology systems. The cost of commercial systems need not prevent a school from using an LMS.

Learning management systems are versatile tools for teaching and managing the many tasks involved in the daily life of an educator, including assessing student learning. You likely have had some experience with an LMS in college, but only from the perspective of the learner. We hope that experience will encourage you to use any LMS that may be available to you as a teacher in your own classroom.

Integrated Learning Systems

Learning management systems can deliver instruction and assist in assessing student learning, but they require active involvement of the teacher in creating and gathering resources, organizing them, and making them available to students. An **integrated learning system (ILS),** in contrast, is designed to deliver instruction, assess learning, and remediate as needed to attain specified standards, all with little or no teacher involvement.

A typical ILS is a self-contained combination of computer-assisted instruction, **computer-based testing**, and an intelligent tutoring system. The ILS presents the content, often using a full range of multimedia approaches, and quizzes the learner at varying intervals as formative assessment. Using artificial intelligence, it adapts the presentation to the learner's needs, based on the formative assessments. When the system determines that the learner appears to have reached the desired level of proficiency, it gives a summative assessment, which is commonly an adaptive test that varies the items based on the learner's responses and from learner to learner. Tests can be much more sophisticated than traditional assessments because the system judges achievement based on response patterns and moves quickly over areas the student clearly understands, then probes more deeply those areas of potential weakness, varying the difficulty of the items to determine the level of attainment.

Among many ILS providers, Pearson Digital Learning (www .pearsondigital.com) offers the Waterford system for foundational learning in reading, math, and science for the lower elementary grades, Success-Maker for K–8 individualized instruction building on the early foundations, KnowledgeBox for multimedia content aimed at grades K–6, and NovaNET for online courseware for grade 6 through adult learners. Extensive research documents each system's benefits based on assessment data, and many less successful schools have seen marked improvement in student learning after implementing an ILS (see Gallagher, 1997, for significant gains among students in a failing elementary school in Chicago). High cost, however, has always been a barrier to wider adoption of ILS.

Integrated learning systems such as the Pearson products typically include content and assessments for multiple subject areas. There are also more focused products such as the widely used Accelerated Reader and Accelerated Math from Renaissance Learning (www.renlearn.com). Both products meet the requirements of No Child Left Behind for scientifically based research, according to their producer. Neither is designed to stand alone; but rather they are intended to complement and support regular classroom instruction in their respective areas. The common element is continual assessment and guidance for the teacher about each student's achievement and suggestions, even prescriptions, for the next step in learning. The teacher's role becomes one of monitor and tutor when assessments indicate more support is necessary.

Computer-Assisted Instruction

Our final topic within integrated technologies is **computer-assisted instruction (CAI).** The origins of CAI go back to the 1950s and research efforts at IBM. CAI is often categorized under such terms as *tutorials, simulations, drill and practice,* and *instructional games.* In each case there is computer software designed to help learners master some discrete part of the curriculum. Some CAI products have become classics, including Oregon Trail, Reader Rabbit, and Math Blaster. You are probably familiar with at least one of those titles.

Individual CAI titles do not seek to provide the entire curriculum, as does an integrated learning system. Rather, CAI typically offers an engaging supplement to the curriculum, whether to assist students who are having difficulty with the content as presented or to stimulate students who have grasped the prescribed materials quickly and are ready for a greater challenge. CAI can help teachers achieve the elusive goal of individualized learning. Many educators particularly favor simulation software for its power to support constructivist learning by allowing learners to experiment, to try multiple options, and to learn from their mistakes.

The instruction provided by CAI may be adaptive, changing the order and even the nature of the presentation based on student responses along the way, just as good teachers have always done based on observed responses. At the least, individual CAI titles will have self-check formative assessments within the software and may have summative assessments as well. These assessments also may be adaptive, as previously described in an ILS.

In addition to electronic assessments comparable to traditional ones, CAI has the potential to provide a much fuller, richer understanding of student learning and even thought processes through **logging.** Logging records the path taken by each learner through the materials and also measures the time taken at each step. Analyses of times and paths can point to misunderstandings of specific content that may warrant reteaching to benefit the entire class. CAI developers may provide for assessment printouts, or the teacher may have to create further assessments to document the learning that has taken place.

Behavior Matrix software (Hung & Lockard, 2007) illustrates yet another approach to helping learners develop important skills through problem-based learning (PBL), which we discussed in Chapter 8. This software models expert problem solving by guiding preservice teachers to analyze classroom behavior problems. Users identify a problem, then consider and select from multiple possible responses, all presented in a matrix that fits on a single screen for ease of use (Figure 15.9). Starting on the left side, the teacher selects the observed behavior of concern, then moves to the right to review and consider potential responses. At each stage, the learner can access detailed explanations and both written

Figure 15.9 *Behavior Matrix for Problem-Based Learning of Classroom Behavior Management*

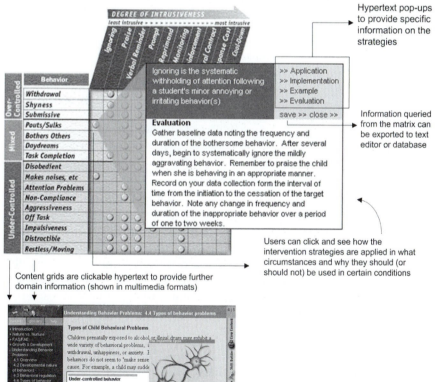

Resource for Your Assessment Toolkit
Checklist for Using Technology in Assessment

The following items can help you to consider appropriate ways in which to enhance assignments or simplify the assessment processes using various technologies. No single assessment is likely to use more than one or at most a few technologies, but considering them all is beneficial as you develop your assessment expertise.

- Use basic software (word processing, spreadsheet) to develop a paper assessment, perhaps in more than one version.
- Use an online site to create a worksheet, puzzle, quiz, or text.
- Use a publisher's test bank as a source of assessment items or use an online resource.
- Develop your assessment rubric using an online resource such as Rubistar.
- Require students to submit electronic documents that you will review and return electronically.
- Plan appropriate data analysis and recording procedures.

- Develop an assessment rubric as a checklist to complete during observation of student performance, such as class presentations.
- Plan appropriate means for students to share their work with the entire class, including reserving necessary equipment.
- Consider whether the assignment may yield student portfolio artifacts and whether slight changes to the assignment could enhance their value for inclusion in a portfolio.
- Identify potential modifications to the assessment to assist learners with special needs, especially adaptive technologies.
- If research on the Web is appropriate, develop a WebQuest to provide focus and direction and to maximize learning within available time.
- Develop the assignment and/or assessment for use with any available student response system or learning management system.

and multimedia examples of applying specific techniques. Assessment of learning can be practical (on the job), by printout of the decisions made while using the matrix, or by self-reflection on the goals and outcomes. Initial research supports the developers' hypothesis that this PBL approach can help learners move from novice toward experienced and even expert problem solver through meaningful experiences.

Ask Yourself

Reflect on any experience you may have had as a student with a learning management system. In most cases this is likely to be in higher education, rather than in your K–12 years as elementary and secondary schools are more recent adopters of such systems. What was your initial reaction to using this system, particularly its role in assessment? Did you submit work through the system? Did you receive feedback and assessments through the system? How did your response to it change during and beyond the first semester? Would you like to have access to such a system for use with your students? If so, how would you use it? If not, what are your concerns?

If you have had any experience with an integrated learning system, describe how it served both to deliver instruction and to provide assessments. Did you find the ILS helpful? What benefits did you perceive and what concerns do you have about such a system?

Think about any experience you have had with either computer software for learning (CAI) or technology-supported problem-based learning. What were the assessment components? Did you even think about being assessed as you used the technology? What uses can you envision for these technologies in your teaching, especially as part of your assessment approach?

Digging Deeper
Future Shock

In 1970 Alvin Toffler introduced the notion of "future shock." According to Toffler, contemporary society was permeated by too much change in too short a time. This accelerated pace differed from other eras in that human beings were so overwhelmed by change that they were entering a state of shock. By shock, he meant that human beings were shutting down, unable to respond to innovations, and, for this reason, technology was taking over society. Toffler forecasted that since humans were no longer able to critique or question new technologies because they were developing so quickly, eventually technology would run societies, and humans would be subject to technology (Toffler, 1970).

At first this idea was ridiculed, but over time many sociologists and futurists have come to agree with Toffler's forecast. According to Toffler, once a technology is developed, it is implemented, and there are fewer and fewer obstacles to its implementation. People use the technology and eventually accommodate it into their lives without questions. It is considered hip or fashionable to keep up with the newest innovations.

There is a growing concern today that the benefits of technology are making work easier and more efficient at a great cost to human beings. People work 24-7 because they can. E-mail, Blackberries, cell phone connections to the always available Internet are virtually requirements for the contemporary professional.

Toffler's solution to this problem of unbridled technological development was simple—humans needed to question new technologies, to critically analyze possible consequences to their lives, and to carefully evaluate the human price versus the possible technological good. He suggested that people needed to question things even though they did not yet have all the facts, rather than hold back their opinion until they were certain that they understood the technology itself. Toffler called on schools to teach such critical dispositions.

Summary

- Technologies as basic as word processing increase a teacher's efficiency and flexibility in developing assignments and assessments. Free online tools can assist in creating worksheets and puzzles of all kinds as well as quizzes and tests, and test banks provide resources to speed the development of assessments.

- Many resources exist to assist in creating rubrics, which help assure fair and consistent assessment of student work.

- Electronic grade books simplify record keeping, while data analysis software supports both determination of grades and possible weaknesses in the assessment instrument itself.

- Multiple techniques support qualitative assessment of student performances, including direct observation and interviewing. As well, technology can enhance sharing of student work, such as projecting an electronic document or an individual's computer screen in a lab setting for teacher or peer review.

- Student response systems engage all students and provide instant formative feedback to the teacher as to whether students understand the lesson.

- E-portfolios document student learning comprehensively over an extended time period, and avoid the concern that assessment is often just a snapshot of one moment in time. As well, reflective journaling provides deeper insight into students' learning and cognitive processes.

- Students with special needs benefit greatly from adaptive technologies that allow fuller participation in the learning process, including assessment activities.

- WebQuests direct learning from Internet resources and help avoid inefficient or inappropriate surfing within a learning activity. Student-created WebQuests offer a unique way for students to demonstrate learning.

- Learning management systems such as Blackboard assist teachers in the countless managerial and clerical tasks that all teachers must complete, including creation, delivery, and management of assessments.

- Integrated learning systems deliver instruction, assess achievement, and provide remediation tailored to the needs of individual learners across broad curriculum areas.

- Computer-assisted instruction individualizes learning experiences at the lesson level and typically includes assessment items at varying points in the lesson.

Key Terms

adaptive or assistive technologies (440)

asynchronous (444)

computer-assisted instruction (CAI) (448)

computer-based testing (447)

integrated learning system (ILS) (447)

journaling (438)

learning management systems (LMS) (443)

logging (448)

student response system (SRS) (436)

synchronous (444)

Tablet PC (431)

template (427)

WebQuest (440)

For Further Discussion

1. Discuss the benefits of test banks. Then reflect on possible weaknesses or limitations as well.

2. Describe any experience you may have had developing a rubric and explain how technology could have helped you in the process.

3. Assessments require data recording and analysis. Discuss ways in which technology could assist with these processes.

4. Discuss potential benefits of student response systems. What concerns do you have about using them?

5. Recall any experience you have had with portfolios and reflective journaling. Discuss the benefits of these forms of assessment based on your experience. How do you envision using one or both with your students?

6. Why are adaptive technologies growing in importance to teachers? Describe any experience you have had with adaptive technologies. How would they enhance assessment for special needs learners?

7. Discuss the challenges that arise when students use the Internet for research. How could a WebQuest reduce potential problems? How could a WebQuest be a form of assessment?

Comprehension Quiz

Directions: For each of the numbered assessment purposes or activities below, indicate which technologies from the list on the right are *most appropriate*. Write the letter(s) in the blank to the left of each item. Reflect on your choices and be prepared to justify them.

Assessment Activities / Purposes	Technologies
1. Data recording	a. Student response systems
2. Summative assessment	b. Integrated learning systems
3. Diagnosis of misconceptions	c. Online tools
4. Formative assessment	d. WebQuests
5. Data analysis	e. Word processor
6. Demonstrating learning over time	f. E-portfolios
7. Creating written assessments	g. Computer-assisted instruction
8. Meeting individual needs	h. Reflective journaling
9. Providing feedback to learners	i. Spreadsheet
	j. Adaptive device
	k. Test banks
	l. PDA (Palm, PocketPC, etc.)
	m. Tablet PC
	n. Electronic grade book

Relevant Website Resources

4Teachers

www.4teachers.org

Among the resources accessible via this site are QuizStar for online quiz creation and Rubistar, a popular resource to help develop sound rubrics. This site is a must for any teacher.

Advanced Learning Technologies Project (ALTEC)

www.altec.org

The site focuses on web-based resources, including professional development and special needs. There are many links to other excellent sites for technology in education.

Discoveryschool

school.discovery.com

Discoveryschool offers a vast repository of materials and links to assist any teacher. In addition to lesson plans and teaching tools, this is also the portal to Kathy Schrock's Guide for Educators, one of the oldest and best online resources for teachers by teachers.

Educational Software Directory

www.educational-software-directory.net

A one-stop site for education software. Follow the Teachers link to find categories including grade book software and assessment resources. However, many are commercial products, not freeware.

Electronic Portfolios

electronicportfolios.org

Helen Barrett's website is the essential first stop for information and examples of electronic portfolios and digital storytelling.

IBM

www.ibm.com/ibm/ibmgives/grant/education/programs/reinventing

Although most people think of IBM primarily as a computer firm, the company also has a strong involvement in improving education. The link here is to the introductory page for many projects. You can follow links to grant sites around the world and to specific technology solutions such as the Watch Me! Read speech recognition software, which IBM developed jointly with the Philadelphia schools.

Microsoft Education

www.microsoft.com/education

This is Microsoft's repository for product tutorials, lesson plans, how-to articles, and links to clip art, clip media, and product templates specifically designed for use by educators. It has a wealth of free materials.

Microsoft, Inc.

www.microsoft.com

Visit this site for all the official information about and many illustrations of educational uses of key products. Use the search box to find OneNote and tablet PCs as two technologies discussed in this chapter.

Moodle

www.moodle.org

Organizations that cannot afford the cost of a commercial learning management system may turn to free, open source software such as Moodle. Moodle is in use in over 150 countries around the world, with over 150,000 registered users in early 2007.

National Educational Technology Standards (NETS)

cnets.iste.org

The International Society for Technology in Education (ISTE) is also home to the National Educational Technology Standards Project. The CNETS page provides links to the standards themselves, the conditions required to achieve them, and full documentation of the standards for students, teachers, and administrators, including profiles of individuals who meet the standards. There are also numerous resources for integrating technology into the curriculum K–12, as well as the latest updates to the standards.

Pennsylvania Department of Education

www.pde.state.pa.us

Among many resources available to teachers everywhere from the state of Pennsylvania is a test item bank, found at www.pde.state.pa.us/a_and_t/site.

Schools of California Online Resources for Education (SCORE)

score.rims.k12.ca.us

SCORE offers a wide range of resources especially for teachers of history and social sciences. Among the resources is a test item bank at score.rims.k12 .ca.us/sub_standards/alt_assessment_res_on_web .html.

Technology and Media Division (TAM)

www.tamcec.org

The Technology and Media Division of the Council for Exceptional Children provides a range of special needs products and resources.

WebQuest Portal

webquest.org

This site is the entry point for the most extensive collection of resources related to WebQuests. It was created and is maintained by Bernie Dodge, the originator of the WebQuest concept, and is therefore the most authoritative source.

References

Blackboard. (2006). *Blackboard K–12 learning management platform.* http://library.blackboard.com/docs/as/ Bb_K12_Brochure.pdf. Accessed May 27, 2007.

Dodge, B. (1997). *Some thoughts about WebQuests.* http:// webquest.sdsu.edu/about_webquests.html. Accessed December 1, 2006.

Fewell, P. J., & Gibbs, W. J. (2006). *Microsoft Office for teachers,* 2nd ed. Upper Saddle River, NJ: Prentice-Hall.

Fletcher, J. D. (2002). Is it worth it? Some comments on research and technology in assessment and instruction. In National Research Council, *Technology and assessment: Thinking ahead: Proceedings of a workshop* (pp. 26–39). Washington, DC: National Academy Press.

Gallagher, E. M. (1997). Utilization of an ILS to increase reading comprehension. *Dissertation Abstracts International, 58*(5), 1591A. (ProQuest No. AAT 9733534).

Hung, W. C., & Lockard, J. (2007). The design and impact of using an advance organizer guided behavior matrix to support teachers' problem solving in classroom behavior management. *Journal of Special Education Technology, 22*(1), 21–36.

International Society for Technology in Education. (2006). *Use of NETS by state.* http://cnets.iste.org/docs/States_using_NETS.pdf. Accessed November 6, 2006.

Marino, M. T., Marino, E. C., & Shaw, S. F. (2006). Making informed assistive technology decisions for students with high incidence disabilities. *Teaching Exceptional Children, 38*(6), 18–25.

National Research Council. (2002). *Technology and assessment: Thinking ahead: Proceedings of a workshop.* Board on Testing and Assessment, Center for Education, Division of Behavioral and Social Sciences and Education. Washington, DC: National Academy Press.

O'Bannon, B. W., & Puckett, K. (2007). *Preparing to use technology. A practical guide to curriculum integration.* Boston: Pearson/Allyn & Bacon.

Penuel, W. R., Boscardin, C. K., Masyn, K., & Crawford, V., (2007). Teaching with student response systems in elementary and secondary education settings: A survey of study. *Educational Technology, Research, and Development, 55,* 315–346.

Phipps, J. J. (2005). E-journaling: Achieving interactive education online. *Educause Quarterly, 28*(1), 62–65. http:// www.educause.edu/ir/library/pdf/EQM0519.pdf. Accessed November 18, 2006.

Toffler, A. (1970). *Future shock.* New York: Random House.

Williams, S. M. (2002). Speech recognition technology and the assessment of beginning readers. In National Research Council, *Technology and assessment: Thinking ahead: Proceedings of a workshop* (pp. 40–49). Washington, DC: National Academy Press.

CHAPTER 16

Reflective Self-Assessment

Chapter Objectives

After reading and thinking about this chapter, you will be able to:

- Explain why the heart of assessment is self-development and growth rather than evaluation or judgment.

- Describe formal ways that teachers can assess their own practice and learning.

- Show that self-assessment can and should be integrated with instruction.

- Clarify that self-assessment is a necessary component of learning.

- Identify ways that students can be taught to self-assess.

- Elaborate on the importance of teacher self-assessment.

We have taken you on a journey through the many facets of assessment in our complex, contemporary society. The journey began with the problem of defining assessment and clarifying its purposes. From the very beginning, you probably noticed that the world of assessment is by no means simple or one-dimensional. Your task as a teacher is to constantly revisit the many metaphors, purposes, and techniques of assessment as you make daily decisions about the its use in your classroom.

Because there are conflicting purposes for assessment, we have challenged you to explore foundational questions about the complex nature of assessment. Any area that has conflicting purposes and vested interests is an area that is in flux. So we have chosen to end this text about assessment with a call for ongoing reflective self-assessment. We do so because, in the end, you can never stop learning and questioning your own understandings about the nature of knowledge, about the competing standards from vested interest groups, and about the assessments that you employ. Often issues of justice and equity will arise, and you must be flexible and aware enough to tackle these questions and refrain from complacency.

We also have challenged ourselves to provide you with some tools and advice on how to develop a program of self-assessment both for yourself and for your students. Although reflection is an important skill for students to practice, it is also important for teachers to see themselves as learners and to understand and enhance their development through an informed, deliberate process of reflection. That is why this final chapter describes how teachers can continue to use the assessment process to improve their teaching and learning.

Foundational Questions for Your Consideration

- Do you think it is useful to constantly reevaluate what you do in the classroom or does such reflection intrude on your focus or make you insecure?
- Do you think students should be allowed to help teachers design and write assessments? Why or why not?
- Is it a good idea to invite students to critique an assessment that they have just completed? Why or why not?

Reflective Self-Assessment: The Heart of Exemplary Teaching and Learning

In this section, we describe a variety of perspectives for developing a self-assessment program. We also remind you of the importance of always linking assessment to your specific classroom setting. Finally, we clarify how you can incorporate self-assessment approaches as an integral part of your instructional practice.

Foundations as a Basis for Teacher Self-Assessment

Throughout this text we have anchored much of our thinking and writing in the foundations of educational assessment. As we discussed in Chapter 1, the *foundational approach* of this book threads philosophical, psychological, sociological, and historical perspectives in an effort to help you see assessment from a wider point of view. The term *foundations* has other connotations that go beyond examining ideas from different disciplines of study. It can also mean the examination of underlying principles or theoretical bases of ideas. Foundations can imply that you examine the assumptions and beliefs that underlie your ideas about the world. In this sense, the term *foundations* also suggests the use of *interpretive, normative,* and *critical* approaches to examine the things you do and the positions you take. These perspectives are especially powerful when it comes to developing a personal approach to self-assessment.

Using an **interpretive perspective** to develop a self-assessment approach to your teaching and assessment practices requires that you spend time analyzing the intent, meaning, and effect that your actions may have in diverse contexts. The concept of meaning is critical to this point of view. Meaning is the way a person sees something; meaning is ultimately personal interpretation. You cannot assume that because you use an educational approach that is meaningful to you that the same educational approach will be meaningful to the student, parent, or administrator. People interpret things differently based on their unique sets of experience, family background, culture, religion, and so on.

An assessment of the meaning you attach to your practice is important so that you can take steps to determine how you can communicate your interpretation to others. In addition, such an assessment of meaning implies you need to be a good listener and find ways to understand the meanings that others (parents, administrators, and students) attach to your practices. You may find that their meanings require you to change a well-intentioned educational practice. For example, it is possible to develop an interesting story or metaphor to explain a concept. However, without even knowing it, the story may contain images or character names or even activities that are unfamiliar to some students or have different connotations than you intend. So, the story line you constructed to make things clearer may interfere with students' ability to grasp the concept that you have in mind.

An Interpretive Self-Assessment Scenario   *After carefully designing a lesson aimed at introducing the concept of community helpers, Mr. Carl Ramirez asks his third-grade urban students to read a short story about a police officer who is called to save a cat caught in a tree. After safely bringing the cat down from the tree, the police officer brings the cat to animal control to verify its health and rabies status. At the end of the story, students are puzzled and concerned about the police officer taking the cat from its owner. Mr. Ramirez struggles to explain the importance of health and safety, but students simply do not seem to understand his logical explanation.*

This situation implies that the students' perspective about the police officer's action differs from Mr. Ramirez's perspective. Students interpret the police officer's removal of the cat from the owner (even though such removal is logical) as wrong or improper. Such an interpretation could come from their experiences in a neighborhood filled with crime and arrests. Perhaps some of the students have witnessed a family member taken away by a police officer.

What different meanings are students attaching to the police officer's actions? How might reflecting on the way students focused on the action of the police officer help Mr. Ramirez in re-assessing his use of the story?

Using a **normative perspective** to self-assess means that you regularly examine and explain your practices in light of your values, you probe the normative assumptions underlying educational thought and practice, and you encourage students to develop value positions on the basis of study and reflection. Everything you do, every educational practice you incorporate, and every assessment method you employ is steeped in beliefs, values, and norms. There is no such thing as objective or absolutely correct. Inevitably, the practices we develop and the educational programs we design are based on preexisting conceptions of truth and value. So, it is important to always examine and question the educational programs you use, as well as the textbooks and assessments that you purchase.

A Normative Self-Assessment Scenario   Ms. Shanika Robertson is enthusiastic about a schoolwide motivational program aimed at improved reading achievement. The program provides rewards to students who read and write reports about books they read over a month's time. Ms. Robertson introduces the program and incorporates it into her grading by giving extra credit to the top ten students.
   How do the perspectives of Ms. Robertson and the students differ? How would you describe their perspectives? What do these perspectives suggest to you about the different understandings of the situation? How might we understand the students' reaction as an example of difference in perspectives? How might a reflection on the values implicit in this reading achievement program affect Ms. Robertson's enthusiasm?

Using a **critical perspective** means that you employ democratic values to assess educational policies and practices in light of their effects. You identify contradictions and inconsistencies within social and educational practices and examine their underlying values. A critical approach implies that you have a responsibility, as teacher and assessor, not merely to understand what schools *are* doing but also what schools *ought to be* doing. You have the right and obligation as a participant in the profession to question policies and practices and to develop ideas and suggestions to improve the profession.

A Critical Self-Assessment Scenario   Ms. Riva Jones donates food on a regular basis to her school's outreach program designed to help poor families in the community. As a middle school teacher, she notices that, despite the school's efforts, many students come to class hungry. She speaks about her concerns with her principal but is told that there is only so much that can be done to help students with difficult problems like these.
   In what ways might a critical self-assessment influence Ms. Jones's response to the principal?

Assessment Standards for Teachers: A Basis for Self-Assessment

In 1990, as noted in Chapter 1, the American Federation of Teachers, the National Council on Measurement in Education, and the National Education Association published a set of standards for teacher competence in educational assessment. The standards organize the teacher's professional role and responsibilities into activities occurring before, during, and after classroom instruction. These roles and responsibilities provide an excellent set of questions that you can and should reflect on throughout your entire teaching career. We believe that these broad standards provide a basis for ongoing reflection and a useful starting place in the development of your self-assessment practice. The following is a set of questions, each of which relates to one of the seven standards:

- Is the assessment method that I intend to use appropriate for the type of instruction that I have planned?

- Does the assessment that I have designed really match the instruction that I have implemented?

- Have I carefully thought through the administration and context of the assessment environment? Have I thought through the scoring protocol so that I am focused on the specific instructional objectives of interest? Am I certain that my interpretation strategy is proper?

- How am I using assessment results to make decisions about individual students, to direct my teaching, to improve curriculum, and to make recommendations for school improvement?

- What types of cultural, physical, and mental considerations should I include when I am developing a specific assessment?

- How can I improve the ways that I communicate assessment results to my students, parents, educators, and other audiences?

- Are there any legal or ethical issues that I need to review in an effort to protect my students from harm?

In addition to building in a time and a place to regularly review each of these questions, you will always want to be on the lookout for new documents about the nature and proper use of assessment. One that you may want to consider is *Knowing What Students Know: The Science and Design of Educational Assessment*, released by a panel of experts through the National Research Council in 2001. Also, *The Student Evaluation Standards* published by the Joint Committee on Standards for Educational Evaluation (2003) provides a thoughtful set of statements that lend themselves to your self-assessment growth. (See Appendix B for a list of these standards.)

Student Motivation as a Basis for Ongoing, Reflective Self-Assessment

Educational psychology has a long history of inquiry into how people learn. In your preparation for a career in education, you will likely become familiar with such theories—cognitive constructivism, social constructivism, behaviorism, and many others. Often, however, teachers forget that these theories do not describe just the ways in which children learn but rather how we all learn. Further, the deeper you explore learning theories, the more you will find that although one theory may appear to contradict another, no single theory adequately explains all human learning. In fact you will probably find elements of all these theories in yourself and in your students.

The same holds true for ways in which we are motivated to learn. The various theories of motivation are beyond the scope of this book, but each of them explains in somewhat different terms why and how students are motivated to learn. Consider your experiences as a student. Why did you enjoy one subject more than another, say English over chemistry? Was it the subject itself that grabbed you? Was it a particular teacher who inspired you? Did your parents pursue careers in the field?

At the end of the day, how much do you know about your students? You will probably know who has been sick or whose parents are divorced or who have exceptional talents. And you will certainly know how well your students are performing in your class: A students, underachievers, college-bound, hard workers. But how often do we stop to think about *how* our students learn? Or why one student seems deeply engaged only when the subject is insects? To be fair to our students, when we administer an assessment of any type, shouldn't we take into account the many personal factors that surround the individual lives of our students?

Several years ago, a number of colleagues were invited to a two-day seminar conducted by an eminent thinker in the area of student learning and motivation. One invited guest, a teacher of a highly specialized branch of mathematics, declined the invitation and said, in effect, that if he did not even know how he himself learned, why should he be concerned with how his students learned? Think about how much more his students might have learned or perhaps how much more his students might have appreciated his perspective if only this professor had reflected on his own learning and on how his students encountered math in his class.

Using Formative Assessments as Opportunities for Self-Assessment

Throughout this text we have operated on two important assumptions: that teaching and learning are interactive and that assessment is the tool that

Resource for Your Assessment Toolkit

Students' Sociocultural Context as a Basis for Ongoing, Reflective Self-Assessment

Social context issues such as race, ethnicity, gender, and socioeconomic status provide a key perspective to guide your ongoing self-assessment. As a teacher, it is critical to carefully examine the sociocultural context in which your students live. The following questions are worth asking yourself on a regular basis:

- What are the specific characteristics of the environment in which my students live? Are there any school norms, traditions, or rituals that conflict with the social environment of the community?
- Do my expectations for student achievement and growth differ based on race, ethnicity or primary language? Do I think of students with low prior achievement as unable to learn?
- Does my behavior in any way indicate a lack of confidence in some students' ability to learn? If so, why?
- Do I carefully choose examples in my teaching and assessment that relate to the lives of students?
- Do I consider the economic requirements for completing homework assignments? Do I unintentionally give assignments that give an advantage to students with greater income and opportunity?

- Do I have expectations for parents that may be unrealistic given their educational backgrounds, opportunities, and time available?
- Do I inadvertently call on males more than females or vice versa? Do I challenge males more than I challenge females?
- Do I treat females differently than males in mathematics or science?
- Do I treat students with a special education designation in a way that implies that they cannot learn?
- What can I do differently to meet the various needs of my students?
- What can I do to improve school safety? How can I make my classroom a place where students are free to express themselves without fear of bullying or ridicule?
- In what ways can I involve parents in the academic development of their students? What barriers may make it difficult for parents to get involved and how can I overcome these barriers?

Sources: Colton & Sparks-Langer, 1993; Secada, 1992.

enables you to recognize what needs to be taught next and that enables students to recognize what they need to learn next.

As you teach, you need to know about the difficulties your students are having; and you need to know these difficulties *while* you are teaching, not just at the end of a unit of instruction. You will recognize that we are talking here about *formative* assessment, aimed at determining students' misunderstandings or learning gaps and what can be done next to help them learn. The careful use of formative assessments is a key opportunity for self-reflection and self-assessment of your instructional methods.

There is nothing new about the importance of formative assessment. Despite its obvious importance, however, there is a wealth of evidence that the everyday practice of assessment in the classroom is beset with shortcomings. Paul Black and Dylan William (1998) completed a major meta-analysis of research related to the use of assessment in public schools and concluded that three serious issues needed attention.

The Disconnect Between Assessment and Learning The first serious issue that the researchers identified regarding assessment practices was that there is a disconnect between assessment and intended learning. They describe this issue as follows:

- "The tests used by teachers encourage rote and superficial learning even when teachers say they want to develop deep understanding. Teachers do not seem to notice the inconsistency between what they measure and what they think they are measuring."

- "The assessment methods teachers use are not shared with other teachers in the same school, and there is little continuity in the assessment practices across grades or classrooms."

- "For primary teachers in particular, there is a tendency to emphasize quantity and presentation of work and to neglect comprehension and understanding."

These findings provide an excellent set of cautions for you to use as self-reflective prompts to develop better assessments. A specific assessment practice that you might consider is to encourage students, throughout the learning process, to participate in regular discussions about their understanding of the concept being taught. Listen carefully to the way students describe what they know and take good notes about the misconceptions students express. Then take action to help them overcome their specific difficulties.

Negative Impact and Assessment A second issue that plagues assessment practices is negative impact. Black and William describe the assessment weaknesses that cause negative impact as follows:

- "The grading function is overemphasized while providing useful advice and meaningful information to students about their progress and understanding is underemphasized."

- "Assessment methods that compare students in the class are used most frequently. Yet when teachers are asked about the purpose of such assessments, they state that individual development and improvement is their intended focus."

These findings also provide excellent cautions that you can use as part of your ongoing self-assessment program to help you develop assessments that have a positive rather than a negative impact on students. One way to avoid some of this negative impact is to provide written feedback on tests and quizzes rather than grades or percentages. Then allow students to use your feedback to prepare again and to retake the assessment.

Managerial Instead of Instructional Role A third issue of concern that Black and William uncovered relates to the managerial role of assessment. They found that teachers' feedback to pupils seems to serve a management function, often at the expense of the learning function.

- "Teachers often are able to predict students' results on external tests because their own tests imitate them, but at the same time the classroom tests do not uncover pupils' learning needs so that they can be remediated."

- "The collection of grades is given higher priority than the analysis of pupils' work to discern their learning needs."

Once again, we offer these compelling insights from research about teacher use of assessments, not to criticize, but rather to help you recognize potential pitfalls in using classroom assessment. Here is the critical point: The underlying component of each of the three findings is the use of assessment solely for evaluation at the end of the learning process, rather than as a formative component of teaching and learning.

Recall that assessment has many purposes, and only one of those purposes should be to make a judgment about students' work. There are many other purposes for assessments that relate to providing feedback that is informative, helpful, corrective, encouraging; these types of assessments do not require the use of a grade or percentage or a statement about whose work is best or whose work is worst. When such comparative judgments are removed from the assessment context, the assessments become formative rather than judgmental. We cannot emphasize strongly enough the benefits, for both teacher and student, of ongoing formative assessment as an integral component of the instructional cycle.

Ask Yourself

Recall an assessment that one of your teachers used to specifically help you understand what it is that you needed to learn rather than to provide you with a grade. What did the assessment look like? How did you feel when the teacher provided the feedback? Did you actually learn something new as a result of the experience or was there no follow-up? How often did you receive this type of formative assessment throughout your years as a student?

Helping Students Develop into Self-Assessors

Self-assessment does not belong exclusively to teachers. Self-assessment is an integral part of learning, and so it also belongs to students. In this section we describe ways that you can teach students to self-assess, to reflect on their thinking processes, and to develop probing self-questioning skills that will help them uncover problems, gaps, and confusions.

Helping Students Learn to Reflect

Of all the assessment techniques you are learning, the most important aspect of each one is to help students learn to reflect on their own learning. In this textbook, we have shown you how to develop an assessment that is valid and reliable. We have also emphasized, however, that having a valid and reliable assessment does not help the learner unless the learner understands the feedback from the assessment. Any effective assessment must be one in which students understand the results of the assessment in a way that helps them take action. The best way to make this happen is to provide opportunities for self-assessment and to specifically teach techniques for self-assessment. Just like any other skill, self-assessment must be taught. You will need to explain the vocabulary, teach the relevant skills, and give students opportunities to practice.

One key way to begin the process is to provide time for students to examine and accumulate evidence about something that they think they have learned. Students can learn a lot simply by being asked to support and find evidence for what they think they know. In the process of gathering evidence, students may uncover facts that conflict with what they think. This allows them to self-correct along the way. Students will also find out that, when they cannot find evidence for something they think they know, this aspect of their understanding should be called into question and re-examined. As a result, the simple use of an ongoing reflective assignment that requires students to support their understandings with evidence is a teaching method for developing self-reflection.

Another way to assist students in the development of self-reflection is through the use of portfolios. Asking students to create a portfolio of evidence that shows what they are learning and providing time each day to work on their portfolio and reflect on its contents build an opportunity for self-reflection into each school day. Some prompts that you could use to vary each day's reflection are

- Select something you wrote today with which you were not satisfied. Place it in your portfolio and describe what you think it is missing or what is wrong with it.

- Select something that you completed today that you are proud of and place it in your portfolio. List the strengths you see in this piece of work.

- Select a piece of work that was assigned that you could not complete. Show it to another student and ask the student to share his or her work on the same assignment. Write down what you learned from reviewing the other student's work.

- Select a piece of work and identify what help you need to make it better. What could I (your teacher) have done better today to improve your understanding?

- What did you learn today that changed your perspective or point of view or understanding about something?

Another way to assist students in the development of self-reflection is through the use of learning logs and journals, as we discussed in Chapter 8. Learning logs and reflective journals provide opportunities for students to reflect on their progress along the way.

Learning logs consist of short entries such as data tables, drawings and illustrations, lists of readings, unanswered questions, homework assignments, and so on. In general, learning logs are collections of information and questions related to different learning assignments or projects.

Reflective journals are usually written in narrative form and deal more with feelings, opinions, or personal experiences. They are often used to respond to pieces of literature or as a way of recording how a concept relates to one's personal life (Burke, 2005).

The key to using these logs and journals effectively is to develop specific questions that prompt students to use them in a reflective manner. For example, you might ask students to examine their data tables in light of specific criteria such as the precision of the recorded data, or the detail that was provided in a reading list, or the vocabulary and precision in which they formulated a question. Or you might ask students to share their reflective journals with a partner and then develop a comparison of the likenesses and differences between their experiences. The key is to provide time—for students to both record information in logs and journals and to evaluate the recordings in light of different, valued criteria.

These and other related questions can be helpful in assisting students to practice self-reflection on a regular basis. Keep in mind, however, that asking students to take part in these types of reflective activities is sometimes difficult. Students (and teachers too) will go to great lengths to maintain an internal sense of competence and to deny or fail to see flaws in their work (Covington, 1992). So you may need to provide lots of positive reinforcement to students when they admit some difficulty. You will also need to model the process yourself by self-reflecting on your performance as a teacher in front of students.

Another way to make self-reflection less threatening is to ask the whole class to collaborate as a team to compose a hypothetical self-reflection on a particular problem that you pose. The important thing is to make self-reflection safe and rewarding. The key is to remove grades and their judgmental atmosphere from the exercise.

Attributes of Good Self-Reflection

It is helpful to examine the characteristics of good self-reflection so that you can use them to determine if students are making progress in the development of this important disposition. Unfortunately, there is no unified list on which all theorists agree.

Perhaps the key to good self-reflection lies in a vision of a classroom of self-reflective learners. Imagine a classroom filled with students honestly sharing their confusions, making and defending judgments about their learning, and taking part in the assessment process itself.

There are many different specific attributes that are implicit in this vision of students taking an active role in the assessment process. For example, this vision suggests that students are taking charge of their learning and that the teacher has given students the right to do so. The image implies that the teacher takes time to allow studentms to express their needs and points of view and that students feel safe to make mistakes and to share their confusions. *This image implies that teaching is no longer limited to the teacher and that learning is no longer limited to the students.*

Remind yourself often of this picture and ask what can you can do to enable your students to take part in such a classroom setting. You can also invite your students to develop their own picture of what self-reflective learners do and involve them in discussions about the criteria or key elements that fit their views.

The work of Judith Arter and Vicki Spandel (1992) gives some additional ideas worth considering. These two theorists have developed several specific dimensions that they contend underlie effective self-assessment and reflection. You can use these dimensions to determine what skills you might teach your students.

- *Coverage.* Does the reflection address all the important indicators of learning that are part of the task? As you try to teach students what indicators and criteria are relevant, you could make a checklist and simply have students note whether their products have each of the indicators of learning. As students get better at recognizing which indicators and criteria are relevant, students can make their own checklists.

- *Accuracy.* Are students developing correct sense of their learning achievement and development? One technique to help students determine this is to have them compare their evaluation of themselves with your evaluation or with the evaluations of peers. Then, discuss the similarities and differences between the student's perspective and that of others.

- *Specificity.* Do students' reflections include clear examples to support the ideas that are expressed in their self-reflections? Once again, you could assess the specificity provided by each student and suggest what evidence or specificity is missing.

- *Integration.* Have students appropriately developed interpretations or conclusions about their achievement based on specific evidence? One way you could help students with this dimension is to work with them to be sure they understand how to draw an inference based on data.

- *Revelation.* Does self-reflection help students develop new insights about their learning? Since students may not have experience in developing insights, you could best help them by adding a new insight of your own and explaining how you arrived at that insight.

Teaching Students How to Describe Their Thinking (Metacognition)

As we have discussed earlier in this book, metacognition is the ability to describe the process of one's thinking with clarity and elaboration. This is not a simple skill. In fact, experts often have difficulty doing this because their understanding in their area of expertise—and the process by which they arrived at this knowledge and understanding—seems self-evident to them. The reason this happens to experts is that they have so internalized and applied their understanding and skills that they can no longer recall what their original confusions and difficulties were when they were still in the process of learning.

Describing what is going on in students' heads as they are learning is therefore a skill that must be learned. This skill of describing what one is thinking is not simple. As we have noted earlier (Covington, 1992), students are sometimes unwilling to say what they are thinking because they believe they have to be correct or they will receive a lower grade. So, they sometimes refuse to admit or recognize errors in their work. Students also may fear that if they identify errors or inefficiencies in their work, they will sound foolish. It is important to help students practice communicating their uncertainties and confusions in an environment that is safe and rewarding.

There is no magic formula for teaching metacognition. The key is to simply provide safe opportunities, in as many ways as you can, for students to show their thinking processes. Allow students to talk about their thinking, draw images of their thinking, use graphic organizers, write a list of their thinking, show how they are trying to solve a problem, discuss the questions they have, write a paragraph that describes their thinking, and so on.

In addition to providing multiple ways for students to show their thinking, have students listen to others describe their thinking. Then ask students to identify some technique that other person mentioned that they had never used in the past. Taking the time to describe one's thinking will

Digging Deeper
The Origins of the Term Metacognition

Known for their work in social cognitive development, John Flavell of Stanford University, wife Ellie Flavell and colleague Frances L. Greene coined the term *metacognition* and introduced the concept to the world of education by studying preschoolers' thinking skills in the 1970s at the Bing Nursery School on the Stanford campus. Their research led to their published works, including *Young Children's Knowledge about Thinking* (1997).

In their research, Flavell and his team found that preschoolers understand that thinking is a human, mental activity and that it can involve things that are in the past or in the present, real or imaginary. Even preschoolers can distinguish thinking from other activities such as talking, feeling, seeing, or knowing.

However, preschoolers greatly underestimate the amount that they and others think, and they have difficulty perceiving that other people think. Flavell found that preschoolers often know that rocks do not think, but preschoolers also often believe that their parents do not think very much. Flavell concludes that, because of this misconception about how much thinking is done by others, preschoolers do not fully develop their sense of self.

Metacognition includes knowledge and regulation of cognition. Knowledge about cognition consists of (1) *person variables*, that is, knowledge about one's self and others' thinking; (2) *task variables*—knowledge that different types of tasks exert different types of cognitive demands; and (3) *strategy variables*—knowledge about cognitive and metacognitive strategies for enhancing learning and performance.

in and of itself help students develop this skill. The following provide some other useful teaching strategies.

- Have students monitor their learning and thinking by pairing students for a learning task and assigning one student to act as the listener and the other student to think out loud throughout the assignment. Reverse the roles for another assignment.

- Have students make predictions about information to be presented next based on what they have read.

- Have students relate ideas to existing experiences and prior knowledge.

- Have students develop and ask questions of themselves about what is going on around them.

- Encourage students to know when to ask for help by modeling an example yourself.

- Show students how to transfer knowledge and skills to multiple situations by explicitly naming the skill or concept when you are applying it to a new situation or using it in a new way.

Resource for Your Assessment Toolkit
Developing Metacognition Through a Plan of Action

The North Central Regional Educational Laboratory (1995) has developed the following approach to teaching metacognition. In this approach they conceptualize metacognition as a series of steps focused on a plan of action. The steps are

- *Develop* a plan of action.
- *Maintain/monitor* the plan.
- *Evaluate* the plan.

They suggest that you explicitly tell students the names of each of these steps and that you let students know how important it is to make a plan of action related to their learning. They recommend that you provide the following questions as students move through the three key steps.

Before: When you are *developing* the plan of action, ask yourself,

- What in my prior knowledge will help me with this particular task?
- In what direction do I want my thinking to take me?
- What should I do first?

- Why am I reading this selection?
- How much time do I have to complete the task?

During: When you are *maintaining/monitoring* the plan of action, ask yourself,

- How am I doing?
- Am I on the right track?
- How should I proceed?
- What information is important to remember?
- Should I move in a different direction?
- Should I adjust the pace depending on the difficulty?
- What do I need to do if I do not understand?

After: When you are *evaluating* the plan of action, ask yourself,

- How well did I do?
- Did my particular course of thinking produce more or less than I had expected?
- What could I have done differently?
- How might I apply this line of thinking to other problems?
- Do I need to go back through the task to fill in any blanks in my understanding?

Teaching Students to Ask Probing Questions

David N. Perkins (1986, 1993) contends that one cannot ask a question unless one already knows something about the topic. He suggests that in order for students to uncover what they do *not* understand, they must first understand *something*. Real learning, according to Perkins, is *iterative*—that is, one first takes a stab at something, expresses some understanding, and begins to analyze what looks askew or what does not fit. The next step is to ask a question and get more information.

This use of questioning to gain new insights is what is meant by the term *probing questions*. How to formulate probing questions, just like any other skill, must be taught. It is not something one automatically knows how to do.

How can a teacher help students develop this important self-assessment skill? Here are some suggestions:

- Provide students with multiple opportunities to express what they know at this time. Have students try to create a visual graphic that shows what they know, share the graphic with others, and then ask others for feedback. Have students describe what they know using a graphic organizer that you have developed and see what they put in the various fields of the organizer. Then, again have them share their different graphics and allow students to change their graphic organizers after they have seen the work of other students.

- Model the use of probing questions by having students share their understandings with you in an interview setting. As you ask probing questions about their work, have students write down your questions. After the interview, have them try to answer the questions in writing and hand these written responses back to you. In this way students become familiar with this kind of question and over time learn to use similar questions on their own.

- Put a general probing question on the board each day and have students use that question throughout the learning activities of the day. Some of these general probing questions might be
  - What strengths do you see in your work and why do you think these are strengths?
  - What does not fit into your understanding about today's topic? In what way does it differ from the rest of your understanding?
  - Describe the steps that you used to answer today's assignment. What steps were necessary and what steps were unnecessary?

Developing a Disposition for Lifelong Learning Through Self-Assessment

Ultimately, we have tried to share a vision for assessment that shows you how essential this task is to the learning process. In the end, no one ever finishes learning and so no one ever finishes self-assessing. Remember the image of sitting beside a student and asking questions to learn what the student knows and can do? Now put yourself into *both* roles. In self-assessment, you are both the asker and the answerer, the teacher and the student. Ask yourself, "What is it that I know and can do?" And, just as important, "What else do I need to know and do?"

You have chosen a profession that is full of challenges and that, in turn, offers abundant rewards. Good teaching requires effort, enthusiasm, and a mind always open to better ways of approaching things. We wish you success in a life of continual questions and learning, for these are the heart of assessment.

?Ask Yourself

Many college students do not think that taking time to show one's thinking is useful. They often want to be given information and take tests rather than spend time talking about their ideas to others. Is it possible that we have consistently given students the impression that the only thing that counts in learning is the correct answer and that the process itself is irrelevant?

Summary

- Reflective self-assessment is essential to improving your teaching and learning.

- The foundations of educational assessment include philosophical, psychological, sociological, and historical perspectives. But the term *foundational* also suggests interpretive, normative, and critical approaches to self-assessment.

- Assessment standards for teachers that suggest actions before, during, and after classroom instruction can provide a good basis for your self-assessment practice.

- Reflecting on different notions of cognition—of what it means to know or understand something and of the various ways that individuals learn—can enrich your approach to both instruction and assessment.

- Ongoing self-assessment can increase your awareness of the uniqueness of each of your students and can help you find ways to encourage and support their learning.

- As a teacher, it is critical to keep in mind the sociocultural situation of your students. Self-reflection increases your sensitivity to these factors.

- Formative assessments are an essential tool for gauging where students are in the learning process and where they should go next. These assessments are equally valuable assessing teaching approaches and techniques.

- Self-assessment is not the sole province of teachers. It can and should be taught and fostered in students. The classroom can become a self-assessment laboratory where students explore how they learn and how to be better learners.

- According to Arter and Spandel, effective student self-assessment has the characteristics of adequate coverage, accuracy, specificity, integration, and revelation.

- Metacognition is the process of thinking about and describing the thinking process itself. Encouraging students to do this increases their self-reflection skills.

- Asking probing questions is an important self-assessment method; teaching students to formulate and use such questions will greatly increase their ability to assess their own progress.

Key Terms

critical perspective (460)

interpretive perspective (459)

normative perspective (460)

For Further Discussion

1. How can ongoing self-assessment improve your teaching skills?

2. What self-assessment practices can you see yourself incorporating into your teaching routine?

3. Can you remember being aware of any of your teachers actively assessing their teaching approaches and then self-correcting by changing an approach? Was that surprising to you or did it seem natural?

4. What student self-assessment practices can you see yourself implementing?

5. How might teaching and encouraging students to self-assess affect the learning process? The atmosphere in the classroom?

Comprehension Quiz

Rather than develop a comprehension assessment focused on your ability to restate the ideas of this chapter, we thought it appropriate to provide a metacognitive assessment that asks you to practice self-reflection. In this assessment we pose several self-reflective exercises that we hope relate to your life and experiences. They are designed to help you to assess your progress and make decisions concerning what it is you might want to learn next about the topic of assessment.

• Make a list of statements that represent what you really understand about assessment.

• Now, think about the type of classroom filled with students that you would like to work with once you complete your degree. Return to your list of statements and circle those that will be especially helpful in that classroom.

• Now consider what is missing on your list of understandings that will be critical to your work in your imaginary classroom. Make a list of things that you do not yet understand well but need to master for this classroom setting.

• Where can you get some more information about these critical issues, and what are some specific strategies that you can use to learn what you still need to know?

• How can you know that you are really learning? How can you spot errors if you make them? Consider the type of resources and tasks you will need to employ to help you monitor your learning.

• Now outline a personal plan to strengthen your understanding of the field of assessment.
  • Consider what you need to do first.
  • Develop a set of individual tasks and order them.
  • Estimate the time you will need to complete each task. Place this time allotment next to each task.
  • Target specific dates to complete each task.

Relevant Website Resources

Metacognition and Self-Talk

http://ozpk.tripod.com/0meta

The Teacher Development Network website offers a comprehensive list of links on metacognition. There are articles on what metacognition is and how to use it. This website is a good place to start your learning about metacognition.

Metacognition: What It Means and How to Use It

http://www.ncrel.org/sdrs/areas/issues/students/learning/lr1metn.htm

The website for Learning Points Associates provides a definition for metacognition and a clear description of a process to employ metacognition effectively.

Learning to Learn/Metacognition

http://www.studygs.net/metacognition.htm

Author Joe Landsberger has created this website titled Study Guides and Strategies. One of the study guides includes learning to learn, or metacognition. He offers questions to help the learner use the metacognitive process.

Examples of Prompts for Student Self-Reflection on a Course or Program

http://uwadmnweb.uwyo.edu/acadaffairs/assessment/Docs/Cap_12.doc

This document offers examples of student self-reflection concerning a course or program. Questions and reflective statements are provided for students to ponder and clarify their reflections and experiences.

Questions for Student Self-Reflection

http://oncampus.richmond.edu/~jbaker/documents/portfolioreflectionquestions.doc

This website provides another example of student self-reflection. This reflection is more focused on the student's assignment/project. Students are able to provide reflective thoughts and experiences.

Southern Illinois University, Edwardsville: Classroom Assessment Teaching Goals Inventory

http://www.siue.edu/~deder/assess/cats/tchgoals.html

SIU's Teaching Goals Inventory provides educators with a mechanism for self-reflections on teaching and ways to allow students to learn better. An inventory is available for educators to critique themselves. There is also a self-scoring guide with an explanation of what it means.

References

American Federation of Teachers, National Council on Measurement in Education, National Education Association. (1990). *Standards for teacher competence in educational assessment of students.* http://www.unl.edu/buros/article3.html.

Arter, J., & Spandel, V. (1992). Using portfolios of student work in instruction and assessment. *Educational Measurement: Issues and Practice, 11*(1), 36–44.

Black, P., & William, D. (1998). Inside the black box: Raising standards through classroom assessment. *Phi Delta Kappan, 79*(2), 139–148.

Burke, K. (2005). *How to assess authentic learning.* Thousand Oaks, CA: Corwin Press.

Colton, A. B. & Sparks-Langer, G. M. (1993). A conceptual framework to guide the development of teacher reflection and decision-making. *Journal of Teacher Education 44* (1), 45–54.

Covington, M. (1992). *Making the grade: A self-worth perspective on motivation and school reform.* New York: Cambridge University Press.

Flavell, J. H. (1994, January 1). Preschoolers don't think much about thinking. *Stanford News.*

Flavell, J. H., Green, F. L., & Flavell, E. R. (1995). Young children's knowledge about thinking. *Monographs of the Society for Research in Child Development, 60*(1), 1–96.

Flavell, J. H., Green, F. L., & Flavell, E. R. (1997). Development of children's awareness of their own thoughts. *Journal of Cognition and Development, 1,* 97.

Flavell, J. H., Green, F. L., & Flavell, E. R. (2000). *Young children's knowledge about thinking.* England: Blackwell.

Joint Committee on Standards for Educational Evaluation. (2003). *The student evaluations standards: How to improve evaluations of students.* Thousands Oaks, CA: Corwin Press.

National Research Council. (2001). *Knowing what students know: The science and design of educational assessment.* Committee on the Foundations of Assessment. M. Pelligrino, H. Chudowsky, & R. Glaser, eds. Board on Testing and Assessment, Center for Education. Division of Behavioral and Social Sciences and Education. Washington, DC: National Academy Press.

North Central Regional Educational Laboratory. (1995). *Strategic teaching and reading project guidebook.* Naperville, IL. http://www.ncrel.org.

Perkins, D. N. (1986). *Knowledge as design.* Hillsdale, NJ: Erlbaum.

Perkins, D. N. (1993). *Teaching for understanding. American Educator, 17*(3), 8, 28–35.

Secada, W. G. "Race, ethnicity, social class, language and achievement in mathematics." In Douglas A. Grouws (ed.) (1992). Handbook of research on mathematics teaching and learning. New York: Macmillan Publishing, pp. 623–660.

Appendix A

National Standards Groups and Publications

Civics Standards

Center for Civic Education (www.civiced.org)
National Standards for Civics and Government

Fine Arts Standards

Consortium of National Art Education Association (www.naea-reston.org)
National Standards for Art Education

Foreign Language Standards

American Council for Teachers of Foreign Language (www.actfl.org)
Standards for Foreign Language: Learning in the 21st Century

Geography Standards

National Geographic Society (www.nationalgeographic.org)
National Geography Standards

History Standards

National Center for History in the Schools (nchs.ucla.edu/standards)
National Standards for History

Language Arts Literacy Standards

National Council of Teachers of English (www.ncte.org)
National Reading Association (www.reading.org)
Standards for the English Language Arts

Mathematics Standards

National Council of Teachers of Mathematics (www.nctm.org)
Principles and Standards for School Mathematics

Science Standards

American Association for the Advancement of Science (www.aaas.org)
Benchmarks for Science Literacy
National Academies of Science: National Research Council (www.nrc.org)
National Science Standards

Social Science

National Council for the Social Studies (www.ncss.org)

Expectations of Excellence: Curriculum Standards for Social Studies

Physical Education and Health Education Standards

American Alliance for Health, Physical Education, Recreation, & Dance (www.aahperd.org)

National Health Standards

National Physical Education Standards in Action

National Standards for Dance Education

Appendix B

Student Evaluation Standards*

The Student Evaluation Standards presents and elaborates 28 standards for use in a variety of educational institutions. The standards provide guidelines for designing, implementing, assessing, and improving student evaluation. Each of the 28 standards has been placed in one of four essential categories to promote student evaluations that are proper, useful, feasible, and accurate.

- The *propriety* standards help ensure that student evaluations are conducted lawfully, ethically, and with regard to the rights of students and other persons affected by student evaluation.
- The *utility* standards promote the design and implementation of informative, timely, and useful student evaluations.
- The *feasibility* standards help ensure that student evaluations are practical; viable; cost-effective; and culturally, socially, and politically appropriate.
- The *accuracy* standards help ensure that student evaluations will provide sound, accurate, and credible information about student learning and performance.

Although intended for broad application, the primary focus of these standards is to promote sound, credible, and accurate evaluations that foster student learning and development at the classroom level. These standards are intended for teachers and others who evaluate students as well as those who use and are affected by student evaluations.

*Drawn from the Joint Committee on Standards for Educational Evaluation. 2003. *The Student Evaluation Standards.* Thousand Oaks, CA: Corwin Press.

Summary of the Student Evaluation Standards (2003)

Propriety Standards

The propriety standards help ensure that student evaluations will be conducted legally, ethically, and with due regard for the well-being of the students being evaluated and other people affected by the evaluation results. These standards are as follows:

P1: *Service to Students*   Evaluations of students should promote sound education principles, fulfillment of institutional missions, and effective student work, so that the educational needs of students are served.

P2: *Appropriate Policies and Procedures*   Written policies and procedures should be developed, implemented, and made available, so that evaluations are consistent, equitable, and fair.

P3: *Access to Evaluation Information*   Access to a student's evaluation information should be provided, but limited to the student and others with established legitimate permission to view the information, so that confidentiality is maintained and privacy protected.

P4: *Treatment of Students*   Students should be treated with respect in all aspects of the evaluation process, so that their dignity and opportunities for educational development are enhanced.

P5: *Rights of Students*   Evaluations of students should be consistent with applicable laws and basic principles of fairness and human rights, so that students' rights and welfare are protected.

P6: *Balanced Evaluation*   Evaluations of students should provide information that identifies both strengths and weaknesses, so that strengths can be built upon and problem areas addressed.

P7: *Conflict of Interest*   Conflicts of interest should be avoided, but if present should be dealt with openly and honestly, so that they do not compromise evaluation processes and results.

Utility Standards

The utility standards help ensure that student evaluations are useful. Useful student evaluations are informative, timely, and influential. Standards that support usefulness are as follows:

U1: *Constructive Orientation*   Student evaluations should be constructive, so that they result in educational decisions that are in the best interest of the student.

U2: *Defined Users and Uses*   The users and uses of a student evaluation should be specified, so that the evaluation appropriately contributes to student learning and development.

U3: *Information Scope*   The information collected for student evaluations should be carefully focused and sufficiently comprehensive, so that the evaluation questions can be fully answered and the needs of students addressed.

U4: *Evaluator Qualifications*   Teachers and others who evaluate students should have the necessary knowledge and skills, so that the evaluations are carried out competently, and the results can be used with confidence.

U5: *Explicit Values*   In planning and conducting student evaluations, teachers and others who evaluate students should identify and justify the values used to judge student performance, so that the bases for the evaluations are clear and defensible.

U6: *Effective Reporting*   Student evaluation reports should be clear, timely, accurate, and relevant, so that they are useful to students, their parents/guardians, and other legitimate users.

U7: *Follow-Up*   Student evaluations should include procedures for follow-up, so that students, parents/guardians, and other legitimate users can understand the information and take appropriate follow-up actions.

Feasibility Standards

The feasibility standards help ensure that student evaluations can be implemented as planned. Feasible evaluations are practical, diplomatic, and adequately supported. These standards are as follows:

F1: *Practical Orientation*   Student evaluation procedures should be practical, so that they produce the needed information in efficient, nondisruptive ways.

F2: *Political Viability*   Student evaluations should be planned and conducted with the anticipation of questions from students, their parents/guardians, and other legitimate users, so that their questions can be answered effectively and their cooperation obtained.

F3: *Evaluation Support*   Adequate time and resources should be provided for student evaluations, so that evaluations can be effectively planned and implemented, their results fully communicated, and appropriate follow-up activities identified.

Accuracy Standards

The accuracy standards help ensure that a student evaluation will produce sound information about a student's learning and performance. Sound information leads to valid interpretations, justifiable conclusions, and appropriate follow-up. These standards are as follows:

A1: *Validity Orientation*   Student evaluations should be developed and implemented so that the interpretations made about the performance of a student are valid and not open to misinterpretation.

A2: *Defined Expectations for Students*   The performance expectations for students should be clearly defined, so that evaluation results are defensible and meaningful.

A3: *Context Analysis*   Student and contextual variables that may influence performance should be identified and considered, so that a student's performance can be validly interpreted.

A4: *Documented Procedures*   The procedures for evaluating students, both planned and actual, should be described, so that the procedures can be explained and justified.

A5: *Defensible Information*   The adequacy of information gathered should be ensured so that good decisions are possible and can be defended and justified.

A6: *Reliable Information*   Evaluation procedures should be chosen or developed and implemented so that they provide reliable information for decisions about the performance of a student.

A7: *Bias Identification and Management*   Student evaluations should be free from bias, so that conclusions can be fair.

A8: *Handling Information and Quality Control*   The information collected, processed, and reported about students should be systematically reviewed, corrected as appropriate, and kept secure, so that accurate judgments can be made.

A9: *Analysis of Information*   Information collected for student evaluations should be systematically and accurately analyzed, so that the purposes of the evaluation are effectively achieved.

A10: *Justified Conclusions* The evaluative conclusions about student performance should be explicitly justified, so that students, their parents/ guardians, and others can have confidence in them.

A11: *Metaevaluation*   Student evaluation procedures should be examined periodically using these and other pertinent standards, so that mistakes are prevented or detected and promptly corrected, and sound student evaluation practices are developed over time.

Glossary

academic skills Observable and measurable performances students demonstrate in content areas such as reading, mathematics, science, social studies, language arts, and foreign language.

accommodations Test-taking practices designed to support students with special needs.

accountability Process of holding teachers and administrators responsible for helping students meet stated learning goals, usually measured by standardized, normed tests.

achievement gap Significant differences in measures of educational attainment among groups of students.

achievement test An assessment that measures students' accumulated knowledge in a particular discipline or skill.

adaptive technologies Hardware and software designed to enable use of technology by individuals with special needs. Also called *assistive technologies*.

analytic rubric A scoring guide that lists individually each aspect of knowledge or skill that is required in a piece of student work and the criteria for judging each aspect.

anecdotal note or record A factual description of an incident that the teacher personally observes in which the facts are recorded without an emotional accounting or evaluation.

aptitude test An assessment that measures a student's capacity to achieve or perform in certain areas.

artifact A piece of evidence that displays some valued skill, ability, knowledge, or approach; sometimes called a *folio*.

assessment A broad term that includes the practice of testing but also includes a variety of formal and informal methods of gathering information about student learning, understanding, and performance. It is the art of placing learners in a context that brings out or clarifies what a learner knows and can do, as well as what a learner may not know or be able to do.

assistive technologies See *adaptive technologies*.

asynchronous Events that are related but that occur at different times. In an asynchronous online discussion, for example, participants read previous entries and create their responses at their convenience.

authentic task A task that is similar to the activity that practicing professionals perform or that naturally occurs in a real-world context.

benchmark A specific expectation of student performance at a grade or grade span (for example, K–3 or 4–6); an intermediate level of standard in some states, used to define learning goals to be achieved by a particular grade or grade span.

benchmark or performance competency A specific accomplishment that shows progress toward a larger standard or goal.

big ideas or themes Large concepts that cut across many different disciplines and can be taught across a variety of grades.

bimodal The presence of two modes in a distribution of scores.

capstone performance A performance that occurs at the end of a program of study and enables students to show knowledge and skills in a context that matches the world of practicing professionals.

celebration portfolio An organized collection of evidence that shows students' favorite works or accomplishments.

central tendency A way of summarizing the typical performance in a set of assessment scores.

cognitive map   A set of abstract structures or big ideas (such as interaction, cause-effect, equilibrium, dissonance) that connects and organizes conceptual information.

completion item   A test question constructed of a sentence from which one or more words are missing. A blank line is inserted in the sentence, and the student is to write in the missing words at that point. Also called *fill-in-the-blank item*.

computer-assisted instruction (CAI)   Computer software designed to help learners master some discrete part of the curriculum.

computer-based testing   Assessment completed by the student at a computer, often with immediate feedback for each item as well as automatic scoring and record keeping.

constructed-response assessment   An assessment that requires students to use their own words to communicate a unique answer to a question.

content validity   The degree to which a test measures the multiple dimensions of the content it is intended to measure.

contract grading   A grading method in which a teacher and student set individual learning goals for the student and then develop a plan to determine the grade the student will receive for meeting the goals.

course management system (CMS)   A computer system that assists teachers in managing all aspects of instruction, such as Blackboard, WebCT, LiveText, and Moodle.

criterion-referenced grading   A method that grades student achievement by matching it to predefined standards set by the teacher, school district, state, or national groups.

criterion-referenced test   An assessment that measures a person's skill or understanding by comparing it to an established standard or criterion.

criterion validity   The degree to which a particular assessment correlates with another measure that would be expected to show similar outcomes.

critical perspective   Ongoing examination of one's educational practices in light of their effects on students' lives, by applying democratic values and goals as criteria.

demonstration task   A task that requires a student to explain, describe, or show how something works.

descriptive rating scale   A rating scale consisting of a series of adjectives or thumbnail sketches that portray degrees of progress toward a desired learning outcome.

descriptors   Explanatory words or phrases that specify the characteristics, attributes, or properties of a performance or product.

differentiation   Changing instruction to meet the academic needs of diverse learners.

disaggregation   Separating test score data into subcategories for purposes of comparison.

dispositions   Tendencies or habitual behaviors valued by society; for example, persistence and ability to work with others.

distracter   A plausible alternative to the correct answer in multiple-choice items.

dynamic assessment   An interactive approach to assessment focusing on the ability of the learner to improve his or her skills following specific intervention and rich interaction with a teacher.

English Language Learner (ELL)   A person in the United States who is learning English as a second language. Such a student is exceptional but not disabled.

enrichment   Adding deeper understanding by exploring the curriculum in greater depth.

e-portfolio   An electronic collection of samples of student work.

Equal Protection Clause   A clause in the Fourteenth Amendment to the U.S. Constitution that entitles similarly situated individuals to equal rights.

equivalent forms reliability   The degree to which two tests present students with items that are comparable in form, length, and difficulty. Equivalent forms reliability is more common in standardized testing, where tests often have two or more forms.

essay test   See *constructed-response assessment*.

establishment clause   A clause in the First Amendment to the U.S. Constitution that prohibits the government from "establishing" or endorsing a particular religion.

exhibit   A visual presentation or display that explains, demonstrates, or shows something in a way that needs little or no additional explanation from the creators.

fairness A quality that teachers aspire to by making their judgments of students impartial and free of bias.

Family Educational Rights and Privacy Act (FERPA) A federal law that protects the privacy of students' educational records.

feedback A verbal or written method to communicate assessment results to students in order to help them modify, correct, or strengthen their work.

fill-in-the-blank item See *completion item*.

flow A motivational state characterized by moments of optimal experience.

folio See *artifact*.

formative assessment Assessment aimed at determining students' misunderstandings or learning gaps and what can be done next to help them learn.

foundational approach The study of an idea through different perspectives drawn from philosophy, history, and the social sciences. Also, the critical, interpretive, and normative examination of assumptions and beliefs that underlie the idea being studied.

free exercise clause A clause in the First Amendment to the U.S. Constitution that prohibits the government from preventing individuals from freely participating in a religion of their own choosing.

frequency polygon A line graph representation of data, similar to a histogram, with the X-axis (horizontal axis) representing the distribution of assessment scores from lowest to highest, and the Y-axis (vertical axis) representing the frequency of each assessment score.

frequency table A representation of data in the form of a table, with the first column listing each possible assessment score from lowest to highest, and the second column listing the frequency of each possible assessment score (the number of times a score is earned).

generalized rubric A set of rules that specifies the criteria for judging large, important tasks as they would be by experts, such as a complex piece of writing or a scientific experiment.

giftedness In a school setting, evidence of outstanding capability in areas such as general intellectual ability, academic aptitude, visual and performing arts, or leadership capacity.

grade equivalent (GE) score A normative score that describes a student's level of performance in terms of a year and month in school. A grade equivalent score of 3.4 means performance representing the fourth month of third grade.

grading The process of holistically evaluating student performance and assigning a symbol to represent what a learner knows and can do, or may not know or be able to do.

growth portfolio An organized collection of evidence that displays a student's changes and accomplishments over time.

halo effect Allowing generally positive or generally negative feelings about a student to inappropriately affect the evaluation of a particular piece of a student's work.

high-stakes testing Any test for which there are significant consequences for the student, for the teacher, or for the school.

histogram A representation of data in the form of a bar graph, with the X-axis (horizontal axis) representing the distribution of assessment scores from lowest to highest, and the Y-axis (vertical axis) representing the frequency of each assessment score.

holistic rubric A scoring guide that focuses on scoring a performance as a whole based on an overall description, rather than specifying individual criteria separately.

indicator A behavior or performance that points to or indicates the presence of some larger trait or ability. For example, being able to answer questions about a reading passage is an indicator of reading comprehension. Some states also use this term as the name of their grade-specific learning outcomes within the state's standards.

Individualized Education Plan (IEP) The legally mandated plan to assure that each special needs student receives the most appropriate education possible.

Individuals with Disabilities Education Act (IDEA) A federal law that provides disabled students with the right to a free, appropriate public education.

innate Present in a person from birth.

inquiry task A type of performance task that requires students to collect their own data when learning about a topic or issue.

integrated learning system (ILS) A computer system designed to deliver instruction, assess learning, and remediate as needed, with little or no teacher involvement. Typically a combination of computer-assisted instruction, computer-based assessment, and intelligent tutoring system.

internal consistency reliability The degree to which an assessment appropriately focuses on just one concept or specific area.

interpretive perspective Ongoing examination of one's educational practices in light of the intent, meaning, and effect of one's actions.

inter-rater reliability The degree to which two or more scorers consistently rate the same student responses similarly, often used when scoring constructed responses or performances.

interviewing An interaction in which the teacher presents a student with a sequence of questions and listens to the responses, asks further questions, and records data.

item analysis A set of procedures, including *item difficulty* and *item discrimination*, that measure the quality of test items.

item difficulty An item analysis statistic that measures how difficult a test item is.

item discrimination An item analysis statistic that measures how well a test item differentiates between those who have a high level of achievement and those who have a low level of achievement.

journaling Maintaining a record of one's thoughts, reasoning, and/or activity to document learning in a qualitative manner and to provide additional insights.

journal portfolio An organized collection of student products that provides a structure for students to reflect on their work.

learning log A detailed record of experiences or events that relate to some inquiry or learning event; an ongoing record of observations, drawings, insights, charts, and tables students use to collect data during a performance assessment or other learning situation.

Lemon **test** A judicial test sometimes employed by courts to aid in determining whether a practice would violate the Establishment Clause.

logging Recording the path taken by a learner through electronic learning materials during computer-assisted instruction and the amount of time spent on each step.

mastery goal orientation An orientation characterized by a desire to learn for the sake of learning, to master new skills, to meet personally established goals, and to monitor one's own learning.

matching test Assessment that asks students to associate an item in one column with a closely related item from a second column.

mean A measure of central tendency; the arithmetic average of a set of assessment scores.

meaning making The natural process of the human brain to make sense of things based on one's experiences and personal point of view.

median A measure of central tendency; the middle score in a distribution of scores. Half of the scores are above the median, half are below the median.

metacognition Reflection on, awareness of, or analysis of the way that one understands an idea or event or the way that one processes information. Simply stated: thinking about one's own thinking.

mode A measure of central tendency; the most frequent score in a distribution of scores.

multimodal The presence of three or more modes in a distribution of scores.

multiple-choice test An assessment that presents a stem or question with usually three to four possible responses. The task of the test taker is to determine which of the options is correct or the best answer.

multiply focused and extended constructed-response items Questions that allow students to show their understanding of a concept, use their own wording, make some choices about how they will approach the responses, and then elaborate on their understanding in a way that demonstrates how they think about that concept.

multiply focused task A task that encompasses a variety of related tasks that work together as part of a larger action, such as solving a multipart problem or developing a position about a complex issue.

narrative evaluation A statement of a student's strengths and weaknesses related to learning goals, given by the teacher in written form, rather than simply as a grade or a numerical score.

National Assessment of Educational Progress (NAEP) A standardized test designed to assess the academic performance of children in public and private schools over time. It is given to a sample of schools across the United States.

negatively skewed distribution A distribution of scores that is distorted (pulled) lower because of low outliers (unusually low scores).

normal curve (normal distribution) A theoretical, mathematically derived frequency distribution of scores that is symmetrical, with the mean, median, and mode all the same score.

normative perspective Ongoing examination of one's educational practices in light of personal beliefs, values, and societal rules and expectations.

norm-referenced grading A method of assigning grades to students by comparing their achievement to the achievement of other students.

norm-referenced test A standardized test that provides normative scores and is developed and evaluated by experts to ensure that the test has appropriate reliability and validity.

normative scores Test scores that compare one student's performance with that of a norm group.

norms Statistics that summarize the performance of a large group of test-takers during the final stages of creating a norm-referenced test. These statistics are used as the basis of comparison when students later take the published norm-referenced test.

numerical rating scale A scale that associates numbers with descriptions along the scale; lower numbers indicate lower accomplishment, and higher numbers indicate higher accomplishment.

objective Fair to all students; free from personal feelings or prejudice; unbiased.

observation The act or practice of noting and recording facts and events; a direct means for learning about students, including what they do or do not know and can or cannot do.

observation checklist A clear and concise list of behaviors that is used when observing a student's skills and behavior.

observation validity The accuracy and completeness of information collected on a targeted behavior or skill.

offensiveness A quality of an assessment that creates a negative atmosphere for particular students because it upsets, distresses, or angers them.

outlier A score that is very different from the rest of the set of scores (either extremely high or extremely low).

pass/fail grading A system used in universities to encourage students to take more challenging courses or courses outside their majors, also used in early elementary school to avoid the emphasis on letter grades for younger students.

percent correct A score calculated by dividing the raw score (the number of items answered correctly) by the number of items on the test.

percentile rank The most typical normative, it gives a student's score based on the percentage of those who scored below that student.

performance-based assessment An assessment where students are placed in a particular context and asked to show what they know or can do within that context.

performance competency See *benchmark or performance competency.*

performance criteria A set of expectations or descriptors that provide directions for performing a task as well as guidelines for determining a student's score.

performance goal orientation An orientation characterized by a desire to learn and demonstrate a new skill for the sake of comparing oneself to others.

performance task An assigned task that permits students to show in front of an observer and/or audience both the processes they use and the products they create.

portfolio A purposeful organized collection of evidence (called *artifacts* or *folios*) that documents a person's knowledge, skills, abilities, or dispositions.

positively skewed distribution A distribution of scores that is distorted (pulled) higher because of high outliers (unusually high scores).

presentation task A task performed in front of an audience.

problem-based learning (PBL) An approach to learning and assessment that requires students to make sense of complex, ill-structured problems that come from real-life situations.

procedural due process The right given by the Fourteenth Amendment in the U.S. Constitution, which requires that before an individual's life, liberty, or property can be taken, the person must receive notice and some type of hearing.

process criteria Procedures used to create student grades that focus not only on the final examination scores or final products but also on how the students worked to achieve the final products.

process skills The skills and procedures used to create a product.

product criteria Measures used to create student grades that focus on final examination scores, final products, or other culminating demonstrations of learning.

product portfolio An organized collection of evidence that focuses on the end products of a completed project or task rather than on the process by which the product was developed.

progress criteria Measures used to create student grades that focus on how the students improved over time.

project portfolio An organized collection of evidence that shows both the steps and the results of a completed project or task.

prosocial skills Affective skills such as listening and cooperating that students need in order to interact with others appropriately in school or elsewhere.

psychological foundations A field that explores the theories and principles of how people learn and attempts to identify effective classroom practices through applications of those principles.

psychomotor skills Skills related to physical action such as playing sports, keyboarding, tying shoes.

Public Law 94-142, the Education for All Handicapped Children Act A federal law addressing the needs of disabled students; the precursor to the Individuals with Disabilities Education Act.

range A measure of variability; the difference between the highest score and lowest score in a distribution of score.

rating scale A list of descriptive adjectives or numbers for judging a product or a performance; the list is arranged from lowest to highest in quality.

rational basis test A test used by the courts to determine if the government is violating the U.S. Constitution by treating people differently for relatively inconsequential differences.

raw score The simplest method of indicating performance on an assessment, describing the performance by the number of items answered correctly.

reliability The degree to which assessment results are consistent across repeated administrations (*test-retest reliability*) or consistent no matter who collects the evidence (*inter-rater reliability*) or consistent in presenting students with items that are comparable in form, length, and difficulty (*equivalent forms reliability*).

Response to Intervention (RtI) An alternate way of identifying and serving students in need of special assistance. RtI is a multi-step problem-solving approach that involves the use of research-based alternative instructional methods for students experiencing academic or behavior problems.

rubric A guide that spells out the standards and criteria for scoring student work.

schemas Meaningful units within an expert's memory that allow the expert to quickly retrieve and use a large body of knowledge.

scoring guide See *rubric*.

Section 504 of the Rehabilitation Act of 1973 A federal law specifying that individuals with disabilities have the right to participate in and have access to the same programs, benefits, and services as non-disabled persons.

selected-response items An assessment in which students demonstrate their knowledge or understanding by choosing one of the responses that is offered as part of each question.

self-assessment Examining one's own actions and abilities in an effort to determine what one knows and can do as well as what one needs to know and do.

self-efficacy A feeling of competence to achieve a desired outcome within a particular context.

self-reflection Thinking about learning experiences and trying to make sense of them.

short-answer items Questions that ask students to supply a focused answer by constructing a response

singly focused constructed-response items Essay questions that allow students to use their own vocabulary but have a very narrow range of acceptable responses. There is one correct answer, but students may use different wording.

singly focused task A task that is restricted in scope, such as solving an equation or reading a paragraph.

skewed distribution A distribution of scores that is distorted (pulled) higher or lower due to the presence of outliers.

social learning theories Theories of human behavior that focus on the interaction between learners and their social environments, that is, the people around them.

standard A vision of excellence or a world-class performance or worthy achievement; broad large-scale learning objectives identified by each state for public school students to achieve; large learning goals and objectives identified by professional organizations for all students to achieve in their academic areas.

standard deviation A measure of variability; the average distance each score is from the mean of a distribution of scores.

standardized test A test that is administered and scored using a procedure that is the same for each test taker. Most standardized tests are norm-referenced tests.

standards-based portfolio An organized collection of evidence showing achievement as it relates to particular learning standards.

standards framework A description of how standards fit both larger learning goals and smaller benchmarks or performance competencies.

stanines Short for "standard nine," stanines indicate where student performance falls on a scale of 1 to 9; a type of normative score.

state actor Any individual employed by and acting on behalf of the state or federal government. Teachers are state actors in this legal sense.

stereotypes Images that conform to a fixed or general pattern and are held in common by a group; often simplified, prejudiced, and/or uncritical.

strict scrutiny test A test used by the courts to determine if the government is violating the U.S. Constitution by treating people differently based on certain characteristics that historically have been the subject of discrimination, such as treating African American and Caucasian students differently.

standards-based report card A report card that describes a student's progress toward meeting specific educational standards that are listed on the report card.

structured interviews Interviews in which the teacher prepares written questions in advance and standardizes the procedure by using the same directions and materials for all students.

student-led conference A conference that students conduct with peers, teacher, or parents to discuss their understanding of key concepts in their work samples and portfolios, reflect on their learning, and set new learning goals.

student response system (SRS) A hardware and software system that provides each student with a "clicker" or response device that resembles a remote control. The teacher's computer runs the software that receives responses entered by students using their clickers. The software tallies and records the responses, allowing the teaching to monitor the performance of all students rather than only those who respond verbally in class.

substantive due process The right given by the Fourteenth Amendment of the U.S. Constitution requiring that the actions of *state actors* be fair before an individual's life, liberty, or property may be taken.

summative assessment Evidence that is collected to show what a learner knows and is able to do at the end of a learning period.

synchronous Occurring at the same time, in real time; a form of online discussion that requires participants to be at computers at the same time.

tablet PC A notebook computer with which the user may interact by writing, drawing, and tapping directly on the screen with a stylus, in addition to normal use of its keyboard.

template A document, such as a word processor document, that provides the structure for the student to add desired text.

testing An assessment by which educators evaluate students' knowledge or skills by their performance on a particular instrument or task. In general tests are intended to serve as objective measures of learning.

test-retest reliability The degree to which a test consistently yields the same result, determined by administering the same test to the same group of students at two different times and then comparing the scores on the first and second testing. Comparable scores between the two testings indicate stability over time.

thinking strategies or tactics Sets of thinking skills that are used together, such as a logical sequence used when conducting experimentation, a set of steps used to write a paper, or an appropriate method used for solving an ill-structured problem.

true-false test An assessment that presents a statement or proposition for which the test taker must determine which of two options (usually true or false) is correct. Also called an alternative response or binary choice test.

unfair penalization Occurs when the content of an assessment disadvantages students because it makes it difficult for some groups of students to do well, unrelated to their true ability and knowledge in the area being assessed.

unpacking the standard Breaking the larger goals and standards of the curriculum into the key ideas and skills stated in the standard.

unstructured interviews Interviews in which the teacher asks students questions that occur naturally in a conversation and that evolve depending upon students' responses to the questions.

validity The extent to which an assessment clearly relates to and measures what it is that we are trying to assess, including the degree to which a test measures the multiple dimensions of the content it is intended to measure (*content validity*), the degree to which a particular assessment is correlated with another measure that would be expected to show similar outcomes (*criterion validity*), and the accuracy and completeness of information collected on a targeted behavior or skill (*observation validity*).

WebQuery An inquiry in which learners find and collect evidence primarily drawn from resources available on the Internet; may be teacher-created or a constructivist learning activity for students.

zone of proximal development The range of skills that exist between what a learner can do independently and with the support of a teacher or other skilled person.

Comprehension Quiz Answer Key

Chapter 1

Part One

1. d

2. b, c

3. e

4. a

Part Two

1. a

2. a, b

3. b, c

Chapter 2

1. Educational testing is one type of assessment. It takes place in a structured environment, is administered in a standardized way, and is designed to produce a particular kind of score. Educational assessment, the broader term, is any planned method of gathering useful information about a person's learning, whether it be skills and knowledge already attained or a readiness to learn.

2. Assessments must be administered at critical developmental ages. A student's readiness for a greater level of complexity in problem solving and conceptual understanding can be gauged with indicators such as observation, interviews, and classroom performance. Differences in developmental ability call for differing assessments.

3. A student's single test score is insufficient for a teacher to "size up" the student. The teacher will need to sit individually with that student, asking questions and observing the student work on relevant tasks. By determining the student's zone of proximal development, the teacher will be in a position to appropriately prepare instruction with that student.

4. Goal orientation consists of performance goal orientation, a learner's inclination to learn and demonstrate a new skill in comparison to others' skills and mastery goal orientation, and a desire to learn for the sake of learning. Self-efficacy constitutes one's feeling of competence to achieve a desired outcome. Flow represents a learner's moments of optimal experience.

5. Various aspects of motivation have an impact on student learning and performance in the classroom. It is useful to know a student's interests, goal orientation, and perceived self-efficacy in preparing to teach the student most effectively.

Chapter 3

1. IQ tests, test formats, norming, and viewing tests as fair and equitable means of understanding student ability are some of the trends that have roots in the early twentieth century.

2. Gender issues related to abuse and health negatively affect the academic achievement of females, as well as biases and stereotypes that prohibit females from taking courses and excelling in challenging classes in math, science, and technology.

3. Possible answers include: Curriculum, academic knowledge and skills of teachers, teacher experience and attendance, class size, technology-assisted instruction, and school safety. Students from lower socioeconomic and diverse backgrounds have fared worse than other students on these factors, thus disadvantaging them in academic arenas.

4. Classroom teachers can avoid bias in assessments by consciously working to ensure that assessments do not include stereotypes, offensiveness, or unfair penalization. These attributes could jeopardize the validity of the assessments.

5. Pros include (1) the inclusion of all students, especially English language learners and students with disabilities, in accountability systems, and (2) the requirement for disaggregated data, so that the scores of students who are disadvantaged can be clearly identified. The cons include (1) unfairly labeling schools as failures, even when progress is being made, (2) limiting of the curriculum to tested subjects and areas, (3) pushing students out of school in an effort to meet AYP.

Chapter 4

Part One

1. c	**2.** b
3. a	**4.** b

Part Two

1. b
2. a
3. c

Chapter 5

1. • Stem is grammatically incorrect (comma splice).
  • Stem asks about major viewpoints, but the answers are the theorists.
  • Freud is in three of the answers, so if students recognize that he is not a cognitive theorist, it only leaves one possible answer.

There are two major viewpoints about children's cognitive development embraced by educators today. Which two psychologists embody these viewpoints?

  a. Piaget and Vygotsky
  b. Erickson and Piaget
  c. Skinner and Vygotsky
  d. Piaget and Skinner

2. • Answers are punctuated as sentences but are awkwardly worded fragments.
  • "Making" is misspelled. (d)
  • "Person" should be possessive. (a)
  • "Characteristics" is not grammatical. (a)
  • The definition should probably be in the stem, with four different concepts listed as answers.

Temperament is generally defined as

  a. a person's distinctive thoughts and beliefs about the world.
  b. an individual's way of adapting to the world.
  c. an individual's ability to solve personal problems and make decisions.
  d. a person's behavioral style and characteristic ways of responding.

3. • Stem is awkwardly stated. Try reading it aloud.
  • Answers a, b, and c are also punctuated as sentences but are fragments.

Early-maturing girls differ in some ways from late-maturing girls. Which of these is one way that they differ?

  a. probability of developing an eating disorder
  b. age at beginning to date

     c. level of interest in school activities

     d. probability of developing depression in adolescence

4. The question as worded is probably acceptable, but this question demonstrates the common, limited use of a true-false item. The writer simply inserted B. F. Skinner for Pavlov to make the item false. The writer might have instead written a question that assesses students' understanding of behaviorism, such as the difference between classical and operant conditioning.

True or False:

A cat running into the kitchen when someone in the kitchen uses the electric can opener is an example of operant conditioning.

5. This is a proposition that is so large that it can be reasonably justified as true or false from a variety of perspectives. Think about B. F. Skinner above and how you might instead ask a question about the nature of learning.

True or False:

According to B. F. Skinner, learning is best assessed through direct observations of behavior.

Chapter 6

There is no single correct response to the Comprehension Quiz, so we will present a possible revision of the question with criteria that, if this were an actual essay question, you might choose to include in your assessment of student responses.

As you develop your scoring guide to assess the responses, you should take into account the relative weight of each of the criteria that you identify as being important to a constructed response.

Revised Question 1 Compare the developmental theories of Jean Piaget and Lev Vygotsky, showing key similarities and differences. Using a fifth-grade mathematics class as an example, how might these two theorists interpret differently the difficulties a student is having with the concept of fractions?

Criteria that might be used in scoring guide:

- Appropriate evidence of similarities between Piaget and Vygotsky
- Appropriate evidence of differences between Piaget and Vygotsky
- Proper transfer of understanding of theories to student's difficulty with mathematics

Revised Question 2 Darwin's theory of natural selection has had an impact on disciplines beyond biology. Select one discipline (psychology, for example) and identify three ways in which Darwin's ideas have influenced thinking in the field.

Criteria that might be used in scoring guide:

- Equal weight should be assigned to the identification of each of the five responses.

Revised Question 3   This question has two parts. First, I would like you to take the perspective of the president of the United States and enumerate the reasons for and the reasons against involving the United States in the Vietnam conflict. Second, taking the point of view of a historian, evaluate the social, political, and economic consequences of the decision to become involved.

Criteria that might be used in scoring guide:

- Evidence for becoming involved in the Vietnam conflict
- Evidence against involvement
- Evidence of understanding of the social, political, and economic consequences of involvement

Chapter 7

1. This is an emotional response rather than a record of observable, measurable behaviors. The teacher needs to use data from other assessments to make a valid assessment of the student's skills. A better anecdotal record might read as follows:

   Juanita has not answered any math problems correctly. She consistently reversed numbers. She also stopped after attempting four of the computation problems. I tried to assist her when I noticed she stopped, but she did not respond to my prompts. I will set up an interview with her so that I find out more about her mathematics difficulties.

2. This checklist lists skills not directly observable in the classroom (1, 2, and 6). It also lists a skill not related to reading comprehension (8).

3. No value has been assigned to the number categories: is "1" most desired or least desired? Too many behaviors are listed for one observation. Several points are not observable or measurable (8, 10, and 12). Many points need further qualification (3, 4, 7, 13, and 14).

Chapter 8

1. Performance assessments are easier to score than paper-and-pencil assessments. *False.* Reasons: Performance assessments require the development of scoring tools that are more complex than simply

indicating that a question is correct or not as with paper-and-pencil assessments.

2. Performance assessments target complex tasks that require higher-order thinking skills. *True.* Reasons: As soon as you attempt to complete a task that includes a process and a product, there is an automatic opportunity to display higher levels of thinking. The very act of making a decision, or developing a product on your own, or developing a position engenders more advanced thinking

3. Checklists can be used at regular intervals to evaluate a student's progress toward completing a performance task. *True.* Reasons: Checklists provide a convenient method of recording data about specific aspects of learning across multiple tasks. These types of scoring tools provide an efficient way of recording data and specifying these data points across different time intervals.

4. Performance tasks simulate real-life experiences. *True.* Reasons: One of the important characteristics of performance tasks is their authenticity. The tasks should be closely related to the real-life experiences that students and adults encounter every day. These realistic experiences require decision making, problem solving, and creativity.

Chapter 9

Part One

1. S
2. C
3. G

Part Two

1. A
2. A
3. A
4. D
5. A
6. D

Part Three

1. A
2. G
3. A
4. H

Chapter 10

Case Study 1

Although answers will vary, the underlying rationale for determining what goes into the grade should be primarily based on the intended learning outcomes and the clear connection between those outcomes and the assessment pieces that relate to the outcomes. Weighting the four assessment pieces in light of importance and difficulty is another component of the underlying rationale. For example, it is appropriate to give more weight to the final, multiple-choice examination and performance assessment than to the quizzes. Finally, the rationale should reflect an awareness that homework assignments should not be counted heavily in the final grade. Homework is often considered practice, and there is no clear evidence that the homework was completed by the student.

Case Study 2

Things you should consider when you determine these students' grades:

1. Jody's scores were improving for each writing assignment. She started with a score of 50 percent (usually an F) for her first narrative paper and progressed to a score of 85 percent (usually a B) for her final research paper. Since many educators feel the later grades should be weighted more than the earlier grades to reflect academic achievement, Jody could receive a B for the final marking period. The F she received on the original short story, however, will pull down her average considerably. We recommend that you penalize Jody's cheating with the use of detentions, referrals to administrators, referral to an honors court, conferences with the counselors and parents, removal of privileges, or your refusal to provide letters of recommendation for honor societies, awards, or college scholarships. Despite her lapse in judgment, Jody should have to write the story before school, during lunch, or after school in your presence because her final grade should reflect her mastery of language arts.

2. Kevin started off the course earning a 95 percent on his first narrative paper and an 85 percent on his informative paper. He was on track to earn a B+ or possibly an A for the course. By receiving a zero on his persuasive paper, however, his average plummeted from 90 percent or a low A to 60 percent or an F. First, you need to talk to Kevin to find out the circumstances surrounding his not turning in the persuasive paper. He may be experiencing personal problems or may have lost

some interest in doing a good job on his later papers because he realized the one mistake—his zero—would cause his course average to go down, despite his best efforts on subsequent papers. Kevin should also be permitted to submit a make-up persuasive essay since it is a major requirement of all state standards. You also might consider allowing all students to either drop their lowest grade or rewrite papers on which they received low scores to see if they can improve their writing skills.

3. Juan started poorly with a 50 percent on his first paper but through hard work on his part, he gradually improved his writing on each assignment. By the last assignment, Juan had improved from an F grade to a strong C. According to many educators, you should weight the later grades more heavily than the earlier grades to show progress and improvement over time. Another equitable method to justify giving Juan a higher grade than a C would be to allow him to use his constantly improving mastery of the writing standards to rewrite his earlier papers. If he re-submitted the first few papers, you could be more comfortable re-averaging his grade based upon his most recent work because they most accurately reflect his mastery of writing skills at the end of the course. Be careful, however, not to inflate Juan's grade based solely on his effort, progress, or process, since the final grade should reflect his academic achievement related to the course goals and standards.

Chapter 11

1. The mean of 40 would tell you that overall the class performed fairly well on the test. The score of 40 suggests that, on average, students answered about 80 percent of the items correctly. Other information about variability (SD) or item difficulty would give us a more complete picture, however.

2. The class with the standard deviation of 10 shows more variability of scores, and the class with the SD of 5 suggests that the scores are more closely clustered around the mean score of the class.

3. This indicates item difficulty. It would tell us how students performed overall on a single item. In this case, we might infer either that the item was too easy or that students truly understood that particular concept well. We would want to look at item difficulty on other items covering the same concept.

4. The mean is the measure of control tendency most influenced by outliers. The median is much less influenced by a few extremely high or extremely low scores than the mean. The mode is unaffected by the presence of a few high or low scores.

Chapter 12

1. a. norm-referenced

   b. criterion-referenced

   c. criterion-referenced

   d. criterion-referenced

2. a. Stanine: Indicates where student performance falls on a scale of 1 to 9, with 1 being in the lowest range and 9 being the highest. An average score would fall in the 4, 5, 6 range.

   b. Percentile rank: Reports a student's performance as a percentage relative to all other test takers. For example, a score at the 75th percentile means that a student performed better than 75 percent of the test takers.

   c. Grade equivalent: Communicates a level of performance relative to test takers in the same month and grade in school.

   d. Raw score: Indicates the number of correctly answered items.

   e. Percentage: Indicates the number of correctly scored items divided by the total possible multiplied by 100.

3. • Stanines are easy to interpret and communicate a student's relative performance, but they are not precise measures for comparison.

   • Percentile rank is a more precise indicator than stanines in that it communicates in percentages how a student performed relative to all test takers.

   • Grade equivalent communicates how a student performs with respect to year and month in school, but it is also easy to misinterpret in that it does not imply that a student is necessarily ready for work at the grade level indicated in the GE score.

   • Raw scores are not as helpful as percentage correct, but for both it is imperative to know what the highest possible score on a particular assessment is.

4. • Communicate to students why they will be taking the test and what the results can mean to them.

   • Prepare students for the types of items that they will encounter on the test and the organization and format of the test.

   • As a regular practice, provide students with prompt and constructive feedback on tests so that they make the exercise part of their reflective learning.

5. a. The student performed better than 74 percent of students who took the same test.

    b. The student performed on the test at a level that one would expect an eighth-grader in the seventh month of school to perform on the same test.

    c. This represents an "average" score, but with 4, 5, 6 considered average in the stanine range of 1–9, it is probably on the lower end of students who scored roughly in the middle third.

Chapter 13

1. False. Not only *may* special education students be tested, NCLB *requires* that members of this subgroup be tested.

2. True. As long as the questions are pedagogically related to the curriculum and they are presented in a nonproselytizing manner, assessments may include factual questions about religion.

3. False. While NCLB does require states to use standardized tests to assess students, there is no requirement that states require students to pass a high-stakes assessment in order to receive a high school diploma.

4. False. Directory information such as telephone numbers, addresses, and so on is not considered to be an educational record covered under FERPA.

5. False. Student performance can be taken into account for both teacher tenure/promotion and merit pay decisions.

6. True. State requirements vary, but all have some form of preservice teacher qualifying test.

7. False. Each state individually determines AYP benchmark scores. The same is true for the assessment used: Each state is free to select whichever one(s) they choose.

8. True. The Fourteenth Amendment also provides students with equal protection rights.

9. True. In addition to publishing general results, the scores of four different subgroups must be separately reported.

10. True. For example, Title I schools that fail to make AYP for a series of consecutive years can be required to offer tutoring services (paid for by the district).

Chapter 14

1. a. below average IQ: a, c, e, f, g, j

    b. poor auditory perception: c, d, h

    c. time constraints: a, j, k

    d. limited English proficiency: a, c, d, e, f, g, j

    e. poor visual perception: a, d, e, f, g, i, j

    f. anxiety: a, b, e, f, h, j, k

2. Mr. Ortiz correctly: provided examples of question formats; provided sample test questions; provided a separate set of directions for students with special needs; underlined key words where deemed appropriate; and kept the testing area quiet by placing a sign on the door.

    Mr. Ortiz failed to provide assessment accommodations by: overwhelming students by putting so many test questions on a page; setting a time limit for the test; and not permitting questions during the test at all.

3. Ms. Jackson observed some of Renee's behaviors, such as being distracted easily and not completing assignments, that alerted her to the possibility of Renee having a learning disability. Ms. Jackson properly followed the steps of documenting test scores; however, there is *not* an indication of ongoing documentation of Renee's other achievement information or other related classroom behaviors. Also, Ms. Jackson did not make special efforts to help Renee prior to the referral. In addition, there is no reference to Renee's standardized test scores or to conferences with Renee's parents. All of these steps need to be followed *prior* to a referral for identification of a learning disability.

4. a. PBA

    b. DA

    c. PBA

    d. PBA

    e. DA

    f. DA

5. Setting

- Can the student take the test in the same way as it is administered to the other students?
- Can the student focus on the task at hand with other students present?
- Are there other distractions that prevent the student from completing the assessment?

Presentation

- Can the student read?
- Can the student see and hear?
- Can the student understand English at grade level?

Timing

- Is the student able to work continuously for the length of time that the test is typically administered?

- Do the accommodations or special devices the student is using require extra time in order for the student to complete the test?

Response

- Can the student manipulate a writing instrument?
- Can the student follow from a test to a test-response form?
- Can the student speak or write English as needed?

Scheduling

- Does the student experience excessive anxiety during a certain content-area test? If so, should that test be administered when the assessments for all of the other content areas have been completed?
- If the student takes a medication that wears off over time and testing is scheduled during that time, should testing occur at a more optimal time of the day?

Other

- Is the student equipped with the necessary test-taking skills?
- Is this assessment the first time the student will be taking a formal district or state test?

Chapter 15

This quiz is good for leading to discussion. Many different answers are possible.

Suggested Answers

1. i, l, n
2. b, c, f, g, k
3. a, b, g, h
4. a, b, g, k
5. g, h, i
6. b, f
7. e, i, k, m
8. b, g, j
9. a, e, m

Chapter 16

Answers will vary.

Credits

Text and Art Credits

p. 12, Resource for Your Assessment Toolkit: From *"Standards for Teacher Competence in Educational Assessment of Students"* developed by the American Federation of Teachers, the National Council on Measurement in Education, and the National Education Association. Used with permission. **p. 15**, Figure 1.2: From *Critical Thinking: A Statement of Expert Consensus for Purposes of Educational Assessment and Instruction,* (1990), p. 25, by Peter Facione, Insight Assessment. Used with permission. **p. 32**, Figure 2.1: From Ormrod, Jeanne Ellis, *Human Learning*, 5th Edition, ©, Pg. 309–318. Reprinted by permission of Pearson Education, Inc., Upper Saddle River, NJ. **p. 40,** Resource for Your Assessment Toolkit: *Teaching and Teacher Education* by Megan Tschannen-Moran and Anita Woolfook Hoy. Copyright 2001 by Elsevier Science & Technology Journals in the format Textbook via Copyright Clearance Center; and, Perez, E. & Baltramino, C. (2001), Multiple Intelligences Self-efficacy Inventory: Development and Validation. *Revista Iberoamericana de Diagnostico y Evaluacion Psicologica*, 12(2), pp 43–55. Used with permission. **p. 78**, Figure 4.1: From *Frames of Mind* by Howard Gardner © 1993. Reprinted by permission of Basic Books, a member of Perseus Books Group. **p. 82**, Resource for Your Assessment Toolkit: From *Knowing What Students Know: The Science and Design of Educational Assessment* by Committee of Foundations of Assessment. Copyright 2001

by National Academies Press. Reproduced with permission of National Academies Press in the format Textbook via Copyright Clearance Center. **pp. 85–87**, Resource for Your Assessment Toolkit: Adapted with permission from a presentation by Robert J. Marzano, McREL Institute. Copyright © 1995. All rights reserved. **p. 170**, Figure 7.2: From *Standards to Rubrics in Six Steps: Tools for Assessing Student Learning, K–8* (Hard) by Burke, K. Copyright © 2006 by Sage Publications Inc. Books. Reproduced with permission of Sage Publications Inc. Books in the format Textbook via Copyright Clearance Center. **p. 183**, Figure 7.10: From *What To Do With The Kid Who—* by Burke, K. Copyright © 2008 by Sage Publications Inc. Books. Reproduced with permission of Sage Publications Inc. Books in the format Textbook via Copyright Clearance Center. **p. 185**, Figure 7.11: From *How To Assess Authentic Learning* by Burke, K. Copyright © 2005 by Sage Publications Inc. Books. Reproduced with permission of Sage Publications Inc. Books in the format Textbook via Copyright Clearance Center. **p. 211**, Figure 8.3: From Grant Wiggins, Authentic Education. Used with permission. **p. 220–221**, quote: *Integrating Science with Mathematics & Literacy: New Visions for Learning and Assessment* by Hammerman & Musial, Copyright 2008 by Sage Publications Inc Books. Reproduced with permission of Sage Publications Inc Books in the format Textbook via Copyright Clearance Center. **p. 222**, Resource for Your Assessment Toolkit: The activities in this performance assessment are based on an activity called *The Big Banana Peel!* Developed by the AIMS Education Foundation (www.aimsedu.org). **p. 224,** Figure 8.9: From *Standards to Rubrics in Six Steps: Tools for Assessing Student Learning, K–8* (Hard) by Burke, K. Copyright © 2006 by Sage Publications Inc. Books. Reproduced with permission of Sage Publications Inc. Books in the format Textbook via Copyright Clearance Center. **p. 226**, Figure 8.10: From *How to Assess Authentic Learning* by Burke, K. Copyright © 2005 by Sage Publications Inc. Books. Reproduced with permission of Sage Publications Inc. Books in the format Textbook via Copyright Clearance Center. **p. 252,** Figure 9.2: From *Educative Assessment* by Grant Wiggins, Copyright © 1998. Reprinted with permission from John Wiley & Sons, Inc. **pp. 255–256,** Figure 9.4: *Integrating Science with Mathematics & Literacy: New Visions for Learning and Assessment* by Hammerman & Musial, Copyright 2007 by Sage Publications Inc Books. Reproduced with permission of Sage Publications Inc Books in the format Textbook via Copyright Clearance Center. **p. 258**, Figure 9.6: 2000–2007 Copyright © ALTEC at the University of Kansas. Development of this educational resource was supported, in part, by the US Department of Education award #R302A000015 to ALTEC (Advanced Learning Technologies in Education Consortia) at the University of Kansas. **p. 261**, Figure 9.8: Copyright © 1997–2008, Illinois State Board of Education, reprinted by permission. All rights reserved. **p. 262**, Resource for Your Assessment Toolkit: Copyright © 2000, Chicago Board of Education, reprinted by permission. All rights reserved. **p. 270**, excerpt: From *Developing Grading and Reporting Systems for Student Learning* by Guskey and Bailey. Copyright © 2001 by Sage Publications Inc. Books. Reproduced with permission of Sage Publications Inc. Books in the format Textbook via Copyright Clearance Center. **p. 282**, Resource for Your Assessment Toolkit: Adapted from Frisbie, D.A. & Waltman, K.K. *Developing*

a Personal Grading Plan. Educational Measurement: Issues and Practice, 11(3), 35–42. Used by permission of the authors. **pp. 287–288,** quote: From "The case against the zero." by D.B. Reeves from *Phi Delta Kappan*, Vol 86, No 4, pp. 324–325. Published by Kappan Magazine (December, 2004.) **p. 320,** Figure 11.5: From Collins, Harold W., et al. *Educational Measurement and Evaluation: A Worktext*. Published by Allyn and Bacon, Boston, MA. Copyright © 1976 by Pearson Education. Adapted by permission of the publisher. **p. 326**, Resource for Your Assessment Toolkit: Reprinted with permission from the National Board for Professional Teaching Standards, www.nbpts.org. All rights reserved. **p. 347**, Figure 12.5: Reproduced with permission of CTB/McGraw-Hill LLC. **p. 362**, Figure 13.1: Blank, R.; Cavel, L.; Toye, C.; & Williams, A. (Eds.). (2007). *Key State Education Policies on PK-12 Education: 2006*. Washington, DC: Council of Chief State School Officers. **p. 373**, Figure 13.2: Adapted from *Report CardsZ: Title I, Part A Non-Regulatory Guidance*, US Department of Education, September 12, 2003. Used with permission. **p. 380,** Figure 13.4: Adapted from "High School Exit Exams Meet IDEA—An Examination of the History, Legal Ramifications, and Implications for Local School Administrators and Teachers" by Jennifer R. Rowe from the *Brigham Young University Education and Law Journal* (2004, Issue No. 1). Used with permission of the BYU Education and Law Journal, A Joint Publication of the J. Reuben Clark School of Law and the Brigham Young University Department of Educational Leadership. **p. 385,** Figure 13.5: From Azordegan, J. (2004) *Initial Findings and Major Questions about HOUSSE*. Denver, CO: Education Commission of the States. Used with permission. **p. 411,** Resource for Your Assessment Toolkit: Wood, Judy W. *Adapting Instruction to Accommodate Students in Inclusive Settings*, 4th Edition, © 2002, Pgs. 567–568. Reprinted by permission of Pearson Education, Inc., Upper Saddle River,

NJ. **p. 430**, Figure 15.2: 2000–2007 Copyright © ALTEC at the University of Kansas. Development of this educational resource was supported, in part, by the US Department of Education award #R302A000015 to ALTEC (Advanced Learning Technologies in Education Consortia) at the University of Kansas. **p. 431,** Figure 15.3: Used with permission from LiveText Inc., LaGrange, IL. **p. 443,** Figure 15.6: Used with permission from Bernie Dodge, Department of Education Technology, San Diego State University, San Diego, CA. **p. 445,** Figure 15.7: Used with permission from Blackboard, Inc., Washington, DC and Northern Illinois University. **p. 446,** Figure 15.8: Used with permission from LiveText Inc., LaGrange, IL. **pp. 464–465,** quote: Inside the Black Box © Paul Black and Dylan Wiliam, 1998. Reproduced by permission of GL Assessment. www.gl-assessment.co.uk. All rights reserved. **p. 471,** Resource for Your Assessment Toolkit: From *Strategic Teaching & Reading Project Guidebook* (1995, NCREL, revised) info@ ncrel.org Copyright © North Central Regional Educational Laboratory. Used with permission of Learning Point Associates, Naperville, IL.

Photo Credits

p. 2, CO1: © Jim Cummins/Corbis. **p. 26,** CO2: © Cindy Charles/PhotoEdit. **p. 48,** CO3: © David Young-Wolff/PhotoEdit. **p. 74,** CO4: © Michael Newman/PhotoEdit. **p. 106,** CO5: © Bob Daemmrich/The Image Works. **p. 136, 162,** CO6, CO7: © Ellen B. Senisi/The Image Works. **p. 202,** CO8: © Bob Daemmrich/The Image Works. **p. 236,** CO9: © Michael J. Doolittle/The Image Works. **p. 266,** CO10: © Eddie Keogh/ Reuters/Corbis. **p. 298,** CO11: Ryan McVay/ Getty Images. **p. 330,** CO12: © Michael Newman/PhotoEdit. **p. 358,** CO13: © Royalty-Free/ Corbis. **p. 396,** CO14: © Elizabeth Crews/The Image Works. **p. 424,** CO15: © LWA-Dann Tardif/zefa/Corbis. **p. 456,** CO16: © David Young-Wolff/PhotoEdit.

Index

DA